T0230030

Timos Sellis (Ed.)

Rules in
Database Systems

Second International Workshop, RIDS '95
Glyfada, Athens, Greece
September 25-27, 1995
Proceedings

 Springer

Series Editors

Gerhard Goos, Karlsruhe University, Germany

Juris Hartmanis, Cornell University, NY, USA

Jan van Leeuwen, Utrecht University, The Netherlands

Volume Editor

Timos Sellis
Division of Computer Science, National Technical University of Athens
GR-157 73 Zographou, Athens, Greece

Cataloging-in-Publication data applied for

Die Deutsche Bibliothek - CIP-Einheitsaufnahme

Rules in database systems : second international workshop ;
proceedings / RIDS '95, Glyfada, Athens, Greece, September
1995. Timos Sellis (ed.). - Berlin ; Heidelberg ; New York ;
Barcelona ; Budapest ; Hong Kong ; London ; Milan ; Paris ;
Tokyo : Springer, 1995
  (Lecture notes in computer science ; Vol. 985)
  ISBN 3-540-60365-4
NE: Sellis, Timos [Hrsg.]; RIDS <2, 1995, Glifada>; GT

CR Subject Classification (1991): H.2

ISBN 3-540-60365-4 Springer-Verlag Berlin Heidelberg New York

© Springer-Verlag Berlin Heidelberg 1995
Printed in Germany

Typesetting: Camera-ready by author
SPIN 10485600   06/3142 – 5 4 3 2 1 0   Printed on acid-free paper

Springer
Berlin
Heidelberg
New York
Barcelona
Budapest
Hong Kong
London
Milan
Paris
Santa Clara
Singapore
Tokyo

Lecture Notes in Computer Science 985

Edited by G. Goos, J. Hartmanis and J. van Leeuwen

Advisory Board: W. Brauer   D. Gries   J. Stoer

Preface

This book is the proceedings of the Second International Workshop on Rules in Database Systems (RIDS '95) held at Athens in September 1995. Rules have been a major focus of research interest in database systems for more than a decade, the initial focus on deductive rules and integrity constraints being augmented by recent research into active rules. The aim of this workshop, which was the second after a very successful first workshop in Edinburgh (Scotland) in September 1993, was to bring together researchers working on both theoretical and practical aspects of rules in database systems, to examine the current state of the art, to explore relationships between different categories of rule systems, and to identify complementary areas for further development, as well as interesting applications.

The workshop was organized by the members of ACT-NET, a "Human Capital and Mobility" network of universities and research institutes funded by the European Union in order to foster collaboration on research in the area of active database systems. The network currently includes Aberdeen, Athens, Darmstadt, Heriot-Watt, Karlsruhe, Linkoping, Pais Vasco, Skovde, Versailles, and Zurich.

In response to the call for papers for RIDS '95, the program committee received 47 submissions indicating strong interest in the area. Each submission was reviewed by 3 members of the program committee, and comments were returned to the authors. After a thorough evaluation, 22 papers were selected for inclusion in the proceedings and presentation in the workshop. These papers covered several aspects, including:

Semantics for active database systems
Active behaviour
Rule base organization and modeling
Rule analysis
Deductive databases
Implementation and benchmarking of active database systems
Cooperative system support.

In addition, there were two panel discussions, one addressing the "The Active Database Management Systems Manifesto", which is an attempt to set the scene on what an active database management system should be, and a second one on implementation and application experiences.

We wish to express our appreciation to all the authors of submitted papers, to the program committee members and their referees, and to the organizers of the panels.

Athens, September 1995   Timos Sellis

Acknowledgments

We are indebted to the program committee members for their assistance in evaluating the 47 papers submitted. The committee consisted of:

M. Bouzeghoub (Univ. de Versailles, France)
A. Buchmann (TH Darmstadt, Germany)
G. von Bueltzingsloewen (FZI, Germany)
S. Chakravarthy (Univ. of Florida, USA)
O. Diaz (Univ. del Pais Vasco, Spain)
K.R. Dittrich (Univ. of Zurich, Switzerland)
P.M.D. Gray (Univ. of Aberdeen, UK)
H.V. Jagadish (AT&T Bell Laboratories, USA)
M. Kersten (CWI, The Netherlands)
M. Koubarakis (UMIST, UK)
R. Manthey (Univ. of Bonn, Germany)
N.W. Paton (Univ. of Manchester, UK)
T. Risch (Linkoping Univ., Sweden)
T. Sellis (Nat. Tech. Univ. of Athens, Greece)
E. Simon (INRIA, France)
J. Widom (Stanford Univ., USA)

We are also grateful to the following who helped with reviews: A. Ait-Braham (UMIST, UK), J. Barros (Univ. de Versailles, France), M. Berndtsson (Univ. of Skovde), B. Boss (FZI, Germany), S. Embury (Univ. of Aberdeen, UK), H. Fritschi (Univ. of Zurich, Switzerland), S. Gatziu (Univ. of Zurich, Switzerland), A. Geppert (Univ. of Zurich, Switzerland), U. Griefahn (Univ. of Bonn, Germany), A. Jaime (Univ. del Pais Vasco, Spain), Z. Kedad (Univ. de Versailles, France), M. Kradolfer (Univ. of Zurich, Switzerland), T. Kudrass (TH Darmstadt, Germany), G. Levreau (Univ. de Versailles, France), E. Metais (Univ. de Versailles, France), B. Rieche (Univ. of Zurich, Switzerland), and D. Tombros (Univ. of Zurich, Switzerland).

Finally, we would like to express our gratitude to the National Technical University of Athens for providing financial support to the workshop.

Contents

The Active Database Management Systems Manifesto

The Active Database Management System Manifesto: A Rulebase of ADBMS Features

Edited by[1]
Klaus R. Dittrich, Stella Gatziu, Andreas Geppert

Institut für Informatik, Universität Zürich
Winterthurerstr. 190, CH-8057 Zürich, Switzerland
{dittrich,gatziu,geppert}@ifi.unizh.ch

Abstract. Active database systems have been a hot research topic for quite some years now. However, while "active functionality" has been claimed for many systems, and notions such as "active objects" or "events" are used in many research areas (even beyond database technology), it is not yet clear which functionality a database management system must support in order to be legitimately considered as an active system. In this paper, we attempt to clarify the notion of "active database management system" as well as the functionality it has to support. We thereby distinguish mandatory features that are needed to qualify as an active database system, and desired features which are nice to have. Finally, we perform a classification of applications of active database systems and identify the requirements for an active database management system in order to be applicable in these application areas.

1 Introduction

Active database management systems (ADBMSs) [e.g., 4, 6, 15] have recently become a very attractive database research topic. Many different systems and models have been proposed which claim to be "active". However, it is still unclear what the term "active database management system" really means. Under which condition can you legitimately claim that your system is "active"?

Authors often define the term ADBMS along the lines of "being able to react automatically to situations in the database and beyond" or "allowing the specification and implementation of reactive behavior". Some of these definitions are not very precise, and often there is no broad agreement on how to explain the term "active". This may be due to the fact that the proposals for systems and architectures have preceded the formal and conceptual groundwork.

In this paper, we describe what, in our opinion, the characteristics are that a database management system must exhibit in order to be legitimately called "active".

---

1. This paper and the underlying agreement on the characteristics of ADBMSs are actually among the results of ACTNET, where we initially have realized the need for a common understanding of ADBMSs. ACTNET is a network in the "Human Capital and Mobility" programme funded by the commission of the EU. The current participants in ACTNET are the Universities of Aberdeen, Athens, Darmstadt, Edinburgh (Heriot-Watt), Karlsruhe, Linköping, San Sebastian, Skövde, Versailles, and Zürich.
We gratefully acknowledge the contributions of the participants of the ACTNET-meeting in Versailles (January 1995). In particular, we are indebted to Günter von Bültzingslöwen and Norman Paton for further detailed comments and discussions.

However, while trying to find a definition and to define essential characteristics, we encountered two problems:

1. Many different ADBMSs and systems with some sort of "active functionality" have been defined so that simply taking the commonalities among these systems as the definition of an ADBMS would easily result in a collection of general and meaningless statements.

2. For a deeper understanding of ADBMSs and maybe different classes thereof, it is useful to look at their intended application domains and the facilities they require. Otherwise, the implications of specific system characteristics are difficult to grasp. For instance, is it mandatory for an ADBMS to support composite events? The answer is that for some "reactive" applications composite events are needed, for others they may be convenient to have, and again for others they are not needed at all. The same holds for coupling modes — not all conceivable coupling modes are required for simple applications.

Concerning the second observation, note that the development of ADBMSs is motivated by the application areas in mind, probably even more than has been the case for object-oriented DBMSs. We therefore think that one cannot simply abstract from the application domains when defining ADBMSs. Instead, we propose to specify some general features required for all ADBMSs and to define more specific features depending on the application domains the system in question is appropriate for (similar to the classification of object-oriented DBMSs [10]).

The remainder of this paper is organized as follows. The next section introduces the terminology and basic concepts of ADBMSs. Section 3 describes characteristics of ADBMSs and distinguishes between required and optional features. Section 4 introduces a classification of ADBMSs based on the requirements of the types of intended application domains.

2 Terminology

Before we introduce the characteristics of an aDBMS, we attempt to establish a common terminology.

A *database management system* (DBMS) is a software system for reliably and efficiently creating, maintaining, and operating large, integrated, multi-user databases. It implements storage and retrieval of data, secondary storage management for large sets of objects (including access paths, clustering, etc.), concurrency control, and recovery. The collection of data including secondary information is stored in the *database*. The structure of the database is defined by the *database schema*. Schemas are specified using the data definition language (DDL), and access to the database is by means of a data manipulation language (DML). Both together represent a so-called *data model*. Finally, a *database system* (DBS) is a DBMS together with a concrete database.

In a nutshell, ADBMSs extend "passive" DBMS with the possibility to specify *reactive behavior*. Below, we introduce the concepts relating to the specification and implementation of this additional DBMS-functionality.

ECA-rules (event-condition-action rules) consist of events, conditions and actions. The meaning of such a rule is: "when an event occurs, check the condition and if it holds, execute the action". Other terms are used synonymously in active database systems, for example *triggers*.

Once a set of rules has been defined, the active database system monitors the relevant events. In this way, it *detects* the occurrence of each relevant event and afterwards it notifies the component responsible for rule execution about this occurrence. We call this notification the *signalling* of the event. Consecutively, all rules which are defined to respond to this event are *triggered* (or *fired*) and must be *executed*. Rule execution incorporates condition evaluation and action execution. First, the condition is evaluated and if it is satisfied, the ADBMS executes the action.

More precisely, an event can be conceived as a pair (*<event type>*, *<time>*) where *<event type>* denotes the decription of occasions upon which a reaction must be performed, and *<time>* represents the point in time when such an occasion actually occurs. What the user determines within the event definition is only the event type (synonymously: event description, pattern, definition); at runtime, multiple events may occur for a given event type. Event types may be determined by occurrences in the database system or in its environment. For example, they can be specified as the beginning or the end of a data modification operation. In the case of a relational database system, a data modification operation is one of the three operations `insert`, `delete` or `update` on a particular relation. In the case of an object-oriented database system, the creation or the deletion of objects or the invocation of methods are regarded as events. Ultimately, an event type may also be directly specified as an absolute point in time e.g., "at 12:00 on 1.6.94", as a relative or periodiccally occuring time ("each Monday on 8 am").

An event can be *primitive* or *composite*. Primitive events correspond to elementary occurrences and can be mapped directly to a point in time determined by something occurring in the database system (e.g., a data modification operation), or by something occurring in the database environment (e.g., an absolute point in time). Composite events are defined as combinations of other primitive or composite events using a set of *event constructors* such as disjunction, conjunction, etc. Composite events are mapped to a point in time based on information about their component events, e.g., the point of time when the last component occurred.

Generally speaking, the point in time when an event occurs is a parameter of the event occurrence. Further parameters are possible, such as the transaction in which an event occurs, or the name of the user who has started this transaction.

In the case of composite events, *event restrictions* specify conditions the components must fulfill in order to form a (legitimate) composition. One way to specify such restrictions are predicates on the *event parameters* (such as the occurrence time), but more general predicates are possible, too. For instance, it may be required for a composite event that all of its components have occurred within the same transaction, or all refer to operations on the same database instance.

The *event history* or *history* consists of all occurrences of the defined event types (including components of composite events). Such an event history exists for any operational active database system. The history begins at the point in time when the first event type is defined. The history may last over many sessions and over several transactions. Thus, it might then be possible to signal a composite event based on events that have occurred during different application sessions or transactions.

A *condition* formulates in which state the relevant part of the database has to be in order to execute the action, i.e. it shows *what* must be checked. It is checked when the rule is triggered. A condition may be either a predicate on the database state like the "where"- part in an SQL-statement, or a database query with an empty or non-empty result. The condition is satisfied if either the result evaluates to true or is non-empty.

An *action* formulates the reaction to an event and is executed when the rule is triggered and its condition holds. An action may contain data modification or data retrieval operations, transaction operations like commit or abort, call of arbitrary procedures/ methods, etc. The fact that the action may execute data operations may cause the occurrence of other events. This leads to the *cascaded triggering* of rules.

Event occurrences are typically *bound* to data items (i.e., an event is bound to the data item for which the event occurred). The kind of binding determines the *granularity* of events as well as the data items that conditions and actions of rules associated to the event can refer to. Different kinds of bindings have been proposed [14]: *instance-oriented* binding means that the particular instances for which an event occurred can be referred to by conditions and actions. If the binding is *set-oriented*, then an event occurrence is associated with a set of instances for which the particular event occurred (e.g., all modified tuples of a relation). Conditions and actions can then refer to this set of instances. Finally, if the binding is *prior*, then the condition can also refer to the state of instances prior to the event occurrence.

In analogy to a data definition language which supports the modeling of data structures (and behavior in the case of object-oriented DBMS), an ADBMS provides a *rule definition language* as a means to specify ECA-rules. The rule language consists of constructors for the definition of rules, events, conditions, actions and execution constraints. The *rulebase* of an ADBS contains meta information on defined ECA-rules.

In addition to rule specification and event detection, an ADBMS has to support rule execution. It thus needs an *execution model*. An execution model determines when rules are executed, and which properties rule execution has.

In general, events triggering rules occur within transactions, and rules are executed in transactions. The execution model thus has to suit the transaction model of the DBMS. If in a transaction an event occurs that triggers a rule, then this transaction is commonly called the *triggering transaction*. If the rule is executed in one or more transactions, these are called *triggered transactions*.

The execution model defines the relationships between triggering and triggered transactions in terms of commit and abort dependencies as well as the semantics of rule execution with respect to concurrency control and recovery. The most common framework for specifying these relationships are nested transactions [13]. A triggered transaction is either a subtransaction of the triggering transaction, or it is independent from the triggering transaction. In the latter case, rule execution means spawning a new transaction tree.

The second relationship determined by the execution model is the time when a triggered transaction is executed with respect to the triggering transaction or event. The triggered transaction can be started immediately after the event has been signalled, or at the end of the triggering transaction (i.e., directly before commit).

Both relationships are usually specified through *coupling modes*. The originally proposed coupling modes [12] are:

- *immediate*: the triggered transaction is executed directly after the event has been signalled.
- *deferred*: the triggered transaction is executed at the end of the triggering transaction, but before commit.
- *decoupled*: the triggered transaction is started as a separate transaction.

In the first two cases, triggered transactions are essentially subtransactions of the triggering transaction. In the decoupled case, the triggered transaction can be started directly after event signalling, but it is independent from the triggering transaction. Especially, the commit and abort dependencies as present in the immediate and deferred cases do not exist in the decoupled case. A decoupled transaction can commit or abort regardless how the triggering transaction terminates. Additionally, the triggered transaction runs concurrently to the triggering one.

Further coupling modes have been proposed in the literature. In [9], the decoupled case is subdivided into causally dependent and independent transactions. In the first case, the triggered transaction can commit only if the triggering transaction also commits, and is serialized after the triggering transaction. The causally dependent coupling mode has been refined in [3]. Two new subcases of this coupling modes are proposed: the *sequential causally dependent* mode means that the triggered transaction can only start after the triggering one has committed. In the *exclusive causally dependent* mode, the triggered transaction may commit only if the triggering one has failed.

Coupling modes only define the relationship between triggering and triggered transactions. In addition, it can happen that multiple triggered transactions are to be executed at a given point in time. The ADBMS must then perform *conflict resolution*, i.e., either determine a serial order in which these triggered transactions are executed or control their concurrent execution in some way. Conflict resolution is also part of the execution model. *Priorities* are one possibility for conflict resolution in ADBMSs [1].

3 Characteristics of ADBMSs

In this section we describe the features any ADBMS must/should have, regardless of its applications. We first describe the features an ADBMS must support ("essential features"), followed by a list of features that are desirable (optional features).

3.1 Essential Features

Feature 1. An ADBMS is a DBMS.
All the concepts required for a passive system are required for an ADBMS as well ("passive" modeling facilities, query language, multi-user access, recovery, etc.). That means, if a user ignores all the active functionalities, an ADBMS can be worked with in exactly the same way as a passive DBMS.

Feature 2. An ADBMS supports definition and management of ECA-rules.
An ADBMS extends a passive DBMS in that it supports *reactive behavior*. Reactive behavior must be specifiable/definable by the user. The means to define rules together with the data definition facilities are sometimes also called the *knowledge model* [8]. The other way round, the DBMS-interface (e.g., the data definition language) is extended or complemented by operations for defining rules.

Feature 2.a. An ADBMS has to provide means for defining events, conditions, and actions.
We require that situations are described by (event/condition)-pairs. We also demand that the ADBMS supports the *explicit definition of events*. In some cases it may be useful to let a compiler or the ADBMS itself generate the event definition. In this case, we say that the event is defined *implicitly*. The user then specifies conditions and actions, and the ADBMS determines the event automatically (e.g., consider a consistency enforcement mechanism where only constraints and repairs are specified, but the system internally uses events signalled upon modification of data items to determine when the consistency constraint has to be checked). Nevertheless, the ADBMS also has to offer the possibility for the user to define events explicitly at the ADBMS-interface. If explicitly definable events are not provided, ECA-rules are solely an internal implementation mechanism for tasks that could also be implemented "passively", and there is no general support for reactive behavior. Thus, an ADBMS should support the notion of "event" to determine when reactions have to be performed (i.e., full-fledged ECA-rules). This is one major distinction of ADBMSs from other rule-based DBMSs, such as knowledge-based management systems (expert database systems, deductive DBMSs).

In general, we require that — wherever meaningful — *before* and *after events* can be defined. In case of database operations, for instance, a before event is signalled directly before the operation is actually executed. An after event is signalled directly after the operation has been performed.

If the event part is mandatory, the condition part might be omitted. We then refer to event-action rules. In this case, however, it should be possible to specify conditions as parts of actions.

All parts should be fully integrated with the (passive) data model. The event types supported should at least subsume the DML-operations and transaction statements. This means that, for example, the update of a specific relation can be defined as an event of interest. Conditions should be expressible as queries against the database, whereby the retrieval facilities supported by the DBMS should be applicable. Actions are principally any executable code fragment. It should at least be possible to use DML-commands in actions, including transaction commands (e.g., such that the triggering transaction can be aborted).

Ultimately, it has been mentioned before that the ADBMS distinguishes *event types* and *event occurrences*.

Feature 2.b. An ADBMS must support rule management and rulebase evolution.
The set of rules defined at a given point in time forms the *rulebase*. The rulebase should be managed by the ADBMS, regardless of whether the rules are stored in

the database proper or separately. In other words, definitions of ECA-rules are a part of the DBMS meta information and the database. The ADBMS should store information about which rules currently exist and how they are defined. This stored information on ECA-rules should be visisble for users and applications.

Furthermore, the rulebase must be changeable over time: it is neither sufficient to support a fixed set of ECA-rules, nor is it appropriate to support reactive behavior as ECA-rules that are hard-wired into the DBMS-code. An ADBMS must therefore allow new ECA-rules to be defined and old ones to be deleted. It should also be possible to modify event, condition, or action definitions of existing rules.

Rules can be *disabled* and *enabled*. Disabling a rule means that the rule definition remains in the rulebase, but that it will not trigger upon subsequent occurrences of its event. Enable is the inverse operation to disable: enabling a disabled rule means that the rule afterwards will trigger again upon occurrences of its event.

Feature 3. An ADBMS has an execution model.

Feature 3.a. An ADBMS must detect event occurrences (situations).
Ideally, an ADBMS detects event occurrences of all sorts automatically, i.e., event occurrences do not have to be signalled by the user/application. Otherwise, if application programmers or users are responsible for the correct signalling of *all* sorts of events, this system is just a syntactic variant of a passive DBMS (although users may in addition to other things also have the right to signal events).

Feature 3.b. An ADBMS must be able to evaluate conditions.
An ADBMS must be able to evaluate conditions subsequent to event detection.

It should also be possible to pass information from events to conditions. If an event has occurred for a specific object or a set of tuples in a relation, it must be possible to refer to this information in the condition. In addition, queries over the database state should be possible in conditions.

Feature 3.c. An ADBMS must be able to execute actions.
An ADBMS must be able to execute actions upon event detection and after the condition is known to hold. It must be possible to pass information from the condition to the action (e.g., information on the object for which the condition held). It should be possible to execute actions as part of the triggering transaction, and as such the action execution should be subject to concurrency control and recovery.

Feature 3.d. An ADBMS has well-defined execution semantics.
In order to have a "well-defined" execution semantics, the following properties with respect to events have to hold:
- event consumption must be well-defined,
- event detection and signalling must be well-defined.

If composite events are supported by the ADBMS, event consumption must be well-defined. Event consumption determines which component events are considered for a composite event, and how event parameters of the composite event are computed from its components. Different application classes may require different consumption modes, such as "recent", "chronicle", "continuous", and "cumulative" [5]. Either an ADBMS follows a fixed strategy for event consumption, or it offers the choice out of a collection of consumption modes.

In addition, rule execution must have a clear semantics, i.e., must define when, how, and on what database state conditions are evaluated and actions executed. The execution model hereby has to obey the restrictions imposed by the transaction model, e.g., transaction structures etc.

First, the relationship of condition evaluation and action execution with the triggering transaction must be defined. *Coupling modes* define *when* a condition is evaluated (an action is executed) with respect to the triggering event occurrence, and *what* the relationship to the triggering transaction is (e.g., the triggered transaction is a subtransaction of the triggering one). As mentioned above, it should at least be possible to execute actions as part of the triggering transaction. Thus, at least the coupling modes immediate and/or deferred must be provided.

Second, it must be defined whether events are *instance-oriented* or *set-oriented*. Instance-oriented events relate an event to a single instance. Set-oriented events relate *one* event to a collection of instances for which the event has occurred (recall the elaboration on binding modes in section 2).

Finally, it must be defined which database state is visible for condition evaluation and action execution. One possibility is the state upon event signalling; in this case the condition evaluation "sees" the database state as it was when the event had been detected. Another possibility is the *actual* database state, i.e., the current state at condition evaluation or action execution time. It may also be possible (or necessary) to see multiple states in conditions and actions. In this way, it is possible to refer to the state before, say, a modification and the state after a sequence of modifications. In this case, the binding mode *prior* is supported; the part of the database that actually represents the change is referred to as a *delta*.

It is desirable but not mandatory for an ADBMS to offer multiple alternatives for each (or some) of these features. Where such flexibility is supported, rule definitions also specify a selection for each feature where choices are possible. The rule specifier can then to some extent determine the desired semantics of rule execution. Otherwise, one specific strategy is selected by the ADBMS-designer and applied for all rules. This information is then hard-wired into the ADBMS and thus cannot be determined by the user. However, note that sometimes even for simple application classes, different possibilities (e.g., for coupling modes) are required.

Feature 3.e. Conflict resolution must either be pre-defined or user-definable.
In an ADDS it can happen that multiple rules have to be triggered at the same point in time (e.g., because multiple rules have been associated with the same event, or a transaction triggers several rules which all have the coupling mode deferred). The ADBMS must then be capable of performing conflict resolution, i.e., to determine in which order the rules must be executed. Since conflict resolution typically depends on the semantics of the rules (which in general is only known by the user), the rule specifier must have the opportunity to define how conflicts are resolved, e.g., by means of priorities. If the user, however, does not want to define conflict resolution, he/she is not obliged to do so, and the ADBMS will either determine some order or execute rules non-deterministically.

3.2 Optional Features

Feature 4. An ADBMS should represent information on ECA-rules in terms of its data model.

If an ADBMS represents rules with the constructs of its data model, the possibility to inspect the rulebase with the retrieval facilities comes for free. Users can then query the rulebase like any other database, without being forced to learn a new representation formalism.

Feature 5. An ADBMS should support a programming environment.

It goes without saying that an ADBMS must be *usable*. The bottom line for usability is the availability of a rule definition language (which of course, may be part of the DDL; see Feature 2 above). In order to assist the user in beneficially using the ADBMS, a number of tools should be provided:

- a rule browser,
- a rule designer,
- a rulebase analyzer,
- a debugger,
- a maintenance tool,
- a trace facility, and
- performance tuning tools (see below).

These tools may be separate tools dedicated for an ADBMS-programming environment, or may be extensions of already existing DBMS- or CASE-tools. Note further that it is not intended to require that all tools are separate systems, we are simply interested in their functionality.

A *rule browser* allows inspection of the set of currently existing rules. The rulebase is the extension of the catalogue (or data dictionary) in passive DBMSs, since it contains meta-information on defined ECA-rules. Clearly, when defining ECA-rules the possibility to conceive which rules have already been defined is essential.

The ADBMS should offer a *design tool* that assists users in defining new rules. Such a tool support is crucial when the reactive behavior as required by the universe of discourse has to be systematically mapped into ECA-rules. This support is possible in two not necessarily mutually exclusive ways: either a general design tool also covers ECA-rule design, or the reactive behavior is specified using dedicated high-level languages, such as a constraint definition language.

A *rulebase analyzer* is a tool that allows certain properties of the currently existing rulebase to be checked. Examples of such desired properties of rule sets are termination, confluence, and observably deterministic behavior [2]. If the ADBMS supports cascaded rule execution, it is important to ensure that rule execution terminates under all circumstances. Together with the other properties, termination ensures that the current rulebase is safe and correct with respect to the intended reactive behavior. In general, these properties cannot be proven automatically, but an analyzer might assist a DBA in proving them or at least in detecting inconsistencies.

A *debugger* is a tool that allows the controlled execution of rules (and applications) and helps to check whether the rulebase implements the required reactive behavior adequately. Thus, in contrast to proving properties with an analyzer, a debugger supports test-modify cycles.

A *maintenance tool* for an ADBMS supports the user in performing rulebase evolution. In addition to the rule definition facility, it supports deletion and modification of
existing rules.

Finally, a *trace tool* is a facility that records event occurrences and rule executions,
such that a DBA[2] is enabled to realize which actions the ADBMS has triggered automatically. If such a tool is not supported, the ADBMS might perform actions that users
never become aware of.

Feature 6. An ADBMS should be tunable.
An ADBMS must be useful in its application domain. Especially, the ADBMS solution
must not show significantly worse runtime performance than equivalent solutions on
top of a passive system. There is little experience with current ADBMSs how to measure their performance systematically. However, it is apparent that a practically useful
ADBMS should offer the possibility to tune its rulebase (whereby of course the semantics of the rules should not change due to tuning!). A problem with tuning in current
ADBMSs is that the specification of rules (their conditions and actions) is essentially
given by their implementation, i.e., as queries and code fragments. A feasible approach
might be the equivalent to the three-schema-architecture [11]: at the external level, us-
er- or application-specific rules are specified (e.g., for consistency constraints), the
conceptual level contains all rules relevant for the community of all users/applications,
and the internal level specifies the implementation details. The internal level should
then provide for the means for performance improvements, and all details concerning
efficient rule execution are captured on this level.[3]

4 A Classification of ADBMSs

Based on the statements made in the previous section, we would like to be more concrete, especially with respect to the way of instantiation of the "essential features" determined above (i.e., composite events, execution semantics, and so forth).
Nevertheless, in general this is not possible, since ADBMSs can be used for quite different purposes, and in doing so must offer varying degrees of expressive power. One
way to overcome the remaining vagueness is to consider application classes, to determine their requirements, and then to identify classes of ADBMSs that are appropriate
for these application classes. In this way, we do not necessarily add additional features
to the functionality of an ADBMS, but can determine appropriate and required realiza-
tions of the features described above (much alike the description of dimensions and
possible instantiations described by Paton et al. [14]).

In order to classify ADBMSs according to the application classes they are useful
for, we consider two dimensions:
- the role of the ADBMS in an application system (*supervision* or *control*), and
- the degree of integration of the application system (*homogeneous* or *heterogeneous*).

---

2. DataBase Administrator
3. In other words, in analogy to passive DBMSs we require physical database design for
   ADBMSs.

Supervision means that the ADBMS verifies requests for database operations against the database (or vice versa), and eventually performs simple actions (e.g., notification, transaction abort, update propagation). An ADBMS that controls the application system is in addition, able to trigger external functions, e.g., application programs. In this case, the ADBMS is able to control the behavior of the entire application environment (and not only the state of the database), and can do so possibly over a period of time spanning many sessions.

We call an application system "homogeneous" if all of its components are applications of the ADBMS in question, i.e., they share a common schema and common databases. Otherwise, we say that the application is "heterogeneous". Particularly, the ADBMS may have to control systems that are implemented on top of other platforms. Combining these dimensions leads to three classes of ADBMSs, since the combination supervision/heterogeneity is not regarded as meaningful.

4.1 ADBMSs for Supervision in Homogeneous Application Systems

The simplest case is ADBMSs for supervision in homogeneous application systems. Such an ADBMS recognizes certain user/application requests and verifies them against the database state (or verifies the database state against the most recent application requests). In this case, the (meta) rules on how to operate the entire application system are still with the user/operator of the application system, but are not necessarily expressible with ECA-rules of the ADBMS. Despite its ability to notify the user (e.g., printing messages on the console) and to abort transactions, the ADBMS has no control over the application system, i.e., it will not cause complex application programs to execute.

The kinds of events it can detect are given by the data model, it specifically does not need composite events. Thus, maintaining the event history is not necessary. For conditions, it is sufficient to query the database state and the data dictionary, and actions are DML-commands (including transaction abort).

Such a system is useful for implementing the "usual" DBMS tasks, such as (simple) consistency constraints, authorization, updates of materialized views, etc.). Furthermore, note that some of these DBMS-tasks might use the active functionality only internally as an implementation mechanism that might also be provided in a "passive" way. The benefit of active functionality is then not the support of functionality that would not be possible otherwise, but the uniformity and minimality of implementation concepts.

In general, composite events etc. are not necessarily required, but may be beneficial in some situations. Depending on the concrete application in mind, different kinds of execution semantics may be necessary (the coupling mode deferred for consistency maintenance, immediate for authorization). For (advanced) consistency maintenance, deltas ("before values") are required.

Not all the functionality required for a given application class might be implementable in this way. However, we would claim that in most cases the aforementioned ADBMS characteristics are sufficient. See Table 1 for a summary of the ADBMS features required by this application class.

Feature	Instantiation
Events (2.a)	DML-operations, not necesarily composite
Conditions (2.a)	predicates on database state / queries
Actions (2.a)	DML-action, user notification
Rule evolution (2.b)	create/delete, enable/disable
Consumption modes (3.d)	chronicle
Coupling modes (3.d)	at least immediate, deferred
Execution (3.d)	under local control

Table 1. ADBMSs for Supervision in Homogeneous Application Systems (Summary)

4.2 ADBMSs for Control in Homogeneous Application Systems

The second class is formed by ADBMSs that are capable of controlling not only the database, but also its environment (i.e., the applications). The ADBMS is able to encode (at least a substantial part of) the information about the application environment in the form of ECA-rules. The ADBMS is able to detect states or sequences thereof of the application system and to perform automatic reactions, including the automatic spawning of application programs. Applications are tightly integrated, and the active mechanisms are part of the homogeneous DBMS underlying the application system.

Everything that is provided by the first class of ADBMSs must be available in this kind of system, too. Additionally, in order to control the DBS-environment, including the applications, more event types are necessary (e.g., time events). The ADBMS has to keep track of the relevant part of the event history, and must also be able to evaluate restrictions on this event history. Technically speaking, composite events, event restrictions, and monitoring intervals (or equivalents thereof) must be provided. Composite events are necessary in order to control and monitor complex sequences of situations in the DBS-environment. Composite event restrictions (such as referring to the triggering transaction —"same transaction"—) must also be provided. Likewise, a broad variety of rule execution semantics must be supported (i.e., when the rule is executed, and how its execution relates to the triggering transaction). In other words, the coupling modes immediate, deferred, and decoupled are the bottom line.

This class of ADBMSs is characterized through feasibility for control in "tightly integrated applications". All the application programs use the same schema, transaction model, DML, etc. Particularly, it is possible to run all triggered activities under the control of the local (ADBMS-) transaction manager.

An example application domain for this type of ADBMS are stock trading application systems. See Table 2 for a summary of the ADBMS features required by this application class.

Feature	Instantiation
Events (2.a)	DML-operations, external events, composite
Conditions (2.a)	boolean function, including predicates on database state / queries
Actions (2.a)	DML-action, user notification, external programs
Rule evolution (2.b)	create/delete + modification and event history adaption, enable/disable
Consumption modes (3.d)	choice, including chronicle
Coupling modes (3.d)	at least immediate, deferred, decoupled
Execution (3.d)	under local control

Table 2. ADBMSs for Control in Homogeneous Application Systems (Summary)

4.3 ADBMSs for Control in Heterogeneous Application Systems

The third class is formed by ADBMSs that are capable of integrating possibly heterogeneous and autonomous systems. The active mechanism enables the ADBMS to perform control of such heterogeneous, loosely integrated component systems.

In addition to the capabilities of the second class described above, such an ADBMS has to be able to detect situations in other application systems (which themselves may be based on other DBMSs), thus affecting the event definition and detection facilities. It might also be necessary to detect events from external devices.

Most important, powerful rule execution mechanisms are necessary, since it might be the case that triggered actions cannot be executed under the control of the local transaction manager. The rule execution model must support complex relationships among application steps (e.g., compensation, ordering of application steps, dependencies).

Furthermore, if such an ADBMS is intended for real-time applications, it should support the specification of timing constraints for rule executions. The rule definition should also comprise contingency actions, which are executed whenever the timing constraint of a rule cannot be met. Clearly, an ADBMS for real-time applications should also possess the properties required for a "passive" real-time system.

Summarizing, in this type of ADBMS parts of the "middleware" can be moved into the DBMS, i.e., the active mechanism contributes to implementing the middleware in the ADBMS. Since the ADBMSs of this class are intended for loosely-coupled, possibly heterogeneous systems, their integration into software architectures that aim at mediation in such environments should be possible. Especially, it should be possible to integrate ADBMS-functionality into OMG's CORBA architecture [7]. Relevant services provided by the ADBMS would then refer to event definition, registration, notification, etc.

Example application domains are advanced workflow management systems, reactive behavior in heterogeneous DBSs, real-time plant control systems, and process-centered software development environments. See Table 3 for a summary of the ADBMS features required by this application class.

Feature	Instantiation
Events (2.a)	DML-operations, external events, composite
Conditions (2.a)	boolean function, predicates on database state
Actions (2.a)	DML-action, user notification, external programs, contingency actions
Rule evolution (2.b)	create/delete + modification and event history adaption, enable/disable
Consumption modes (3.d)	choice, including chronicle
Coupling modes (3.d)	`immediate, deferred, decoupled +` causal dependencies
Execution (3.d)	not completely under local control

Table 3. ADBMSs for Control in Heterogeneous Application Systems (Summary)

5 Conclusion

In this paper, we have described what in our opinion the term "active database management system" means. We have identified mandatory and optional features, and have attempted to identify "classes" of ADBMSs with respect to the application classes they are useful for.

The intention of this paper is to clarify teminology in a specific area of database research. Establishing a common teminology is among the prime objectives of research; and using such a common language instead of ever more buzzwords helps to prevent misunderstandings.

In our opinion, it is not wise to collect all somehow "reactive" system under the "ADBMS-umbrella"; maybe different terms might be more appropriate for other systems. For example, it can be more useful to term a system without explicit events an "expert database system" — which would by no means suggest that expert database systems were less good, useful, etc. than ADBMSs. Our intention is to establish agreement on teminology, concepts, and systems, and not to start a manifesto war.

6 Acknowledgments

We gratefully acknowledge the funding of ACTNET by the Commission of the European Union (contract no. CHRX--CT93-0089). The University of Zurich acknowledges the funding of its ACTNET participation by the Federal Department for Education and Science (Bundesamt fuer Bildung und Wissenschaft, BBW, contract no. BBW Nr. 93.0313).

7 References

[1]   R. Agrawal, R.J. Cochrane, B. Lindsay: *On Maintaining Priorities in a Production Rule System*. Proc. 17th Intl. Conf. on Very Large Data Bases (VLDB), Barcelona, Spain, September 1991.

[2]   A. Aiken, J. Widom, J.M. Hellerstein: *Behaviour of Database Production Rules: Termination, Confluence, and Observable Determinism*. Proc. ACM-SIGMOD Intl. Conf. on Management of Data, San Diego, CA, June 1992.

[3]   H. Branding, A. Buchmann, T. Kudrass, J. Zimmermann: *Rules in an Open System: The REACH Rule System*. Proc. Rules in Database Systems. Workshops in Computing, Springer-Verlag, 1994.

[4]   A.P. Buchmann: *Active Object Systems*. In A. Dogac, T.M. Ozsu, A. Biliris, T. Sellis (eds): Advances in Object-Oriented Database Systems. Computer and System Sciences Vol 130, Springer, 1994.

[5]   S. Chakravarthy, D. Mishra: *An Event Specification Language (Snoop) for Active Databases and Its Detection*. Technical Report UF-CIS TR-91-23, CIS Department, University of Florida, September 1991.

[6]   S. Chakravarthy (ed): *Special Issue on Active Databases*. Bulletin of the TC on Data Engineering 15:1-4, 1992.

[7]   *The Common Object Request Broker: Architecture and Specification*. OMG Document 91.8.1, August 1991. © Digital Equipment Corp., Hewlett-Packard Company, HyperDesk Corp., ObjectDesign Inc., SunSoft Inc.

[8]   U. Dayal: *Active Database Management Systems*. Proc. 3rd Intl. Conf. on Data and Knowledge Bases, Jerusalem, 1988.

[9]   U. Dayal, M. Hsu, R. Ladin: *A Transactional Model for Long-Running Activities*. Proc. 17th Intl. Conf. on Very Large Data Bases (VLDB), Barcelona, Spain, September 1991.

[10]   K.R. Dittrich: *Object-Oriented Database Systems: The Notions and the Issues*. In K.R. Dittrich, U. Dayal, A.P. Buchmann (eds): On Object-Oriented Database Systems. Topics in Information Systems, Springer 1991.

[11]   R. Elmasri, S.B. Navathe: *Fundamentals of Database Systems*. Benjamin/Cummings Publishing, 1989.

[12]   M. Hsu, R. Ladin, D. McCarthy: *An Execution Model for Active DBMS*. Proc. 3rd Intl. Conf. on Data and Knowledge Bases, Jerusalem, Israel, June 1988.

[13]   J.E.B. Moss: *Nested Transactions: An Approach to Reliable Distributed Computing*. MIT Press, 1985.

[14]   N.W. Paton, O. Diaz, M.H. Williams, J. Campin, A. Dinn, A. Jaime: *Dimensions of Active Behaviour*. Proc. Rules in Database Systems. Workshops in Computing, Springer-Verlag, 1994.

[15]   N.W. Paton, O. Diaz: *Active Database Systems*. Technical Report, Heriot-Watt University, Edinburgh, Scotland, November 1994.

Semantics for Active Database Systems

Formal Specification Of Active Database Functionality: A Survey

Norman W. Paton[1], Jack Campin[2], Alvaro A.A. Fernandes[2] and M. Howard Williams[2]

[1] Department of Computer Science
University of Manchester, Oxford Road, Manchester
[2] Department of Computing and Electrical Engineering
Heriot-Watt University, Riccarton, Edinburgh

Abstract. This paper reviews research on the formal specification of active behaviour, indicating both what has been done in this area, and how. The scope of different approaches is compared within a common framework, which reveals that although many aspects of active behaviour have been described formally, no single proposal covers all phenomena associated with active database systems.

1 Introduction

Database research has often been characterised by a close association between theory and practice, with formal results being used to guide and underpin the development of novel database systems. The presence of a widely accepted formal description of a language or model can encourage a more focused development effort than generally emerges from empirical work on constructs or systems.

In the area of active databases, most research has been empirical in nature, with no widely accepted formal model acting as a starting point for the development of implementations for different data models or systems. As a result, the most prominent proposals for active database systems, while sharing a range of basic notions and constructs, support widely differing languages and execution models. A preliminary, informal framework for the comparison of active database systems and applications, designed to highlight common ground and key differences, is given in [15]. However, no formal model has yet been developed that encompasses the range of facilities supported by different active database systems. Despite this, an increasing number of researchers have been working on the formal specification of different aspects of active database functionality, with a range of different aims in mind. This paper reviews a number of approaches to the formal specification of active behaviour, with a view to indicating what features have been formally specified, illustrating the formal methods that have been used, and allowing a comparison of the principal results to date. The paper is structured as follows: section 2 indicates what might be sought from a formal specification of active behaviour, sections 3 to 10 describe individual approaches from the literature, section 11 provides some pointers to other representative examples in the literature, section 12 summarises the approaches considered in this paper, and section 13 presents some conclusions.

2 Context: Active Database Systems

Active database systems are able to respond automatically to situations that arise inside or outside the database itself. The active behaviour of a database is generally described using rules, which most commonly have three components, an *event*, a *condition* and an *action*. A rule with such components is known as an event-condition-action rule, or *ECA-rule*. Such a rule lies dormant until an occurrence of the event that it is monitoring, when the rule is said to be triggered. The condition of a triggered rule is subsequently evaluated, and if true, then the rule is added to the *conflict set*, which is the store of triggered rules accessed by the scheduler which selects rule actions for execution.

The structural and behavioural characteristics of active database systems can be classified according to a number of dimensions, as outlined informally in [15]. For the purposes of this paper we classify the aspects to be described into three areas: *knowledge model*, *execution model*, and *management model*.

The knowledge model represents the syntactic view of active rules as seen by the rule programmer. This has three main facets: *Event language:* a notation in which the situations that trigger a rule can be specified; *Condition language:* a notation used to express additional constraints which must be satisfied by the database before the triggered rule is added to the conflict set; *Action language:* a notation used to specify the effect that the rule must have when it is executed.

The execution model describes how rules interact in the context of the whole database system. It has the following aspects: *Transition granularity:* the nature of the binding between event occurrences and rule activations – it is possible that an individual event occurrence will trigger a rule, or that a collection of occurrences of an event will together trigger a rule; *Coupling mode:* the temporal and causal relationship between triggering and execution – for example, it is possible that the action of a rule is executed as soon as possible after the evaluation of the condition of the rule (immediate), or at a later point, such as at end of transaction (deferred); *Priority scheme:* an ordering specifying which rules are considered first when several have been triggered at the same time (i.e. when the conflict set contains more than one rule); *Nett-effect policy:* which may allow intermediate state changes internal to a transaction to be ignored by the rule system.

The management model comprises properties of the rule base taken as a whole, as well as operations for modifying the rules: *Operations on rules:* some active databases allow rules to be created or removed, and activated or deactivated, during execution; *Termination:* whether or not the execution of a given rule set must reach a final state; *Confluence:* whether the (in general nondeterministic) rule set defines a unique final state given any context of initiation; *Equivalence Model:* a notion of semantic equivalence between rule sets, which is a prerequisite for optimisation.

Specific proposals for formal descriptions of active behaviour will be examined using the above dimensions to highlight the scope of different proposals; a comparison of the different proposals within this framework is given in section 12. Furthermore, for each approach presented the following issues are addressed:

Motivation: why the formal specification was developed.
Formalism: what formal technique was used.
Limitations: what issues were not considered, and why.

There will also be a description of each approach to give a flavour of how the formal specification has been achieved.

3   Starburst in Denotational Semantics

Motivation: to establish how readily the execution model of an existing active database system can be specified formally.
Formalism: denotational semantics.
Limitations: the specification focuses upon the execution model, and abstracts over the condition/action languages of Starburst.

The denotational model of the Starburst active rule system in [21] provides a semantics for a rule base considered as a function mapping user inputs (requests made during a transaction) and prior database states into subsequent database states. This approach emulates semantic models for conventional programming languages.

The core idea in the specification is the notion of a *set of changes* – this models both a user transaction and the effect of a rule. A rule is considered (simplifying slightly) to be a function mapping sets of changes and database states to new sets of changes and new database states. The top level of the specification is a *meaning function* which gives a denotation for a rule system (set of rules ordered by priority). Several supplementary functions are used as intermediates in the definition of this meaning function. These intermediate functions play a purely technical role; they do not correspond to data structures or natural units of behaviour in the Starburst system.

An example of this style is provided by the denotational definition of rule priority. In Starburst, this is an arbitrary partial ordering. The specification defines this informally, and makes use of it by a function *Eligible* which selects candidate rules for firing among those with highest priority:

$$Eligible : \mathcal{RC} \times \mathcal{O} \to \mathbb{P}\,\mathcal{R}$$
$$Eligible = \lambda\{\langle r_1, \delta_1 \rangle, ... \langle r_n, \delta_n \rangle\}, o \bullet$$
$$\{r_i \mid 1 \leq i \leq n \wedge r_i(\delta_i, \varnothing) \downarrow 1 = true \wedge$$
$$\{r_j \mid 1 \leq j \leq n \wedge r_j(\delta_j, \varnothing) \downarrow 1 = true \wedge$$
$$r_j > r_i \in o\} = \varnothing\}$$

$\mathcal{O}$ is the domain of rule orderings; $\mathcal{RC}$ is the domain of *sets of rule-change pairs*, pairings of a rule and an elementary change to the database. $\mathcal{R}$ is the domain of rules. The functions r_i representing the denotations of rules return a triple of values, the first of which (accessed by the $\downarrow$ selection operator) is a Boolean value indicating whether the rule has been triggered.

This notation is extremely concise; a syntactically sugared variant, like those of functional programming languages, might make for more maintainable specifications. Formal reasoning about this model is not straightforward; there are few tools available for analyzing general denotational specifications, and the general problem is intractable.

4   An Object-Oriented Framework for Specifying Active Rule Systems

Motivation: the development of a framework for formally specifying the semantics of different rule systems, with a view to allowing a detailed comparison of proposals. To date, the framework has been used to define the semantics of the Starburst[22], POSTGRES[18] and Ariel [8] rule systems [4, 5].
Formalism: Object-Z [17], an object-oriented extension of Z.
Limitations: As in the Starburst specification of section 3, details of event, condition and action languages are not included in the specifications.

The formalism of Object-Z, sharing with Z its characteristics of being a first-order theory of an evolving state, frequently gains in simplicity of expression over the functional, domain-based denotational approach, but at the expense of considerably greater length. The constraints on allowable operations on the database are introduced by *subclassing*; a very abstract description of a highly generic active database is progressively refined to converge on the functionality of specific rule systems. This incremental refinement of specifications contrasts with the denotational model, where the domains and functions are introduced all at once, and the type system of the semantics prevents extensive generalisation.

To illustrate the approach, figure 1 gives part of the Object-Z class *SRule*, a subclass of the generic class *Rule* used to model Starburst specific behaviour. The rule has stored properties *a*, *d* and *r* which log the nett-effect of changes to the table monitored by the rule. It is these sets of changes which, respectively, describe the append, delete or replace operations which are relevant to the event that is being monitored by the rule. The *Fire* operation tests the *Condition* of the rule, and if it is true, executes its *Action* (both *Condition* and *Action* are inherited from *Rule*); after the *Fire* operation has been carried out, the logs of changes being monitored by the rule are cleared.

The benefits of the Object-Z framework include the clarity and tailorability of the resulting specifications, which make explicit the differences between proposals for active rule systems. However, in describing the active capabilities of a range of systems, the current framework abstracts over many other features of these systems, such as the data models, query languages, etc.

5   Heraclitus: An execution model description language

Motivation: to provide a language which can be used to support alternative execution models for active database systems.

$$
\begin{array}{l}
\rule{0pt}{0pt}\\
\end{array}
$$

```
┌─ SRule ─────────────────────────────────────────────────
│ Rule
│
│ │ store : SStore
│
│ ┌──────────────────────────────────────────────────────
│ │ a : SetLog[Object]
│ │ d : SetLog[Object]
│ │ r : SetLog[Object × State]
│ ├──────────────────────────────────────────────────────
│ │ ┌─ INIT ──────────────────────────────────────────────
│ │ │ emptylog
│ │ └──────────────────────────────────────────────────────
│ │
│ │ ┌─ ClearRuleLog ──────────────────────────────────────
│ │ │ Δ(a, d, r)
│ │ ├──────────────────────────────────────────────────────
│ │ │ a'.INIT ∧ d'.INIT ∧ r'.INIT
│ │ └──────────────────────────────────────────────────────
│ │
│ │ ┌─ Fire ──────────────────────────────────────────────
│ │ │ Δ(adb.stores)
│ │ ├──────────────────────────────────────────────────────
│ │ │ Condition ⇒ Action
│ │ │ ¬ Condition ⇒ adb.stores' = adb.stores
│ │ │ ClearRulelog
│ │ └──────────────────────────────────────────────────────
└──────────────────────────────────────────────────────────
```

Fig. 1. Class *SRule* in Object-Z.

Formalism: a hybrid operational/algebraic approach.
Limitations: does not directly lend itself to formal reasoning.

Hull and Jacobs [10] describe a database programming language, Heraclitus, that is used to model active database constructs. The essential new concept in Heraclitus is the *delta*: a denotable value in the language representing a proposed change to the database. These can be inspected by the rule system and algebraically combined to return new deltas; their times of creation and manipulation are decoupled from the time when they are applied to the database (they need not be applied at all). This supports hypothetical reasoning about the state of the database; it also makes it possible to implement a variety of coupling modes with little difficulty, although this is not done in the paper.

This methodology goes some way towards implementing a desideratum identified earlier in our discussion of the denotational semantics of Starburst; providing a 'syntactic sugar' for the semantics. However, the Heraclitus language is imperative; this makes it a good prototyping language, but a declarative language with similar primitives would lend itself better to transformational reasoning.

As an example, in [10] it is shown how the execution model of Starburst can be supported using Heraclitus. The specification involves writing rules as Heraclitus functions, which are then processed by a Heraclitus program which schedules rules for execution in response to relevant updates. In this context, rules directly access the *deltas* which represent the changes to which they must respond. The following rule condition, expressed in (slightly modified) Heraclitus notation, returns *true* if there are tuples being inserted into the **tube** relation (`<+tube(tid,_,_,type)>` in change), the **type** attribute of which is neither stored in the database nor scheduled for insertion:

```
function condition@1(change,curr:delta):bool
return exists tid,type such that
                (<+tube(tid,_,_,type)> in change and
                 not tube_type(type,_,_) when curr)
```

In the above function, **change** represents the updates monitored by, but not yet processed by, the rule, and **curr** represents the updates of the current transaction. In the above rule, the **in** operation tests for the presence of an inserted tuple in the delta **change**, while the **when** operation tests to see if a relevant **tube_type** tuple will be stored in the database once the updates in **curr** have been applied.

The principal strength of the work on Heraclitus is that the formal definition of the algebra of deltas can be exploited within an implemented database programming language, thereby allowing experimentation with different flavours of active rule system.

6   A logic framework using the Event Calculus

Motivation: to establish what characteristics of active functionality can be captured within a framework based upon first order logic [6].

Formalism: event calculus [13].

Limitations: resorts to an operational semantics to describe execution model features.

This approach relies on the database case of the Kowalski-Sergot event calculus (EC) [13], which is based on a history of events. The set of all logical consequences derived from the history by the EC gives rise to a sequence of fact-sets, each of which can be viewed as the extensional part (EDB) of a deductive database (DDB). Adding an intensional part (IDB) in the form of a deductive rule (DR) set that operates over each (and all) of the clause sets characterises a complete DDB framework that only differs from the standard case in having access to the multiple states generated by the succession of events.

In the context of this paper, the main contribution of [6] is to define specification languages for events, conditions and actions in such a way that event detection, condition verification and action execution have a logical semantics.

The event specification language is a Datalog-equivalent language over the event occurrences recorded in the history. Event composition is modelled by the intensional definition of event-occurrences using DRs over the history. Ascertaining that an event (possibly a composite one) has occurred is equivalent to evaluating a query over the DDB composed of the history (as the EDB) and the DRs over it (as the IDB). This DDB defines, by logical consequence, all the events of interest in the application. Analogously, the condition specification language is a Datalog-equivalent language over the logical consequences of the DDB comprising, as its EDB, the logical consequences of the application of the EC to the history, and, as its IDB, application-specific DRs. Ascertaining that a condition holds in a database state is equivalent to evaluating a query over the induced sequence of DDBs. Finally, the action-specification language can be reduced to the monotonic appending of new event occurrences to the history.

For example, assuming **append** as a primitive action on the history, the following ECA rule (of the form $E : C \rightarrow A$) specifies that if a salary alteration occurred that raised the salary of some employee to a higher level than that of his or her manager, an action should be taken to raise the salary of the manager to the same level as that of the employee:

```
    happened(_EventId, put_salary(EmployeeSalary)@Employee),
  : holdsAt(property(Employee,manager,Manager), Now),
    holdsAt(property(Manager,salary,ManagerSalary), Now),
    ManagerSalary < EmployeeSalary, current_time(Now)
-> append(put_salary(EmployeeSalary)@Manager)
```

Note that the predicate **happened** is used to query the event history, and **holdsAt** is used to query the database. Variable bindings are assumed to flow by unification between the different parts of the rule.

The distinguishing aspect of this proposal is that it tightly integrates deductive and active rules without attempting to merge their semantics into a whole since there are grounds to believe that by merging them the whole could turn out to be less than the sum of the parts.

7   An Operational Semantics For Rule Base Analysis

Motivation: to develop a formalism for rule execution which allows reasoning about the properties of rule bases [24].

Formalism: operational semantics.

Limitations: focuses upon a single condition-action rule language.

The techniques of [24] give an operational semantics for rule systems expressed using a simple condition-action rule language. While the language is quite restrictive, user transactions can be arbitrarily complex. Only one coupling mode (immediate execution) is supported.

To give a flavour of the specification, the following function defines the effect of executing the rule α on the database state s as a result of the update u:

$$f_\alpha(s, u) = u \cup \bigcup_{(c_1 \cdots c_n) \, \in \, \varepsilon[C_\alpha(x_1 \cdots x_n)]su} U_\alpha[c_1 \cdots c_n]$$

The function indicates that the updates resulting from u and the firing of the rule α are u unioned with the updates which results from executing the action of the rule ($U_\alpha[c_1 \cdots c_n]$) for each of the tuples for which the condition of the rule is true ($\varepsilon[C_\alpha(x_1 \cdots x_n)]su$).

The execution sequences modelled by this formalism are a subset of those described in sections 3 and 4, as a constraint requires updates to accumulate monotonically. Together with syntactic constraints on rule bases which maintain this monotonic behaviour, this gives sufficient conditions to guarantee termination and confluence; however, these constraints (on variable sharing, and a prohibition on the generation of new identifiers) are too strong to be realistic for most database applications. For example, it would not be possible to write a rule with an action that increases the salary of each employee by a fixed percentage. Approaches to the analysis of rule bases are considered further in sections 8 and 9. Further work on rule analysis based upon operational semantics is described in [20].

8 Reachability analysis by graph theory

Motivation: to develop a framework within which analysis of rule bases can be conducted [1].

Formalism: graphs which represent rule execution.

Limitations: depends upon user input or unspecified analyses of rule conditions and actions.

This work, although described in the context of the Starburst rule system, presents a generic framework for establishing three properties of rule bases, namely termination, confluence and observable determinism. The analysis method proceeds in a similar way to that in section 7, but allows for more fine-grained information to be considered (e.g. by examining the effect of rules on individual tuples, and by incorporating a priority scheme to make a larger class of rule bases provably terminating and confluent). The conditions that guarantee confluence and termination (commutativity of rules) are less restrictive, but correspondingly harder to check; the authors suggest that they might be worked out interactively with user input, although the later work described in section 9 can do this automatically.

The analysis is a hybrid of syntactic and semantic reasoning; its correctness is defined in terms of *execution graphs*. The nodes n of an execution graph represent a database state D_n and a set of triggered rules TR_n, such that each rule is associated with the updates that have caused the rule to be triggered. Any edge between nodes i and j has the following characteristics [1]:

- A label r, such that $r \in TR_i$.
- There is some (possibly empty) set of operations O performed by r such that the triggered rules in TR_j can be derived from the triggered rules in TR_i by:
  1. Removing rule r.
  2. Removing some subset of the rules that can be untriggered by the action of r.

3. Adding all rules in the rule base that may be triggered by that action of r.

Properties of rule bases are then defined in terms of such graphs. For example, a rule base is confluent if every execution graph for the rule base has at most one final state.

A useful contribution of this paper is the notion of *partial confluence*, where confluence is only required to hold for part of the database state. Verification of this proceeds in the same way as for full confluence, but considers only the subset of the rules affecting the relevant part of the database.

9 Applying Relational Algebra to Rule Analysis and Optimisation

Motivation: to support analysis [3] and optimisation [2] of condition-action rules.

Formalism: relational algebra.

Limitations: execution model issues and events are not considered.

An important question in rule analysis, which must be addressed, for example, in the context of the graph analyses of [1], is 'which rule actions may activate other rules?'. A conservative approach to this problem might work on the basis that any rule action that writes to a relation can potentially activate any rule with a condition that monitors the relation. However, such an approach may detect a potential activation dependency between rules which in fact does not exist (for example, because the tuples updated by one rule always yield the value false when the condition of the potentially dependent rule is evaluated).

The work described in [3] shows how the action of one rule can be 'pushed through' the condition of another. This process of pushing an action through a condition is achieved by applying propagation rules. For example, if the rule condition contains the join $E_1 \bowtie E_2$, and the action to be propagated is represented by the insertion E_{ins} to the relation E_1, then the effect of the insertion on the result of the join is $E_{ins} \bowtie E_2$. The successive application of such propagation rules yields a relational algebra expression which may or may not be satisfiable, thereby indicating whether the action may or may not trigger the rule. In general, the satisfiability of relational expressions is undecidable, so automatic analyses must use conservative techniques which are not described in [3].

Further exploitation of relational algebra transformations for active databases is presented in [2], with a view to supporting the optimisation of rule processing. In this case, rule conditions are rewritten to exploit delta relations which represent the changes made to the database since the rule was last evaluated, exploiting knowledge as to the truth (or otherwise) of the condition of the rule when it was last evaluated. This enables a form of preprocessing to be performed on active rule conditions expressed using relational algebra, prior to the application of standard query optimisation techniques.

A strength of this work is that it effectively adapts a proven database formalism for use in active databases. The principal limitations are the close association with the relational model, and limited consideration of the impact of different execution models on rule analysis and optimisation.

10 Event Description Using Petri Nets

Motivation: to provide a formal, abstract and readily implementable description of a rich event description language [7].
Formalism: coloured Petri nets.
Limitations: no specification of features of active behaviour other than events.

The SAMOS active database has a comprehensive language for defining composite and temporal events. This comprises a wide range of primitive events (time events, transaction boundary events, events raised by method calls, user-defined events raised by explicit exception statements) and composite events built from these by composition operators (conjunction, disjunction, sequencing, negation, and counting the number of times an event has occurred).

The formalism used to model composite event detection is Petri nets; this is also used as an implementation technique. Each operator in the event algebra can be modelled as a generic fragment of net; these fragments can be glued together (making the appropriate identifications) to generate a composite net for arbitrarily complex compositions. This is represented in a manner familiar from Petri net theory – a matrix represents the static topology of the net while a vector of places represents its (dynamically changing) marking.

The following example shows how sequential composition of two events (**E1;E2**) is supported. Each occurrence of events **E1** and **E2** generates a new token. The place **H** and transition $t3$ have the effect of ignoring occurrences of **E2** occurring before **E1**. This diagram can be glued into further constructs; **E1** and **E2** can be simple events or the output places of nets representing composites.

Petri nets permit optimisation by algebraic techniques; these techniques are not applied in SAMOS – instead the nets are directly executed from the original matrix/vector representation.

11 Further Work on Formal Approaches to Active Databases

Space limitations preclude detailed descriptions of other formal work on active databases. There have, however, been several significant projects not described in previous sections, a number of which are outlined below. These projects either cover ground which is beyond the scope of this paper (e.g. design), or represent alternative approaches to those presented earlier in the paper.

Harrison and Dietrich [9] provide a Datalog-based formalism which extends previous event algebras in permitting *recursive* complex events – those affecting recursively defined relations in the intensional database. Events and conditions

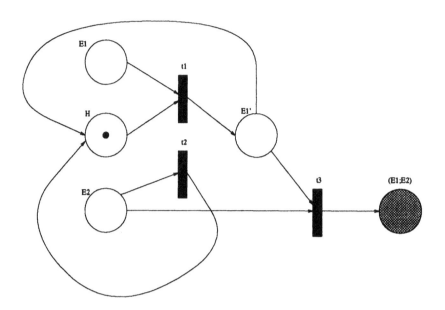

Fig. 2. Petri net for sequential composition.

are treated uniformly, with conditions permitted to examine the previous state of the database. The techniques of the paper also go beyond [7] in providing an optimisation technique for complex event detection, and handle modifications to deductive rules uniformly with modifications to data. This paper does not consider the action part of rules at all; hence issues like termination are beyond its scope.

Zaniolo [23] describes a fixpoint interpretation extending the classical operational semantics of deductive databases to provide them with a common view with active databases. The thrust of [23] is that there is a basic computational engine that can process pure deductive rules and yet simulate the effect of active behaviour. Unfortunately, it seems clear that some of the expressive power of active database systems is not easily captured in a purely declarative framework (e.g., the possibility of specifying particular coupling modes).

Teisseure, Poncelet and Cichetti [19] extend the formally defined semantic data model IFO to support mechanisms for characterising events within an application. An algorithm is presented for generating a set of ECA rules equivalent to a schema of events. This provides a structured methodology for creating rule bases, with potential to reduce design errors. However, the rule generation algorithm neither guarantees nor checks for good behavioural properties (termination and confluence), and expresses only a subset of the functionality of recent active database systems.

Raschid [16] has focused upon a rule execution mechanism for an extended relational database system with condition-action rules, and has shown how rules can be partitioned into non-interacting cliques. Correct rule systems are defined semantically as those that terminate and produce a least fixpoint as a result; a syntactic criterion for this is that they should be *partitioned* so as to limit undesirable interactions between *cliques*, which are defined by reachability. The clique construct is also used to identify nondeterminism (non-confluence).

Karadimce and Urban [12] present an approach to rule analysis based upon conditional term rewrite systems. It is shown how active rules can be mapped onto conditional term rewrite rules (CTRRs) for both execution and analysis. Execution is performed by rewriting the rules using the term rewriting system. Analysis is performed by applying results from the theory of conditional term rewrite systems to the CTRR representation of the active database rules. In this context, termination can be guaranteed when all rules have a specific syntactic property, and confluence is ensured by unifying and comparing pairs of rules in which a single term may be rewritten in different ways.

12 Comparison

The following tables summarise the strengths and weaknesses of the approaches presented in the preceding sections. A – sign indicates that an active database aspect is not represented at all; a + means that it is, but not in a manner lending itself to tractable analysis; a ++ means that formal reasoning about the aspect is supported (formal reasoning about the equivalence model amounts to optimisation capability). Entries in brackets mean that the methodology could be straightforwardly extended to describe (+) or reason about (++) the relevant feature. A less focused consideration of the merits of different formal techniques for use with active systems is given in [4].

12.1 Knowledge Model

Formalism	Event Language	Condition/Action Language
Denotational[21]	–	–
Object-Z[4]	–	–
Algebraic Semantics[11]	+	+
Event Calculus[6]	++	++
Operational Semantics[24]	+	++
Graph Theory[1]	–	–
Relational Algebra[21]	–	++
Petri Nets [7]	++	–

In certain cases, it would be possible to extend the scope of the existing specifications to include comprehensive descriptions of the event and condition/action languages (e.g. using Denotational Semantics or Object-Z), but to do so would be a significant task. In Heraclitus, reasoning about the condition/action language is complicated by the fact that algebraic and imperative constructs are used together in the complete system.

12.2 Execution Model

Formalism	Transition Granularity	Coupling Mode	Priority Scheme	Nett-Effect Policy
Denotational[21]	+	+	+	+
Object-Z [4]	+	+	+	+
Algebraic Semantics[11]	+	+	+	++
Event Calculus[6]	+	+	+	+
Operational Semantics[24]	+	+	- (+)	- (+)
Relational Algebra[21]	-	-	-	-
Graph Theory[1]	-	-	+	-
Petri Nets[7]	-	-	-	-

In a number of the above cases, only one transition granularity or coupling mode is supported, but this could often be extended to cope with description of more complex systems. In [6], the execution model has been described formally using an operational semantics, rather than within the event calculus itself. It is not clear how generally useful an ability to reason about the execution model is in isolation, but it is evident that certain aspects of the execution model do affect analysis results and optimisation potential, so access to a formal description of the execution model can be seen as important to mainstream tasks relating to active rule systems.

12.3 Management

Formalism	Operations on rules	Termin- -ation	Conflu- -ence	Equivalence Model
Denotational[21]	- (+)	-	-	-
Object-Z [4]	+	-	-	-
Algebraic Semantics[11]	- (+)	-	-	-
Event Calculus[6]	- (+)	- (++)	- (++)	- (++)
Operational Semantics[24]	- (+)	++	++	++
Graph Theory[1]	- (+)	++	++	-
Relational Algebra[21]	-	++	++	++
Petri Nets[7]	-	-	-	(++)

A number of remarks which were made in section 12.1 are also of relevance here, as, in general, reasoning about features such as termination and confluence is dependent upon event and condition/action languages being amenable to automatic analysis. In the deductive context of [6], termination and confluence analyses could exploit related work on deductive databases [14].

13 Conclusions

This paper has described and compared a range of approaches which have been adopted to the formal specification of different aspects of active behaviour. A number of points can be made in concluding:

1. Individual proposals rarely support the formal specification of a complete system, which is probably because different formalisms seem to be best suited to different tasks.
2. Despite the above point, it is relatively unusual for different formalisms to be used together (although exceptions are presented in sections 5 and 6). In other domains, it is common for multiple formalisms to be used together (e.g. for specifying the syntax and semantics of programming languages).
3. Implementations are rarely derived from formal specifications (exceptions include Heraclitus and SAMOS), although formal specifications are sometimes derived for existing systems (e.g. Starburst).
4. The potential for reasoning about specifications has rarely been exploited in implementations, and there is little evidence that working optimisers or analysers have been developed from formal specifications described in the literature.

It can be hoped that future work will: lead to formal specifications of all aspects of implemented active databases; exploit formal techniques during the implementation of systems; and develop useful tools which assist in the design and implementation of applications which use active database facilities.

Acknowledgements We are pleased to acknowledge the support of the UK EPSRC (grant GR/H43847) and the EU HC&M (ACT-NET) programme in funding active database research at Heriot-Watt. This work has also benefited from useful discussions with Andrew Dinn and Oscar Diaz.

References

1. A. Aiken, J. Widom, and J.M. Hellerstein. Behaviour of database production rules: Termination, confluence, and observable determinism. In *ACM SIGMOD*, volume 21, pages 59–68, 1992.
2. E. Baralis and J. Widom. Using delta relations to optimize condition evaluation in active databases. Technical Report Stan-CS-93-1495, Department of Computer Science, Stanford University, 1993.
3. E. Baralis and J. Widom. An algebraic approach to rule analysis in expert database systems. In J. Bocca, M. Jarke, and C. Zaniolo, editors, *Proc. 20th VLDB*, pages 475–486. Morgan-Kaufmann, 1994.
4. J. Campin, N.W. Paton, and M.H. Williams. A Structured Specification of an Active Database System. *Information and Software Technology*, 37(1):47–61, 1995.
5. J. Campin, N.W. Paton, and M.H. Williams. Specifying Active Database Systems in an Object-Oriented Framework. *submitted for publication*, 1995.
6. Alvaro A.A. Fernandes, M. Howard Williams, and Norman W. Paton. A Logic-Based Integration of Active and Deductive Databases, 1994. Submitted for publication.
7. S. Gatziu and K.R. Dittrich. Events in an active object-oriented database. In N.W. Paton and M.H. Williams, editors, *Rules in Database Systems*, pages 23–39. Springer-Verlag, 1994.
8. E.N. Hanson. Rule Condition Testing and Action Execution in Ariel. In *Proc. SIGMOD*, pages 49–58. ACM, 1992.

9. J.V. Harrison and S.W. Dietrich. Integrating active and deductive rules. In N.W. Paton and M.H. Williams, editors, *Proc. 1st Int. Workshop on Rules In Database Systems*, pages 288–305. Springer-Verlag, 1994.

10. R. Hull and D. Jacobs. Language constructs for programming active databases. In R. Camps G.M. Lohman, A. Sernadas, editor, *Intl. Conf on Very Large Data Bases*, volume 17, pages 455–467. Morgan Kaugmann, 1991.

11. D. Jacobs and R. Hull. Database Programming With Delayed Updates. In P. Kanellakis and J. Schmidt, editors, *Third International Workshop on Database Programming Languages*. Morgan-Kaufmann, 1991.

12. A.P. Karadimce and S.D. Urban. Conditional Term Rewriting as a Basis for Analysis of Active Database Rules. In J. Widom and S. Chakravarthy, editors, *Proc. IEEE RIDE-ADS Workshop on Active Database Systems*, pages 156–162. IEEE Press, 1994.

13. R. Kowalski. Database updates in the event calculus. *Journal of Logic Programming*, 12:121–146, 1992.

14. A.Y. Levy and Y. Sagiv. Queries independent of updates. In R. Agrawal, S. Baker, and D. Bell, editors, *Proc. 19th VLDB*, pages 171–181. Morgan-Kaufmann, 1993.

15. N.W. Paton, O. Diaz, M.H. Williams, J. Campin, A. Dinn, and A. Jaime. Dimensions of active behaviour. In N.W. Paton and M.H. Williams, editors, *Proc. 1st Int. Workshop on Rules In Database Systems*, pages 40–57. Springer-Verlag, 1994.

16. L. Raschid. A semantics for a class of stratified production system programs. *J. Logic Programming*, 21(1):31–57, 1994.

17. G.A. Rose. Object-Z. In S. Stepney, R. Barden, and David Cooper, editors, *Object-Orientation in Z*, pages 59–77. Springer-Verlag, 1992.

18. M. Stonebraker, A. Jhingran, J. Goh, and S. Potamianos. On rules, procedures, caching and views in database systems. In *Proc. ACM SIGMOD*, pages 281–290, 1990.

19. M. Teisseire, P. Poncelet, and R. Cichetti. Towards event-driven modelling for database design. In J. Bocca, M. Jarke, and C. Zaniolo, editors, *Proc. 20th Int. Conf on VLDB*, pages 1–12. Morgan-Kaufmann, 1994.

20. L. van der Voort and A. Siebes. Enforcing confluence of rule execution. In N.W. Paton and M.H. Williams, editors, *Proc. 1st Int. Workshop on Rules In Database Systems*, pages 194–207. Springer-Verlag, 1994.

21. J. Widom. A Denotational Senmantics for the Starburst Production Rule Language. *ACM SIGMOD Record*, 21(3):4–9, 1992.

22. J. Widom and S.J. Finkelstein. Set-Oriented Production Rules in Relational Database Systems. In *Proceedings of the ACM SIGMOD International Conference on Management of Data*, pages 259–270, 1990.

23. C. Zaniolo. A unified semantics for active and deductive databases. In N.W. Paton and M.H. Williams, editors, *Rules in Database Systems*. Springer-Verlag, 1994.

24. Y. Zhou and M. Hsu. A theory for rule triggering systems. In F. Bancilhon and et al., editors, *Proc. Extending Database Technology (EDBT)*, pages 407–421. Springer-Verlag, 1990.

Denotational Semantics for an Active Rule Execution Model

Thierry Coupaye and Christine Collet

LGI-IMAG, University of Grenoble
BP 54 38041 cedex 9, France
e-mail: {Thierry.Coupaye, Christine.Collet}@imag.fr
Phone: (33) 76 51 44 73
Fax: (33) 76 44 66 75

Abstract. In the last few years, many active database models have been proposed. Some of them have been implemented as research prototypes. The use and study of these prototypes shows that it is difficult to get a clear idea of the proposed approaches and to compare them. More generally there are some unquestionable difficulties in understanding, reasoning about and teaching behavior of active database systems. We think there is a need for formal descriptions of the semantics of such systems in order to describe and to understand them with less ambiguities, to compare them and to come up with some progress in defining standard concepts and functionalities for active databases.

This paper presents an informal and then a formal semantics of the execution model of an active system we developed at the University of Grenoble, France. We show that such a formal description is adequate for comparing our proposal with existing ones and for identifying and classifying functions of an active database system.

1 Introduction

In the last twenty years, a great deal of progress has been made in Programming Languages toward the definition of a theoretical framework which allows to reason about the semantics of these languages. These works [Sto77] show that formal semantics is useful for language designers, programmers and serious users (!) since it provides respectively:

- a tool for design and analysis, as it can suggest elegant and efficient implementations,
- a precise basis for a computer implementation, as it guarantees that the implementation matches the designers wishes and that the language is implemented the same way for different systems or machines,
- useful user documentation, as a trained user is able to read a formal semantics definition and use it to answer subtle questions about the language.

We believe formal semantics is also useful for *active databases* which support automatic triggering of actions as response to events. In the last few years, many active database systems have been proposed. Most of them use more or less the paradigm of *active rule* built on the *Event-Condition-Action (ECA) formalism*. Active rules allow the specification of some actions (A) including database operations that are executed automatically as a response to events (E) and whenever conditions (C) hold. Events are generated by some operations and then detected by the active rule system or generated explicitly (user-defined events). Generally speaking, events are generated in the context (of the execution) of a data base application including transactions. Therefore, the processing of rules is handled in a specific environment defined as a data base application. Active rule systems differ from one another by (1) the underlying data model (relational, object-oriented, etc.), (2) the integration of active rules in this data model (rules as first class objects, rules as part of class definition, etc.) and also (3) rule expressivity. But the most crucial differences arise from (4) choices about the overall behavior of the rule system. This behavior, or *rule execution model* defines the actual semantics of the rule system. It mainly covers two aspects: (1) when and how (in which order) rules are executed and (2) what are the effects of rule executions on the environment of the other rules and on further rule executions.

In most of the active systems proposals, the semantics is given in an informal, natural language description as in [HLM88]. The use of these prototypes or the attempt to understand them shows that it it is difficult to have a clear idea of the approaches and to compare them. More generally there are some unquestionable difficulties in understanding, reasoning about and teaching behavior of active database systems.

We think there is a need for formal descriptions of the semantics of such systems in order to describe and to understand them with less ambiguities, to compare them and to come up with some progress in defining standard concepts and functionalities for active databases.

They have been already a few attempts to give a formal semantics to active systems:

- The database programming language *Heraclitus* [HJ91, SGJ93] is an extension of C that supports the relational algebra and novel constructs related to the specification of the semantics of active database systems.
- An operational semantics for the Activity Description Language ADL [Beh93] is given in [Beh94]. It uses Gurevich's evolving algebras. An evolving algebra can be seen as an abstract machine which uses a set of universes, a set of functions and a set of transition rules. Universes and functions define algebras that can evolve dynamically according to transitions rules.
- Finally, a denotational semantics of the Starburst Production Rule Language is given in [Wid92]. Denotational semantics can be used as a methodology for giving mathematical (functional) meaning to active rule systems. Its high-level structure makes it useful for designers, programmers and users. A denotational definition is made of a set of algebras and a set of valuation functions on these algebras. An algebra is defined as a semantic domain and a set of operations on this domain.

This paper gives a formal semantics of the execution model of the Native Active Object System (NAOS) [CHCA94, CCS94] developed at the University of

Grenoble, France. This system has been designed in the framework of the GOOD-STEP project[1] for developing an object-oriented database system dedicated to support Software Development Environments(SDE) [GOO94]. Active rule facilities have been incorporated into the object database system O_2 [BDK92, Tec95] as a means to support some aspects of these environments.

For defining the semantics of NAOS, we found *Heraclitus* not convenient mainly because this language is purely relational. In object-oriented databases, all possible operations (creation, update of objects, method and program calls, etc.) cannot be expressed only in terms of insertions, deletions as in relational databases. Combined effects of operations (executed by applications or rule processing) cannot thus be calculated using *Heraclitus* constructs. We were largely inspired by the work presented in [Wid92] and we also chose denotational semantics because a denotational definition is more abstract than an operational one, for it does not specify computation steps. Another reason for choosing denotational semantics is that we think like R. D. Tennent in [Ten76] that this "general language-independent framework of semantical concepts would help to standardize terminology, clarify similarities and differences between" active rule systems.

The denotational semantics of the NAOS execution model is defined as a meaning function $\mathcal{M}$ that takes any set of rules and produces the function that maps a set of events (produced by a set of operations in a transaction or by rule executions) and a database state into the new database state that results from processing those rules.

The paper is organized as follows. Section 2 gives an informal description of the execution model of the NAOS rule system. Sections 3 and 4 introduce respectively semantic domains and valuation functions used to build the complete formal semantics of the system. Then, Section 5 shows that the formal description of NAOS is well suited for comparing our proposal with existing ones and for identifying and classifying functions of an active database system.

2 NAOS Rule Semantics

A complete description of NAOS and numerous examples of rules are given in [CCS94] which presents the overall system and in [CHCA94] which mostly details the event types provided by the system. In the following we only adress aspects which are relevant to the semantics of rule execution.

A rule definition is made of three main components. An event part, a condition part and an action part. The event part specifies which event(s) will trigger a rule. In the current prototype we detect both primitive and composite events, ut for the time being and in this paper we consider only internal primitive events for rule executions. Thus, this paper does not deal with composite and temporal events[2] and the word *event* will be used for *internal primitive event*. There are

---

[1] GOODSTEP is an Esprit-III research and development project funded by the CEC under contract No 6115

[2] Thus it does not deal with *simultaneous events*.

two kinds of primitive events: entity manipulation events and applicative events. Entity manipulation events are generated by the manipulation of an entity (an entity is either an object or a value) or part of an entity. In the latter case a path in the entity type has to be specified in the event type. Operations that may generate events are the creation, deletion, access to an entity, update of an entity, the fact that this entity become persistent or transient, the insertion and deletion in a collection attribute of the entity and method calls. Applicative events are associated with the beginning or end of a transaction, a program or an application. The condition part is an O_2SQL query (O_2SQL is a SQL-like language). The action part is made of an O_2C code[3].

When considering a rule execution model, four points have to be taken into account: the coupling modes, multiples rules triggered by the same event, cascading executions of rules, and repercussion of rule executions on further rule executions.

Coupling modes specify when and how rules are executed. Based on the atomic transaction model of O_2, we have defined two kinds of rules: (1) *immediate rules* which are executed right after the occurrence of an event of their associated event type (*event-instance-oriented semantics*) and (2) *deferred rules*, corresponding to cumulative changes on entities (*event-set-oriented semantics*), which are executed at the end of the transaction (just before the validation of the transaction) in which instances of their associated event types have occurred.

When an event occurs, several rules may be triggered. One then has to know in which order these rules will be executed. In NAOS this order is given by *priorities* between rules. The system assigns default priorities based on rule definition order and the programmer can overwrite these priorities by specifying *precedence relationships* between couples of rules. This mechanism allows to define a total order which ensures a deterministic behavior of the rule system.

When a rule is executed, the system first evaluates its condition and if it holds it executes its action. The execution of the action part may generate new events that may trigger other rules an so on. Once again one has to know in which order all these rules will be executed. To establish this order we have introduced the notion of *execution cycle*. An execution cycle is a succession of operations that are executed in a transaction (the current transaction is referred to as cycle 0) or during the execution of the action part of a rule. Whatever the coupling mode, rules are always executed in a new execution cycle different from the one in which triggering event(s) occurred. If several rules have to be executed in the same execution cycle, they are executed according to their priorities as we have seen before. Immediate rules are executed in a *depth first order* while deferred rules are executed in a *width first order*. Furthermore, Immediate rules have an implicit priority on deferred rules.

When a rule is triggered, a data structure representing the rule execution environment is built by the system. This structure, called a *delta structure*, is named by the programmer in the event part and can be accessed in the condition

---

[3] O_2 and all product names derived from it (O_2SQL, O_2C, O_2API) are registered trademarks of O_2 Technology.

and action parts. The type of a delta structure depends on the kind of the rule and its event type. As an example for an immediate rule triggered by the update of an attribute (the operation type is *UPDATE*), the delta structure built contains the entity concerned by the update operation plus the new value of the attribute.

Last but not least, when executing a rule, only significant events should be considered. If a rule is triggered by the creation of an entity but this same entity happens to be destroyed before the actual execution of the rule, the rule should not be executed. Choice of rules to be executed and construction of delta structures are thus made considering the *net effect* of operations performed in the triggering transaction. In NAOS the calculation of net effect is based on the classical composition of pairs of operations performed on the same entity.

Assume for instance that a rule r is triggered by the insertion of elements in an attribute s of collection type:

- if elements a,b,c are inserted into s and then elements a,b are deleted from s, the only event (resulting from the calculation of net effect) taken into account for the execution of r is the insertion of element c,
- if elements a,b are inserted and then elements a,b,c are deleted, the only event taken into account is the deletion of the element c, and r is not executed,
- finally, if elements a,b,c are inserted and then deleted, there is no resulting event so again r is not executed.

3   Semantic Domains

As we said previously, an algebra is defined as a semantic domain and a set of operations on this domain. In our case, we do not need operations on the domains we define. Thus, in the following, we only use domains. In programming languages and systems, a semantic domain is a space of values. A domain may have a structure different than a set, but sets are adequate for all situations discussed in this paper.

3.1   Domain of Database States

Let DBS be the domain of database states. The formal definition of a database state can be found in [LRV92]. Informally a database state is mainly a type system Π together with a consistent set of objects and values that represent instances of the types of Π at a given time.

Events detected and treated by NAOS are generated by the execution of O_2 applications which are written using O_2C and O_2SQL. As we already said, NAOS rule conditions are written in O_2SQL and NAOS rule actions are written in O_2C. In order to give a formal semantics of the whole NAOS system we would need a formal semantics of the O_2 Object Model, O_2C and O_2SQL.

However, since our goal is to help in understanding the behavior of NAOS rules, i.e. the semantics of the NAOS execution model, we will not use the formal definition of a database state in the rest of this paper. We claim that for the comprehension of the reader, he/she has just to know that, at a given time, the database is in a state that could be formally described.

3.2 Domain of Events

The domain of events E is one of the most important since it allows to define **both a particular event and the environment of this event**.

Let OPT be the domain of operation types, $OPT = \{CREATE, DESTROY,$ $, RETRIEVE, UPDATE, INSERT, DELETE, ATTACH, DETACH,$ $METHOD\_BEGIN, METHOD\_END\} \cup AOPT$ where $AOPT$ is the set of applicative operation types that denote the begin and end of transactions, programs and applications.

In the O_2 kernel, all entities are uniquely identified. We can thus consider EID as the domain of entity identifiers.

Let P be the domain of *paths*. Let p be a path in P; p allows to reach a component value in a entity - for instance, the attribute **children** of an instance of the class **Person**. A path can be specified for the operation types $RETRIEVE$, $UPDATE$, $INSERT$ and $DELETE$ but it is not mandatory. In case a path is not given (e.g., if we are interested in by the event $UPDATE$ **Person**), we will denote this kind of *empty path* by $\perp^4$ ($\perp \in P$).

The three domains OPT, EID and P allow to represent an event itself, i.e., an happen of interest. The two last domains, V and Δ allow to represent the environment associated with an event.

V is the domain of values. Let v be a value in V; v is the value of an entity (or part of an entity).

We call δ such that $\delta \in \Delta$, an *update value*. If the associated operation type is $UPDATE$ then the update value denotes the new value of the entity (or part of the entity if the path is not empty). If the associated operation type is $INSERT$ or $DELETE$ then the update value denotes the elements inserted or deleted from the entity (or part of the entity if the path is not empty).

Let E be the domain of events, $E = OPT \times EID \times P \times V \times \Delta$. Let e be an event in E, $e = (opt, eid, p, v, \delta)$ where:

- $opt \in OPT$ is an operation type,
- $eid \in EID$ is an entity identifier,
- $p \in P$ is a path in the entity identified by eid,
- $v \in V$ is the value of the entity identified by eid ($p=\perp$) or the value of the subpart of this entity which can be reached by p ($p \neq \perp$),
- $\delta \in \Delta$ is the update value of the considered entity ($p=\perp$) or the update value of the subpart of this entity which can be reached by p ($p \neq \perp$).

---

[4] In the following, $\perp$ will represent the non-termination, a null value or no value at all, i.e., a lack of information. To be completely clean, we should have a different $\perp$ for each domain. But we consider that, in our case, using the same symbol is not ambiguous.

As an example, consider the event e generated by the insertion of instances of class **Person** in an attribute **children** of type **set(Person)**. This event is denoted by: $e = < INSERT, eid, p, v, \delta >$. In this case v is the old value (before the insertion) of **children** and δ the set of elements inserted into **children**. Note that for applicative events, the operation type denotes completely an event. As an example, an event generated by the beginning of a transaction is denoted by $< TRANSACTION\_BEGIN, \perp, \perp, \perp, \perp >$.

Event Orderings. Let O_E be the domain of event orderings. Let o_E be an ordering in O_E, such that $o_E = \{e_i \leq_E e_j\}$ where e_i and e_j are in E and $\leq_E$ is reflexive, transitive, antisymmetric and total ($\forall e_i, e_j \in E$, $e_i \leq_E e_j$ or $e_j \leq_E e_i$).

Intuitively, the relation $\leq_E$ allows to order events over time: $e_i \leq_E e_j$ iff e_i has occurred before e_j. One can consider that when an event is detected, a timestamp is assigned to it. Timestamps are then used to build event orderings.

Domain of set of events. Let S be the domain of set of events, $S = P(E)$ where P is the powerset operator. Let s be a set of events in S, $s = \{e_1, ..., e_n\}$ where $e_1, ..., e_n$ are in E. Note that $(s, \leq_E)$ **is a totally ordered set (chain).**

3.3 Domain of Rules.

Let R be the domain of rules. $R = IR \uplus DR$ where IR is the domain of immediate rules, DR is the domain of deferred rules and the symbol $\uplus$ denotes the disjunct union (sum) of domains.

Note that it is useless to tag the elements of R since $IR \cap DR = \emptyset$ (a rule is either immediate or deferred).

A rule can be activated or deactivated for a given rule execution. This can be considered as a dynamic feature of a rule. Let ACM be the domain of rule activation modes, $ACM = \{A, D\}$ where A denotes an *activated* rule and D a *deactivated* rule. The activation mode of a rule is important since a deactivated rule will not be executed.

Domain of Immediate Rules. Let IR be the domain of immediate rules. Let r be an immediate rule in IR. r is a function that takes an activation mode, a database state dbs and an event e. It returns a boolean value, a new database state and the set of events produced by the execution of r. That is:

$$r : ACM \rightarrow DBS \times E \rightarrow \text{ß} \times DBS \times S$$

$r(A)(dbs, e) \downarrow 1 = true$ iff r is triggered by e^5. If $r(A)(dbs, e) \downarrow 1 = false$ then $r(A)(dbs, e) \downarrow 2 = dbs$ and $r(A)(dbs, e) \downarrow 3 = \emptyset$. If $r(A)(dbs, e) \downarrow 1 = true$ then (i) $r(A)(dbs, e) \downarrow 2$ is the result of the execution of rule r with dbs as the initial database state and e as the event environment (delta structure) and (ii)

---

[5] We use $\downarrow i$ to denote the projection on the ith element of a Cartesian product.

$r(A)(dbs, e) \downarrow 3 = \{e_1, ..., e_n\}$ where $\{e_1, ..., e_n\}$ is the set of events produced by the execution of rule r.

Note that if the condition is evaluated to false then $r(A)(dbs, e) \downarrow 2 = dbs$ and $r(A)(dbs, e) \downarrow 3 = \emptyset$ (we assume that the evaluation of a condition does not have side-effects).

Note also that $r(D)(dbs, e) \downarrow 1 = false$ since a deactivated rule is not executed.

Domain of Deferred Rules. Let DR be the domain of deferred rules. Let r be a deferred rule in DR. r is a function that takes an activation mode, a database state dbs and a set of event s. It returns a boolean value, a new database state and a set of events (produced by the execution of r). That is:
$$r : ACM \rightarrow DBS \times S \rightarrow \text{ß} \times DBS \times S$$
The definitions given in Sect. 3.3 are valid for deferred rules too, considering a set of events s instead of an event e (because deferred rules have a set oriented semantics).

Rule Orderings. Let O_R be the domain of rule orderings. Let o_R be an ordering in O_R, $o_R = \{r_i \leq_R r_j\}$ where r_i and r_j are in R and $\leq_R$ is reflexive, transitive, antisymmetric and total. The relation $\leq_R$ allows to order rules:
$$r_i \leq_R r_j \text{ iff } r_j \text{ has a higher priority than } r_i.$$

3.4 Other Domains

Let RSC be the domain of rule-events-cycle triples. $RSC = R \times S \times \mathbb{N}$ where $\mathbb{N}$ is the set of natural integers. Let rsc be a rule-events-cycle triple in RSC, $rsc = < r, s, c >$ where $r \in R$, $s \in S$, $c \in \mathbb{N}$. The set of events and the cycle considered for the selection and the execution of rule r are denoted by s and c respectively.

Let $SRSC$ be the domain of sets of rule-events-cycle triples. $SRSC = P(RSC)$ where P is the powerset operator.

4 Valuation Functions

The valuation functions given in this section can be divided into two groups:

- functions of the first group (Sect. 4.4 to 4.8) concern the choice of rules to be executed considering multiples rules triggered by the same event and cascading executions,
- functions of the second group (Sect. 4.9) concern the actual rule execution and the calculation of net effect. Due to a lack of space all these functions cannot be given in this paper.

For each function defined, we give an informal description and a formal (functional) one. The formal description is given using the Church λ-calculus [Hin86].

We use the *let* abbreviation defined as:

$$(let\ x = expr_1\ in\ expr_2) \equiv (\lambda x.expr_2)\ expr_1.$$

We also use:

- the *cases* notation which is like the C `switch` notation
- sometimes a Prolog-like notation in which the character "_" stands for any value in the considered domain.

4.1 $\mathcal{M}$

$\mathcal{M}$ takes a set of rules $\{r_1, ..., r_n\}$, a rule ordering o_R and an event ordering o_E. The meaning of $\{r_1, ..., r_n\}$, o_R and o_E, denoted $\mathcal{M}[\{r_1, ..., r_n\}, o_R, o_E]$ is a function which takes a database state *dbs*, a set of events s and a cycle number c. It returns a new database state and a new set of rule-events-cycle triples that results from processing the rules in $\{r_1, ..., r_n\}$ starting from the initial set of events s (these events occurred in cycle 0, which corresponds to the triggering transaction) and the initial database state *dbs* using the orderings o_R and o_E. This processing may not terminate. In that case, the function returns $\bot$ (bottom). Otherwise, the function returns a set of rule-events-cycle triples in which all set of events are empty. This means that all events have been treated and all rules associated to them have been executed.

$\mathcal{M}$ is defined as follows:

$$\mathcal{M} : P(R) \times O_R \times O_E \rightarrow DBS \times S \times \mathbb{N} \rightarrow (DBS \times SRSC) \cup \{\bot\}$$
$$\mathcal{M}[\{r_1, ..., r_n\}, o_R, o_E] = \lambda dbs, s, c.$$
$$\mathcal{M}'(o_R, o_E)(< dbs, Distrib(s, c, \{r_1, ..., r_n\}) >)$$

4.2 Distrib

Distrib takes a set of events s, a cycle c and a set of rules $\{r_1, ..., r_n\}$. It returns the set of rule-events-cycle triples that results from distributing s and c to each rule in $\{r_1, ..., r_n\}$. *Distrib* is defined as follows:

$$Distrib : S \times \mathbb{N} \times P(R) \rightarrow SRSC$$
$$Distrib = \lambda s, c, \{r_1, ..., r_n\}.$$
$$\{< r_1, s, c >, ..., < r_n, s, c >\}$$

4.3 $\mathcal{M}'$

$\mathcal{M}'$ takes a rule ordering o_R and an event ordering o_E. It returns the least fixed point of a function $\mathcal{F}$. Function $\mathcal{F}$ takes a database state *dbs* and a set of rule-events-cycle triples $\{< r_1, s_1, c_1 >, ..., < r_n, s_n, c_n >\}$. It returns $< dbs, \bot >$ if no rules are triggered by the events in $s_1 \cup s_2 \cup ... \cup s_n$. Otherwise, $\mathcal{F}$ calls function *Choose-Triggered* to choose a rule r and then applies itself to the new database state and set of rule-events-cycle triples that results from calling function *Execute* with r, *dbs* and $\{< r_1, s_1, c_1 >, ..., < r_n, s_n, c_n >\}$. $\mathcal{M}'$ is defined as follows:

$$\mathcal{M}': O_R \times O_E \to DBS \times SRSC \to (DBS \times SRSC) \cup \{\bot\}$$
$$\mathcal{M}' = \lambda o_R, o_E. \; Least\text{-}Fixed\text{-}Point(\lambda \, \mathcal{F}.$$
$$\lambda < dbs, srsc >\}.$$
$$\quad if \; (Eligible-I(srsc) \cup Eligible-D(srsc)) = \emptyset$$
$$\quad then \; < dbs, \bot >$$
$$\quad else \; let \; r_i = \; Choose\text{-}Triggered(srsc, o_R, o_E)$$
$$\quad in \; \mathcal{F}(Execute(o_E)(r_i, dbs, (srsc)))$$

Proving that a least fixed point of function $\mathcal{F}$ exists is not trivial and beyond the scope of this paper. One can notice that this problem is very similar to the one encountered when one wants to define the semantics of a `while` statement in imperative languages: it is possible that a program using a `while` statement never ends, however, it is possible to give a formal semantics of a `while` statement. This point is discussed in [Ten76, Sto77].

4.4 Eligible-I

Eligible–I takes a set of rule-events-cycle triples and returns the set of immediate rules that are triggered by at least one event in their associated set of events. $Eligible-I$ is defined as follows:

$$Eligible-I : SRSC \to SRSC$$
$$Eligible-I = \lambda srsc.$$
$$\{< r_i, s_i, c_i >\in srsc \mid r_i \in IR \wedge (\exists e_j \in s_i \mid r_i(A)(\_, e_j) \downarrow 1 = true)\}$$

4.5 Eligible-D

Eligible–D takes a set of rule-events-cycle triples and returns the set of deferred rules that are triggered by events in their associated set of events. $Eligible - D$ is defined as follows:

$$Eligible-D : SRSC \to SRSC$$
$$Eligible-D = \lambda srsc.$$
$$\{< r_i, s_i, c_i >\in srsc \mid r_i \in DR \wedge r_i(A)(\_, s_i) \downarrow 1 = true\}$$

4.6 Choose-Triggered

Choose-Triggered takes a set of rule-events-cycle triples, a rule ordering o_R and an event ordering o_E; it returns a rule that will be next executed. *Choose-Triggered* first tries to choose a rule among immediate rules. If no immediate rule has to be executed then it chooses a rule among deferred rules. This shows that **immediate rules have an implicit priority on deferred rules**.

Choose-Triggered is never applied on a set of rule-events-cyle triples containing no eligible rules.

Choose-Triggered is defined as follows:

$$Choose\text{-}Triggered : SRSC \times O_R \times O_E \to R$$
$$Choose\text{-}Triggered = \lambda srsc, o_R, o_E.$$
$$\quad if \; Eligible-I(srsc) \neq \emptyset$$
$$\quad then \; Select-I(Eligible-I(srsc), o_R, o_E)$$
$$\quad else \; Select-D(Eligible-D(srsc), o_R)$$

4.7 Select-I

Select−I takes a set of rule-events-cycle triples *srsc*, a rule ordering o_R and an event ordering o_E. It first searchs the set of rules associated with the greatest cycle by calling function *Greatest-Cycle*. Afterwards, by calling function *First-Event-Cycle*, it chooses the rule that is triggered by the first occurred event. If there are several, it chooses the rule with the highest priority. Note that function *Select−I* illustrates the **depth first execution order of immediate rules**. *Select−I* is always called with a set *srsc* containing only immediate rules. *Select−I* is defined as follows:

$$Select-I : SRSC \times O_R \times O_E \rightarrow R$$
$$Select-I = \lambda srsc, o_R, o_E.$$
$$First\text{-}Event\text{-}Rule((Greatest\text{-}Cycle(srsc), o_R, o_E)$$

4.8 Select-D

Select − D takes a set of rule-events-cycle triples and a rule ordering o_R. It returns the rule with the highest priority triggered by events that occurred in the smallest cycle. *Select−D* illustrates the **width first execution order of deferred rules**. *Select − D* is always called with a set *srsc* containing only deferred rules. *Select−D* is defined as follows:

$$Select-D : SRSC \times O_R \rightarrow R$$
$$Select-D = \lambda srsc, o_R.$$
$$r_i \; where$$
$$< r_i, s_i, c_i > \in \; srsc \; \wedge$$
$$\{< r_j, s_j, c_j > \in \; srsc \; | \; c_j < c_i \vee (c_j = c_i \wedge r_j \leq_R r_i)\} = \emptyset$$

4.9 Execute

Execute takes a event ordering o_E, a rule r_e, a database state *dbs* and a set of rule-events-cycle triples containing the triple $< r_e, s_e, c_e >$ where r_e is the rule to execute. It returns:

1. a new database state resulting from executing r_e starting with database state *dbs* and;
2. a set of rule-events-cycle triples which reflects the actual execution of r_e on that set. As a matter of fact, the execution r_e may generate new events that may modify the environment of rules in the given set of rule-events-cycle. In particular, these events were not in the given event ordering o_E but they should be for further rule executions. In a way, the function *Extend* inserts these events in o_E. Because of these generated events, some rules that were triggered before may not be executed (because of net effect), some others that were not triggered before may be triggered by these new events. Thus, for each rule-events-cycle triple $< r_i, s_i, c_i >$, s_i and c_i have to be re-calculated. Note that the calculation of the environment differs for r_e and for other rules. That is why the two functions *Reflect-e* and *Reflect* (resp.) are defined.

Execute is a bit more tricky if r_e is an immediate rule because one has to know the event e which has triggered r_e. Event e is the first occurred event in $\{e_1, ..., e_n\}$ that triggers r_e. *Execute* is defined as follows:

$Execute : O_E \rightarrow R \times DBS \times SRSC \rightarrow DBS \times SRSC$

$Execute[o_E] = \lambda r_e, dbs, srsc.$

$\quad let\ rsc_e =< r_e, s_e, c_e >\in\ srsc$

$\quad\quad new\_dbs = r_e(A)(dbs, e) \downarrow 2,$

$\quad\quad s_g = r_e(A)(dbs, e) \downarrow 3$

$\quad in$

$\quad if\ r_e \in IR$

$\quad then\ let\ e = First\text{-}Triggering\text{-}Event(r_e, s_e, o_E)\ in$

$\quad\quad < new\_dbs,$

$\quad\quad Reflect\text{-}e(Extend(o_E, s_g))(s_g, < r_e, s_e - \{e\}, c_e >) \cup$

$\quad\quad Reflect(Extend(o_E, s_g))(s_g, srsc - \{< r_e, s_e, c_e >\}) >$

$\quad else$

$\quad\quad < new\_dbs,$

$\quad\quad Reflect\text{-}e(Extend(o_E, s_g))(s_g, < r_e, s_e, c_e >) \cup$

$\quad\quad Reflect(Extend(o_E, s_g))(s_g, srsc - \{< r_e, s_e, c_e \}) >$

5 Comparisons with Others Works

This section compares the NAOS rule execution model with other active rule execution models; it mainly concerns NAOS and Starburst[Wid92] as they are the only two active rule systems for which the execution model have been formally described. In these two systems, three kinds of domains can be distinguished:

- First, domains describing database states: S in Starburst and DBS in NAOS. Differences most important come from the fact that the underlying data model is relational in the first case and object-oriented in the other. We consider that the DBS domain is not crucial because, as we said before, we are just interested in describing the active rule **execution** model and not the entire active rule model.
- Second, domains describing situations that can trigger rules. They are Δ, the domain of sets of database changes for Starburst and S the domain of sets of events for NAOS. Elements of S are somewhat more complicated than elements of Δ because once again of the underlying object-oriented data model and because events "carry" a lot of semantics.
- Finally, domains describing rules (mainly R in both cases). Note that the ACM domain (the domain of activation modes) does not exist for Starburst since the notion of dynamic deactivation/reactivation of rules does not exist in this system.

If we discard $\mathcal{M}, \mathcal{M}'$ and *Distrib* which are very general functions common to Starburst and NAOS semantics, valuations functions can be divided into two groups:

– The first group is made of functions *Run-Rule*, *Add-Changes* and *Net-Effect*
for Starburst, *Execute*, *Reflect*, *Net-Effect*, *Compose* and *Compose-events* for
NAOS. These functions deal with the actual execution of one single rule and
the effects of this particular execution on further executions of rules and on
the database state. Calculation of net effect is a bit more tricky in NAOS
because they are other operations than insertions, deletions and updates
that have to be taken in account. Reflection of the execution of a rule on the
database state is, in a way, more complete in Starburst semantics. This is
due, for some part, to the fact that O_2SQL and O_2C which allow respectively
to express conditions and actions in NAOS do not have a formal semantics.

– The second group is made of functions *Choose-Triggered*, *Eligible* and *Select*.
These functions deal with the execution of a set of rules. Problems addressed
here are when and how rules have to be executed. These problems are generally referred as *multiple rule executions* and *cascading rule executions*. In
Starburst there is only one kind of rules which executions are deferred to
some execution points. A system-defined execution point is the end of the
triggering transaction. Other execution points during the triggering transaction are user-defined. Starburst rules have a set oriented semantics and the
net effect is always taken into account. For a given execution of multiple and
cascading rules, there is only one set of *eligible* rules. Rules to be executed
are picked up from this set according to priorities which define a partial order among rules. One can talk of a *flat execution* of multiple and cascading
rules. In NAOS, there are two kinds of rules with two very different semantics: (1) *immediate rules* which have a event-instance-oriented semantics and
(2) *deferred rules* which have a event-set-oriented semantics[6]. Execution of
multiple and cascading rules is based on the notion of *execution cycle*. Immediate rules are executed in a depth-first order while deferred rules are
executed in a width-first order (cf. Sect. 2). In a given execution cycle, rules
are executed according to priorities between rules as in Starburst. *Net-effect*
is also always taken into account.

Like in Starburst, there is only one kind of rules in Postgres [SJG90]. These
rules have a instance-oriented semantics and are always executed right after
their triggering event. The execution model of Postgres is very simple. Multiple
rules are not really considered: several rules can be triggered simultaneously but
the system chooses and executes only one of them based on numeric priorities.
Cascading rules and *net effect* are not considered at all. Nevertheless this lack of
multiple and cascading rules allows to give a precise semantics to the cancellation
of the triggering operation (**instead** clause) which is not the case for NAOS.

Most research on Active Databases concerns the way rules interact with other
concepts or modules of the database system supposed to support those rules,
the expressiveness of the rule language or the event description language. There
have been only few works on execution models: the description of the Samos
rule semantics[GGD91], the work of Beeri and Milo [BM91] (which surprisingly

---

[6] That is why we have functions *Eligible–I* and *Eligible–D*, *Select–I* and *Select–D*.

does not speak about multiple and cascading rules) and HiPAC [HLM88]. These systems are based on extended transaction models.

In this paper, we prefer to restrict our study to active systems based on atomic transaction models and in which rules are always executed in the triggering transaction. The use of an extended transaction model can be seen as a mean for optimizing rule executions. As an example, one can notice that the notion of *execution cycle* of HiPAC and NAOS for managing cascading rules are very similar. One difference is that, in HiPAC, a cycle is "physically" represented by a (sub)transaction.

6 Conclusion

In this paper, we have presented the informal and (most of the) formal semantics of the NAOS rule execution model. We showed that the ideal situation would be to have a formal semantics of most active systems at one's disposal. Using the same formalism, namely Denotational Semantics, as for Starburst and NAOS would allow to share some domains or functions and thus to easily compare these systems as it is shown in the previous section. Comparing active systems is important because it could allow to propose some sort of standard for actives databases or to propose flexible execution models in which several sets of rules could have different semantics according to their application domain (rules for integrity constraint management, rules for derived data calculation, notification, etc.). Then, this would also allow to build generic tools for visualizing, debugging or browsing large rule sets.

7 Acknowledgments

We would like to thank Fabienne Lagnier for her careful reading of this paper and her suggestions in improving some function definitions. Thanks also to Ahmed Bouajjani for useful discussions on formal semantics, to Javam Machado for his comments on an early draft of this paper and François Paradis for his comments on the final version of this paper.

References

[BDK92] F. Bancilhon, C. Delobel, and P. Kanellakis. *Building an Object-Oriented Database - The story of O_2*. Morgan Kaufmann, 1992.

[Beh93] H. Behrends. ADL-Activity Description Language. Technical Report 3-93, Rostock university, 1993.

[Beh94] H. Behrends. An Operational Semantics for the Activity Description Language ADL. Technical Report 4-94, Oldenburg university, 1994. To be published.

[BM91] C. Beeri and T. Milo. A Model for Active Object Oriented Database. In *Proc. of the 17th International Conference on Very Large Data Base*, pages 337–349, Barcelona, Spain, September 1991.

[CCS94] C. Collet, T. Coupaye, and T. Svensen. NAOS Efficient and modular reactive capabilities in an Object-Oriented Database System. In *Proc. of the 20th International Conference on Very Large Data Bases*, Santiago, Chile, September 1994.

[CHCA94] C. Collet, P. Habraken, T. Coupaye, and M. Adiba. Active rules for the Software engineering platform GOODSTEP. In *Proc. of the 2nd International Workshop on Database and Software engineering - 16th international conference on Software Engineering*, Sorrento, Italy, May 1994.

[GGD91] S. Gatziu, A. Geppert, and K.R. Dittrich. Integrating Active Concepts into an Object-Oriented Database System. In *Proc. of the 3rd International Workshop on Database Programming Languages: Bulk Types & Persistent Data*, pages 399–415, Nafplion, 1991. Morgan Kaufmann.

[GOO94] GOODSTEP Team. The GOODSTEP Project: General Object-Oriented Database for Software Engineering Processes. In *Proc. of the Asia-Pacific Software Engineering Conference, Tokyo, Japan*, pages 410–420. IEEE Computer Society Press, 1994.

[Hin86] J. R. Hindley. *Introduction to Combinators and λ-Calculus*. Cambridge University Press, Cambridge, England, 1986.

[HJ91] R. Hull and D. Jacobs. Language Constructs for Programming Active Databases. In *Proc. of the 17th International Conference on Very Large Data Bases*, pages 455–467, Barcelona, Spain, 1991.

[HLM88] M. Hsu, R. Ladin, and D. McCarthy. An Execution Model for Active Database Management Systems. In *Proc. 3rd International Conference on Data and Knowledge Bases*, pages 171–179, June 1988.

[LRV92] C. Lecluse, P. Richard, and F. Velez. O_2, an Object-Oriented Data Model. In *Building an Object-Oriented Database - The story of O_2*, chapter 4, pages 77–97. Morgan Kaufmann, 1992.

[SGJ93] R. Hull S. Ghandeharizadeh and D. Jacobs. On implementing a language for specifying active database execution models. In *Proc. of the 19th International Conference on Very Large Data Bases*, pages 441–454, Dublin, Ireland, 1993.

[SJG90] M. Stonebraker, A. Jhingran, and J. Goh and S. Potamianos. On rules, procedures, caching and views in data base systems. In *Proc. of the ACM SIGMOD*, pages 281–290, Atlantic City, USA, May 1990. ACM Press.

[Sto77] J. E. Stoy. *Denotational Semantics: The Scott-Strachey Approach to Programming Language Theory*. The MIT Press, Cambridge, Massachussets, 1977.

[Tec95] O_2 Technology. The O_2 User Manual. Technical Documentation - Version 4.5, O_2 Technology, March 1995.

[Ten76] R. D. Tennent. The Denotational Semantics of Programming Languages. *Communications of the ACM*, 19(8):437–453, August 1976.

[Wid92] J. Widom. A Denotational Semantics for the Starburst Production Rule Language. *SIGMOD Record*, 21(3):4–9, September 1992.

Activity Specification Using Rendezvous

Chawki **Tawbi**, Ghaleb **Jaber** and Marc **Dalmau**
IUT de Bayonne - Centre de Recherche
3 Avenue Jean Darrigrand
64115 Bayonne Cedex- FRANCE
Tel (33) 59.52.89.91   Fax (33) 59.52.89.89
E.mail <tawbi, jaber, dalmau>@iutbay.univ-pau.fr

Abstract

The aim of this paper is to present an active relational DBMS which is typed and extensible (its domains are extended to Abstract Data Types). We were inspired by the notion of tasks in the Ada[1] programming language to specify the activity in the system. Users dispose of a constructor to create rule behaviour models (called *rule type*) for describing the behaviour of objects of this type when activated. Users can therefore create object "rules" and define relation attributes as rules.

Like an Ada task, each rule is a program unit that runs in parallel with other rules or programs. Its role is to execute services in response to requests. Synchronisation between the appellant and the rule is achieved using the principle of rendezvous. When an event occurs the system generates a rendezvous request with the concerned rules and services. We use the rendezvous principle to implement composite events.

Key words: Active DBMS's, Ada Tasks, Composite Events, Type.

1. Introduction

Activity in DBMS is one of the indispensable feature of the next generation DBMS due to its ability to support the classic functionalities of such systems (e.g., IC, view, derived data, authorisation), as well as the requirements of new applications such as multimedia or cooperative systems. That is why many research projects [5, 6, 8, 10, 12, 13, 14] have been conducted in the active database domain which lead to a set of prototype under construction.

Active behaviour is obtained by integrating Event-Condition-Action rules (ECA rules), which are inspired by production rules in AI, within the DBMS[2]. These rules give users the possibility of indicating the events that they want to react to, as well as the conditions under which an action has to be performed in reaction to the events. In other words, E determines when a rule should be evaluated, C ascertains if A can be performed, and A indicates the operation to be executed if C is satisfied. An Event can be primitive or composite. A primitive Event may be either a database operation, a temporal event, or an abstract one (i.e., user-defined). On the other hand, composite events are considered by composing primitive events. A Condition may be either a predicate or a database query (in the latter case the Condition is satisfied if the query result is not empty). Authorised operations at the Action stage will depend on a particular system as well as the domain of the application; they may range from a simple database operation to any application program. An Action may also be an operation on events or rules (activate, deactivate).

---

[1] Ada is a registered trademark of the DoD.
[2] The ECA formalism was proposed for the first time in [4].

The definition of rules and events in an active DBMS is usually carried out with the help of its query language which has to be extended for the specification and manipulation of rules and events. In the case of a primitive triggering event, the specification language is easy to use, but when it is a matter of specifying composite events, it becomes very complex. Some event specification languages, such as Snoop [3] and COMPOSE [7], have been specially designed for composite event specification. On the other hand, many systems offer a set of operators to specify composite events (HiPAC, SAMOS, EXACT...). This declarative way to specify composite events by means of a fixed set is not sufficient because of the difficulty to foresee the requirements of an application in term of event consumption policy. In the system we propose, we have been inspired by the task notion in the Ada language [1] which was conceived to design real-time applications. However, we have adapted this notion in order to make up the activity under all its aspects. The user can define *rule type* using a type constructor. Thus, rules will be specified as instances of a *rule type*.

Like a task in Ada, a rule is a program unit that runs in parallel to other units where the synchronisation between them is done using the principle of rendezvous. When an event occurs the system automatically generates rendezvous requests with its associated rules. We have adopted this principle to implement and detect composite events. So, a composite event is seen as a rule that waits for rendezvous with its composing events (which can themselves be composite).

We use the relational model extended to abstract data types (ADT's) [2] as the data model. Users can specify attributes which have a *rule type* as definition domain. In this way, it will be possible to associate a rule to each tuple of a relation and to deactivate rules (if necessary) for some specific tuples.

The remainder of this paper is organised as follows: firstly we introduce our motivations, then we analyse how activity is specified in our system and the way in which we integrate the notion of task. Next we present the execution model and architecture of our system. Before concluding we compare our system with some already existing active DBMS's.

2. Motivations

As events reflect the ability of a system to react to changes in a DB and its environment, considerable attention has been focused on it especially in the case of composite events. Event specification languages such as Snoop and COMPOSE were therefore designed to allow composite event specification.

The use of a declarative language with a fixed set of operators, even if very rich (Snoop, COMPOSE), provides a limited approach and cannot envisage respond to all the needs of applications. On the other hand, it is difficult to foresee which the features and consumption policies of the composite events required by an application could be. Thus, using a pre-defined set of operators will oblige the application to be conformed to this fixed set.

We suggest to provide implementation tools which allow the user to build the composite event required. Thus a composite event may be specified, by users, as a rule which will be informed about the occurrences of its component events using rendezvous. On the other hand the classic operators such as disjunction, conjunction and sequence can be specified into generic packages which can be reused easily.

We then supply a language which can operate at two levels: a upper one where classic operators can be offered as generic units, and a lower one were users can specify their own policy of event consumption in a procedural way.

3. Activity Specification

Before presenting how activity is implemented in our system we will now introduce briefly our system data model.

3.1 Data Model

Our DBMS is based on the relational model which we have extended to support abstract data types (ADT) as domains of attributes [ANIORTE 93]. The ADT are specified using Ada packages where users can implement their own data type according to their application needs. The query language is also an extension of the SQL language in which users can combine data access operations with ADT operations. This logic gives users more expressiveness without losing the easy-use of a relational model. Here are two examples of a relation creation and a database request:

○ *CREATE TABLE RECT(r_num integer, rect_colour colours, form rectangle)*
   Where *colours* and *rectangle* are two ADT's.
○ *select *, surface(form)*
   from RECT

This request returns all rectangles and their surfaces (*surface* is an ADT operation).

3.2. Rule specification

Primitive events in our system, are the database operations (including transactional ones), temporal and abstract events. We will present how abstract events can be used to specify composite events (§ 3.3.2). Rule activation is obtained by its associated event occurrences or explicitly by users.

3.2.1. Rules and Tasks

A rule is defined by its behaviour model (carried out using behaviour type) which describes its activity model and its coupling mode. The former describes the behaviour of the rule (C-A) when it is activated, and the latter indicates its binding with current transaction.

Like an Ada task, a rule is a program unit that operates in parallel to other units. Its function is to service other units (another rule or a program) after a solicitation. Synchronisation between units is carried out by the principle of rendezvous where a *calling* unit asks for a rendezvous with the *called* one in order to obtain its service.

The description of the activity model is carried out using *activity type*. As the *task type* in Ada the description of an *activity type* is composed of a specification part (interface with other units) and a body. The execution of an *activity type* instance (rule) is terminated after the execution of its body:

❶ **An activity model interface**
```
activity type A_Rule is
    entry service_1 ;
    ...
    entry service_n ;
end A_Rule ;
```

❷ **Implementation of model**
```
activity body A_Rule is
    accept service_1 do
        -- service_1 implementation
    end service_1;
    ...
    accept service_n do
        -- service_n implementation
    end service_n;
end A_Rule ;
```

The entries *service_1*, ..., *service_n* represent the rendezvous points with the rule. If we need a rendezvous request with a rule R1, having this activity model, in order to get the *service_i*, we can do this by the message *"R1.service_i"*. Multiple requests of the same entry are managed using a FIFO queue. The rendezvous points in this example are sequential -i.e. the associated services are executed in the sequence of their implementation. In other words, a rendezvous with the entry *service_i* will be suspended while all services *service_j* ($j<i$) are being executed. Each service is executed once and the rule is terminated after the execution of its nth service. The control structure **loop...end loop** permits the restart of the execution of a rule body. However, the clause **select** can be used allowing selective rendezvous (to be accepted in any order).

For a time limited acceptance of rendezvous, the clause **delay** can be specified in the alternative of **select** as we show in the following example:

```
activity  type  alarm  is
          entry  ALERT;
          entry  STOP;
end alarm;

activity  body  alarm  is
begin
loop
          accept  ALERT;
                  -- an alert has been  given wait 15 seconds the time to stop
                  -- it (in the case of a wrong alert) or give the alert
          select
                  accept STOP;      -- Stop "wrong alert"
          or
                  delay 15.00;      -- wait 15 seconds before giving the alert
                  put("ALERT!!!");
          end  select;
end  loop;
end alarm;
```

In this example, once the control reaches at the **select** clause, a 15 second delay starts, and if there is no rendezvous request with the entry STOP before the expiration of delay, the alert will be given (i.e., the instructions following the delay statement will be executed). Note that a clause *accept* may be without body (e.g., ALERT) and serve only as a rendezvous point.

In our approach, each entry will be associated with its proper events. The occurrence of one of them will generate a rendezvous request with this entry.

When events occur in an application, the system stops it in order to process them. Once this process terminates, the application resumes. During event processing, the system identifies the relevant rules and generates rendezvous requests with them. These requests wait in the queue of the relevant rule entry point and the system processes all the rule entries that are waiting for a rendezvous request. It is possible that a rendezvous request with a E' entry will not be processed during this cycle if in the rule behaviour a previous entry E has been specified, which must be processed before E'. In this case, the rendezvous requests with E' are kept and may be processed in the next cycle if the entry E has been processed.

The semantics of the acceptance and request for rendezvous in Ada (blocking waiting until the end of the activity body execution) are not appropriate for action parts which may contain an *accept* or a *delay*. For example, if we take an aeroplane reservation system where a rule must verify after 24 hours whether the ticket has been confirmed or not: this rule must be triggered after each insertion of a tuple in the table "reservation". If the rendezvous request is a blocking one, then the transaction in which the reservation has been carried out will be blocked for 24 hours. In order to solve this problem we have modified the rule behaviour from that of the Ada task. So after accepting a rendezvous request for an entry, the relevant body is executed either to the end of the specified action or to the meeting of another rendezvous point (delay or accept). However a temporal waiting (delay) will be processed as a waiting-for-rendezvous with the system's internal clock. Note that, the operations allowed in the action part of a rule entry are DB operations (except a "commit"), abstract event triggering, rule firing, activation and deactivation of rules and events.

3.2.2. Behaviour Model
A behaviour model is carried out using a behaviour type which is specified by means of a constructor having two parameters: the activity model and the coupling mode. In our system, rules are seen as instances of a behaviour type. Some operations are defined on objects of this type such as **fire** (triggers a rule), **activate** (activates a "deactivate" rule) and **deactivate** (deactivates an "activate" rule).

The binding of a rule with current transaction is expressed by means of coupling modes. In our system the C-A coupling mode is always immediate[3], but we offer three coupling modes for the E-C part: Attached (immediate), Detached-Dependent, and Detached-Independent. In the Attached mode, all operations performed by the rule are considered as a part of the transaction in which the event has occurred. The Detached-Dependent mode means that the rule will be executed in a different transaction T2 than the triggering one T1, but T2 is dependent on T1 -i.e. T2 can be committed only if T1 has executed a commit, and if T1 is aborted T2 will be aborted in its turn (more details are given in the execution model). However, with the Detached-Dependent mode, operations performed by the rule will be a part of a transaction which is totally independent of the triggering transaction. In both detached modes, the new transaction will be executed in parallel with the triggering transaction.

3.2.3 Rule Specification Language
The system query language has been extended in order to support rule and event definition, rule behaviour type definition, and event-rule association. In the case of a rule that does not have an associated event, this rule may be activated using the command **fire** which can be integrated into an application program.

➢ The following syntax is used to define a rule behaviour model:
● *define type <behaviour_model>*
as rule_behaviour(<activity_model>,<mode>)
rule_behaviour is the constructor of a behaviour model (*behaviour type*),
<behaviour_model> is the type identifier into the system,
<mode> indicates the coupling mode with the triggering transaction,

---

[3] We can simulate other coupling modes by using two rules.

<activity_model> is the activity model which describes the rule activity (C-A).

As a general case, the rule must be associated with all the tuples of a relation (e.g., constraint integrity verification) and will be triggered when the triggering event occurs on any of those tuples. But sometimes, it is interesting to associate a rule only with some tuples (e.g., if we do not want to change a displayed object). For that reason, users can define attributes as rules (associated to tuple). In this case, if the triggering event occurs on a specific tuple, then its own rule will be triggered (i.e., we will have a rule per tuple).

➤ The definition of a general rule:
● *create rule <ident_rule> as <behaviour_model>*
   <ident-rule> is the rule identifier,
   <behaviout_model> specifies the rule behaviour.

➤ The declaration of a tuple-associated rule in a relation R is made out by the definition of an attribute of R having a *rule type* as definition domain.

● *create table R(X integer, Y string, ..., Z <behaviour_model>)*
   <behaviour_model> specifies a behaviour model.

➤ The association between a rule and an event is made using the following syntax:
● *fire [<relation_name>.] <ident_rule> [.<entry>] [when <ident_event>]*
   <relation_name> is used in the case of a tuple-associated rule to indicate the attribute which is specified as a rule (illustrated in § 3.5 by an example),
   <entry> indicates the entry name of a rule (if there are several entries and we do not want to generate a rendezvous request with each one belong them)
   <ident_event> is the event identifier which, when it occurs, generates automatically a rendezvous request with the rule specified entry.

3.3. Event Specification

The primitive events supported by our system are: database events, temporal events (absolute, relative and periodic), and abstract events. The composite and relative-temporal events are specified as abstract events (see § 3.3.2).

3.3.1. Primitive Events

➤ A database or an abstract event is specified in our system using the following syntax:

● *define event <ident_event> [<before/after> <db_operation>*
   [on <relation_name[.attribute]>]]
   <ident_event> is the event identifier into the system.
   In the case of a DB event, *before* and *after* specify the moment of the event detection (before or after the operation execution),
   <db_operation> indicates the triggering operation,

<relation_name[.attribute]> specifies the concerned relation; however event can be associated to only one attribute.

➤ Absolute- and periodic-temporal events are specified using the following syntax:

- *define event <ident_event> at <time_specification>*   for absolute events
- *define event <ident_event> every <period_specification>* for periodic events
  <time_specification> indicates a time and/or a date at which the event will occur,
  <period_specification> specifies the frequency of the event occurrence; to do that the following key words can be used preceded by a number: minutes, hours, days, weeks, months, years.

Examples

○ *define event E2 at 10:30 April 20 1995*
○ *define event E3 every 2 days*

E2 will be signalled by 20 April 1995 at 10:30, and E3 each two days.

➤ On the other hand, relative events are specified as abstract events and signalled using rules. For instance, an event "E_relative = Ei + 4 minutes" is defined as follows:

⇨ *define event E_relative*
⇨ *define type relative as rule_behaviour(rel_E, Attached)*
⇨ *create rule rel_Ei as relative*
⇨ *fire rel_Ei.Execute_Rule when Ei*

activity type rel_E is
        entry Execute_Rule;
end rel_E;

activity body rel_E is
begin
        accept Execute_Rule do
                delay duration("4 minutes); -- *wait 4 minutes*
                                              -- *duration is a predefined*
function
                        raise(E_relative);   -- *signals event to Event Detector*
                end Execute_Rule;
end relative_event1;

3.3.2. Composite Events

A composite event is defined as an abstract event and its detection is assured by a rule that indicates (using the command **raise**) the associated event occurrence. This rule is informed of the events, which compose the composite event, using the rendezvous points.

Any composition operators (e.g., disjunction, conjunction, sequence, negation) can be made out using this technique. Here are two examples showing how to perform the conjunction and the negation:

O conjunction: In this example event E3 (conjunction of two arbitrary events E1 and E2) will occur if E1 and E2 occur within an interval of one minute in either order:

```
⇨ define event E3
⇨ define type  conjunction as  rule_behaviour(conj12, Attached)
⇨ create rule conjunction-E1-E2 as  conjunction
⇨ fire conjunction-E1-E2.Execute_Action1  when E1
⇨ fire conjunction-E1-E2.Execute_Action2  when E2
⇨ Rule activity-model implementation:
activity   type conj12 is
           entry Execute_Action1;
           entry Execute_Action2;
end conj12;
activity   body conj12 is
begin
select
           accept   Execute_Action1;              -- if E1 occurs before E2
           select
                     accept  Execute_Action2 do    -- wait for E2
                             raise(E3);            -- signal E3 to the system
                       end  Execute_Action2;
              or
                       delay duration("1 minute");  -- wait for E2 only one minute
               end  select;
     or
           accept Execute_Action2;                -- if E2 occurs before E1
           select
                     accept  Execute_Action1 do    -- wait for E1
                             raise(E3);            -- signal E3 to the system
                       end  Execute_Action1;
              or
                       delay duration("1 minute");  -- wait for E1 only one minute
               end  select;
end  select;
end conj12;
```

O Negation: Suppose we want to specify the negation of an event E. From a specific time, if E doesn't occur during the next 5 minutes for example, then raise NOT_E. This specific time can be an absolute-temporal event or any other event (e.g., begin of transaction):

```
⇨ define event NOT_E
⇨ define type  negation as  rule_behaviour(not, Attached)
⇨ create rule NOT1 as  negation
⇨ fire NOT1.start when b-o-t
⇨ fire NOT1.stop when E

activity   type not is
           entry start;
           entry stop;
end not;
```

```
activity   body not is
begin
        accept start;
        select
                accept stop;
        or
                delay duration("5 minutes");
                raise(NOT_E);
        end select;
end not;
```

3.4. Event-Condition-Action Binding

The rules are activated each time a relevant event occurs or at a user's request. The system requests rendezvous with the concerned rules and associates with each of them the event context which contains, among other things, the event parameters and the concerned tuple value (in the case of a database event) before and after the operation. The current context associated with a rule entry is obtained by using the suffix "current" after the entry name (entry_name.current). Two key words, **old** and **new**, are used to get, respectively, the old and new value of the current tuple.

In the case of a rule (R2) entry that is activated from the action part of another rule R1, the current context in R1 will be passed to R2. However, in the case of a rule having several entries (this, in general, is the case of rules defining a composite event) there is a need to find out which context has to be passed to an entry in addition to its proper context. This problem has been studied in [3] and solved by the definition of several kinds of contexts. Another semantics will be to query the histories of events and rules. We have chosen the last solution in the present version of our system where users have the tables that describe the histories of events and rules at their disposition where they can pick up events in any order they want using a procedural way.

3.5. Examples of Application

O The first example is defined in a stock management database. The rule presented here supervises a product quantity that should not be less than a specified threshold. This rule will be triggered each time a product quantity is updated.

```
⇨ create table Product(produit_num integer, product_name string, quantity
     integer, threshold integer)
⇨ define event modif_quantity after update on Product.quantity
⇨ define type verif as  rule_behaviour(control_quantity, Attached)
⇨ create rule verif_threshold as verif
⇨ fire verif_threshold when modif_quantity
⇨ The rule activity-model implementation:
activity   type control_quantity is
     entry Execute_Rule;
end control_quantity;

activity   body control_quantity is
begin
loop
     Accept Execute_Rule do
        if new.quantity < new.threshold then -- new contains the tuple new  value
                put("You should buy some");
                put(new.product_name);
```

```
     end  if;
       end Execute_Rule;
  end  loop;
  end control_quantity;
```

O The second example details a rule in an aeroplane reservation system that cancels a unconfirmed reservation after 24 hours of its creation:

⇨ *define type control*
   as rule_behaviour(control_rule, Detached-Dependent)
⇨ *create table Reservation(ResNum string, VolNum integer, Name string,*
   Surname string, supervisor control)
⇨ *create table Ticket(TicketNum integer, ResNum string)*
⇨ *define event insert_res after insert on Reservation*
⇨ *fire Reservation.supervisor when insert_res*
⇨ The behaviour implementation of the rule associated to the attribute supervisor:
activity type control_rule is
       entry Execute_Rule;
end control_rule;

```
activity  body control_rule is
begin
      Accept Execute_Rule do
            delay   duration("24 hours");          -- wait 24 hours
            if not exists(" select * from Ticket        -- the Condition
                       where Ticket.ResNum = new.ResNum") then
                  execute("delete * from Reservation     -- The Action
                       where Reservation.ResNum = new.ResNum")
            end if;
      end Execute_Rule;
end control_rule;
```
Note that this rule can be implemented using a relative event.

The following request deactivates the rule associated to the reservation number X:
       select deactivate(supervisor)
       from Reservation
       where ResNum = X

4. Execution Model

The execution model is the part of the system which specifies the way in which rules are executed after the occurrence of a relevant event. It is specially responsible for the order of rule execution if there is a priority between rules and if several rules are triggered at the same time. It also ensures the execution of rules according to their coupling modes.

When one or several events occur during a transaction execution (user's request or application program) the application will be suspended while the rule manager (RM) treats the activated rules. For each event, the RM determines the set of activated rules and classifies them into three categories: the attached rules (AR), the detached dependent rules (DDR), and the detached independent rules (DIR). For each DDR and DIR the system creates a process and a transaction to process the rule, and generates a rendezvous request with the relevant entries. These transactions will be executed in parallel with the initial one. In the case of an AR, the system generates the rendezvous requests with all the concerned entries; it chooses the entry to process according to the method described in [9].

The system accepts the first rendezvous request for the current entry E of a rule and executes all the associated operations either until its body ends or until another rendezvous point (another entry) or until a temporal waiting (a delay statement). Then, the RM examines all the events triggered by the entry treatment, re-orders all the entries to treat and restarts the process. Once all the triggered rules are treated, the initial application can resume.

A dependent transaction can execute a "commit" only if the initial transaction is terminated successfully; if not, it must be aborted. However, a transaction can make a "commit" if there are no activated attached-rule waiting to be treated. On the other hand, if there are some attached-rules waiting for a temporal rendezvous, the system waits for the rendezvous request and for execution of the action. When there are no more rules with temporal waiting, all the rules that are waiting for a rendezvous (other than with the internal clock) are killed and "commit" can be executed.

If a transaction executes an "abort", all rules activated are killed and all dependent transactions are aborted. Whereas if a dependent transaction executes an "abort", this has no effect on the initial transaction.

5. Implementation issues

5.1. System Architecture

The architecture of the system (Figure 1) is made up of the following modules: the Analyse/Process of users' commands (APC), Event Manager (EM), Context Manager (CM), Rule Manager (RM), and Transaction Manager (TM).

The database operations and the definition of events and rules in the application will be processed by the APC module. After analysing, the APC passes the event definition to the EM, the rule definition to the RM, and the database requests (after decomposing them into a list of database commands) to the TM.

The TM signals the DB operations, before and after execution, to the EM in order to detect possible events, and then continues processing after getting permission from the EM. At an event occurrence the EM, after a request to the CM to record the event context, signals the triggered event to the RM which activates the concerned rules and requests rendezvous with them. The verification of condition and the execution of action of a triggered rule are treated in the same way as the application itself.

The other types of events (temporal, abstract and composite) are directly signalled to the EM which signals them to the RM which then treats them as database events.

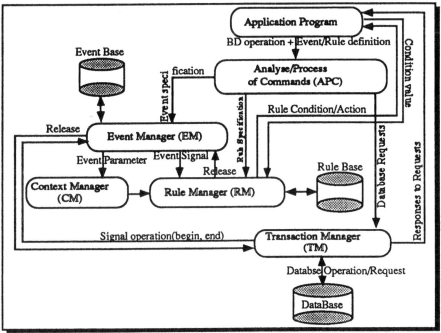

Figure 1.

5.2. Event Management

Database events are stored into a table called *eventbase* where we find for each event the triggering operation, the concerned relation (and attribute), and the triggering moment (before or after). Every database operation is signalled before and after their execution to the event manager which inspects the *eventbase* to detect a potential event.

To manage absolute- and periodic-temporal events we have adopted the solution proposed in SAMOS [6]. This solution consists of using the UNIX system command *cron*. So each temporal event specification is transformed into commands to be inserted into a *crontab* file. However as we have introduced before, the composite and relative-temporal events are specified using rules. So no additional mechanism is required to manage these kinds of events.

5.3. Rule Management

We use two kind of processes to implement rules: (i) processes associated to attached rules and (ii) processes associated to detached rules. The former run into the triggering transaction, whereas the latter have their own transactions.

5.3.1. Attached rules

A process associated with an attached rule may have the following states: Non-Active, Waiting for Selection, Active, or Temporal Waiting (i.e., a delay). Transitions between states are shown in Figure 2.

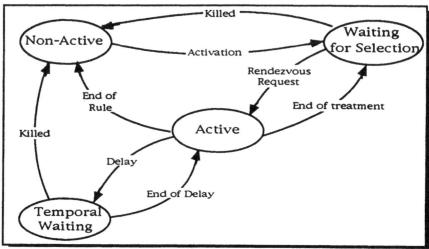

Figure 2.

A rule will be activated at the occurrence of a relevant event, it waits for a rendezvous request to be executed. When it is being executed, it may pass to one of the two states waiting-for-selection (when there is another accept) or temporal-waiting (when there is a delay). An attached rule can be killed if the triggering transaction aborts.

5.3.2. Detached rules

We are able to distinguish four states for the process associated with such rules (Figure 3): Non-Active, Waiting for Rendezvous, Active, Blocked (when it triggers an event, it will be blocked during the treatment of this event).

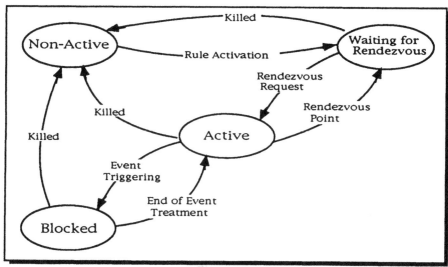

Figure 3.

When a detached rule is being executed, it may pass to one of the two states waiting-for-rendezvous (when there is another accept) or blocked (it can signal an event). A detached rule is killed if its own transaction aborts.

6. Related Work

SAMOS [6] offers six operators to specify composite events: disjunction, conjunction, sequence, *-constructor, history, negative. Composite events are detected using Petri nets where each event specification is translated to an equivalent Petri net. The validity interval introduced in SAMOS and required for the last three operators can be achieved in our system using the delay statement. In Sentinel the event specification language Snoop [3] offers a rich set of operators. A composite event is considered as an object and it will be notified by the occurrences of its component events using a pre-defined method *notify*. So users cannot specify their own event consumption policy. The notion of contexts introduced in Snoop gives it more flexibility but they are specified according to specific applications. COMPOSE is another event specification language introduced in the active DBMS Ode. Automata and generic automata are used to detect composite events. The set of operators offered by COMPOSE are more or less difficult to be interpreted. The immediate and separated coupling modes in HiPAC [10] are similar to the attached and detached-dependent modes in our system. The HiPAC execution model is based on a nested transaction model [11] that we have adopted. But with HiPAC, rules cannot be associated to only one object as they can in our model. In contrast to our system, Starburst [14] only supports database events and it provides only one composition operator: the disjunction. Since POSTGRES [13] support ADT specification, an attribute of a relation can be specified as a procedure or a query but cannot be manipulated as a rule like in our system. In POSTGRES, similarly to our system, users can reference, in the condition and action parts, the data which is the cause of rule triggering. ALERT [12] like POSTGRES and our own system, allows data that causes the rule triggering to be referenced in the rule condition and action. The active DBMS ARIEL [8], again similar to our system, enables users to reference data triggering, the rule. Like in our suggestion, the rule specification language in EXACT [5], is based on a programming language (PROLOG). However composite events in EXACT are specified in a declarative manner, whereas in our system they are specified using a procedural way. However, users of EXACT can also deactivate rules for some objects like they can in our system.

7. Conclusion

In this paper we have presented an approach inspired by the notion of an Ada task in order to introduce activity into a relational database.

Our system has the advantage of specifying relation attributes as rules, which is not the case in any active relational DBMS to date. In addition, the specification of composite events is performed in the rule action part (using a procedural manner) without needing any special event language or mechanism. This allows the use of the same language for specifying active rules either with simple or composite events.

Until now, only composite events which occur in the same transaction have been taken into consideration to make up a composite event. In future work we will be extending our model to incorporate any composite event.

We are, currently, implementing a prototype of our system under UNIX on the HP9000 station.

REFERENCES

[1] Department of Defence, Ada Joint Program Office - *Reference Manual for the Ada Programming Language*, ANSI/MIL-STD-1815A. Washington, D.C.: Government Printing Office, January 1983.

[2] ANIORTE P. and JABER G. - *The Implementation of an Expandable and Typed RDBMS*. Indo-French Workshop on Object Oriented System. Goa (India), 1992.

[3] CHAKRAVARTHY S. and MISHRA D. - *Snoop An Expressive Event Specification Language for Active Databases*. Technical Report, University of Florida, UF-CIS-TR-93-007, March 1993.

[4] DAYAL U. - *Active Database Management System*. 3rd International Conference on Data and Knowledge Base. Jerusalem, June 1988.

[5] DIAZ O. and JAIME A. - *EXACT an EXtensible approach to ACTive object-oriented databases*. Technical Report, University San Sebastian, May 1992.

[6] GATZIU S. and DITTRICH K.R. - *Events in an Active Object-Oriented Database System*. Proceedings of the 1st International Workshop On Rules in Database Systems, Edinburgh, 1993. Springer-Verlag (1994), pp 23-39.

[7] GEHANI N.H., JAGADISH H.V., and SHMUELI O. - *COMPOSE A System For Composite Event Specification and Detection*. Technical Report, AT&T Bell Laboratories, December 1992.

[8] HANSON E.N. - *The Design and Implementation of the Ariel Active Database Rule System*. Technical Report, University of Florida, UF-CIS-018-92, September 1991.

[9] JABER G. - *An Extension of a RDBMS towards an Active RDBMS*. Proceedings of BIWIT 94 on Information Systems Design and Hypermedia. Biarritz, February 1994, pp 299-309.

[10] McCARTHY D.R. and DAYAL U. - *The Architecture of an Active Data Base Management System*. Proceeding ACM-Sigmod Conference. Portland, May 1989, pp 215-224.

[11] MOSS E. - *Nested Transactions : An approach to Reliable Distributed Computing*. MIT Press (1985).

[12] SCHREIER U., PIRAHESH H., AGRAWAL R. and MOHAN C. - *Alert An Architecture for Transforming a Passive DBMS into an Active DBMS*. Proceedings of the 17th International Conference on Very Large Data Bases. Barcelona, September 1991, pp 469-478.

[13] STONEBRAKER M., JHINGRAN A., GOH J. and POTAMIANOS S. - *On Rules, Procedures, Caching and Views in Data Base Systems*. Proceedings of SIGMOD. Atlantic City, June 1990, pp 281-290.

[14] WIDOM J., COCHRANE R.J. and LINDSAY B.G. - *Implementing Set-Oriented Production Rules as an Extension to Starburst*. Proceedings of the 17th International Conference on Very Large Data Bases. Barcelano, September 1991, pp 275-285.

Active Behaviour

Reactive Behaviour Support:
Themes and Variations

Ray Fernández[12], Oscar Díaz[2]

[1] ADOS Soluciones Software S.A.
Mugako Ibilbidea 1, Of 4. 20160 Lasarte, Spain
[2] Departamento de Lenguajes y Sistemas Informáticos,
Universidad del País Vasco / Euskal Herriko Unibertsitatea
Apd. 649, 20080 San Sebastián, Spain
e-mail: <jipferur,jipdigao>@si.ehu.es ***

Abstract. Unlike previous behaviour models, reactive behaviour description includes not only *what* to execute but also *when* to execute it. Programming languages, database systems and graphical user interfaces are being enhanced to provide explicit support for reactive behaviour due to the large range of application which naturally express their semantics using this paradigm. This paper presents a common framework in which current alternatives to reactive behaviour support in object-oriented systems can be placed and compared. This framework imposes some clasification features, that suggest some new approaches for the reactive behaviour support.
Keywords: reactive behaviour, event detection, triggers/rules, active database sytems

1 Introduction

With the blooming of the object-oriented paradigm, applications are modeled as a set of interacting objects which require and provide services. This approach assumes that each object knows where the service is and directly applies or call for it. However, this call-driven approach is not the only manner to invoke behaviour. Expert Systems practitioners proposed *situation-action rules*, a *data-driven* mechanism where rules are fired (i.e. the action executed) depending upon the current state of the system [6]. Active database proponents have proposed *event-condition-action rules*, a mechanism where behaviour is automatically invoked as a response to events but without user intervention [4]. Here, it is a change of state (or event) rather than the state itself what makes the rule to be fired. Such approach is more akin with the object-oriented philosophy where the object state is encapsulated and state changes are achieved only through

*** This work has been supported by the Commission of the European Communities under the AC-NET network of the Human Capital programme and the Department of Industry and Energy of the Basque Government.
Ray Fernández has been funded by the Technology Specialist Program of the Science and Education Department of Spain.

messages (i.e a service request to a client). Therefore, message-sending events play a paramount role in the support of reactive behaviour in object-oriented systems.

Reactive behaviour support mainly concerns event detection and reaction execution, whereas the actors involved are the client, the server and the system itself. How to achieve and distribute reactive behaviour support among the actors, admit distict options, depending on whether the user has access to the client, the server or the system code.

This paper presents a common framework in which current alternatives to reactive behaviour support in object-oriented systems can be placed and compared. Section 2 outlines the fundamentals of the object-oriented paradigm, introducing the concepts used later. Section 3 introduces *the theme* that is, the main concepts behind the reactive behaviour notion. *Variations* concerning where, when and how message sending events can be trapped, are described in sections 4 and 5. Section 6 provides a comparison of the different approaches presented. Conclusions are given in Sect. 7.

2 Framework

The term **application** is used to refer to the set of elements developed by the user to achieve a certain objective with a program, and **development** system (or just **system**) to refer to the set of software and hardware elements that allow the user to develop such applications from its creation to its use; the execution of the application is referred to as **run-time**, as opposed to **definition time**, by which the process of creating the application is meant.

The user **defines** an application at definition time, whose elements describe what the application will be at run-time; those elements may or may not be part of that application at run-time; we have used the term **interpreted** for the former case and **compiled** for the later.

In an object-oriented approach, system and application definitions have been modeled as objects, and its run-time behaviour as a collection of interacting objects interchanging requests to accomplish any aim.

The term **class** is broadly used to refer to the definition of an object. Objects are created at run-time according to their classes described at definition time. Several objects of the same class can co-exist at run-time.

Extending on the metaphor of interacting objects, the term **dynamics** is used to refer to the run-time interactions of the system and the application; **messages** are then requests from one object (the **sender**) to another (the **receiver**), instructing it to carry out one action; and the process of interchanging such requests in the form of messages is called **message-passing**

The set of messages that can be answered by an object is described in its **interface**. The definition of the action to be carried out by an object as an answer to a message is called **method**: messages represent request units, whereas methods are implementation units. To be callable, a method has to be included in its object's interface. Several methods with the same name (the method selector) can exist in different classes. A method can require **parameters** to carry out its action, and yield an answer as an explicit result of the request. Equally, information about the right or wrong fullfilment of the method could be obtained from method's execution.

Certain features[4] may prevent the system from knowing at definition time which method will be executed at run-time for a certain message, given that distinct methods can share the same name, so a given selector can refer to several of these methods (name overloading).This forces the presence of run-time mechanisms able to solve this: **dynamic binding**, whereby method selection is done when the message is being processed and not earlier, or **method lookup**, whereby information is added to each object about the method that implements each valid selector it answers. These mechanisms are only required for those methods on which name overloading occurs.

Summing up, a *system* offers a framework for defining applications by supplying certain primitive constructs (e.g. the notion of *message* or *class*), and enforces the expected meaning (i.e. semantics) of those primitives present at the run-time of the application by supplying **run-time support** for them (e.g. method lookup).

The diagrams presented throughout the paper use the Martin/Odell [9] graphical notation, as shown in Fig. 1. Rectangles represent operations, arrow points represent the situation after the execution of an operation. Grayed operations are used to highlight new or changed operations respect to the previous version of the diagram. Dotted lines link one operation to a sequence of operations that show its details.

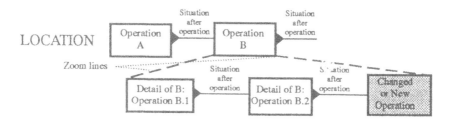

Fig. 1. Diagram notation used throughout this document

3 Reactive Behaviour Elements

According to the dictionary, an event is a circumstance or fact that happens, specially when it has some *relevance*. *Relevance* in a software system means that

---

[4] Namely those promoting polymorphism, the ability of an object to refer at run-time to instances of various classes [12].

some sort of action has to be taken; consequently, an **event** in a software system can be seen as a specific situation upon which reactions *may* be necessary.

Two types of events can be distinguished, namely *internal events* (i.e. those generated inside the system of interest) and *external events* (i.e. those relevant circumstances taking place outside the system of interest). Typical external events include the clock, the user, the operating system[5], or the user-interface part of the application (when the system of interest is the non-user-interface part of the application), etc.

The user can be interested in undertaking an action linked to a certain event or set of events, such as showing a new window when the mouse is moved over a certain rectangle of the display, or updating the valid domain of x when y is changed and both are related by $x + y = 1$. This *behaviour in which actions are carried out as a consequence of certain circumstances* (events) is known as **reactive behaviour**. The term *reactive development systems* (or **reactive systems**) is used to refer to those systems explicitly supporting the use of reactive behaviour to create applications (i.e., offering on-purpose primitives and run-time support).

A simple schema of reactive behaviour encompasses: (1) **defining** the relevant circumstance (*event*) and the reaction; (2) **detecting** when the relevant circumstance has taken place and **signaling**; (3) **reacting** to the event, i.e. carrying out the operations which are triggered by the event.

Table 1. System classification based on reactive behaviour support

Event Detection	Reaction Execution	Classification
Development System	Development System	Active
Development System	Application	Event-driven
Application	Development System	Event source
Application	Application	Call-driven

Table 1 classifies systems according to who is responsible for event detection and reaction execution:

- **Active**: the system supports both event detection and reaction execution (i.e. reacts *automatically* to events). The response is achieved through the run-time support part of the development system, according to the reaction definitions given by the application. Examples are active database management systems, constraint based programming systems, etc.

---

[5] These are usually detected by an interrupt mechanism (when the circumstance requires, the application is interrupted, the circumstance processed, and an event generated) or continuous polling (the interested object cycles through a cycle inspecting the external event sources).

- **Event-driven**: the system does support event detection. The application can explicitly request about events detected by the system, but the application is responsible for consuming the event and carrying out the reaction. This is usually achieved by continuously polling the system or by *call-back* mechanisms: in the first case, the names *event bus, event queue* are also used for the polled system; in the second case, the application is awaken at a certain point of execution when the interesting event happens, much like interruptions are used to signal external events. Example include most Graphical User Interface (GUI) subsystems.
- **Event source**: the application detects the event and signals it to the runtime part of the development system or to another application. The later system perceives the event as an external event. Examples: security alerters in computer-controlled machines; hardware drivers (apart from their hardware encapsulation functionality, they must signal problems to the operating system.
- **Call-driven**: the system does not support reactive behaviour. The application has to detect relevant circumstances and execute the reactions. Reactive behaviour can be *programed* in *any* development system which is provided with a conditional branch primitive construct (i.e., *if* relevant-circumstance-has-occurred *then* do-required-action).

3.1 Message Sending Events

Among internal events, **message sending events (MSE)** are those rised as a result of the occurrence of a message in the system of interest. The detection of MSEs is then, the corner stone for the creation of active systems in a message-passing environment. This justifies a detailed description of the life cycle of a message which can be described as follows (see Fig. 2):

- *Create.* When the calling object reaches a point of execution in which a message has to be sent, the message is first created, i.e., the triplet $[R, M, P]$ is obtained with receiver R, selector M and parameters P.
- *Pass.* The message is passed to the system for processing. The system can suspend the processing on the calling object or not. Messages can be created both explicitly (via code in the application) or implicitly (via semantics of code, i.e. type conversion mechanisms in C++, invariant checks in Eiffel).
- *Dispatch.* Message processing begins by verifying the message (e.g. if there is a type checking mechanism, the parameters P will be checked against the method M signature). Once this is satisfactorily achieved, the sender is not liable for M's syntax. If the triplet is not a proper message, an error is raised by the system.
  Once the verification is successfully passed, the right implementation of method M on receiver R is found. This process is called binding. On purely interpreted systems, this is done at run-time; on purely compiled systems, some bindings could be done at compile time and others cannot be resolved until execution time (e.g. *dynamic binding* mechanism described in Sect. 2)

– *Accept*. The method M on receiver R is called with parameters P. As in any method execution, it can be accepted or rejected (e.g. access denied, preconditions are not fullfiled. If rejected, an error or exception signal arises. If accepted, execution proceeds. We use the *contracting objects* approach to a message's semantic validation [12] in which M defines pre and postconditions, and the run-time support dynamically checks for its fullfilment before and after execution of M. When the system does not provide this contracting approach, M itself does the checks and indicates errors or raises exceptions it parameters are wrong, resources unavailable, etc.

– *Execution* of the method is carried out by the receiver.

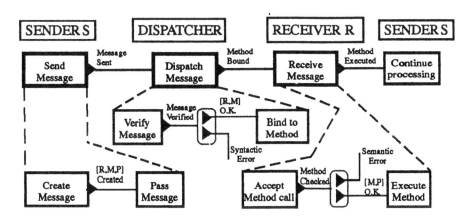

Fig. 2. The message life cycle

According with the terminology introduced in previous section, MSE **signaling** refers to how the system detects, acts or informs of the occurrence of such MSE, the signal being the creation of an element carrying the information; the message that will be signaled is called a **monitored message**, whereas the methods that can be executed as a consequence of monitored messages are called **monitored methods**). The rest of this paper studies how MSEs can be and have been signaled[6]. The themes relate to *how* can MSEs be signaled, and *where* (static view) or *when* (dynamic view) are MSEs signaled in a message's life cycle.

4   Where / When: Variations on MSE Detection and Signaling Location

Responsibility for detecting MSEs (the *event detection*), can be undertaken by any of the main components involved in the' message life cycle, namely:

---

[6] See [3], [1], for an approach to other aspects of events and active systems. [10] includes also a paragraph dealing with signaling events.

— *By the sender.* The sender invokes the method via the environment's creation and sending mechanisms. The sender is usually an application object, which has to be modified to detect a new event: besides invoking the method, the sender has to signal that this method has been called (this is the MSE *detection*).

— *By the receiver.* The receiver refers to the place where the selected method's implementation is executed. The receiver is usually one of the objects involved in the application; hence, besides executing the method, the receiver has to be extended with the MSE signaling. Each time a monitored message is received, some signaling mechanism is called by the receiver.

— *By the dispatcher.* The dispatcher carries the message from the sender to the receiver. The dispatcher is usually part of the development system's run-time support to the application, at least at the system's level in which the message is a primitive construct. Unlike previous approaches, this alternative does not require modifying the involved objects but the system: besides checking and binding the message, the dispatcher signals the occurrence of the event.

5 How: Variations on Event Detection and Signaling Support

MSE detection mechanisms can differ greatly. This section describes the different approaches; the next section presents a comparison based on expressive power, maintenance costs, efficiency and requirements.

5.1 Sender-based Approach

As the sender is typically an application object or program, a sender-based approach requires changing the application, by either detecting a MSE for every message sent, or changing the application each time a message starts to be monitored. The signaling must be done where the message could be sent (see Fig. 3), i.e. in every place where the text of the application could generate the sending of the message at run-time. Thus, the user has to inspect and potentially make changes throughout the whole application each time a new MSE is required.

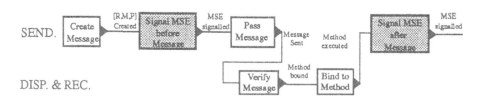

Fig. 3. Sender-based MSE signaling

Besides forcing the user of a service to do more than the simple invocation of the service, the main drawback stems from the detection being distributed among the customers, thus jeopardising encapsulation and maintenance [1]. The ILOG Server system [5] follows this approach.

5.2 Receiver-based Approach

Receiver-based approaches are based on wrapping mechanisms (see Fig. 4): a monitored message must activate a method that extends the original method with a MSE signaling mechanism, *without* changing its name (thus without impacting, at least syntactically, any use of the method in the application's code). The extra code needed to do the signaling is called **wrapper**, because it is typically executed before and after the original method. The wrapping mechanism can be offered by the system itself as a primitive construct.

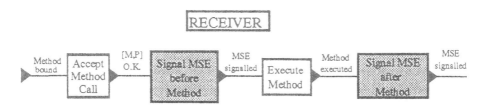

Fig. 4. Receiver-based MSE signaling

The receiver's method can perform the MSE signaling. Being the receiver an application object, this approach also requires changing the application. However, unlike the previous approach, here the detection is centralised in a single place (i.e. where the service stays) rather than being distributed among several sites (i.e. where the service is required). Furthermore, a higher degree of transparency is achieved as the user of the service is unaware of whether the message is monitored or not. The alternative sites where the wrapper-like behaviour can be placed are:

1. In the method: replace the original method by a new one which contains the implementation of the original method and adds MSE signaling code at the beginning and end of this code. The wrapped version of a method is created as soon as the method becomes monitored. This alternative requires recompilation. In some systems the ability to generate wrappers is implemented in a separate class from which all classes with active features must be derived. This solution only traps messages for which the corresponding method's definition has been modified with the wrapping. The main drawback is that the method itself is changed, thus changing the previous semantics (although this is what the addition of the active behaviour intends, users and inheritors may

be unaware of the new semantics). It can jeopardise method inheritance (e.g. overriding). An example of this approach is presented in [8] where the Gemstone object-oriented DBMS (based on Smalltalk) is extended with active capabilities.

2. In the class (*twin method*): create a new *twin* method whose signature is the same as the original method. As a class cannot have two methods with same full signatures, the new twin method hides the previous definition. This solution does not require access to the method's definition since no update on method is done. The SENTINEL system [3] is an example of this approach.

3. In another class (*twin class*): create a new class C' for each class C with monitored methods. C' inherits from C, and extends the monitored method: it signals the MSE, and then calls the ancestor's version of the method. As no two classes can exist in a system with the same names, the original class has to be hidden under other name. This approach has been used in [7] where Eiffel is extended to integrate application and rule-based expert system capabilities.

5.3 Dispatcher-based Approach

MSE signaling can be obtained by altering or extending the dispatcher semantics as perceived by the application. This can be achieved with definition-time mechanisms (extending the development system so that the application's definition, as the run-time system perceives it, is altered) or run-time mechanisms (altering the run-time system behaviour).

Definition-time Mechanisms. Figure 5 details the *dispatch* function of Fig. 2: after accepting the message as such, the dispatcher locates the right method to be bint to the message. This is achieved by a lookup on the table which supports the mapping function between the message's selector and the right method definition for it[7]. This lookup can be extended to support MSE signaling as shown in Fig. 6. For a message $MS = [O, M, P]$, the lookup function binds a different method, say MM. MM signals the occurrence of MS, and then calls the original method M of object O. Every message MS is now bound to the dummy method MM by the dispatcher. But this includes the message that MM sends to M on object O to perform the *actually desired* function, so as to keep the original semantics of MS unchanged. This requires MM to access the original M, but the message to be sent must be different (or it will be bound to MM): it issues a distinct message MS2, that the lookup function has to bind to M of O.

This lookup cross-naming can be obtained without impact on the application's code[8] by using *name space management* mechanisms or *forwarding* techniques.

---

[7] On systems supporting *static binding*, this lookup is done once and hence, it is saved for subsequent messages.

[8] Or, at least, maintaining user transparency by not forcing any change to be done by the user.

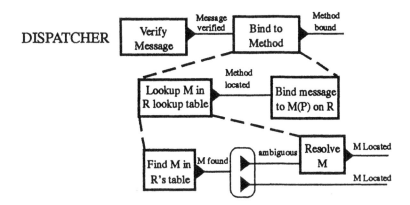

Fig. 5. Detail of the dispatching process

Name Space Management Mechanisms are available in some object-oriented systems to avoid clashes on names (of classes, methods, attributes, etc.). This include the Eiffel LACE renamimg block [11] and the C++ namespacing mechanisms to be approved by the C++ ANSI committee. This characteristic can be used to deviate a message to a wrapper method without accessing the dispatcher nor the user method's code. In [15], this approach is investigated for Eiffel.

This approach requires the name space management mechanism to allow for the definition of triples *[class in-effect, original-name, new-name]*: when the class *original-name* is used within *class in-effect*, the system substitutes all references to class *original-name* for references to class *new-name*. These triples are translated into entries in the lookup table to fullfill its semantics.

Forwarding Mechanisms allow for method name substitution to be done at run-time. Forwarding systems hold a table of name substitution pairs *[method name, physical code address of method]* for each object in the system[9]. When a certain method has to be called (a message sent) the sender has first to ask the run-time system for the list of the methods offered to him by the receiver, and then issue the call by itself. In this approach, the dispatching is sliced between the run-time support system (which creates the list of physical addresses of methods from the lookup table) and the sender, which does the call.

Forwarding mechanisms can provide a base for MSE signalling: For each monitored method M, a wrapping method MM is built. The run-time system can thus be used to supply a slightly altered list (a list that has the pair *[method M, physical address of MM]*) to anyone but MM (which receives the right address for M). The forwarding mechanism is then used to map an original method's name M to a wrapping method MM.

As far as we know, no system has been presented that uses a forwarding system to perform MSE signaling.

---

[9] These can be seen as *compiled interfaces* to the objects.

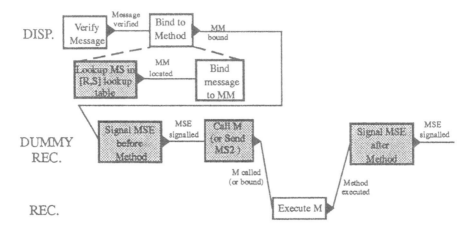

Fig. 6. Altering the lookup operation

Run-time Mechanisms. The run-time support system can be altered in the place where the message's method execution takes place, so that it signals an MSE for every dispatched message, as shown in figure 7.

This can require accessing and modifying the code of the dispatcher mechanism, if that is available. In compiled systems, the extended semantics can be planted either at compile or run-time. In interpreted systems, the system itself has to be changed. An example of the latter is the EXACT system [2].

If the dispatching mechanism is available as a method itself, that method can be specialised to perform the MSE signalling. Object Request Brokers (ORBs) are dispatchers, handlers of the messaging between objects, aiming to integrating heterogeneous and distributed objects by handling all the communication between them. Thus, the ORB can provide wrap-like functionality to a method either by altering registration mechanism in the same way presented either in the *name space management* approach, or as presented in the *forwarding* approach. The latter allows for the addition of newly monitored messages at run-time. As far as we know, no system has been presented that performs MSE signalling from ORB-dispatched messages.

The **main advantages** of the dispatcher-based approach are:

- The system is changed *once*, and then exploited with no need for further modifications: the trapping mechanism is known, but does not force changes in previously created applications, thus being unfelt by the user.
- The changes are done in the semantics of messaging, being thus *orthogonal* to the rest of the system's constructs. [10].

---

[10] Except if some other extension already changes messaging ser. antics in a way that couples, not chains, with the extensions undertaken for the MSE signalling.

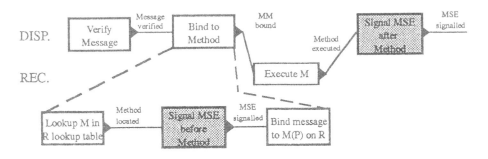

Fig. 7. Wrapping placed on the dispatcher calling operation

— In reactive systems, where the system performs both MSE signaling and the reaction, optimisations can be achieved by enhancing the linking between the event and the action (i.e., directly launching an action instead of signaling an event, if one and only one action is declared to react to a certain event).

5.4 A Note on Layered Approaches

Several of the systems presented simplify the use of their facilities by presenting a layered architecture. A special language is provided to define the reactive part of the application, from which code is generated and joined with the definition of the rest of the application. Such approach introduces a layer above the previously existing one: the user of the system receives a simpler definition mechanism and perceives a simpler semantic extension. But, as happens with layered extensions, the user is no longer able to see the whole system on a single definition layer, thus extending the development cycle, and forcing the use of different development tools (debuggers, compilers, browsers, ...) for each layer. Besides, several extensions on top of the same layer can be incompatible.

This approach tackles only the definition part of the active system. Hence, they have not been included in the comparison because they are not proper MSE signaling mechanisms, but an aid to the use of the mechanism provided by the reactive system. They effect quality of code, maintenance and ease of implementation and use, in the same way that any other layered extension does, without affecting run-time behaviour.

In a compiled OOPL able to change a message's semantics to that of a direct call (due to optimisation), the dispatcher deals only with non-optimised messages; thus, in order to use this approach for MSE signaling, the optimisations must be deactivated for monitored messages; this does not change the semantics of these messages.

6   Comparing MSE Signaling Approaches

Table 2 compares previous approaches according with their expressive power, maintenance and quality, implementation requirements and usage requirements which are all further described in the following sections.

Table 2. Distinctions among different approaches to MSE detection.

CRITERIA	Sender	Receiver	Dispatcher
Expressive Power			
Event detection point	bef-pre,aft-post	aft-pre,bef-post	bef-pre,aft-post
Event granularity	[*, *, *]	[R, *, *]	[*,*,*] / [R,M,*]
Maintenance and quality			
Need of a new MSE	Recompile	Recompile	Recompile/None
Robustness	Lower	Lower	Lower
Extensibility	Lower	Lower	Equal
Reusability	Lower	Lower	Equal
Compatibility	Equal	Equal	Higher
Modularity - reactive part	Low	Medium	Higher
Implementation Requirements			
In interpreted system	Easy	Easy	Medium
In compiled system	Easy	Easy	Diff./Medium
Changes in parser	No	No	Yes
Changes in run-time	No	No	Yes
Extra application objects	No	No	Maybe
Usage Requirements			
Changes in code	o(N MMSG)	o(N MMTH)	No
Performance Penalty			
Monitored message	No	No	No
Non monitored message	No	No	No/Yes

6.1   Expressive Power

Expressive power concerns the type and meaning of a MSE, that is:

- **Event detection point**: If the system allows methods to declare pre and post conditions, (e.g. Eiffel [11], Sather [13]), when should the MSE be signaled, that is, what should *before-method* and *after-method* mean? The ideal situation is that in which (1) before-method means the method's preconditions have been checked, and (2) after-method means the method's postconditions have been verified. This cannot be achieved by any of the presented approaches. Instead, two cases can happen:

- Before precondition and after postcondition: the MSE signals the invocation of the method or the *succesful* end of its execution.
- After precondition and before postcondition (thus the MSE signals the *correct-according-to-specification* invocation of the method or the end of its execution.

The former is exhibited by mechanisms where the signaling is done before properly executing the invoked method. The latter is presented if the signaling is done inside the method, once the preconditions have been checked (thus, only a receiver-based approach offers this semantics).

- **Event granularity.** The system can signal MSEs on messages of structure $S = [R, M, P]$. In which elements of S can the user place wildcards? This deals with class-level or instance-level selectivity [3], ECA or CA rules [14]. Sender-based approaches allow the user to signal exactly what he desires. Receiver-based approaches must know the receiver to be able to select the wrapper method. Dispatcher-based approaches can accept any syntax for S when the user redefines the dispatcher. When the flexibility of the dispatching mechanism is used, receiver and method must be known.

6.2   Maintenance and Quality

Maintenance and quality of the resulting application and reactive system combination [12]):

- **Need of a new MSE,** i.e., cost of the addition of a new element of active behaviour, derived attribute, ... that needs a new monitored message. This can or cannot force a recompilation (rebuild o parse in an interpreted system).
- **Robustness,** i.e., ability to function in abnormal conditions. This is usually linked to the ability to check invariants, pre and postconditions when executing a method (as described in the *event detection point* feature). The different approaches cannot signal MSEs both after correct invocation and after right fullfilment, hence the reactions cannot be executed with certainty about the correctness of the MSE they are reacting on. Sender and dispatcher-based approaches decrease robustness when MSEs are signaled before the execution of the method, and receiver-based ones when MSEs are signaled after the execution.
- **Extensibility,** i.e. ability to acommodate changes in reactive behaviour specifications. Sender-based approaches severely break the encapsulation of functionality by dispersing the points in which MSEs are signaled. Receiver-based lower the extensibility in the same way mentioned for layered approaches: a wrapper is an extension to the method, and as such can interfere with other extensions. Given its orthogonality with other mechanisms, dispatcher-based approaches do not affect extensibility of the previous code.

- **Reusability**, i.e. ability of the application to be reused, in whole or in part, for new applications. The reusability of the original component maybe lowered or maintained. The same arguments used in the previous paragraph are applicable here. The basic reusable element is the object's class code *and* the reactive part of the application linked to that object's monitored messages.

- **Compatibility**, i.e. easiness to be combined with other applications. The application as a whole does not change its interface mechanisms with others in sender and receiver-based approaches. In dispatcher-based approaches, the three alternatives presented are based precisely on mechanisms whose original idea is the combination between applications (via interoperability of classes -name space management- or objects -forwarding-).

6.3 Implementation Requirements

Implementation Requirements concern the changes and effects in the underlying system. Sender, receiver and namespace-based dispatcher approaches all use the existing system primitives to do the MSE signaling; therefore the system thus unaware of it and offers no special syntax or run-time support. Otherwise, any dispatcher-based approach requires hiding the user the internals of the mechanism, that he perceives as a semantic extension: the syntax of the language has to be left unchanged, but its parser has to be modified to do the extra work needed (e.g., creation of either new classes or new lookup-table entries); besides, changing the run-time support or creating extra objects not explicitly defined by the user can be needed. Run-time and parsing code is normally more coupled in an interpreted system, which thus will be normally easier to modify.

6.4 Usage Requirements

Usage Requirements have a twofold implication:

- **Changes in code**, i.e. how the original code has to be changed to account for the reactive behaviour mechanisms. The measure is based on two parameters: N MMSG refers to the number of messages sent that can invoke a monitored method; N MMTH to the number of monitored methods. The cost of declaring monitored methods in a dispatcher-based approach is considered negligible, as it can be obtained directly from the MSEs to which the reactions react, with no further change in the application.

- **Performance penalty** incurred after a MSE signaling mechanism is planted[11]. Sender and receiver-based approaches have no extra cost, as the signaling mechanism only affects compilation/definition time, and the processing of monitored messages is done only to signal MSEs and in no other case; neither do dispatcher-based approaches that use the name space management

---

[11] Besides the time need to create/modify the application so that it uses MSEs, and the time needed to do the signaling when it is needed, there can be an extra performance penalty when processing messages.

facilities, because these alter the lookup tables used at run-time, but do not force any unneeded lookups. By contrast, some dispatcher-based approaches pass every message through a modified dispatching functionality, similar in cost to that used to perform dynamic binding; others (those which wrap the dispatcher code) do a signaling for every message processed.

7 Conclusions

The broad range of applications which exhibit reactive behaviour has led to a growing interest in enhancing traditional systems with reactive capabilities. Approaches can broadly be classified according to whether the researchers have access to the source code of the system (then, using a dispatcher-based approach) or not, in which case a receiver-based layered architecture is commonly used. Whereas the former accounts for maintainability as the reactive capabilities is supported as a system primitive, sender and receiver-based approaches can be more efficient as reactive capabilities are specified at the application level.

References

1. O. Diaz, P.M.D. Gray, and N. Paton. Rule management in object oriented databases: a uniform approach. In R. Camps G.M. Lohman, A. Sernadas, editor, *17th Intl. Conf. on Very Large Data Bases, Barcelona*, pages 317–326. Morgan Kaufmann, 1991.
2. O. Diaz and A. Jaime. EXACT: an EXtensible approach to ACTive object-oriented databases. *Submitted for publication*, 1994.
3. S. Chakravarthy E. Anwar, L. Maugis. A new perspective on rule support for object-oriented databases. *SIGMOD Conference*, pages 99–108, 1993.
4. E. N. Hanson and J. Widom. An overview of production rules in database systems. *The Knowledge Engineering Review*, 8(2):121–143, 1993.
5. Inteligence Logiciel, ILOG. *ILOG Server User Manual*.
6. P. Jackson, editor. *Introduction to Expert Systems*. Addisson-Wesley, 1988.
7. C. Jones. Development of an expert system library using object oriented techniques. Master's thesis, Universidad del Pais Vasco, 1993.
8. A.M. Kotz, K.R Dittrich, and J.A. Mulle. Supporting semantic rules by a generalized event/trigger mechanism. In *Advance in Database Technology, EDBT, Venice*, pages 76–91, 1988.
9. J. Martin and S. Odell. *Object Oriented Analysis and Design*. Prentice Hall Publishing, 1993.
10. C. Medeiros and P. Pfeffer. A mechanism for managing rules in an object-oriented database. Technical report, Altair Technical Report, 1990.
11. B. Meyer. *Eiffel: The Language*. Prentice Hall Publishing, 1993.
12. Bertrand Meyer. *Object Oriented Software Construction*. Prentice Hall Publishing, 1988.
13. S. Omohundro. The sather 1.0 specification. info@icsi.berkeley.edu.
14. N. Paton, O. Diaz, and M.L. Barja. Combining active rules and metaclasses for enhanced extensibility in object-oriented systems. *Data and Knowledge Engineering*, 10:45–63, 1993.

15. R. Fernández Rupérez. Embedding of rule-based expert capabilities in oo applications by using active behaviour. In Bertrand Meyer et al., editor, *TOOLS 94*, page 315. Prentice Hall Publishers, 1994.

Reasoning about the behavior of Active Databases Applications

Opher Etzion

Information Systems Engineering Department
Faculty of Industrial Engineering and Management
Technion - Israel Institute of Technology
Email: ieretzn@ie.technion.ac.il

Abstract. One of the most difficult issues in the design of active database applications is the issue of predicting an application's behavior. In this paper we propose a knowledge based representation of an active database application's meta-data. This representation facilitates reasoning about important dimensions of an application's behavior such as: detecting the consequences of an event, data dependencies, termination and confluence and transactions control flow. This paper describes the meta-data level and some of the reasoning results.

1 Introduction and Motivation

The active database discipline is currently in the phase of moving from theory to practice; numerous applications have been and are being developed using the concepts or tools of active databases. One of the major difficulties in this process is the lack of tools and methodologies for design, debug and analysis of an application's behavior. Recent workshops and discussions [10] concurred this fact.

Active databases provide a *reactive* programming style, in which the operations are divided into operations that are requested by the user and operations that are inferred as a reaction to a detected event. The flow of execution is a mixture of operations in reactive and imperative programming. The design and debug of such an application requires a modelling tool able to reason about the behavior of an application. In particular the following capabilities are required:

1. The ability to reason about all the implications of a certain event. Questions that should be answered are of the type:
   - *which operations are directly or indirectly being activated as a consequence of detecting a certain event?*
   - *which data-elements are directly or indirectly being updated as a consequence of detecting a certain event?*
   - *what is the condition for such an update?*
2. The ability to reason about interactions among different rules. Questions that should be answered are of the type:
   - *can a given set of rules be activated together as a result of the same event?*
   - *does any of these rules issue a contradictory operation?*

Although some recent works are related to some of these questions [1], [4], [2], there has not been a comprehensive model that copes with system design issues of active database applications.

Reasoning about active database applications requires the explicit knowledge about all the application's components. The first step is to define the meta-data elements and their knowledge-based representation; this will be discussed in Section 2. The second step is to devise a reasoning scheme for answering the above mentioned questions; this will be discussed in Section 3. Section 4 concludes the paper.

2 The Meta-Data

The meta-data for an active database application consists of static schema, rules and programs. Reasoning about the application's behavior requires further refinement according to both: rules components and rules type.

2.1 The Knowledge Representation Scheme

The meta-data contains the following components:

Structural Schema: the knowledge representation of the database's **static schema.**

Events: the set of **events,** whose detection or signalling potentially entails rules activations.

Operations: the set of **operations** that are performed by the database during the evaluation and execution of rules. Operations denote the execution of the *condition* and *action* part of the rule.

Auxiliary Programs: Programs that are invoked by operations.

We are using a frame based system to represent the meta-data components. The basic entity is a *frame* that consists of *slots*. Each *slot* can represent an atomic value, a set of homogenous values, a tuple of heterogenous values or a reference to another frame. The latter turns the frame system into an association network. This knowledge base's objective is twofold: to use an inference mechanism in order to reason about dependencies among different entities as required in Section 1, and to facilitate the creation of an executable specification. To satisfy these objectives, the knowledge-base is required to include a complete information about the target system.

In this paper we focus on the first goal. Some aspects of the executable specification architecture are discussed in [5]; [6].

The following Sections describe the different meta-data elements.

2.2 The Static Schema

The static schema describes the database structure. Its representation is required, because a major part of the requested reasoning involves the relationships of data-elements with other meta-data components. The frame type employed is called a **data-element**. We assume that the data model supports operations at the attribute level, thus the term **data-element** denotes an attribute. The representation can be easily modified to represent data-elements in the entity level. A **data-element** is represented by the slots:

<element-id, class, type, cardinality, nested-elements, reference-class, reference-event>,

where:

class represents the class to which the data-element belongs. The term class may denote different terms in various data models, such as: relation in the relational model.

type represents a syntactic type,

cardinality determines if the data-element is an atom, a set or a tuple (nested data-element).

nested elements the elements' components are described by nested-elements, in the nested data-element case.

reference-class If the data-element designates a pointer to another entity then the reference-class designates the class of entities that the data-elements can reference.

reference-event is an association between a data-element and an event. It denotes *data-driven event*, i.e. an event that is signalled as a result of a data element's update.

PDI (Persistent Derived Information) is a data-element whose values are derived by derivation rules and not given directly by the user. The frame type representing PDI is a specialization of the frame type representing data-elements. It inherits all its slots and one additional slot:

<reference-stabilizers >

This slots denotes a reference to stabilizers,[1] an alternative operations that are activated to stabilize abnormal situations [8]. The abnormal situation in this case is direct update of a PDI, bypassing the derivation rule, since the derivation rule no longer reflects the dependency among data-elements, this situation is considered as abnormal. This representation is general enough to represent the static schema of various data models.

2.3 Events

An *event* is an entity, that designates an instantaneous occurrence in the modelled reality, whose detection or insertion of its instance to the database may activate operations.

An event is represented by the frame of the type:

---

[1] stabilizers are further discussed in conjunction with the high level operation stabilize.

<event-id, event-name, event-type, event-expression, reference-events,
reference-operations >

event-type classifies the events to signalled event, reflective event and composite event.

- **signalled event:** This is an event whose occurrence is explicitly signalled to the database either by a user-initiated signal operation or by a sensor that inputs the database. Examples: a trial conviction (signal), a detected airplane invasion (sensor), the time stamp 12:00 (sensor), the beginning of the transaction T1 (signal). Signalled events can be further classified to: explicit database update, temporal event and a other signalled event. This is similar to the partition of events in Snoop [3].
- **reflective event:** A data-driven event that is signalled as a result of a database update. It is called *reflective* due to the fact that if reflective programming is used[6], this event can be inferred. The linguistic issue is outside the scope of this paper.
- **composite event:** This is an event that is detected when an assertion in which other events participate is satisfied.

Event-Expression is the specification of a composite event; in event languages such as Snoop[3], the assertion may include logical quantifiers (any, all) and temporal operators, such as: sequence, during, and periodic.

reference-events: An event *e* may reference a composite events *ce*. In this case all the name of event *e* should appear in the event-expression of the event *ce*.

reference-operations: Operations that are triggered by the event.

2.4 Operations

Operations are executable entities that are (conditionally or unconditionally) activated by an event. Our knowledge base supports two programming styles: the typical active database style, in which actions are arbitrary programs, and the PARDES style[5] that supports a specialized operations for derived data and integrity constraints. The modelled application can use either programming style or a combination of them, this issue is further discussed in [7]. The operations are classified into low-level operations (**assert, update, retrieve, commit, abort**) and high-level operations (**attach, derive, enforce constraint, stabilize**). Low level operations are employed by high level operations.

An operation is represented as the frame type:

< operation-id, operation-type, operation-name, operation-expression,
reference-assertions >

The syntax and semantics of operation-expressions are specific to various operation types, thus a separate discussion for each operation-type is presented. The reference-assertions slot refers to preconditions for the operations execution.

Low Level Operations A Low level operation is a specialization of an Operation, and thus, by inheritance, a low level operation frame inherits all the slot types of operation with two additional slots:

< reference-data-elements, reference-events >

reference-data-elements are data-elements that are potentially being retrieved or updated during the execution of the low-level operation. reference-events are events that are potentially being signalled by the low-level operation. Here, we refer to database events. The set of specializations of low level operations consists of: assert, retrieve, update, commit and abort, each of these types is represented by a frame that inherits all the slots from low level operations with no additional slots.

assert: A low-level operation that denotes verification of a query on the database's values. The **assert** operation returns either "true" (the expression has been asserted) or "false". It has multiple uses within the model:[2]
  1. to denote a prerequisite for the execution of an operation.[2]
  2. To define an integrity constraint expression to be enforced.
The operation-expression is a conjunction of expressions in the form:

< operand1 pred operand2 >

where:
operand1, operand2 consists of constants, data-element names or arithmetic expressions that involve data-element names.
pred is either a logical connector $(=, \neq, \leq, <, \geq, >)$ or a set inclusion operation $(\in, \subset, \subseteq)$.
Examples of assertion expressions are:
  1. Number-of-Days $\leq$ 100
  2. (Department-Budget $-$ Department-Expenses)/ Department-Expenses $\leq$ sum (Project) / 100
  3. Project-Budget $>=$ Project-Expenses
  4. Project-Affiliation $\in$ Project

update: A low level operation that creates a new state of the database, by altering its content. We differentiate a **direct update** that is a part of the user's transaction, from a **derived update** that is triggered by the active database system. The operation-expression is of the form:

< operation-code, class-id, entity-id, $(p_1, \ldots, p_n)$ >

operation-code is one of the set: insert, modify, or delete and $(p_1, \ldots, p_n)$ designate data-elements that can be updated in the defined update operation. For the ease of use, we shall partition any update to a set of *single operations*, each of them updates a *single data-element*.Thus, an update operation creates n references to the updated data-elements.

---

[2] An assertion α is a prerequisite for an operation o if $\alpha \in$ reference-assertion (o).

retrieve: This low-level operation issues a database retrieval request. It is activated as a part of an update flow, or requested by a **derive operation**, or is triggered by an event. The expression is a statement in a query language. It is partitioned to a series of single retrieve operations that retrieve (possibly multiple values of) a single data-element.

abort and commit: The **abort** and **commit** low-level operations obey the standard definitions in transaction processing theory. A single frame in the knowledge base is sufficient to denote each of them.

High Level Operations A High level operation is a specialization of operation. Thus, each frame inherits the slots of a frame of type operation and an additional slot:

< reference-low-level-operations >

This slot denotes the low level operations that are activated by the high level operation. The specializations of high level operation are: attach, derive, enforce and stabilize.

attach A high level operation that invokes an auxiliary program and serves as a channel for database related operations in the called program. In the regular active database programming style, this is the standard (and the only supported type) operation. The frame that represents **attach** inherits all the slots of a frame of type high level operation and in addition the slot:

< reference-auxiliary-programs >

Since we assume a complete knowledge about the application, the attach expression should include all the data elements whose values are potentially retrieved by the program and all the data-elements which the program is required to update. The program communicates with the database using the *attach operation*. The attach expression is represented as:

<attach-id, invoked-program, retrieved-data-elements, updated-data-elements
>

This expression is translated to the appropriate references.

derive derive operation is a high-level operation that uses a declarative definition to support derivations of data elements. derive expression denotes the derivation invariant. The syntax is:

PDI := exp1 [when cond1; exp2 when cond2...]

PDI (persistent derived information) is the derived data-element, exp_i is an arithmetic expression that refers to properties.

enforce Integrity constraint enforcement is an high-level operation that verifies the integrity constraint's satisfaction. if the constraint is not satisfied, then it decides whether to abort, or to activate a stabilizer. An enforce frame is a specialization of high level operation, thus it inherits all its slots, and has an additional slot of:

< reference-stabilizers >.

The consistency enforcement operation can be triggered by a reflective event. Its activation may be contingent upon the result of a condition assertion, while the integrity constraint is also represented by an assertion. The operation-expression is of the form

integrity-constraint when condition, stabilizers= (stabilizer when condition)

Both integrity-constraint and condition are assertions whose evaluation are executed by activating the *assert* operation. stabilizer designates the stabilizer's type or a private stabilizer's name.

stabilize A stabilizer is an high-level operation consistency restorer that is invoked by an enforce operation, in case of failure. The failure means that the current database state is inconsistent with respect to its integrity constraints. There are two types of **stabilizers**: an explicitly specified one (using auxiliary routine) and an inferred one. In the latter case, merely the *stabilization strategy* is specified and the context-sensitive operation is inferred. This is again, a reflective programming style.

A stabilizer is represented as:

< stabilizer-id, strategy, exception-handler-name >

2.5 Auxiliary Program

A program that is being called by an attach operation is represented by a frame type Auxiliary program that consists of the following slots:

< program-id, program-name, program-location >

2.6 The execution associations

Figure 1 shows the associations among different elements that denote references. These associations are the key for the reasoning process. The execution process advances through association links. The execution process starts with a set of frames, that constitute a transaction and are typically frames of the types: event, update operation, retrieve operation. These frames are **activated** (see the activation definition below). The control is (conditionally) passed to all the frames that are referenced by the activated frame. This process continues until it reaches a set of frames that do not have any referenced edges. In Section 3 we discuss the issue of this process' termination.

Definition 1. Frame Activation A frame is activated when the entity it represents is activated in the execution process.

• If the frame represents an operation, activation means the actual activation of the operation.

- If the frame represents a data-element, activation means a database operation that updates or retrieves this data-element.
- If the frame represents an event, activation means the detection of this event.

Whenever the control is passed to a frame, the activation is carried out according to the above definition.

dep. id	de	Association type	dt
1	event	participant in event	composite event
2	data-element	data-driven event	reflective event
3	event	triggered operation	operation
4	enforce	invoked stabilizer	stabilizer
5	PDI	triggering derivation stabilizer	stabilizer
6	operation	prerequisite	assert operation
7	high-level operation	Applying Low-Level Operation	Low-level operation
8	attach operation	Auxiliary program call	Auxiliary program
9	low-level operation	database access	data-element
10	low-level operation	DB event	DB event

Fig. 1. Association Types

Figure 2 shows an association network representation, where each node represents an entity and each edge a reference to another entities.

3 Reasoning

In this section the reasoning capabilities of the knowledge-base are discussed. Section 3.1. discusses the detection of all the consequences of an event. Section 3.2. discusses the detection of all data and operation dependencies. Section 3.3. discusses the rules termination and confluence issue. For simplicity we ignore the case in which an assertion's value can change during the activation execution, this case is dealt with separately. Because of length limitations we omit the proof for all the propositions.

3.1 Event Consequences Detection

Maximal consequences set

Definition 2. Direct Consequences. The set of **direct consequences** $[DCS]$ of a frame (fr) is defined as:

$$DCS(fr) = \{\alpha \mid \exists d \in DEP : [de(d) = fr \wedge dt(d) = \alpha]\}$$

94

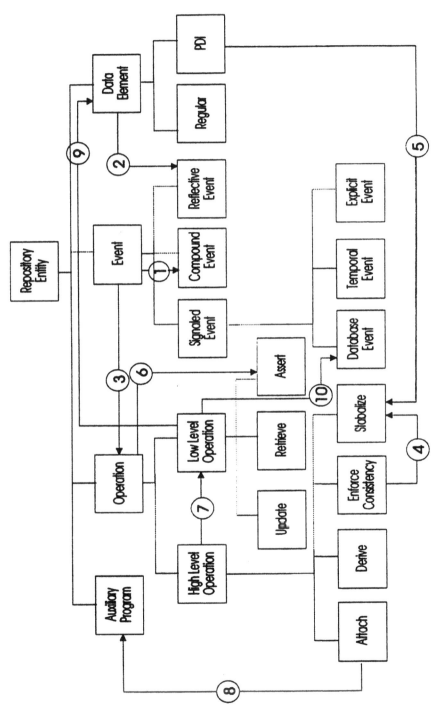

Fig. 2. An association graph representation of meta-data

This set denotes all the frames that have direct association relationships with fr, i.e. the set of frames that are referenced by fr.

Definition 3. Consequences. The set of **consequences** $[CS]$ of a frame (fr) is defined as:

$$CS(fr) = \{\alpha \mid \alpha \in DCS(fr) \vee \exists \alpha' \in CS(fr) : [\alpha \in DCS(\alpha')]\}$$

This recursive definition denotes the transitive closure of the DCS function with respect to dependencies. The set includes all the frames that are directly or indirectly dependent upon fr.

Proposition 4. Maximal activation set: *For any event, ev, the maximal set of frames that can be activated as the result of the event detection is the set $CS(ev)$.*

Elimination of non activating operations: The set $CS(ev)$ defines all the consequences of the event ev; it is a maximal set, and may include entities that are not necessarily activated. These entities are of two types:

1. entities that the decision about their execution is determined only at run-time;
2. entities that we can infer their non execution. Any conditioned execution can be determined only at run-time.

In the latter case, we can use the semantics of derivations and integrity constraint enforcements to eliminate some of the operations dependent upon them, in the cases described below.

Definition 5. Retrieved(RTR). For each operation op, the function RTR is defined as $RTR(op) = \{\alpha \mid \alpha \in DCS(op) \wedge \alpha \text{ is a retrieve operation }\}$.

The RTR function denotes all the retrieve operations that are employed by a certain operation.

Definition 6. Accessed. For each single update or retrieve operation, the function Accessed $(ACC(op))$ denotes the data element that is accessed by this operation.

For convenience reasons, it is assumed that a database operation accesses (possibly many instances of) a single data-element.

Proposition 7. elimination of non activating operations *For any operation ω of type enforce or derive, a retrieve operation ρ in $RTR(\omega)$ can be eliminated from being executed as a consequence of a given event ev , if:*

1. *$\exists$ an update operation u s.t. $u \in CS(ev) \wedge ACC(\rho) = ACC(u)$, or*
2. *ω is incremental.*

The first condition states that if a data-element is updated as a consequence of an event, its value should not be retrieved. The second condition states that if the derivation or constraint enforcement operation can be performed incrementally then there is no need for any retrieve operation. A discussion about incremental derivation can be found in [9].

Definition 8. CCS. Let $ELR(ev)$ be the set of retrieve operations that belongs to $CS(ev)$ and whose execution is eliminated. The corrected consequences of ev

$$CCS(ev) = CS(ev) - ELR(ev)$$

As a result of propositions 4 and 7, we can infer the following propositions.

Proposition 9. *All the operations that are potentially executed as a result of an event ev (in the sense that they cannot be eliminated at compile time) belong to the set* $CCS(ev)$

$CCS(ev)$ is the set that include all the consequences of an event ev. As stated before, some elements of $CCS(ev)$ may not be executed due to failed prerequisites, however they cannot be detected at compile time. $CCS(ev)$ is the minimal set of possible consequences that can be inferred at compile time, thus it is used as a basis for answering queries about the consequences of a given event.

Conditional Execution

Definition 10. Consequent Path. The consequent path between two frames α, γ, denoted as $CP(\alpha, \gamma)$, is a sequence $< \beta_1, \ldots, \beta_n >$, such that:

1. $\beta_1 = \alpha$;
2. $\beta_n = \gamma$;
3. $\forall 1 \leq i \leq n - 1 : \beta_{i+1} \in DCS(\beta_i)$.

A consequent path denotes a chain of frames that connects two frames, using dependencies. Note, that more than one path between two frames is possible. The CP function finds a path, but its definition can be easily extended to find all paths.

Proposition 11. conditional execution *An operation α is executed as a consequence of an event ev iff*
$\alpha \in CCS(ev) \wedge \forall \beta \in consequent-path(ev, \alpha)$: *the assertion designated as a prerequisite to β is evaluated to true.*
    The execution condition $EXCON(ev, \alpha)$ is denoted by:

$EXCON(ev, \alpha) = \bigwedge ass \mid < \beta, ass >\in prerequisite-dependencies \wedge \beta \in consequent-path(ev, \alpha)$

$EXCON(ev, \alpha)$ is the conjunction of all the prerequisite assertions in the path between ev and α and denotes the condition for the execution of α when ev has occurred. An operation without a defined prerequisite is assumed to have a prerequisite that is constantly *true*. If the $EXCON(ev, \alpha)$ is *true* then the operation α is unconditionally executed as a result of an event ev (no prerequisites in the path).

Updated Data-elements set

Proposition 12. Updated data-elements *If an update operation u is (conditionally) executed as a consequence of an event ev then the data-element de = $ACC(u)$ is (conditionally) being updated as a result of this event. The set of all data-elements that are potentially updated as a result of an event ev is:*

$$UDE(ev) = \{de \mid \exists u \in update-operations \cap CCS(ev) : [de = ACC(u)]\}$$

Operation's generators

Definition 13. Generators. An event ev is a generator of an operation α if the operation α is potentially entailed by ev. The set of all generators is denoted by GEN(α).

Proposition 14. equivalence of generators and consequences *From the above definition it is clear that for an operation α*

$$ev \in GEN(\alpha) \; iff \; \alpha \in CS(ev)$$

Inferences To conclude, we show several queries that can be answered by the above mentioned propositions. Each query is answered by the construction of the appropriate set. The construction of each set requires navigation in the knowledge base along the association links. It is possible to compute all these sets at compile time using one scan of the frame, and perform all the desired queries.

- What are all the operations that are executed as a result of the occurrence of an event ev? *the answer is obtained by CCS(ev)*(see Proposition 9).
- What is the condition for the execution of an operation α as a consequence of an event ev? *the answer is obtained by $EXCON(ev, \alpha)$*(see proposition 11).
- Can a data-element de be updated as a consequence of an event ev; what is the condition for this update?
  $de \in UDE(ev)$ (see Proposition 12).
- Is it possible that the operations α, β are executed as a consequences of the same event? *this query evaluates to "true" iff $GEN(\alpha) \cap GEN(\beta) \neq \emptyset$* (see proposition 14).

These queries are useful in the design and debug phases as well as for the evaluation of possible change on the application's behavior.

3.2 Data Dependencies

Definition 15. data dependency A data-element β is dependent upon a data-element α, denoted by the predicate DATA-DEPENDED-PRED (β, α), if any change in the value of α potentially entails the change of the value of an instance (or instances) of β.

Proposition 16. Data dependencies *A data-element β is dependent upon a data-element α iff*

$$\exists u \in update-operations \mid u \in CCE(\alpha) \wedge \beta \in ACC(u)$$

The set of all the data-elements dependent upon the data-element α is denoted by the function data-dependent-set (α)

A data-element can be conditionally dependent upon other data-element, where the dependency condition is similar to the one stated in proposition 11. Queries that can be answered using this data-element are:

- What are all the data-elements that are potentially changed as a result of a change of a given data-element? data-dependent-set (α)(see proposition 16).
- What is the condition by which the value of the data-element β is dependent upon the given data-element α?
  Answer: $EXCON(\alpha, u) \mid u$ is an update-operation $\wedge acc(u) = \beta$.
- What is the influence of a given data-element on the value of another data-element? *this query is meaningful only if all the high-level operations in the consequent-path of these two elements are of type derive.* Possible answers can be: adding, subtracting, counting, complex connections etc..

3.3 Termination and Confluence

Detecting cycles

Definition 17. cyclic application An active database application is cyclic if

$$\exists u \in update-operations \mid u \in CCS(u)$$

(see definition 8. for CCS).

A cycle can be conditioned, where the condition is obtained by EXCON (u,u).

Proposition 18. non termination *A cyclic application will not terminate if the cycle conditions are satisfied and the update operation u is bound to the same value at both ends of the cycle.*

Proposition 19. termination *A cyclic application will terminate if the update operation u is bound in each cycle to a unique member of a finite set.*

Interaction Interaction among rules in active databases [1] can lead to contradiction among update operations, that update the same data-element with different values (*the confluence problem*). Follows is a definition of interaction among frames and its impact on the analysis of the execution.

Definition 20. interaction Two frames fr_1, fr_2 interact if they are disjoined (none of them is a consequence of the other) and they both are generators of an update operation that updates the same data-element. Formally, the predicate $INTERACT(fr_1, fr_2)$ is evaluated to "true" if:
$fr_1 \notin CS(fr_2) \wedge fr_2 \notin CS(fr_1) \wedge \exists u1, u2 \in update-operations : [ACC(u1) = ACC(u2) \wedge u1 \in CS(fr_1) \wedge u2 \in CS(fr_2)]$

Proposition 21. contradicting operations *An event ev can generate contradicting update operations if it includes interacting frames among it consequences, a condition for that is:*

$$\exists fr_1, fr_2 \in CS(ev) : [INTERACT(fr_1, fr_2)]$$

Inferences Examples of useful queries about termination and confluence are:

- *Is the application cyclic? if yes, what are the cycle conditions? Can we analyze the termination status of this cycle?* the answer is obtained using definition 17, and Propositions 18, 19.
- *Do contradictory operations exist as a result of any event? if yes, what are the conditions for this contradiction?* the answer is obtained by using proposition 21.

In applications with many rules, these queries are extremely useful to assess execution problems as a result of wrong coordination among rules.

4 Conclusion

The knowledge-based approach provides a modelling tool and reasoning capabilities about the behavior of active database applications. This approach assists in the task of design and debug of complex active database applications.

The capabilities that have been required in the introduction (the ability to reason about all the implications of a certain event, the ability to plan transactions flow) are all supported by the reasoning facilities of the knowledge base.

The knowledge-based approach holds a substantial promise as a modelling and reasoning tool. This approach can be utilized to analyze other types of dynamic applications, such as workflow models. Future work will also increase the debug facilities by adding explanation power to the reasoning, explaining the results of a query. For example: specifying the members of a cycle. A run-time debugger with a *look ahead* facility based on the knowledge-based execution is also being planned.

The knowledge-base approach can also hold a promise for the purposes of executable specifications; the knowledge base may control the execution of the application and infer decisions at run-time.

The knowledge base is currently under implementation within the PARDES project at the Technion.

References

1. E. Baralis, S. Ceri, and J. Widom. Better termination analysis for active databases. In *Proceedings of the 1st International Workshop on Rules in Database Systems*, pages 163–179, August 1993.

2. H. Behrends. Simulation-based debugging of active databases. In *Proceedings of the 4th International workshop on Research Issues in Data Engineering*, pages 172–180, February 1994.

3. S. Chakravarthy and D. Mishra. An expressive event specification language for active databases. *Data and Knowledge Engineering*, 13(3), October 1994.

4. O. Diaz, A. Jaime, and N. Paton. Dear: a debugger for active rules in an object-oriented context. In *Proceedings of the 1st International Workshop on Rules in Database Systems*, pages 180–193, 1993.

5. O. Etzion. Pardes-a data-driven oriented active database model. *SIGMOD RECORD*, 22(1):7–14, Mar 1993.

6. O. Etzion. The reflective approach for data-driven rules. *International Journal of Intelligent and Cooperative Information Systems*, 2(4):399–424, December 1993.

7. O. Etzion. Tapuz: An information repository approach to active database applications. Technical Report ISE-TR-94-2, Technion -Israel Institute of Technology, Dec 1994.

8. O. Etzion and B. Dahav. Self stabilization in database consistency maintenance. Technical Report ISE-TR-95-1, Technion -Israel Institute of Technology, Feb 1995.

9. S. Koenig and R. Paige. A transformational framework for the automatic control of derived data. In *Proceedings of the VLDB*, pages 306–318, 1981.

10. J. Widom. Research issues in active database systems: Report from the closing panel at ride-ads' 94. *ACM Sigmod Record*, 22(3), 1994.

Extending a functional DBPL with ECA-rules

Swarup Reddi[*], Alex Poulovassilis[+], Carol Small[*]

[*]Dept. of Computer Science, Birkbeck College,
University of London, Malet St. London WC1 7HX.
{carol,swarup}@dcs.bbk.ac.uk

[+]Dept. of Computer Science, King's College London,
Strand, London WC2R 2LS.
alex@dcs.kcl.ac.uk

Abstract. We describe how a functional database programming language can be extended with transactions and ECA-rules. Fundamental requirements of such an extension are that the declarative semantics of the language not be compromised, that the syntax of the language not be disrupted unduly, and that impedance mismatch problems be avoided. We define what we mean by events, conditions and actions and describe the semantics of ECA-rules with reference to event detection, parameter-binding, transaction scheduling and abort handling. We define the execution semantics for the ECA System in the language itself. These semantics form the basis of our implementation of the ECA System.

Keywords. ECA-rules, deductive databases, functional database languages, PFL.

1 Introduction

This paper describes how ECA-rules can be added to PFL, a functional database programming language. PFL is "declarative" in the sense that expression evaluation is confluent i.e. the order in which the sub-expressions of an expression are evaluated does not affect the value of the overall expression. This remains true of expressions which invoke functions that update the database since PFL's type system guarantees that only confluent expressions are accepted for evaluation (see [Sut95] for details). The advantages of confluence of expression evaluation are many, including the possibility of formal proofs of correctness and support for coarse grain optimisations.

PFL is also "deductive" in the sense that it supports extensionally defined relations, and also functions that play the role of intentional relations [Pou91, Sma91]. Recently there has been considerable interest in the integration of active and deductive database technologies - see, for example, [Bay93, Har93, Sim92, Zan93]. There is clearly a degree of overlap in the functionality active and deductive technologies provide, and indeed some researchers have argued that the two paradigms should be kept separate [Wid94]. Nevertheless, we view the functionalities provided by the two paradigms as complementary. For example, to provide the semantics of ECA-rules in a deductive system either the deductive rules must be modified (with the result that application semantics are "embedded" within these rules, and so are hard to manage and modify), or the database must be polled periodically (with the result that if the polling period is too short then system resources are wasted, whereas if it is too long then there is a loss of "currency"). Conversely, considerable investment has been made into query optimisation and theoretical foundations for deductive languages, and it is clearly desirable to use this work in the context of active systems.

This paper describes how ECA-rules can be added to PFL, and indeed any functional database language of similar expressiveness. The challenges involved in this task are two-fold: (i) At the syntactic level, how can ECA-rules be specified in a style that is consistent with the rest of the language? (ii) At the semantic level, how can ECA-rules be supported whilst retaining the declarative semantics of the language?

With respect to the first of these, we first extend PFL to support *transactions*. These are sequences of the form $e_1; \ldots; e_n$ where each e_i is an expression. An ECA-rule then has three components: an expression *events* (the "event query"), an expression *condition* (the "condition query"), and a sequence of expressions, $a_1; \ldots; a_n$ (the "actions"). The firing of an ECA-rule comprises the following steps: the evaluation of *events*, yielding a (possibly empty) list of expressions, *evs*, corresponding to event occurrences; the removal of each element of *evs* which does not satisfy the *condition*, giving a new list of expressions evs' (the "parameter list"); the scheduling of a transaction $a_1 \ evs'; \ldots; a_n \ evs'$.

With respect to the second of the above points, transactions and ECA-rules are not "first class objects" in our language: functions cannot take transactions or ECA-rules as arguments nor can they return them as results and so transactions and ECA-rules cannot be "embedded" within expressions. Also, when processing a transaction $e_1; \ldots; e_n$, each e_i is evaluated in turn and the ECA-rules are fired only when the evaluation of e_i terminates (so our ECA system uses a production system model [Han92]). The evaluation of each expression e_i within a transaction is thus confluent. However, events - such as clock and external events - which need to be detected and acted upon *during* expression evaluation are not supported.

The structure of the remainder of this paper is as follows. In Section 2 we give a brief description of PFL, including its type system and its support for relations, transactions and ECA-rules. In Section 3 we specify the semantics of transaction execution using PFL itself as the meta language. In Section 4 we summarise our contribution and give directions of further work.

2   Preliminaries

PFL supports the following commands each of which is described in this section, apart from command (i) which is discussed in Section 3.3:

(a) the declaration of a new type,
(b) the definition of a type synonym,

(c) the declaration of the type of a new function,

(d) the specification of an equation for a function,

(e) the declaration of a new relation,

(f) the definition of an ECA-rule,

(g) the evaluation of a transaction,

(h) the evaluation of an expression (which is treated as a transaction consisting of a single expression),

(i) the casting of an arbitrary function as a primitive event.

The new features of the language beyond those described in previous papers [Pou91, Sma91] are (f), (g) and (i). In the sequel, we use teletype font for PFL code and *italic* font for syntactic variables. We use $e, e_1, \ldots, e_n$ to denote expressions, $t, t_1, \ldots, t_n$ to denote types, and $e_1, \ldots, e_n :: t$ to indicate that the expressions $e_1, \ldots, e_n$ all have type t.

2.1 Types

PFL is a polymorphic, statically typed, functional database programming language. It is *higher-order* in the sense that functions may take functions as arguments and return functions as results. It is computationally complete, and also update-complete in the sense that any computable transformation over relations can be defined [Sut95].

PFL provides a set of built-in types and facilities for the user to declare new types and their constructors. The built-in types include Num, Str and Chr which are respectively populated by numbers, strings and characters. Also built-in are list, product and function types: for any types $t, t_1, \ldots, t_n$, the type $[t]$ consists of lists of elements of type t; the type $(t_1, \ldots, t_n)$ consists of n-tuples of the form $(e_1, \ldots, e_n)$ where $n > 1$ and each $e_i :: t_i$; and the type $t_1 \to t_2$ consists of functions that map values of type t_1 to values of type t_2. The list constructors are [ ] and (:) where, for all types t, [ ] :: $[t]$ and $(:) e_1 e_2 :: [t]$ if $e_1 :: t$ and $e_2 :: [t]$. The constructor (:) can be written infix, in which case it is unbracketed. We support some syntactic sugar for enumerated lists in that an expression $[e_1, e_2, \ldots, e_n]$ is synonymous with $e_1 : [e_2, \ldots, e_n]$. Also, $\to$ is right-associative so that $t_1 \to t_2 \to t_3$ and $t_1 \to (t_2 \to t_3)$ are synonymous.

New types and type synonyms can be declared at any time. User-declared type names and constructors must start with an upper-case letter. For example, our definition of the ECA system in Section 3 below assumes two types, SMode ("scheduling mode") and AMode ("abort mode"), and two synonyms, TranId ("transaction identifier") and EventId ("event identifier") for the type Num:

```
SMode    ::= Imm | Def;
AMode    ::= ParentChild | ChildParent | Mutual | Independent;
TranId   == Num;
EventId  == Num;
```

Note that ::= and == introduce new types and type synonyms respectively.

2.2 Expressions and Functions

An *expression* in PFL is one of: a variable, a function name, a constructor, or the application of one expression to another. Application is left-associative and has higher precedence than any operator. Variables and function names must start with a lower-case letter and constructors must start with an upper-case letter. The keyword let introduces a local definition for a variable. For example, let x==2; in x*x is equivalent to 2*2 while let a==1; b==2; in (a,b) is equivalent to (1,2).

Also supported are *list comprehensions* [Pey87]. They take the form $[e \mid q_1; \ldots; q_n]$, and are read as "the list of e such that q_1 and ... and q_n". Each q_i is either a boolean-valued expression which must be satisfied, or a generator of the form $p \leftarrow l$ which is read as "the pattern p takes each value in the list l in turn" (a *pattern* being an expression that contains no functions). For example, the expression

$$[(x,y) \mid x \texttt{ <- } xs; y \texttt{ <- } ys; pred (x,y)]$$

returns the subset of the cartesian product of the lists xs and ys which satisfies the predicate pred.

The built-in functions include the usual arithmetic and relational operators, and also the operator ++ which is used both for concatenating two strings and for appending one list to another. The user may define new functions at any time. Functions are defined by means of equations and we give three examples below. The symbol == is used for equation definitions while the symbol = is the equality operator. The type of a function is automatically inferred from its defining equations although the user may optionally pre-declare its expected type. As an aid to readability, we include the expected types in our examples:

```
if :: Bool->a->a->a;
if True  x y      == x;
if False x y      == y;


case :: [(Bool,a)]->a;
case ((bool,val):rest) == if bool val (case rest);


fold :: (a->b->a)->a->[b]->a;
fold op end []        == end;
fold op end (x:xs)    == fold op (op end x) xs;
```

case, when applied to a list of pairs [(b1,v1),...,(bn,vn)], returns the first value vi, such that bi evaluates to True. Given a binary operator op, an expression end and a list of expressions [e1,..,en], fold op end [e1,...,en] is equivalent to

$$\texttt{e1 op (e2 op (... op (en op end) ...)).}$$

2.3 Bulk Data

Bulk data is stored in a class of 0-ary, list-valued functions we term *relations*. The extent of a relation is initially the empty list, and can be updated by means of two built-in functions, include and exclude. These both take as arguments the name of a relation, r, and a value, e. include adds e to the head of the extent of r, provided e is not already present there, and returns r. exclude removes e from the extent of r and returns r.

Although include and exclude update relations by side-effect, PFL's type checker will reject any query or function definition which would compromise the confluence of the language (see [Sut95] for details). For example, if r is an initially empty relation of type [Num] and the function ext returns the extent of its argument, then the expression (ext r, include 1 r) evaluates to either ([],r) or ([1],r), depending on whether the first or second component is evaluated first. Thus, the expression is not confluent and would be rejected by the type checker.

2.4 Transactions

A transaction is specified by a command of the form

$$tranStart;\ e_1;\ e_2;\ \ldots;\ e_n;\ tranEnd;$$

where $e_1, e_2, \ldots, e_n$ are arbitrary expressions and $tranStart$ and $tranEnd$ are built-in functions indicating the start and end of a transaction.

The $n + 2$ expressions comprising a transaction are evaluated in turn. The evaluation of the current expression may cause the occurrence of one or more *primitive events* which are recorded by the evaluator in a system-reserved relation, the delta relation. The invocation of any of the functions include, exclude, transStart and transEnd constitutes a primitive event, as also does the invocation of any other function so declared by the user (see Section 3.3). A further system-reserved relation, the history relation, contains a cumulative record of all primitive events (including those in the delta relation). The history relation is cleared whenever the database is committed while the delta relation is cleared immediately before the evaluation of each e_i.

The delta and history relations cannot be accessed directly because these relations are type-incorrect. Instead, for each class of primitive event an individual history and delta relation are provided which are derived from the overall history and delta relations. In particular, for each relation r::[t], the relations rIncH, rIncD, rExcH, rExcD :: [(EventId,TranId,t)] respectively record the cumulative inclusions, the delta inclusions, the cumulative exclusions, and the delta exclusions with respect to r. Similarly, transStartH, transStartD, tranEndH, tranEndD::[(EventId,TranId)] respectively record the cumulative and delta transaction start events, and the cumulative and delta transaction end events.

Thus, from the user's perspective, each class of primitive event is associated with two relations: a cumulative history that contains a tuple for each event occurrence since the database was last committed and a delta relation that contains a tuple for each event occurrence during the evaluation of the transaction's current expression. These relations are type-correct views of the system-reserved history and delta relations, which, for the sake of simplicity, we have materialised in our current implementation.

The ECA-rules are fired after the evaluation of each expression of the transaction has completed and the occurrence of events (both primitive and composite) is detected by the event queries of the ECA-rules (see Section 2.5), which interrogate the cumulative and delta relations associated with each primitive event.

2.5 ECA-Rules

The user may define new ECA-rules by commands of the form

$\llcorner ecaRule\ i\ ==\ (events, condition, [action_1, \ldots, action_m], sm, am);$

where:

- i is a unique number which defines the priority of the ECA-rule.
- *events* is an expression of type $[t]$ for some type t. It must not update the database. Its evaluation yields a list of expressions, $[ev_1, \ldots, ev_n]$, where each ev_j represents the occurrence of an event during the evaluation of the current expression.
- *condition* is an expression of type $t \rightarrow Bool$ and must also not update the database. *condition* is applied to each element of the list $[ev_1, \ldots, ev_n]$ and only those elements for which *condition* ev_j evaluates to *True* are retained.
- Each *action*$_i$ is an expression (which can, and usually will, update the database) to be applied to the list of events which satisfy the *condition*. Thus overall the user can regard the ECA-rule as specifying the following sequence of "reactions":

  > *let evs* $==\ [e\ |\ e\ \leftarrow\ events;\ condition\ e];$
  >
  > *in* $tranStart;\ action_1\ evs;\ \ldots;\ action_m\ evs;\ tranEnd;$

- *sm* is an expression of type SMode. If the value of *sm* is Imm ("immediate") then a new transaction comprising the reactions will be run prior to resuming the current transaction. If the value of *sm* is Def ("deferred") then a new transaction comprising the reactions will be run after the completion of the top-level transaction.
- *am* is an expression of type AMode representing the abort dependency between the original transaction, $tran_o$, and the reaction transaction, $tran_r$:
  - ParentChild - if $tran_o$ aborts then $tran_r$ is to abort;
  - ChildParent - if $tran_r$ aborts then $tran_o$ is to abort;
  - Mutual - if either $tran_o$ or $tran_r$ aborts then so must the other; and
  - Independent - there is no abort dependency between $tran_o$ and $tran_r$.

To illustrate, suppose that we have three relations: accSite which relates road traffic accidents (acc below) to the grid references (gr below) at which they occurred, and blackSpots and mWayBlackSpots which record the grid references of all accident black spots and motorway black spots respectively (here, a black spot is a grid reference at which six or more accidents have occurred). We can define ECA-rules which (i) enforce the integrity constraint that accidents must occur on roads, and (ii) materialise blackSpots and mWayBlackSpots from accLocation as follows, where $ returns the length of a list, inclist adds a list of tuples to a relation, and error prints its argument and causes the evaluation of the current expression to abort:

```
_ecaRule 1  == (e1,c1,[a1],Imm,ChildParent);
_ecaRule 2  == (e2,c2,[a2,a3],Def,Mutual);

e1          == [tuple | (eId,tId,tuple) <- accSiteIncD ];
c1 (acc,gr) == roadClassAt gr = None;
a1 x        == error "accident not located on road";

e2          == [tuple | (eId,tId) <- tranEndD;
                        (eId2,tId2,tuple) <- accSiteIncH; tId=tId2];
c2 (acc,gr) == $ [gr | (a2,gr2) <- accSite; gr = gr2] > 5;
a2 x        == inclist [gr | (acc,gr)<- x] blackSpots;
a3 x        == inclist [gr | (acc,gr)<- x; roadClassAt gr = MWay]
                       mWayBlackSpots;
```

The ChildParent abort mode of the first rule causes any transaction violating the integrity constraint to be aborted, whilst the Def scheduling mode of the second rule causes re-materialisation of blackSpots and mWayBlackSpots only at the end of a transaction which updates accSite.

3 Transaction Execution Semantics

In this section we specify the semantics of transaction execution using PFL itself as the meta language. We thus obtain a formal declarative semantics for transaction execution which not only forms the basis of our implementation of the ECA System but also is immediately accessible to the PFL user.

For the purposes of manipulation by the ECA System (and also the evaluator) PFL expressions are represented as values of type Expr:

```
Expr ::= C Str | S Str | N Str | Con Str | Rel Str |
         Var Str | Ap Expr Expr | Error
```

Here the constructors C, N, S, Con and Rel are understood to state that the associated string represents a character, number, string, constructor, or relation name respectively. The constructor Error is discussed in Section 3.2 below. The ECA system does not need to distinguish between variables and function names (except relation names) so the constructor Var is used for either of these. For example, the expression head [1,2] is represented as:

```
Ap (Var "head") (Ap (Ap (Con "(:)") (N "1"))
                     (Ap (Ap (Con "(:)") (N "2")) (Con "[]")))
```

3.1 Data Structures Used by the ECA System

The ECA System uses the following type synonyms and functions:

```
Tran       ==  (TranId,[Expr]);
Schedule   ==  [Tran];
```

```
DBState     ==  [(Str,[Expr])];
ECAState    ==  (EventId,TranId,AbortGraph,ECARules,History);
AbortGraph  ==  [(AMode,TranId,TranId)];
ECARules    ==  [ECARule];
ECARule     ==  (Expr,Expr,[Expr],AMode,SMode);
History     ==  (Str,[(EventId,TranId,Expr)]);
nextEv      ::  EventId->EventId;
nextTran    ::  TranId->TranId;
getRel      ::  DBState->Str->[Expr];
incRel      ::  DBState->Str->Expr->DBState;
clearDeltas ::  DBState->DBState;
```

EventId, TranId are synonyms for numbers that uniquely identify events and transactions (see Section 2.1). EventIds and TranIds are totally ordered and the function nextEv (nextTran), when applied to an EventId (TranId), returns the next EventId (TranId) according to the total ordering. EventIds are assigned in the order in which events occur. In contrast, TranIds are assigned in the order in which transactions are scheduled.

Tran is a synonym for a pair comprising a transaction identifier and a list of the expressions comprising the transaction.

Schedule is a synonym for a list of transactions to be executed in sequence.

DBState is a synonym representing the database state. It consists of a list of pairs, the first component being the name of a function and the second being its definition, of type [Expr]. In the case of a non-relational function, the definition consists of a single Expr. In the case of a relation, the definition consists of one Expr for each element of the relation. For example, a relation seen by the user as having name r and extent [1,2] is held in a DBState as the pair ("r",[N "1", N "2"]).

The functions getRel, incRel and clearDeltas interrogate and alter a DBState. For a database state db, relation name r, and expression e, getRel db r returns the extent of r, incRel db r e adds e to the head of the extent of r provided it is not already present and returns db, and clearDeltas db sets to the empty list the extent of every delta relation i.e. every relation whose name ends in "D", together with the system-reserved delta relation.

ECAState is a synonym representing the current state of the ECA System. It comprises the "next" identifier to be assigned to an event; the "next" identifier to be assigned to a transaction; an abort graph which, in the case of a transaction aborting, is used to identify the other transactions to be aborted; the list of ECA-rules; and the system-reserved history relation.

An AbortGraph is a list of triples each of which contains a pair of transaction identifiers and the abort dependency between them.

ECARules is a synonym for a list of 5-tuples representing the ECA-rules of the system. The order of the rules within this list is according to their priority and consequently the user-specified rule identifier (see Section 2.5) is not needed. Each ECA-rule comprises an event and condition (both of type

Expr), an action (of type [Expr]), an abort-dependency (of type AMode) and a scheduling-mode (of type SMode).

3.2 Specification of the ECA System

Our specification of the ECA System assumes a function eval::Expr->DBState ->(Expr,DBState) which takes an expression and a database state, and fully evaluates the expression while logging all primitive event occurrences in the delta relation. eval returns a pair comprising the reduced expression and updated database state. If an error arises during the evaluation of an expression (e.g. an attempt to divide by zero, or an invocation of the error function) then eval reduces the expression to Error and returns the database unchanged. Thus eval is in effect the PFL evaluator which, apart from supporting retrieval from, and update of, relations and logging of primitive events, is much like the evaluator for a conventional functional programming language (for which implementation details may be found in [Pey87]).

At the top level of our specification is execSched, which takes as its argument a triple comprising a DBState, an ECAState and a Schedule. It repeatedly calls execExp (see below) to process the transaction at the head of the schedule (i.e. the *current transaction*) until the schedule is empty. It returns the updated database and ECA states:

```
execSched :: (DBState,ECAState,Schedule)->(DBState,ECAState);
execSched (db,eca,[])          == (db,eca);
execSched (db,eca,(tran:trans)) ==
    execSched (execExp tran (db,eca,trans));
```

execExp, defined below, processes each expression of the current transaction in turn. If the transaction is non-empty, execExp removes its first expression, exp1, and puts the remainder of the transaction back at the head of the schedule. It then clears all the delta relations within the current database state and calls eval to evaluate exp1 with respect to the updated database state. Thus, the delta relation in db2 contains only those primitive events resulting from the evaluation of exp1. If the evaluation of exp1 terminates normally, ecaControl (see below) is called to update the history relation, to do event-detection and to schedule reactions. If the evaluation terminates abnormally, abortHandle (discussed in Section 3.4) is called to abort the current transaction:

```
execExp :: Tran->(DBState,ECAState,Schedule)
          ->(DBState,ECAState,Schedule);
execExp (tId,[]) (db,eca,sched)        == (db,eca,sched);
execExp (tId,exp1:exps) (db1,eca,sched1) ==
    let  sched2    == (tId,exps):sched1;
         (exp2,db2) == eval exp1 (clearDeltas db1);
    in   if (exp2 = Error)
             (abortHandle tId (db2,eca,sched2))
             (ecaControl  tId (db2,eca,sched2));
```

The arguments to ecaControl are the identifier of the current transaction, the current database state, the current ECA state and the current schedule. ecaControl returns the updated database state, ECA state and schedule. The tasks required of ecaControl are twofold. Firstly, the overall history relation and the individual history and delta relations associated with each primitive event need to be updated: this is effected by logEvent whose definition we defer until we have specified event detection and scheduling. Secondly, event detection must be undertaken and any reactions arising must be scheduled (i.e. inserted into the appropriate location in the Schedule):

```
ecaControl :: TranId->(DBState,ECAState,Schedule)
              ->(DBState,ECAState,Schedule);
ecaControl tId (db1,eca1,sched1) ==
   let  newEvents   == getRel db1 "delta";
        (db2,eca2)  == fold (logEvent tId) (db1,eca1) newEvents;
        (eca3,sched2) == detectAndSched tId (db2,eca2,sched1);
   in   (db2,eca3,sched2);
```

In practice, only those ECA-rules whose event expressions reference updated history and/or delta relations need be considered during event detection. However, for the purposes of specifying the event detection semantics we ignore this optimisation. Thus, detectAndSched calls schedRule to process each ECA-rule in turn, and then returns the updated ECAState and Schedule:

```
detectAndSched :: TranId->(DBState,ECAState,Schedule)
                  ->(ECAState,Schedule);
detectAndSched tId (db,(e,t1,g1,rules,h),sched)  ==
   let  (imm,def,t2,g2) ==
           fold (schedRule tId db) ([],sched,t1,g1) rules;
   in   ((e,t2,g2,r,h),imm++def);
```

schedRule lies at the heart of the ECA System. It considers a particular ECA-rule, evaluates the parameter list, and then schedules the reactions and updates the abort graph as necessary. In addition to the current transaction identifier, database state and ECA-rule, schedRule takes as its argument a 4-tuple. The first two components of this are the immediate and deferred reactions so far accumulated (i.e. the reactions arising from the ECA-rules already processed). The third component is the next unassigned transaction identifier and the fourth is the abort graph. schedRule returns an updated version of this 4-tuple. That is, if the ECA-rule under consideration generates a reaction, then this reaction is added to the appropriate list of reactions (according to the rule's scheduling mode), the abort graph is updated and the unassigned transaction identifier is incremented. When processing a rule the evaluation of the parameter list may terminate abnormally. In this case we invoke the abort handler as soon as possible by scheduling as the earliest possible transaction one whose list of expressions is simply [Error]:

```
schedRule :: TranId->DBState->([Tran],[Tran],TranId,AbortGraph)
```

```
                   ->ECARule->([Tran],[Tran],TranId,AbortGraph);
schedRule tId db (imm,def,tid2,graph) (e,c,a,mode,abDep) ==
    let (pl,db) == eval (Ap (Ap (Var "parmList") e) c) db;
        reacts  == [Ap ai pl | ai <- a];
        tran    == (tid2,[transtart]++reacts++[tranEnd]);
        g2      == (abDep,tId,tid2):graph;
        nextId  == nextTran tid2;
    in  case [(pl = Error,    ((tid2,[Error]):imm,def,nextId,g2)),
              (pl = Con "[]", (imm,def,tid2,graph)),
              (mode = Imm,    (imm++[tran],def,nextId,g2)),
              (mode = Def,    (imm,def++[tran],nextId,g2))];
```

Here parmList is a function defined as
parmList events cond == [e | e <- events; cond e];
and stored within the database, db, in the appropriate form.

There are two points to note regarding the event-detection and scheduling. The first is that, since each rule is processed in turn, the order in which reactions are scheduled is the same as the order of precedence of the rules. The second is that, since the event and condition expressions of ECA-rules only query the DBState, all the parameter lists are evaluated against the same DBState.

We now return to the logging of events. To recap, eval evaluates an expression and records in delta the primitive events that occur. In order to undertake event detection, the cumulative history relation and the individual history and delta relations need to be updated to reflect the events recorded in delta. For the history relation this is accomplished by prefixing to it a triple consisting of the current event, the current TranId and the "next" EventId (the EventId in the ECAState is incremented accordingly). The updating of individual history and delta relations is accomplished by incHistAndDelta, defined below. logEvent returns the updated DBState and ECAState:

```
logEvent : TranId->(DBState,ECAState)->Expr->(DBState,ECAState);
logEvent tId (db1,(e,t,graph,rules,history)) event ==
    let eca2  == (nextEv e,t,graph,rules,(e,tId,event):history);
        db2   == incHistAndDelta db1 (e,tId,event);
    in  (db2,eca2);
```

As described in Section 2.4, the individual history and delta relations are views of the system-reserved history relation and we materialise these views for ease of both explanation and implementation. incHistAndDelta first calls the unwind function to unpack the event expression into the name of the function whose evaluation constituted the primitive event (for example include, exclude, tranStart or tranEnd) and the list of that function's arguments. This information is then used to construct the name of the appropriate history and delta relations. The expression to be added to the extents of these relations represents a tuple comprising the EventId, the TranId, and the arguments to the function. The function makeTuple :: [Expr] -> Expr, which we have not specified here, is used to construct this expression: it takes a list of n expressions and returns a single expression representing an n-tuple. Also used is a built-in function numToExpr :: Num->Expr which converts a number into its representation as an Expr. Overall, the functions required for event logging are:

```
incHistAndDelta :: DBState->(EventId,TranId,Expr)->DBState;
unwind          :: (Expr,[Expr])->(Str,[Expr]);
relEvent        :: DBState->[Expr]->Str->EventId->TranId->DBState;
funEvent        :: DBState->Str->(EventId,TranId,[Expr])->DBState;


incHistAndDelta db (eid,tid,exp) ==
    let  (fun,args) == unwind (exp,[]);
    in   case [ (fun = "include", relEvent db args "Inc" eid tid),
                (fun = "exclude", relEvent db args "Exc" eid tid),
                (True,  funEvent db fun (eid,tid,args))];


unwind ((Ap exp1 exp2),args) == unwind (exp1, exp2:args);
unwind (Var fun,args)        == (fun,args);


relEvent db [(Rel r),val] incOrExc eid tid ==
    funEvent db (r++incOrExc) (eid,tid,[val]);


funEvent db fun (eid,tid,args) ==
    let  tuple  == makeTuple (numToExpr eid:(numToExpr tid:args));
    in   incRel (incRel db (fun++"D") tuple) (fun++"H") tuple;
```

3.3 Casting a Function as a Primitive Event

This is analogous to designating the invocation of a method as an event in an active object-oriented system. There are two restrictions on functions that can be cast as primitive events. The first is that the function cannot be called by the event or condition queries of any ECA-rule since these may not alter the DBState. The second is that the function must have a monomorphic type so that the relation in which the event occurrences are recorded only contains tuples of a single type.

For any function $f :: t_1 \rightarrow t_2 \rightarrow \ldots \rightarrow t_n \rightarrow t$ cast as a primitive event, the names of its history and delta relations are the function name suffixed by "H" and "D", respectively, and their types are both $[(EventId, TranId, t_1, \ldots, t_n)]$.

When declaring the function to be a primitive event, the user is required to specify a sequence of inverse events to be executed in the case that an abort occurs (see below). Any primitive events that occur during the evaluation of a function will automatically be compensated. Consequently, the evaluation of the user-specified inverse events can be regarded as a "do instead" activity.

3.4 Abort Handling

As we saw in the definition of execExp above, if an expression evaluates to Error the transaction containing this expression is aborted by the invocation of abortHandle. For reasons of space, we can only briefly describe the functionality of abortHandle here and refer the reader to [Red95] for its definition.

First, the other transactions that must be aborted are identified using the AbortGraph component of the ECAState. Then, rather than being rolled-back, these transactions are *compensated* by compensating each of their constituent primitive events in the reverse order of their occurrence. In particular, inclusions and exclusions of values in relations are compensated by exclusions and inclusions respectively, while user-defined primitive events are compensated by their user-defined sequence of inverse events. A single compensating transaction compensates all the aborted transactions. The compensating events are not logged but instead the events that they compensate are removed from the overall and individual history relations.

4 Conclusions

We have described how the functional database language PFL can be extended with ECA-rules and have given an execution semantics for the extended system by using PFL itself as the meta language. Our approach to ECA-rules can be summarised as follows:

- *No impedance mismatch*: PFL's computational model, type system, and data structures are unaffected by the implementation of the ECA System. No new language need be learnt for specifying events, conditions or actions.
- *Simplicity*: a primitive event occurrence is simply a value in the appropriate history and delta relations. Thus the specification and detection of both composite and primitive events simply comprises the definition and evaluation of queries over these relations.
- *Expressiveness*: events and conditions are specified in a computationally complete language and actions in an update-complete one.
- *Extensibility*: a function can be cast as a primitive event at any time.
- *Generality*: the user has access to both individual history and delta relations and can therefore make explicit choices regarding event consumption for each event instead of having them implicitly assumed and fixed for all events.

Figure 1 summarises our approach to supporting ECA-rules according to the criteria proposed by Paton *et al.* [Pat93]. For reasons of space we can only discuss a few of these criteria here and refer the reader to [Red95] for a fuller discussion.

Condition evaluation occurs when the event is detected, although it can be deferred until, say, the end of the transaction by defining an ECA-rule whose event query detects a tranEnd event. Since both the condition and the action are expressions, a condition can also be moved to the action part of a rule and can hence be evaluated when the action is scheduled to occur.

PFL allows an action to occur either immediately as a sub-transaction, or as a separate transaction. In the latter case the action modes "Detached Dependent" and "Detached Independent" are obtained by using the AModes ParentChild and Independent respectively and the SMode Def. The remaining AModes supported

Events	Type ⊂ { Primitive, Composite } Source ⊂ {Structure Operation, Transaction, Behaviour Invocation, Error } Level ⊂ { Instance, Collection } Role ∈ { Mandatory }
Condition	Mode ⊂ { Immediate, Deferred, Detached } Role ∈ { Optional }
Action	Mode ⊂ { Immediate, Detached Dependent, Detached Independent } Options ∈ { Update-Db, Abort, Do Instead }
Execution Model	Transition Granularity ∈ { Set } Binding Model ∈ { Set } Constraints ∈ { } Scheduling ∈ { All Fired } Priorities ∈ { Numerical }
Management	Operations ∈ { } Description ∈ { Programming Language } Adaptability ∈ { Run Time } Data Model ∈ { Functional }

Fig. 1. Categorisation of PFL's support for ECA-rules

are not covered by the criteria of Paton *et al.* Any sequence of expressions can be specified as the action part of an ECA rule, thus allowing database updates to be performed and transactions to be aborted (by evaluation of an expression leading to Error). The action cannot, however, cause the firing of other ECA-rules to be over-ridden.

At present we do not allow rules to activate or deactivate other rules - although such a facility can be simulated by explicitly checking the value of a switch as part of an event query and turning the switch on or off as part of an action. Rules are not "first class" values: they can be changed only at the command level and cannot be added or deleted *dynamically* by evaluating an expression. However, since rules can be added and deleted once the database is populated we have classified PFL's rule adaptability as "run time". Although we believe that our language could be extended to offer dynamic adaptability of rules, we are uncertain of the desirability of this since it would make the semantics considerably more complicated.

There are a number of areas in which further work is required. Firstly, our current method for assigning priorities to ECA-rules is rudimentary and we plan to provide the user with tools to (re)prioritise ECA-rules. Secondly, we need to investigate optimisation strategies for event detection and condition evaluation. In [Pou91, Sma91] we introduced functions that play the role of intentional relations and in [Red93] developed techniques for the efficient enforcement of integrity constraints over them. We believe that these techniques can be generalised to optimise event detection for event queries that are intentional relations. Thirdly, we need to support the database commands of Section 2 as primitive events and to provide their inverse events. Finally, the database state resulting from the evaluation of an expression e_i followed by the execution of the ECA-rules that it triggers is in general dependent on the order in which sub-expressions of e_i are evaluated. For example, given two relations r1 and r2 of type [Num] the evaluation of the tuple (include 1 r1, include 1 r2) is confluent. However, the detection of a composite event consisting of an update of r1 followed by an update of r2 depends on the order of evaluation of the components of the tuple. Thus we need to explore syntactic criteria which guarantee that a set of ECA-rules gives rise to a unique database state.

Acknowledgements

We are grateful to David Sutton for discussions on PFL's linear type system. This work was supported by EPSRC grant no. GR/J 98134.

References

[Bay93] Bayer, P., and Jonker, W. A framework for supporting triggers in deductive databases, *Proc. 1st Int. Workshop on Rules in Database Systems*, Edinburgh, 1993.

[Han92] Hanson, E.N. Rule condition testing and action execution in Ariel, *Proc. ACM SIGMOD Conference*, San Diego, 1992.

[Har93] Harrison, J.V. and Dietrich, S.W. Integrating active and deductive rules, *Proc. 1st Int. Workshop on Rules in Database Systems*, Edinburgh, 1993.

[Pat93] Paton, N.W. Díaz, O. Williams, M.H. Campin, J. Dinn, A. and Jaime, A. Dimensions of active behaviour, *Proc. 1st Int. Workshop on Rules in Database Systems*, Edinburgh, 1993.

[Pey87] Peyton-Jones, S.L. *The implementation of functional programming languages*, Prentice-Hall, 1987.

[Pou91] Poulovassilis, A. and Small, C. A functional approach to deductive databases, *Proc. 17th VLDB Conference*, Barcelona, 1991. Santiago, 1994.

[Red93] Reddi, S. Integrity constraint enforcement in the functional database language PFL, *Proc. 11th British National Conference on Databases*, Keele, July 1993.

[Red95] Reddi, S. Poulovassilis, A. and Small, C. Extending PFL with ECA-rules, Technical Report, Dept, of Computer Science, Birkbeck College. July 1995.

[Sim92] Simon, E., Kiernan, J. and de Maindreville, C. Implementing high level active rules on top of a relational DBMS, *Proc. 18th VLDB Conference*, Vancouver, 1992.

[Sma91] Small, C. and Poulovassilis, A. An overview of PFL, *Proc. DBPL-3*, Nauplion, 1991.

[Sut95] Sutton, D. and Small, C. Extending functional database languages to update completeness. To appear in *Proc. 13th British National Conference on Databases*, Manchester, July 1995.

[Wid94] Widom, J. Research issues in active database systems, *ACM SIGMOD Record*, 23(3), 1994.

[Zan93] Zaniolo, C. A unified semantics for active and deductive databases, *Proc. 1st Int. Workshop on Rules in Database Systems*, Edinburgh, 1993.

Rule Base Organization and Modeling

Rule Contexts in Active Databases
- A Mechanism for Dynamic Rule Grouping

Martin Sköld, Esa Falkenroth, Tore Risch
Department of Computer and Information Science, Linköping University
S-581 83 Linköping, Sweden
e-mail: {marsk,esafa,torri}@ida.liu.se

Abstract. Engineering applications that use Active DBMSs (ADBMSs) often need to group activities into modes that are shifted during the execution of different tasks. This paper presents a mechanism for grouping rules into *contexts* that can be activated and deactivated dynamically. The ADBMS monitors only those events that affect rules of activated contexts.

By *dynamic* rule grouping the set of monitored rules can be changed during the transactions. In a *static* rule grouping the rules are associated with specific objects during the schema definition.

A rule is always activated into a previously defined context. The same rule can be activated with different parameters and into several different contexts. Rules in a context are not enabled for triggering until the context is activated. However, rules can be directly activated into a previously activated context. When rule contexts are deactivated all the rules in that context are disabled from triggering.

The user defined contexts can be checked at any time in a transaction. Rule contexts can be used as a representation of coupling modes, where the ADBMS has built-in contexts for immediate, deferred, and detached rule processing. These built-in coupling modes are always active and are automatically checked by the ADBMS.

Contexts and rules are first-class objects in the ADBMS. Database procedures can be defined that dynamically activate and deactivate contexts and rules to support dynamically changing behaviours of complex applications.

The context mechanism has been implemented in the AMOS ADBMS. The paper concludes with an example of a manufacturing control application that highlights the need for rule contexts.

1   Introduction

A system for building manufacturing control applications was implemented using an ADBMS [10]. In the system active rules control the manufacturing tasks. Details about the system and examples of active rules are presented in section 4. Experiences from this system integration are:

- These type of engineering applications need to group activities into modes that are shifting during the execution of different tasks.

- Since the ADBMS did not initially have mechanisms for handling mode changes the application had to implement this functionality by introducing state variables in the rule conditions.

- The state variables caused the rules to become complex and unintuitive. A rule would often need to refer to several different state variables.

- The state variables represent control knowledge. It is better to separate rules representing domain knowledge from rules for control knowledge, e.g. by defining *meta-rules* [1][2].

- Implementing mode changes by altering state variables is inefficient since the total number of simultaneously monitored rules will be unnecessary large. By having the ADBMS support mode changes internally the overhead for rule checking can be kept low.

This paper presents an ADBMS mechanism for dynamically grouping rules into *contexts* that are activated and deactivated dynamically. The contexts are associated with different modes in the applications. When the application shifts between modes, the ADBMS is ordered to shift attention, or *focus*, to the associated rule context. Shifting between contexts means that all rules in the old context are ignored and the rules in the new context are monitored instead. There are applications that need to work with modes on different levels where a mode can consist of many hierarchically ordered sub-modes. This means that the ADBMS must be able to handle several rule contexts simultaneously and to support modelling of contexts in the schema. By defining contexts and rules as first-class objects in the ADBMS this is accomplished. This approach also supports the definition of *meta-rules* that are defined over rules and contexts.

Applications must not only have the possibility to create and delete contexts and activate and deactivate them, but must also be able to control when the rules are to be checked. For example, the application might initiate a series of operations and then check if any rules were triggered. This usually falls outside of the general coupling modes defined in ADBMSs. Our contexts therefore have *rule processing points*, which allow applications to define their own coupling modes where the rules can be checked at a user specified time in a transaction.

The contexts are also used internally in the ADBMS to implement system coupling modes. System coupling modes are associated with predefined contexts that are automatically checked by the system.

The paper presents rules and rule contexts as implemented in the AMOS (Active Mediating Object System)[5][13] ADBMS. The paper concludes with an example of a manufacturing control application that highlights the need for rule contexts.

2   Related Work

The idea of grouping rules dynamically into different contexts was initially developed in expert systems[1][17]. Other names for these groups of rules include *worlds* and *viewpoints*. In expert systems these rule contexts are usually used for organizing different *hypothesis* during a deduction process. In an ADBMS the issue is more of organizing the different *activities*.

The contexts were also supported in the rule based expert system Mycin and its successor Oncosin [1]. In Mycin contexts had to be specified as special context variables in rule conditions; in Oncosin a special CONTEXT clause on each rule referred to the context variables. By contrast our contexts completely separate the context specifications (i.e. the control information) from the rules (i.e. the knowledge) and therefore the same rule can occur in many contexts with different control strategies.

The rules in an ADBMS are often defined as first-class objects in the database schemas [3]. In Object Oriented (OO) systems the rules can often be grouped as belonging to a class and rules can be associated with other classes similarly as class methods. KEE [8] used this model for grouping rules into *worlds*. This classification is useful when associating rules with specific objects statically, e.g. when associating some constraint on the possible values of a class attribute or reacting to a user defined event associated with an object. These kinds of rules are usually always active and are triggered when a method is invoked of an instance of the class. However, in many applications there is a need to dynamically group rules that are associated with many different classes of objects.

Both POSTGRES[15] and Starburst[18] allow rules to be members of *rule sets*, which can be ordered hierarchically and where complete rule sets can be activated and deactivated. Rule sets are checked at certain *rule processing points*. The contexts in AMOS are more dynamic since the same rule can be activated in different contexts for different parameters, i.e. for different object instances. The contexts are objects and thus can be stored in any data structure and can be used for relating different data to different contexts. In AMOS contexts are also used for defining built-in coupling modes for rule execution. This means that these contexts have rule processing points that are automatically executed by the system. Since the same rule can be activated into different contexts the same rule can also be given many coupling modes.

In [16] a model is presented for defining applications in terms of *brokers* that represent reactive system components and *roles* that specify the responsibilities of brokers in various situational and organizational contexts. A proposal was made to implement rules using rules and special role dependant state variables. As was mentioned earlier, we believe this kind of modelling is better supported by rule contexts in the ADBMS.

We define rule contexts as first-class objects to enable functions to be parameterized with contexts, organizing them hierarchically in data structures, and defining rules that manage (create/delete, activate/deactivate) other contexts than their own. This makes it possible to define *meta-rules* as in [1][2] where the meta data consists of other rules and contexts.

3 Rules and Contexts in the AMOS Active DBMS

Active rules have been introduced into AMOS[5][13], an Object Relational DBMS. The data model of AMOS is based on the functional data model of Daplex[14] and Iris[6]. AMOSQL, the query language of AMOS, is a derivative of OSQL[11]. The data model of AMOS is based on objects, types, functions, and rules. Everything in the data model is an object, including types, functions, and rules[3]. All objects are classified as belonging to one or several types, i.e. classes. Functions can be stored, derived, or foreign. Stored functions correspond to object attributes in an OO system and to base tables in a relational system, derived functions correspond to methods and relational views, and foreign functions are functions written in some procedural language[1]. Database procedures are defined as functions that have side-effects. AMOSQL extends OSQL[11] with active rules, a richer type system, and multidatabase functionality.

3.1 Contexts

When rules are activated in AMOS, they are always associated with rule contexts. The contexts are first-class objects and are created by the statement:

create context *context-name*

where the *context-name* is a global name. Contexts are deleted by:

delete context *context-name*

The contexts are initially *inactive* which means that before a context is *activated* the events affecting its rules are not monitored (unless the events are monitored by another already active context). Contexts are activated by:

activate context *context-name*

which enables all the activated rules in the context to be monitored. Contexts are deactivated by:

deactivate context *context-name*

which disables all the activated rules in the context from being monitored. Two built-in contexts, named `deferred` and `detached`, are predefined and always active for deferred and detached rules, respectively. These are checked automatically by the system. Deferred rules are checked immediately before transaction-commit and detached immediately after.

3.2 Rules

AMOSQL supports Condition Action (CA) rules. The condition is defined as an AMOSQL query and the action as an AMOSQL procedural expression.
The syntax for rules is as follows:

create rule *rule-name parameter-specification* **as**
    when *for-each-clause* | *predicate-expression*
    do *procedure-expression*
where
for-each-clause ::=
    for each *variable-declaration-commalist* **where** *predicate-expression*

The *predicate-expression* can contain any boolean expression, including conjunction, disjunction and negation. The rules are deleted by:

---

1. In AMOS foreign functions can be written in Lisp or C.

delete rule *rule-name*

The rules are activated and deactivated separately for different parameters. Rules are activated in different contexts, where the default context is the deferred context:

activate rule *rule-name parameter-list* [**strict**] [**priority** 0|1|2|3|4|5] [**into** *context-name*]

deactivate rule *rule-name parameter-list* [**from** *context-name*]

The semantics of a rule in an active context is as follows: If an event in the database changes the truth value for some instance of the condition to *true*, the rule is marked as *triggered* for that instance. If something happens later in the transaction which causes the condition to become false again, the rule is no longer triggered. This ensures that we only react to net changes, i.e. *logical events*. A non-empty result of the query of the condition is regarded as *true* and an empty result is regarded as *false*. Since events are not monitored in inactive contexts, rules in them will not trigger until the context is activated and some event happens that causes the condition to become true. *Strict* rule processing semantics guarantees that a rule is triggered only once for each change that causes its condition to become true. Rule priorities can be used for defining conflict resolution between rules that are triggered simultaneously in the same context.

3.3 Rule Contexts and Rule Processing Points

Each context in AMOS has a separate *rule processing point* where the conditions of the rules in the context are checked and where the corresponding actions are executed if the condition is true. (For strict semantics the action is executed only if the condition was false in the previous processing point of the context).

A processing point is either *explicit* or *implicit*. Explicit processing points are issued by explicit calls from applications to a *check* system procedure. Implicit processing points are issued by the ADBMS at specific database states, e.g. just before (deferred rule processing) and after (detached rule processing) each commit point.

Rule contexts can be used as a representation of coupling modes [4]. The coupling modes are defined as named contexts with implicit processing points. All rules that are activated in the same context also have the same coupling mode, i.e. the same rule processing point. Traditionally coupling modes have been associated directly with individual rules. By associating the coupling modes with rule contexts a more flexible model can be achieved. Since rules can be activated into several contexts they can also be given several coupling modes. Coupling modes for *immediate, deferred,* and *detached* rule processing can be defined as built-in contexts that are automatically checked by the transaction mechanism of the ADBMS (fig. 1). In [4] a separation was made between E-C and C-A coupling modes. When we refer to immediate coupling mode here, we really mean immediate-immediate, and by deferred we mean deferred-deferred. Contexts for other E-C and C-A combinations could also be defined. Immediate rule checking is currently not supported in AMOS, but its processing points would have to be just after (or before) triggering database operations. User defined contexts with explicit processing points can be checked at any time within a transaction. The detached coupling mode is important in a multidatabase architecture like AMOS. In such an architecture one agent or broker may need to monitor the behaviour of another agent[12]. This monitoring must be made on committed data. By using a detached coupling mode the rules that perform the monitoring will never trigger on uncommitted changes.

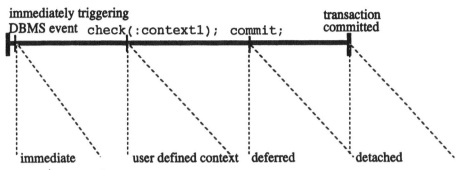

Fig. 1. Contexts as a representation of coupling modes

Decoupled and *causally dependent decoupled* coupling modes [4] can be implemented using general transaction mechanisms for creating sub-transactions and synchronizing transactions.

4   A Manufacturing Control System

The need for a context mechanism became apparent when an ADBMS was used in the implementation of a system for building manufacturing control applications [10]. ARAMIS (A Robot And Manufacturing Instruction System) [9] is a high-level language and a set of tools for designing intelligent behaviour of control systems. The ARAMIS language has similarities with workflow languages [7], but is oriented towards specifying the high-level activities of control applications. The low-level control programs that interact with the physical hardware are isolated from the application programmer by the World Model (WM) metaphor. All the objects in the model of the manufacturing task can be observed and manipulated as objects in the WM. The original ARAMIS system [9] was fully implemented (controlling a robot with various sensors), but with a primitive ADBMS. In [10] a three-level architecture combining the ARAMIS language and an ADBMS is presented. In CAMOS (Control Applications Mediating Object System), see fig. 2, a manufacturing task is expressed in a high-level task language that is partly compiled into an AMOS database that stores the WM and monitors changes to the objects in the WM.

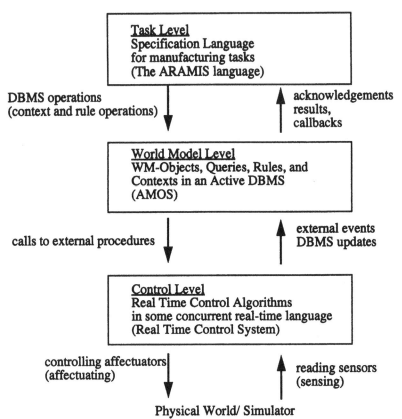

Fig. 2. The three-level architecture of CAMOS

The WM is synchronized with a *physical world* or a *simulator* by cooperation between a *control system* and an ADBMS through a servo mechanism. When the task level updates the WM, the control level affects the physical world to correspond to the WM. Likewise, when the control level sense changes in the physical world, it updates the WM. In the CAMOS architecture the high-level query language and active rules of AMOS are used to support much of the functionality in the WM, e.g. to monitor changes to the WM. Parts of this architecture have been implemented to verify the ideas. Instead of using actual hardware, a simulator of a production cell was used[1]. In the initial implementation state variables were used to model mode changes. Below follows an example of how rule contexts in AMOS can be used instead.

4.1 A Production Cell Simulation

A production cell consisting of a two-armed robot, an elevating rotary table, a press, a

---

1. Based on a simulator developed by Artur Brauer at University of Karlsruhe

crane, and two conveyor-belts produces body parts for cars (fig. 3). Unprocessed parts arrive from the left on the lower conveyor-belt and are transported to the elevating rotary table that puts them into gripping position for the first arm (:arm1) of the robot. The robot moves a part to the press that presses it into a finished body part. The robot then moves the part, using the second arm (:arm2), to the top conveyor-belt that moves to the left. A crane finally picks up the parts and place them on a pallet (lower left of fig. 3).

This is an application that requires a database for storage of data relating to the different parts in stock and also active database management for the actual control of the production task. Another requirement is that the setup should be flexible and the production cell should easily be reconfigured for production of different parts.

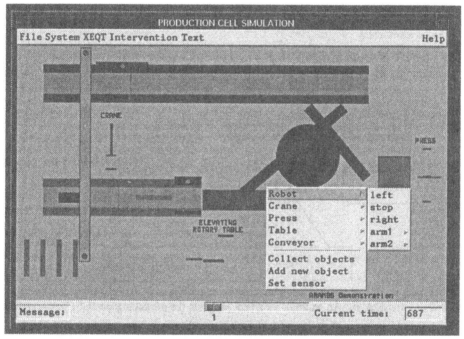

Fig. 3. A top view of a simulated production cell for manufacturing car body parts

Take a scenario where the production cell can alternate between the production of two different parts. This can be modelled by two different contexts (fig. 4). Each context is used to relate to data needed for each part. Rules that are specific for each different part are activated into the respective contexts. Sub-contexts can also be defined for different activities within the cell. This is illustrated here by two contexts used in both production tasks, one for rules relating to the elevating rotary table and one for the press. There will of course be more contexts and rules, but these are enough to illustrate the idea.

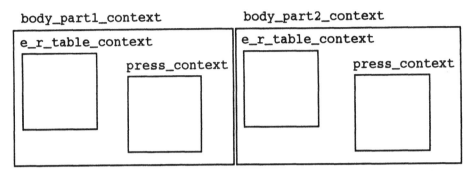

Fig. 4. Example contexts for producing two different parts and two general sub-contexts

An example of a task program for producing part1 is shown in fig. 5. It is a cyclic program that keeps producing parts until it is stopped explicitly.

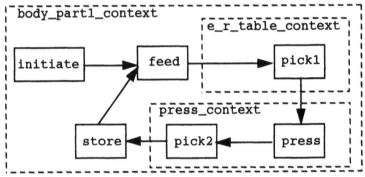

Fig. 5. An example of a task program for producing part1

Below follows part of an example schema in AMOSQL that illustrates the example above. The two main contexts are first defined followed by a context for the elevating rotary table. A rule that defines when the robot can grip a part on the table is activated into the context for the first arm of the robot (:arm1). A context for the press is then created along with a rule that specifies when it is safe to operate the press. The first rule is also activated into this context, but for the second arm of the robot (:arm2) instead. It specifies when the robot can grip an object in the press. Here follows extracts of the context related parts of the schema for this application:

```
create context body_part1_context;
/* Definitions of rules related to part1 */
...
create context body_part2_context;
/* Definitions of rules related to part2 */
...
create context e_r_table_context;
create rule grip_rule(robot_arm a) as
            when for each part prt
            where above(position(a), prt)
            do robot_grip(a, prt);
activate rule grip_rule(:arm1) into e_r_table_context;

create context press_context;
create rule press_rule(robot r, press p) as
            when for each robot_arm a
            where a = arm(r) and
                    outside(position(a), p) and
                    part_in_press_position(p)
            do close_press(p);
activate rule press_rule(:robot, :press) into
            press_context;
activate rule grip_rule(:arm2) into press_context;
```

During the execution the task program for producing part1 the order of database operations initiated from the task level might be:

```
activate context body_part1_context;
...
            check(:body_part1_context);
            ...
            activate context e_r_table_context;
            ...
            check(:e_r_table_context);
            ...
            deactivate context e_r_table_context;
            ....
            activate context press_context;
            ...
            check(:press_context);
            ...
            deactivate context press_context;
```

5 Conclusions and Future Work

The paper presented rule contexts as a mechanism for dynamically grouping rules. Rules are activated into contexts and are deactivated from contexts. When a context is activated it enables all its rules for monitoring. In deactivated contexts all the rules are disabled from being monitored. Events are only monitored if they are referenced from some rule in an active context.

Contexts are used to represent coupling modes where all rules in the same context also share the same coupling mode. Predefined contexts are defined for the usual system coupling modes.

Contexts are first-class objects, which makes it possible to store them in any data structure and to define meta-rules that activate and deactivate them.

Future work includes investigating the need for several contexts belonging to the same coupling mode. This will cause a need for ordering the execution order of different contexts. Using priorities is one way of doing this, but since the conflict resolution between different rules inside the same context is also done with priorities this might lead to an unnecessary complicated model.

The issue of event consumption is also important. If checking of one context consumes events then rules in consecutively checked contexts might not trigger the way they were intended.

Defining meta-rules that manage other contexts is another subject for future research.

6 References

[1] Buchanan B. G., Shortliffe E. H.: Rule-based Expert Systems, *The Mycin Experiments of the Stanford Heuristic Programming Project*, Addison-Wesley, 1984

[2] Davis R., Meta-rules: Reasoning about Control, *AI*, vol. 15, 1980, pp. 179-222

[3] Dayal U., Buchman A.P., McCarthy D.R.: Rules are objects too: A Knowledge Model for an Active, Object-Oriented Database System, *Proc. 2nd Intl. Workshop on Object-Oriented Database Systems*, Lecture Notes in Computer Science 334, Springer 1988

[4] Dayal U., McCarthy D.: The Architecture of an Active Database Management System, *ACM SIGMOD conf.*, 1989, pp. 215-224

[5] Fahl G., Risch T., Sköld M.: AMOS - An Architecture for Active Mediators, *Intl. Workshop on Next Generation Information Technologies and Systems (NGITS '93)* Haifa, Israel, June 1993, pp. 47-53

[6] Fishman D. et. al: Overview of the Iris DBMS, *Object-Oriented Concepts, Databases, and Applications*, ACM press, Addison-Wesley Publ. Comp., 1989

[7] Georgakopoulos D., Hornick M., Sheth A.: An Overview of Workflow Management: From Process Modelling to Workflow Automation Infrastructure, *Distributed and Parallel Databases*, 3, 2, April 1995, pp. 119-153

[8] Hedberg S., Steizner M.: Knowledge Engineering Environment (KEE) System: Summary of Release 3.1, Intellicorp Inc. July 1987

[9] Loborg P., Holmbom P., Sköld M., Törne A.: A Model for the Execution of Task-Level Specifications for Intelligent and Flexible Manufacturing Systems, *Integrated Computer-Aided Engineering* 1(3) pp. 185-194, John Wiley & Sons, Inc., 1994

[10] Loborg P., Risch T., Sköld M., Törne A., Active Object Oriented Databases in Control Applications, *19th Euromicro Conference of Microprocessing and Microprogramming*, vol. 38, 1-5, pp. 255-264, Barcelona, Spain 1993

[11] Lyngbaek P., OSQL: A Language for Object Databases, tech. rep. HPL-DTD-91-4, *Hewlett-Packard Company*, Jan. 1991

[12] Risch T.: Monitoring Database Objects, *Proc. VLDB conf.* Amsterdam 1989

[13] Risch T., Sköld M.: Active Rules based on Object Oriented Queries, *IEEE Data Engineering bulletin*, Vol. 15, No. 1-4, Dec. 1992, pp. 27-30

[14] Shipman D. W.: The Functional Data Model and the Data Language DAPLEX, *ACM Transactions on Database Systems*, 6(1), March 1981

[15] Stonebraker M., Hearst M., Potamianos S.: A Commentary on the POSTGRES Rules System, *SIGMOD RECORD*, vol. 18, no. 13, Sept. 1989

[16] Tombros D., Geppert A., Dittrich K. R.: SEAMAN: Implementing Process-Centered Software Development Environments on Top of an Active Database Management System, *Technical Report 95.03, Comp. Science Dept., University of Zürich*, Jan. 1995

[17] Walters J.R, Nielsen N.R., Crafting Knowledge-based Systems - Expert Systems Made Easy/ Realistic, *John Wiley & Sons*, 1988, pp. 253-284

[18] Widom J.: The Starburst Rule System: Language Design, Implementation, and Applications, *IEEE Data Engineering*, vol. 15, no. 1 - 4, Dec. 1992

Temporized and localized rule sets

Rose Sturm, Jutta A. Mülle, Peter C. Lockemann

Institut für Programmstrukturen und Datenorganisation
Fakultät für Informatik
Universität Karlsruhe, 76128 Karlsruhe
[lockeman|muelle|sturm]@ira.uka.de

Abstract. Constraint management plays an important role in design applications where constraints reflect design restrictions and design decisions. ECA rules are a widely used mechanism to enforce constraints. The paper argues that such rules must be augmented for design environments by a spatial and a temporal dimension of validity, resulting in so-called area-event-condition-action (AECA) rules. The spatial dimension allows to restrict constraints locally in the design space, and to control interaction between designers. The temporal dimension permits designers to retract their designs to earlier stages.

The paper introduces the concept of AECA rules, motivates them by examples from building design, discusses rule management, and then introduces two important issues, conflict detection during collaboration, and backtracking during design revision.

1 Introduction

Active rules (also variously called database triggers, event-condition-action rules, or ECA rules) are perceived, by researchers and database system (DBS) vendors alike, as an ideal means to structure both the static and dynamic properties of complex applications. In an – otherwise critical – paper Simon and Kotz [12] list as two of their benefits a clear separation from and explication of business rules from application programs with better transparency to and control by the business organization, and performance improvement by restricting or concentrating the auditing of applications to well-defined and controllable events. Rules blend in naturally with constraints because constraints have traditionally been used to factor out application semantics common to a number of application programs from these programs.

Since database schemas have over decades been another means for factoring out common semantics, rules have usually become part of a (perhaps extended) database schema. However, such an approach imposes severe penalties: it ties the rules to object types (with "object" being used in a general sense), that is to a class of similar instances, and it also ties them to the entire life time of the type definitions. In other words, it imposes given rules uniformly over space (all instances) and time (the entire life time) of a type.

This work was in part supported by the German Research Council (Deutsche Forschungsgemeinschaft) under contract no. Lo296/11-1

On the other hand, there are applications where it is most natural for the users to confine the validity of constraints in space, i.e., to subsets of instances of one or more types, and the enforcement of the corresponding rules in time, i.e., only to certain periods of time. Besides, technically such a limitation would permit a more selective and, consequently, more efficient constraint evaluation and enforcement.

Restricting rules in space and time depends on the notion of "space" and "time" used. Different applications may use slightly different notions. It makes sense, therefore, to take a top–down approach in order to develop, or select, the appropriate mechanisms for rule management and enforcement. For this paper we choose an application scenario taken from building design. Implementation issues are only briefly touched upon although we are aware that the added expressiveness of these concepts imposes new challenges that may negate some of the technical benefits associated with the restrictions.

The paper ist structured as follows. In chapter 2 we develop the user's perception and needs for highly dynamic rule management. Chapter 3 relates the technical requirements to rule management to previous work. Chapter 4 discusses our basic approach to deal with the localized and dynamic aspects of rules by introducing area-event-condition-action rules and a concomitant execution model which allows to deal with an essential consequence of design activities, conflict detection during collaboration. Chapters 5 and 6 demonstrate the combined effects of spatial and temporal aspects for rule management, with chapter 6 demonstrating a second consequence of design activities, backtracking during design revision. Chapter 7 outlines the system implementation, and Chapter 8 concludes the paper.

2 A design application scenario and its requirements

In applications like building design, the result of the design process is "one-of-a-kind". Common to all such design processes is the dearth of useable earlier results and, hence, the vague, and poorly structured data at the beginning, that become more and more concrete over the course of the process. Initially, the designer's freedom of action is only circumscribed by general design rules and physical laws, but as the design progresses more and more rules are added. Also, design decisions are often revised, and alternatives pursued. Different parts of the design exist in different states of detail at the same time.

The premise of this paper is that design decisions can be considered as constraints on the degrees of freedom that a designer may have. Consequently, the definition and enforcement of constraints and rules must follow the decision process. Constraints develop over time, and they may be retracted or revised, invalidating or modifying some constraints or reverting to earlier constraints. Similarly, constraints evolve differently in different design spaces and, hence, should be tied to particular design spaces.

Design processes are "many–person". To meet short design times under guaranteed quality, the steps of such a process and the experts contributing to them must be closely coordinated, particularly in light of the increasing interleaving of their activities with their tight feedback loops in place of the more traditional sequential processes. Since designers work on different parts and to different degrees of detail, the set of shared constraints is again a subset of all constraints and may vary over time and space.

Let us briefly illustrate these aspects. Figure 1 shows a part of the design of the ground floor of the science wing of a school in Switzerland. All class rooms on this floor (area A) are specialty rooms. Each room has been assigned to a particular teacher. Area B is a free communication zone for the students to meet during their breaks.

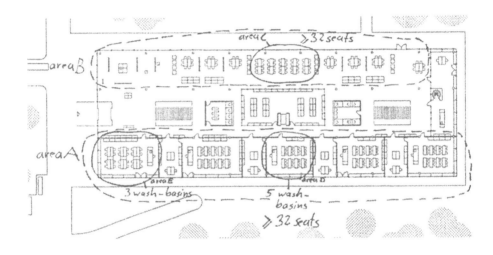

Fig. 1. Design for the Cantonal school of Solothurn

The ultimate goal of the designer is the design of objects with well-defined physical or conceptual boundaries. Examples of these so-called *design objects* are classrooms, seats, exhibition stalls, plumbing and wiring. Design objects may be contained in others, such as seats in a classroom, or may overlap with others, such as plumbing and classrooms. Obviously, then, there is a multitude of relationships between objects, and the designer deals with them by imposing a spatial structure, a *design space*, on them which circumscribes the objects whose interrelationships are of current interest to him. Take as an example a set of classrooms together with that part of the wiring and plumbing that directly affect them, in order to study the effects of a change of the number of water and electricity outlets in a classroom.

Constraints may be bound to design object types and also to individual objects. Specialty rooms may require, in general, water and electricity outlets. Their particular number may, however, be an invariant of an individual room.

For example, it may depend on the number of wash basins desired by each teacher. On the other hand, where an object does not yet exist, constraints can only be associated with design spaces. Consider that the building owner may decide to have a minimum of 32 seats (area C) in some part of area B, without determining the concrete position as yet. Finally, even where all objects are known, a constraint may be more naturally be associated with a design space. Take a geometric area encompassing part of the classroom area and the public area where only a certain maximum number of outlets is permitted in total. Take as another example different levels of detail in planning where the ground floor may already be in the stage of planning the furniture whereas planning of the second floor is still on the functional level. Since design objects have themselves a certain spatial extent, the unifying notion for circumscribing the range of constraints is that of design space (or design area).

Constraints evolve over time. For example, the constraint for area C may only be introduced after the size of the classrooms has been determined, and may later be changed again. Constraints may also be "canned". Consider an expert tool that reflects the work of a specialist, say a sanitary engineer. The tool will in all likelihood include a number of constraints to be satisfied once it gets to work. The constraints "lie in waiting" until then, and become active afterwards, i.e. must be enforced from then on.

The architectural design process is an iterative procedure. Very often, particular parts of the design will be set back to an earlier state, and will then be the new starting point for further design. This feature will cause a backtracking of all relevant constraints in that part of design. For example, suppose new information about the number of future pupils becomes known, causing the need for two more specialty rooms. Therefore area B must be revisited and set back to an earlier state. This area-oriented backtracking concerns physical design decisions as well as constraints related to them, and may affect other areas or objects such as those of the sanitary engineer.

Enforcement of constraints is uneven. A point in time where checking is mandatory in order for the design to proceed is referred to as a milestone. In between milestones, however, only certain consistencies – in particular those that are time–invariant such as zoning and building regulations, building norms, or physcial laws – should continuously be evaluated whereas other inconsistencies regarding, e.g., individual requirements of the building owner or the architect should be tolerated, and not enforced automatically. For example, if a wash basin has been placed one should immediately check if a sewage pipe with enough sloping can be installed. If not, the reaction must also be immediate: Either the wash basin must be placed at a different location, or extensive parts of the existing plan for sewage pipes have to be changed. On the other hand, a constraint such as to have a minimum of 32 seats in the free communication zone, may vary in its importance during the design.

Reactions to a violation even of the same constraint may vary over time and space. For example, a constraint may have low priority at an early stage of the design but may become essential later on, such as the position of the plumbing outlets. A change of the number of wash basins may be prohibited in one classroom but open to negotiation in another.

3   Related work

A standard technique to deal with constraints, with the flexible initiation of constraint checks, and the specification of appropriate responses to violations are ECA rules; these are considered as suitable means to support the above described requirements. An ECA rule is triggered into execution on some event such as a milestone, a vital design operation or a designer's spontaneous wish for a consistency check, causing it to evaluate the associated constraint condition and in case the condition holds, i.e. the constraint is violated, to perform the associated action.

The corresponding concepts, languages and computation models have been widely explored. In most approaches, though, rules are either ubiquitous or tied to object types. For example, ADAM/EXACT [5] indexes rules by class: the class-rules attribute has as its value the set of rules to be verified when a message is sent to any instance of this class. More flexibility can be found in the relational systems Starburst ([14]) and Postgres ([13]), both of which allow to organize rules in rule sets. However, each rule must explicitly be placed in a rule set by the user. This is definitely a too low-level mechanism for our purposes, since we are in a position to attach to rule sets a more specific semantics of areas. In particular, it does not allow to exploit the cross-effects between rule sets arising from the overlap of areas

Flexibility in event handling has recently attracted considerable attention, particularly in the context of object-oriented, active database systems. SAMOS ([7]), Sentinel ([3], and Ode ([9] support simple and complex events, that are constructed with event algebras. REACH [1] also introduces the notion to milestones that are to be detected. SAMOS even takes much broader contexts int account by supporting "event parameters" that may be used to restrict complex events to specific relevant categories, e.g., only to the events within one transaction, or to all events raised by a particular user. Similarly, Sentinel [4] provides four different rule evaluation contexts which differ in the set of relevant events which are used to detect complex events. Some systems allow to relate time stamps to events with the meaning that the rule will fire only if the event arises in the defined time period.

It appears, then, that the modern aproaches to event management are flexible enough to deal with the spatial aspects of our environment. We submit, though, that to do so would overload the event mechanism and blur the distinction between the spatial effects with our special area semantics and the temporal effects.

Finally to the best of our knowledge, temporal validity (or lifetime) of rules has not explicitly been dealt with in the literature (and implicitly only within the context of time stamping of events) and, hence, backtracking of rules has so far not been an issue.

4 AECA rules

Our premise is a clear separation of spatial, temporal and lifetime aspects in rule management. Consequently, we propose to extend ECA rules by a fourth component that explicitly accounts for the spatial aspects, and a rule header to account for the lifetime aspects. The result is what we call *area-event-condition-action (AECA) rules* (or for short: AECARs).

The structure of AECARs is illustrated in the form of a conceptual schema in figure 2. The basic premise for organizing the rules is that each constraint is represented, in the context of an area, by a single rule. Consequently, each AECAR consists of exactly one area and one constraint condition, whereas several events and actions may be associated, so that the validation of a constraint in a specific area may be initiated by different events, and several different actions may be triggered in case of a violation. Clearly, a constraint may appear in as many rules as there are areas which it presently is associated with. Likewise, an area may appear in as many rules as there presently are constraints associated with it. The validity (time) interval for the rule is, through the rule head, associated with the rule as a whole. As we shall see below, this allows to establish a history of design decisions and to permit backtracking of decisions to a specific point in time. The overall structure permits us to leave the condition (and thus, constraint) part and the action part unimpeded by any temporal and spatial considerations.

The application scenario seems to suggest that a design area is a purely two-dimensional geometric affair. However, our partners from the school of architecture define areas in a more far-reaching sense. Areas are placed within a seven-dimensional design space that formalizes all design decisions from all design phases according to the geometrical coordinates, time, resolution, size, type, user, and morphology, etc. in a uniform manner. These attributes are called **dimensions** of the multi-dimensional design space. Within this design space each design object or area represents a hypercube or, if all dimensions are instantiated, a point. (Information about our project and the basic concepts can be found in [10, 11]).

Associated with the AECAR head are attributes which describe the overall state of an area rule: *State of consistency* shows whether the constraint, in the specified area, forces consistency, permits inconsistency, or leaves consistency open. *History* holds the validity interval of the rule. The other two areas have to do with "canned" rules which as part of expert tools come into play only after the design reaches a certain stage. *Nullarea* indicates whether the rule has been predefined but is as yet not associated with any area. The attribute *user* specifies the expert tool owning the rule.

Area definitions, event specifications, constraints, and action specifications are declared individually and are then combined on a case-by-case basis via a rule header into a rule either statically as part of a general framework or expert tool or dynamically as the result of interactive design decisions. In particular, this allows the placement in a library and the reuse of any of them.

Consider as an example rule the application scenario of figure 1. The user

AECAR (Area-Event-Condition-Action-Rule)

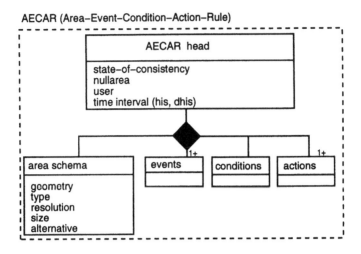

Fig. 2. AECAR schema

may interactively delineate and declare area E together with an event, resulting in the declaration (informally stated)

Area: geometry: (x,y,z)-coordinates of area E in figure 1
    type: {functional planning, installation planning}
    resolution: *,
    size: *,
    alternative: *.
Event: delete (wash-basin),

At some earlier time, he/she may already have entered into the library the desired constraint condition and action ("notify" refers to a programmed procedure).

Constraint condition: number of wash-basins $\geq$ 3,
Actions: notify (installation engineer), notify (user).

The four are combined into a rule by the user with the attributes of the AECAR-head set by the system (for the setting of *History* see chapter 5).

    The rough execution model is as follows. During his/her work a designer designates a working area on which he/she is operating. Note that this area need not be identical to the area of any AECAR or design object. Hence, during the time of operation, all rules whose area overlaps with the working area must be taken into consideration. As such they are active, i.e., they become candidates for possible execution and, hence, for constraint checking. Actual execution takes place on occurrence of the specified event within the working area. This requires an extended notion of event which combinesspatial and temporal aspects into a pair (point in time, area of occurrence). We refer to this kind of event as an area event.

    Fig. 3 gives an example. The user triggers in his/her current working area the events E1, E2, and E3. CC1, CC2 und CC3 are examples of areas of rules.

CC1 is completely located within the current working area, whereas the area of CC2 only overlaps with the current working area, and the area of CC3 falls completely outside of it. Because the user is only able to trigger events within his/her current working environment, only rules CC1 and CC2 are candidates for violation. The spatial dimension of event E1 is completely outside the areas related to CC1 and CC2. Therefore, for the consistency check triggered by event E1 neither CC1 nor CC2 are relevant. E2 lies within the area of CC2, i.e., the effect of E2 in the design overlaps with the position of CC2. In this case CC2 has to be proven valid but not CC1.

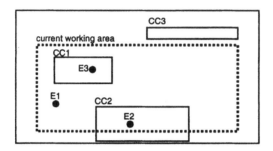

Fig. 3. Relationship between events and constraint areas

AECARs are well-suited to deal with collaborative behavior between several designers. Usually, such collaboration will give rise to conflicts. If we leave it to the persons to detect the conflicts these may go undetected for a long while. Now, if rule execution affects more than one working area, the violation may point to a design conflict. If these areas are the responsibility of more than one person, cross-person conflicts become immediately visible. Take the previous example and suppose that a second designer operates in a working area that is disjoint from the working area shown, but also overlaps with CC2. Then a violation within CC2 may affect him/her as well. This is not the case for E3 and CC1 which are restricted to the user of the working area shown.

In more detail, the execution model looks as follows. Given a specific working area, checking is done in the following steps:

1. Select all rules which overlap with the current working area.
2. From the set of these rules select those for whose related areas events have been raised.
3. Test for these rules whether a given event applies.
4. Where it applies, check the related constraint.
5. If the constraint is violated, take the corresponding action.

Overlapping is defined as an overlap of the geometrical areas together with the identity of the values of the discrete dimensions of the rule area to those of the current working area, provided the current system time is included in the history interval of the rule. As far as the actions are concerned, notification of the designers via the user interface may in many cases be sufficient. Where actions take compensatory steps the database state may change, necessitating a new check of the rules. Note also that because designers may work in parallel, they may generate events concurrently so that the execution model must be able to deal with sets of events.

5 Rule management: Spatial effects

Design decisions will often affect the rules. Consequently, a designer is permitted to redefine the area of a rule, the event that gives rise to the execution of a rule, the condition under which the action will take place, or the action itself, thus adjusting constraints to a modified design status. Take as an example that the designer no longer tolerates that the issue of placing the 32-seat zone remains unresolved. Hence, the area becomes more narrowly circumscribed, events for checking the constraints become more frequent, more constraints must be observed, and violations must immediately be compensated for.

A new design decision results in a new AECAR with a new validity interval whereas the AECAR it replaces remains in the system with a now closed interval. This, incidentally, is another argument for the decomposition of AECARs into independent components.

We illustrate the general principle. Consider the left side of figure 4 as a schematic representation of the various (partially nested) design areas on the graphical user interface.

Figure 4–A1 shows the users' views of the consistencies at design at time t1. The dotted boxes represent the working areas of several users. For each area the figure notes its constraint, related events, and actions. At time t2 the consistency constraints are modified resulting in the view of 4-A2.

The example shows a number of typical changes:

- An existing consistency constraint becomes active in another area, e.g., at point t2 the constraint A is also activated in area7.
- The associated area of the constraint changes, e.g., area2 for constraint B is enlarged to form a new area 8.
- The events change as, e.g., for constraint A in area4.
- The associated actions change as, e.g., for constraint D in area5.
- A consistency constraint becomes inactive in a particular area, e.g., constraint B has been removed from area6.

Figure 4-B shows the corresponding AECARs for times t1 and t3. Compare figures 4-A1 and 4-B1. The consistency constraint A is active at time t1 in two areas, area1 and area4, though with different behaviour. Hence, two rules R1 and R5 are necessary. Similarly, the consistency constraint B is active in two areas, requiring two rules R3 and R6. On the other hand, a single rule R2 indicates that the consistency check of constraint C in area4 may be enforced by two

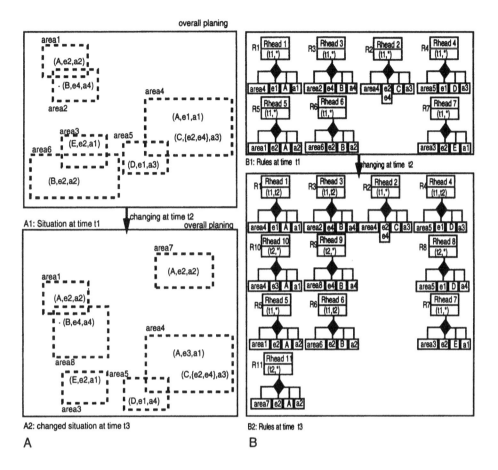

Fig. 4. Dynamic changes of constraints during the design process

events. The consistency constraints D and E are, each, only active in one area. Correspondingly, there exist rules R4 and R7.

Figure 4-B also illustrates the development of the history attributes. Whenever a new rule is created, the endpoint of the history attribute of the old rule it supersedes, and the starting point of the time interval of the new rule are set to the current time. Suppose that rule generation begins with time t1. Therefore, in figure 4-B1 all rules contain the same starting point t1 in their history attribute. The end of the time interval is set to *, which represents a time long way into the future.

At time t2 all rules concerned have to be adapted to reflect the changes. The new set of rules is shown in figure 4-B2. We observe the following effects:

− In area4 event e3, in place of e1, activates the checking of constraint A. Therefore, in rule R1 the history interval is closed, i.e., the end of the time interval is set to t2. To reflect the new situation, rule R10 is generated setting the history interval to start time t2 and end time *.

- Constraint A is added to area7 where it is activated by event e2 and will cause, in case of violation, action a2. This is reflected in the new rule R11, with the history interval beginning at t2 and ending at *.
- Constraint B in area6 is deactivated. Therefore, the history interval of rule R6 is closed by setting the end of the interval to t2.
- Constraint B is also active in area2, which is enlarged at time t2. For that reason, rule R3, in the same way as rule R6 above, is closed and a new rule R9 with the time interval beginning with t2 and ending with * is created, corresponding to the new area8.
- In area5 the violation of constraint D is supposed to invoke action a3 instead of the former action a4. Accordingly, rule R4 is changed in the same way as rule R1 above, and rule R8 is created in a way similar to rule R10 above.
- The changes at time t2 do not affect the rules R2, R5, and R7. These are placed unchanged into the set of rules for time t3. In particular, their history intervals remain between times t1 and *, indicating their continued actuality.

6 Rule management: Temporal effects

As the example demonstrates, the rule base preserves the entire history of design decisions. As an important consequence, the approach introduces the capability to backtrack the design of arbitrary user-defined parts. Very roughly speaking, let a designer specify an arbitrary backtracking area BA, and a setback time t. Within BA the situation is restored to the one that existed at t, that is, all rule areas within BA are recovered as they existed at t, and all decisions taken after t are simply purged from the database.

In fact, there is a complicating factor in backtracking in that the architect may delineate an arbitrary area as a backtracking area. In other words, the backtracking area may not bear a causal relationship to either the current design areas or the earlier ones. Consider figure 5 which continues figure 4 to a point t5 in time. At time t4 the user identifies a backtracking area as shown in the center left. Apparently, the backtracking procedure must somehow involve all areas overlapping with the backtracking area. The question, then, is whether backtracking should affect these areas in their entirety, even those parts that lie outside the backtracking area.

Suppose now that the backtracking area is (at current time t4) to be set back to time t1. In a first step the rules in the current database (B2 in figure 5) with areas overlapping the backtracking area must be identified. In the example there are six such rule areas in the database B2: area3 (with rule R7), area4 (with rules R1, R2 and R10), area5 (with rule R8), area6 (with rule R6), area7 (with rule R11), and area8 (with rule R9). In a second step the status of the constraints of these rules at the time to which the design situation is to be restored (setback time) must be determined.

We illustrate the restore actions with our example.

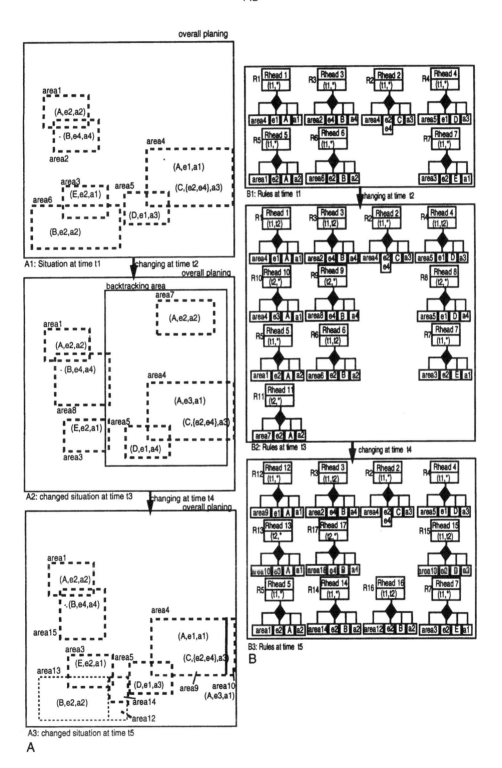

Fig. 5. Dynamically backtracking of parts of the design

- Rule R5 with area1 lies completely outside the backtracking area and, hence, does not change.
- Rule R8 with area5 lies completely within the backtracking area but its validity interval does not include t1 because at t2 the action was changed from a3 to a4. Therefore Rule R8 is deleted. The validity interval of rule R4 with area5 includes t1. Because interval endtime t2 extends into the future as seen from the perspective of t1, R4 is reactivated with the validity interval (t1, *).
- Rule R11 with area 7 lies completely within the backtracking area and was generated at time t2. Because rule R11 was not active at t1, R11 is deleted.
- Rule R7 is not affected although its area3 overlaps with the backtracking area, because its validity interval includes t1.
- The same is true for rule R2 and area4.

This leaves area4 with rule R10 and area8 with rule R9, which overlap with the backtracking area. In order to deal with them we distinguish between *closed* constraints which if valid in an area are valid in each subarea, and *open* constraints, otherwise. For example, physical laws are closed constraints whereas design decisions such as the 32-seat requirement usually are not. We can then establish as a procedure that for closed constraints only the subarea within the backtracking area is rolled back whereas for open constraints the entire area is rolled back. For closed constraints this entails splitting the area. For the pieces inside the backtracking area, the old state must be regenerated whereas outside the current state must be preserved. Note that the change of an area results in the generation of a new rule so that for each split part a new rule must be established. Now suppose that constraints A and B are closed. Accordingly:

- Rule R10 with area4 gives rise to new rules by splitting area4 into two parts. Outside the backtracking area (area10) the same composition of events, condition, actions as in R10 is valid. This is postulated as rule R13 with the area10. Inside the backtracking area (area9) the status at t1 must be regenerated. R12 is the updated rule R1 with the new area area9 and the new validity interval t1 to *. R10 is then deleted.
- For rule R9 area8 must be similarly split. The subarea within the backtracking area would have to be restored to its state at time t1. No corresponding rule can be found inside this area. This leaves R9 adjusted for the area outside the backtracking area area15, which is postulated as rule R17. R9 must be deleted.

Finally, there is the not-so-obvious case of rule R6 which with area6 does not exist any longer at time t4 but existed at restoration time t1 and overlaps with the backtracking area. Its constraint B is closed so that the splitting principle applies again. Rule R6 must be restored for the subarea area14 which lies inside the backtracking area. This is described by rule R14 which is identical to R6 except for the area14. To generate the correct situation outside of the backtracking area, two new (rectangular) areas area13 and area12 must be established. Correspondingly, two new rules R15 and R16 are created, which except for the areas are copies of R6 and hence have a time interval (t1,t2), so that they are not active at time t5.

7 System environment

Rule management as discussed in this paper is part of a three-layered implementation architecture for a CAAD environment. The topmost layer – the representation layer – reflects the users' perceptions of the design process and the design objects and areas. An elaborate user interface allows the architect to deal not only with the geometrical confines of areas but also with the other dimensions ([10]). Specifically for the purposes of this paper, he/she may define and associate rules with areas as a combination of area of activity, events, constraints, and actions, and he/she may delineate working areas and raise events within them. Through the overlap of areas the interaction between different experts during the design becomes immediately visible to them in the form of additional sets of constraints to be observed as the result of a design decision in some other areas.

On the next lower layer all concepts on the user interface are represented in a uniform (conceptual) data structure, the so-called container. For the purposes of this paper, the most important functionality of the layer is the management of the rule base according to sections 5 and 6 as well as provision of the execution machine for the rules according to section 4, essentially as a trigger mechanism.

On the lowest level – the container server – the containers are implemented via an object-oriented database system. This layer also directly utilizes performance enhancing measures such as the precomputation of the set of overlapping rules for a given working area and multi-dimensional access paths to containers and to AECARs to allow arbitrary selection criteria for the rapid identification of relevant AECARs according to our in section 4 introduced event notion.

8 Conclusion

Our paper deals with constraint management. Taking a purely top-down view we have argued that at least in certain design environments ECA-rules have a strong flavor of spatial and temporal validity. We suggested a more discriminating mechanism of area-event-condition-action (AECA) rules. They allow to impose constraints locally in the design space, to control interaction between designers, and to permit designers to retract their designs to earlier stages. We also demonstrated that the combination of these dimensions during backtracking may give rise to complicated situations.

By building AECA rules around the real needs of building designers and their view of the design process and design decisions, we are in the fortunate situation of having a testbed and test persons to evaluate our approach from both a technical and an applications standpoint. We developed an extensive set of constraints for an expert tool, and are currently implementing the testbed.

Much remains to be done. Foremost are experiments with our collaborators from the school of architecture whether AECA rules offer the necessary flexibility without imposing undue technical penalties. If successful, much more attention must be paid to the issue of designing constraints and rules, if possible even spontaneously. Third, while our current testbed implementation does not consider efficiency as an overriding issue, the ultimate success will depend on good performance of the AECA rule mechanism.

References

1. A.P. Buchmann and H. Branding and T. Kudraß and J. Zimmermann. Rules in an Open System: The REACH Rule System. In N.W. Paton and M.H. Williams, editors, *Rules in Database Systems*. 1st Int. Workshop on Rules in Database Systems, Springer Verlag, 1994.
2. S. Chakravarthy, B. Blaustein, A.P. Buchmann, M. Carey, U. Dayal, D. Goldhirsch, M. Hsu, R. Jauhari, R. Ladin, M. Livny, D. McCarthy, R. McKee, and A. Rosenthal. HIPAC: A research project in active, time-constrained database management. Technical Report XAIT-89-02, Xerox Advanced Information Technology, Cambridge, Massachusetts, July 1989.
3. S. Chakravarthy, V. Krishnaprasad, E. Anwar, and S.-K. Kim. Composite Events for Active Databases: Semantics, Contexts and Detection. In *Proc. 20th Conf. on Very Large Data Bases*, pages 606–617, Santiago, Chile, 1994.
4. S. Chakravarthy, V. Krishnaprasad, Z. Tamizuddin, and R. H. Badani. ECA Rule Integration into an OODBMS: Architecture and Implementation. Technical Report UF-CIS-TR-94-023, University of Florida, May 1994.
5. O. Diaz, N.W. Paton, and P. Gray. Rule Management in Object-Oriented Databases: A Uniform Approach. In *Proc. 17th Int. Conf. on Very Large Data Bases*, pages 317–326, Barcelona, Spain, 1991.
6. S. Gatziu and K.R. Dittrich. SAMOS: An Active Object-Oriented Database System. *IEEE Quarterly Bulletin on Data Engineering*, 15(1-4):23–26, December 1992.
7. S. Gatziu and K.R. Dittrich. Events in an Active Object-Oriented Database System. In N.W. Paton and M.H. Williams, editors, *Rules in Database Systems*. 1st Int. Workshop on Rules in Database Systems, Springer Verlag, 1994.
8. N. H. Gehani and H. V. Jagadish. Ode as an Active Database: Constraints and Triggers. In *Proc. 17th Int. Conf. on Very Large Data Bases*, pages 327–336, 1991.
9. N. H. Gehani, H. V. Jagadish, and O. Shmueli. Composite Event Specification in Active Databases: Model and Implementation. In *Conf. on Very Large Data Bases*, pages 327–338, 1992.
10. L. Hovestadt, V. Hovestadt, J. A. Mülle, and R. Sturm. ArchE – Entwicklung einer datenbankunterstützten Architektur - Entwurfsumgebung. Technical Report Nr.23/94, Universität Karlsruhe, November 1994.
11. P.C. Lockemann, J.A. Mülle, R. Sturm, and V. Hovestadt. Modeling and integrating design data from experts in a CAAD-environment. In *Proc. of the European Conf. on Product and Process Modelling in the Building Industry*, to appear, 1995.
12. E. Simon and A. Kotz-Dittrich. Promises and Realities of Active Database Systems. To appear in Proc. Int. Conf. on Very Large Databases, 1995.

13. M. Stonebraker, a.J. Jhingran, j. Goh, and S. Potamianos. On Rules, Procedures, Caching and Views in Data Base Systems. In *Proc. of SIGMOD*, pages 281–290. ACM Press, 1990.
14. J. Widom. The Starburst Active Database Rule System. *IEEE Transactions on Knowledge and Data Engineering*, to appear.

Design and Implementation of an Active Object-Oriented Database Supporting Construction of Database Tools

Ian S. Thomas and Andrew C. Jones

Univ. of Wales Coll. of Cardiff, Dept. of Comp. Maths., PO Box 916, Cardiff. CF2 4YN, UK.
email: {scmist, andrew}@cm.cf.ac.uk

Abstract. We discuss the implementation of GOAD (Gemstone Object-oriented Active Database), an active object-oriented database built on top of GemStone. This system has been developed with the specific aim of supporting interface tools for the creation and maintenance of rule bases, and we give particular attention to explaining how GOAD is designed to meet this aim. We show how objects, classes and metaclasses can support a three level event model which integrates with the underlying system in an 'open' manner. Moreover, by providing a uniform interface to these different objects, we are providing support for the implementation of more generic tools. We discuss the design of the system and how we gather inherited rules at run-time in an efficient manner. We explain the problems that arise as a result of our desired mode of implementation and how they were circumvented. Finally we discuss our future work and specifically how we plan to implement tools for the easier creation of rule bases.

1 Introduction

In recent years there has been a great deal of research effort expended in the area of Active Databases [1,4,6,8,9,12,15,17]. By an Active Database we mean a database which is able to automatically react to certain predefined situations without user intervention. The aim is to develop databases in which knowledge is abstracted from individual applications and centralised within the database itself. This helps to avoid replication of knowledge in each application and the inconsistencies that can be caused by this replication. This knowledge is procedural, rather than declarative in nature: it is generally stored in the form of Event-Condition-Action (ECA) rules. These rules recognise certain 'situations' in the database and react to them, if necessary, in an appropriate manner.

In the literature published to date, particular attention has been given to topics such as the implementation of an Active Database and the specification of events. Less attention has been given to the development of tools to help the programmer through the difficult task of attaching, browsing and deleting events and rules, although the need for such tools has been recognised (see Sec. 2). Our main intention is to develop such tools, and this has had a substantial influence on the design of the underlying GOAD system: the intention is that it should be uniform, open to inspection and integrated in such a way as to make browsing of an object's events and rules seem a natural extension of browsing the object itself.

This paper describes the initial system that has been implemented and describes the ways in which this system will support our eventual aims. It is divided up as follows: Section 2 discusses our motivation for this work and the contribution it makes in the context of the current state of the art. Section 3 describes GemStone, the database on top of which we chose to build our system, and discusses what led us to choose this database as a vehicle for our research. Section 4 deals with the implementation of our system, showing the Gemstone classes that we created to support it. Section 5 discusses the problems that we encountered as a result of using GemStone, and outlines how we circumvented them. Finally, in Sec. 6, we evaluate our achievements to date and discuss our planned future work.

2 Motivation and Aims

As stated above, the purpose of our research is to investigate and implement tools to help in the creation of rule bases. The need for such tools has been highlighted by a number of researchers, e.g. [8,17,19,7,2,3]. These tools can be conveniently divided into two types:

- Design tools to help create the rule base
- Explanation tools to explain the working of an existing rule base

The latter are seen by Stonebraker as an urgent need [19], since given that the purpose of any rule system is to act without user intervention, it is important that users understand what will happen if they are to have any trust in the operation of the system. DEAR [7] is an attempt to write a debugger/explanation tool to demonstrate graphically what will happen when a particular object is changed and a set of rules fired. As we understand it, the debugger only traces integrity rules at the moment and has no support for the tracing of composite or timed events. The work of Behrends [2] also attempts to address this need, although it deals with a relational active database rather than an object-oriented one.

These explanation tools are only part of the solution, however, since before the users can get to this point they have to declare the rules in the first place. This is where the first set of tools come in, and it is in this area that we are planning to work. At the moment most of the work in event/rule creation seems to be directed towards extending possible event specifications and developing declarative languages to allow the expression of events and rules [5,10,11,13,14]. Gatziu and Dittrich, however, state that their long-term aim is the implementation of such graphical design tools [8,10]. This problem is also identified elsewhere [16,17]. A more friendly, possibly graphical way of attaching rules to objects would be another way of helping users gain trust in the system since if they can easily see and understand what they are doing then they will be more willing to accept that what is happening is correct. This is a distinct problem from that addressed in DEAR or the work of Behrends, since there, the rules have already been created and their actions are then traced. A graphical representation for the schemas of active systems is introduced by Bichler & Schrefl [3]. Their system attempts to standardise the design of active database applications during conceptual design before mapping the schema to the object model used for implementation during logical design.

Before we can accomplish our aim of implementing appropriate tools, however, we need an active database system upon which to build and test them. We chose to build our own, and two separate sets of design criteria were identified. The first set comprises criteria which are more 'basic' in that they are concerned with ensuring that our implementation is acceptable for reasons apart from those to do with interface considerations. The second set comprises criteria which we wish to meet so as to ensure that our system is well suited to the development of support tools. We will therefore separate the following aims into these two sets. Firstly, our basic implementation aims are:

- that the rule system should be integrated into the underlying system in an accessible manner, which makes use of all of the benefits of the object-oriented paradigm and of the specific database system we were using;
- there should be no alteration of the behaviour of the underlying database system. We allowed ourselves to *add* new behaviour to some existing classes but did not want to *alter* the behaviour of existing, standard methods in the system as this could have a detrimental effect on some of the existing classes which relied on them; and
- the inheritance mechanism should not have to search the class hierarchy looking for rules that need to be fired. We wanted to find a way of ensuring that the correct rules could be found as quickly as possible and with as little searching as possible.

Our other aims are those that we wish to satisfy to aid us in our subsequent research, namely:

- use of instances, classes and metaclasses to store event objects that are raised on them. This means that each type of object can be queried about the rules that are associated with it;
- the interface to objects, classes and metaclasses should be uniform to ensure that the definition of events is consistent. In this way we can write more generic tools as each of our object types which supports activity responds to a common protocol of messages, and therefore the interface will never need to know what 'kind' of object it is displaying;
- events should be stored with the objects they affect (i.e. no notion of a global 'event manager'). This allows the user to look at an object and see the events (and the rules defined on these events) as a natural extension of looking at the object. Hence we can browse the object's state and the events that have been declared on it;
- the activity model should be highly visible. This is to ensure that there are no 'unaccountable side-effects'; and

- the number and names of parameters should be provided automatically when a new rule is declared on an event. This will ensure that the programmer does not have to go back to the object that raises the event to count the numbers and types of parameters before declaring them in the condition and action code of the rule.

These aims place some restrictions on the choice of underlying database as we shall now see.

3 Choice of Underlying Database

We chose the database GemStone [18] as a vehicle for our system. This was for several reasons. We had previous experience with the Smalltalk programming language, and GemStone is very similar to Smalltalk in many ways, but with some database features added. As in Smalltalk, the source code for all of the system classes is available. Moreover, an incremental approach is taken to compilation as in Smalltalk, which makes prototyping particularly easy. Also, the Smalltalk programming interface that can be used with GemStone allows the use of the excellent development and debugging tools that are available with the Smalltalk language. Finally, and most importantly, GemStone includes features that are useful in satisfying the aims of our project. These features include the ability to:

- compile code at run time, allowing us to implement the visible wrapping of code;
- use objects, classes and metaclasses to hold information which allows us to create a uniform and understandable interface across the three types of objects; and
- query the class hierarchy about itself at run time. This allows us to implement our inheritance mechanism in the desired way.

All of these features were central to the successful implementation of our system.

4 GOAD Implementation

In this section we discuss the major aspects of our implementation. Firstly, we outline the hierarchy of classes that support our implementation. We then discuss the implementation of our ActiveObject class, a superclass to which active objects must belong. We concentrate on the way in which it:

- allows the managing of events;
- wraps and unwraps method code;
- manages the inheritance mechanism for events and rules; and
- provides parameter names and numbers to the events that are declared on it.

4.1 Class Hierarchy

The main classes which make up our system are shown in Fig. 1. Classes shown in italics are those which exist within the standard GemStone system. This hierarchy is consistent with our first two design goals whereby we wished to use the object-oriented paradigm to implement each part of our system and also to ensure that the rule system was an addition rather than an alteration. It has been necessary to *add* code to some standard system classes, but not to *alter* existing code: regular database behaviour remains unchanged.

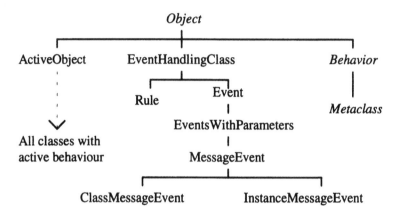

Fig. 1. Class Hierarchy of System

We will now discuss the classes shown above and show how they help to satisfy our design goals.

4.2 ActiveObjects and Events

We shall discuss *ActiveObject* and our *Event* classes together, as their behaviour is very interdependent. Before doing so, it should be noted that ActiveObject contains the behaviour which allows the managing of events; wraps and unwraps method code; manages the inheritance mechanism for events and rules, and provides parameter names and numbers to the events that are declared on the active object. It should also be noted that the code executed by rules in GOAD is stored as standard GemStone *program blocks*.

Managing Events. There are three levels of message event in the GOAD system:

1. *Instance level events* - Events associated with an instance. These events only concern the instance with which they are associated.
2. *Class level instance events* - Events associated with a class. These events concern every instance of the class.
3. *Class level events* - Events associated with a class's class. These events concern methods of the class (i.e. class methods) as opposed to methods of its instances (instance methods).

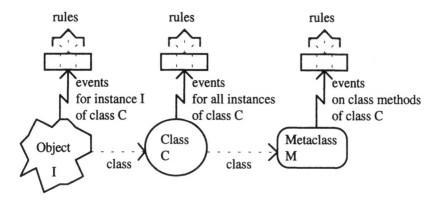

Fig. 2. Event Types Stored at each Level

It is important to recognise that what we have just described is in keeping with the spirit of GemStone; in consequence our model integrates particularly well with the underlying language. In Gemstone *instances* hold information about their own state and hence it is reasonable that they should also hold information about the rules that are fired upon them. *Classes* hold information that is relevant to all instances and therefore they are an ideal place to store rules that apply to all instances. Finally, *metaclasses* hold information on a particular class and therefore are a logical place to store rules that need to be fired when the class's methods are executed.

This is illustrated in Fig. 2. If an event was raised on instance I then we would need to gather any rules attached to the instance and then all of those attached to class C, as these are applicable to every instance of C. We will then know which rules, if any, have been overridden and fire the correct ones. If, on the other hand, we were to run a class method of C that had been declared as an event, then metaclass M would gather all of the rules that are in the metaclass hierarchy for that event and, after the overriding has been accomplished, fire those which are appropriate. (N.B. There were certain constraints imposed by GemStone with regard to the use of metaclasses in this way and these will be discussed in Sec. 5). This behaviour is in line with our aim to make use of not only the object-oriented paradigm in general but also of the special features (like metaclasses) that GemStone, being based on Smalltalk, provides.

To support these different levels, members of classes inheriting from *ActiveObject* have a *beginEvents* and an *endEvents* variable as does the class itself and its metaclass. These variables are members of *EventDictionary* (a specialised form of *Dictionary*). This is similar to the subscription mechanism of Sentinel [1], the main difference being that each selector's event is stored in a dictionary whose key is the selector name. The correct event for the selector can thus be found more quickly.

In addition, *ActiveObjects* have a uniform interface which allows event objects to be created generically. Each of the different levels (instance, class, metaclass) understands the same messages and therefore the event does not need to know what sort of object it is being associated with as it merely 'tells' the object to add itself to the object's dictionary of event objects. For example:

```
MessageEvent on: bedroom
        before: #addCat:
```

declares a message event on an instance 'bedroom' of the class 'Room' before method *addCat:*, i.e. only if a cat enters the room 'bedroom' will this event be raised.

```
MessageEvent on: Room
        before: #addCat:
```

declares a message event on class Room before method *addCat:*, i.e. now if a cat enters any room the event will be raised.

```
MessageEvent on: (Room class)
        before: #new
```

declares a message event on Room class (i.e. the metaclass of Room) before method *new*, i.e. sending the message *new* to the class Room will raise the event. (Obviously, 'before' may be replaced by 'after' in all of the above examples)

Method Wrapping. The method wrapping mechanism of GOAD again works across the three levels of object, with each type of object understanding the message *activate:*. When an attempt is made to declare a selector of an object as an event, the selector is automatically wrapped if required.

The *activate:* method works by taking the original method code and recompiling it with a different selector name. So if the original method was:

```
addCat: aCat
    thingsInRoom add: aCat.
```

it is recompiled thus:

```
uaddCat: aCat
    thingsInRoom add: aCat.
```

and the wrapper code is compiled as:

```
addCat: aCat
    .....
    {Code to gather parameters}
    .....
    self preProc:(paramVals asArray).  "raise begin-
                                                method event"
```

```
result :=  self uaddCat: aCat.   "Do user's meth"
paramVals add: result.
self postProc:(paramVals asArray)."raise end-
                                   method event"
^result
```

Visible or Invisible Wrapping? We considered making method wrapping invisible, so that when the user looked at method *addCat:* he or she would actually be seeing *uaddCat:* and not the wrapper code. We felt, however, that the visibility of what happens is very important as it helps to increase understanding of execution flow. Clearly the visibility of the execution model means it is more important for the user to understand it, but against this possible disadvantage we weighed the following advantages, which led us to our stated goal that the system should have a high degree of visibility:

1. It is far more in the 'spirit' of Smalltalk to have all code visible to the programmer for inspection. In this way the programmer knows exactly when a method is going to have side effects as the whole mechanism is open and accessible.
2. This visibility ensures that tracing of an application does not produce any odd side effects that could confuse the programmer. If a programmer did not know that a particular method was active then the debugger unexpectedly switching to execution of code to raise events rather than proceeding to the next statement in the method could cause substantial confusion.

Inheritance of Rules. In our system, references are automatically maintained, to try and reduce searching for rules. Rather than dynamically searching upwards through the class hierarchy, checking each class to see if it has any rules, each class maintains a direct reference to the inherited event object.

In practice this is accomplished by using event objects to store rules (Fig. 3). An event object is used as a template for an actual event occurrence and stores all the rules that need to be fired when the event occurs. If there are no rules that need to be declared on a particular class for a particular event then we do not need an event object on that class. This means that as a result the position in the event dictionary for that event can just refer to an event object associated with a superclass as the only rules we are interested in are inherited ones. When we wish to *add* rules to a class, however, we must create an event object to store them in. In this case two things happen:

1. A new event object is created and referred to from the event dictionary of the class.
2. All subclasses of this class are updated so that their event dictionary refers to this new event object if they do not have one of their own that should override the new one. This ensures that the subclasses will look for rules in the new event object before the event object that the class was referencing before (see Fig. 4).

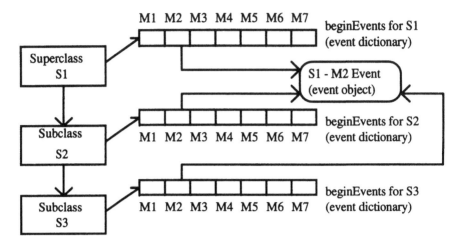

Fig. 3. Situation where only S1 has Rules for Event M2

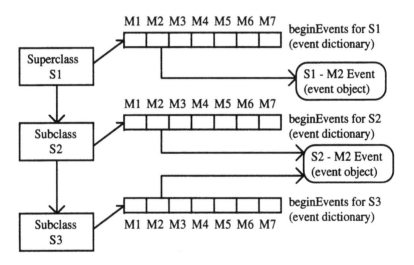

Fig. 4. Updated References after S2-M2 has been Declared as an Event

Instances do not take part in this system described above. This is because we would have too many instances to do this each time we changed the point in the class hierarchy at which an event object is first declared. We therefore test whether or not the instance has any rules before traversing the class hierarchy collecting any inherited ones.

The search which would occur in the absence of our caching techniques simply involves moving up the hierarchy checking at each point whether the current object has any rules to add. In our system the search follows the 'super event' hierarchy. The super event of an event object is the event object belonging to the next object up the hierarchy that has rules. So the 'super event' of the event object for instances is the event object belonging to its class. The super event for classes and metaclasses is the event object belonging to whichever of their superclasses next has an event object.

We also support overriding of rules in subclasses by using a specialised dictionary called *RuleCollectorDictionary*. As we traverse the event hierarchy collecting inherited rules we add them to an instance of this dictionary. Each rule is placed into the dictionary at the position with the key that corresponds to the rule's name. If, when we attempt to add a rule, the position in the dictionary at that rule's name has already been filled then the rule has been overridden lower down in the hierarchy and so that rule is rejected. The event that was raised is eventually returned a collection of rules sorted by priority that need to be fired. We will demonstrate both this and the inheritence mechanism in general in the following example.

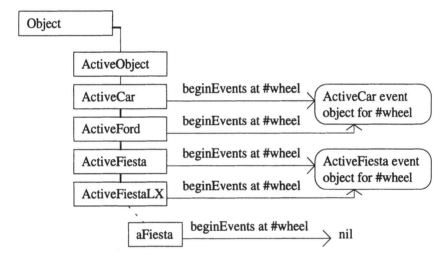

Fig. 5. Example

Example of Inheritance and Overriding. Consider Fig. 5. The system proceeds thus:

1. The instance *aFiesta* asks its *beginEvents* dictionary if it has an event object for the selector *#wheel*. Here it does not, so there are no rules to add so far. It then asks its class to add all the rules in the hierarchy it belongs to. This looks like:

```
collectRules
|collectedRules|
    collectedRules := RuleCollectorDictionary new.
    collectedRules addAll: (triggeredRules values).
    (self superEvent isNil) ifTrue:
        [^collectedRules sortedByPriority].
    ^(self superEvent collectRules: collectedRules)
                            valuesSortedByPriority
```

Here we add all of the rules that this event holds (*triggeredRules*), rejecting those which we find have been overridden (we will know this is the case as we will already have a rule by that name in the dictionary). Next, we check the '*superEvent*'. If the superEvent is *nil* then we can stop as the superEvent refers to the event object of the first class above in the hierarchy that has any rules attached to it. If this is *nil* then there is no event object in the hierarchy to inherit rules from. If the 'superEvent' is not *nil* then we tell it to add its rules to the current collection.

2. By default the event at position *#wheel* in *ActiveFiestaLX*'s *beginEvents* dictionary refers to that of its superclass. We therefore gather the rules that are declared on this event, i.e.

```
collectRules: aRuleCollection
|ruleCollection|
    ruleCollection := aRuleCollection.
    ruleCollection addAll: (triggeredRules values).
    (self superEvent is nil)
    ifTrue: [^ruleCollection]
    ifFalse: [^self superEvent
                        collectRules: ruleCollection].
```

Here the event receives a collection of rules passed from the instance and adds its own rules (again subject to them having not been overridden). It then checks in the same way and if there are more rules to add further up (i.e. the superEvent is not *nil*) then it recursively calls itself on the next event up the class hierarchy.

3. The super event is accessed by asking the event dictionary that the event we just collected rules from is stored in to return the object that it belongs to, in this case the class *ActiveFiesta*.

4. We then access the event in the position *#wheel* of the *beginEvents* dictionary of the superclass of *ActiveFiesta*, which is *ActiveFord*. *ActiveFord* is referring to the event object in *ActiveCar*. We therefore collect all of the rules that are declared on this event and then stop, as we have reached the point in the hierarchy where the method *#wheel* was defined. We then come out of the recursion, eventually returning the list of rules to the event object belonging to *aFiesta* (i.e. the event we started at). This event then fires all of the rules it has been returned by this mechanism.

Automatic Parameter Name Generation. *ActiveObjects*, when queried by events, pass on the number and names of their parameters. Then, when a rule is declared, the names of the parameters that are passed to the rule can automatically be put into place. A method event is raised with the following parameters:

• Object Identifier (OID) of object that is raising the event;
• the selector the event is being raised on;

- a time stamp; and
- the parameters passed to the selector raising the event.

The parameter names generated are intended to be of help to the programmer. As an example, suppose we wish to have a class instance level event on the method with selector:

```
name: aName address: anAddress
```

for the *ActiveObject* subclass *Person*. When the event is created, the class *Person* returns a list of parameter names for the event to store. These are:

```
#('aPerson' 'selectorName' 'timeStamp' 'aName'
'anAddress')
```

Now, if we create a rule on this event, the rule can query the event to get the names of the parameters that its condition and action are passed when the rule is fired and the code can use any of the passed parameters by utilising the names provided by the event.

5 Constraints Imposed by GemStone

There were constraints imposed by GemStone which caused a few problems and prevented our system being implemented exactly as we would have wished:

1. Only single inheritance is supported in GemStone (as in Smalltalk). For our '*ActiveMetaclass*' it would have been easier if we could have inherited from both *ActiveObject* and *Metaclass*. This would have created the class we needed just by inheritance and saved much coding.
2. In GemStone certain classes cannot have subclasses. Among these are *Metaclass* and *Behavior*. This caused extra difficulty as we were unable to create a subclass of *Metaclass* and then copy in the required code from *ActiveObject*. This caused problems in two ways:
   (a) The inability to inherit from *Metaclass* meant that we were unable to have a separate class into which to compile the methods from *ActiveObject*.
   (b) Along the same lines, this inability to have a subclass of *Metaclass* prohibited us from adding the extra instance variables to this subclass that are needed to store events. In addition, the *Metaclass* class description in GemStone cannot be altered and so it was not possible to add the variables to the standard *Metaclass* class.

To get around these problems we had to firstly compile all of the *ActiveObject* methods into the standard *Metaclass* class, and secondly use the *ActiveObject* class as a proxy to store the event dictionary variables for metaclasses of *ActiveObject* classes. Thus:

- *Objects* have *beginEvents* and *endEvents* variables;
- *Classes* have *beginEvents*, *endEvents*, *cbeginEvents* and *cendEvents;* and
- *Metaclasses* have no extra variables.

Therefore when we query a metaclass about its *beginEvents* the metaclass returns the *cbeginEvents* that its class is storing (i.e. 'c' signifies 'class'). None of this is visible to the user in the sense that our interface remains consistent, but it is visible in the sense that all of the code is easily accessible. It is clearly not a perfect solution, but it works correctly and the constraints imposed by the system preclude a better solution.

6 Conclusions and Future Work

6.1 Conclusions

We are currently at the point where we have satisfied the aims stated at the beginning of this paper but, although the system works, there are still things that we wish to change:

- GOAD lacks in support for some essential event types;
- our inheritance mechanism needs updating to cope with composite events; and
- we need a better way of simulating nested transactions.

We feel that any system must have the capability of specifying the most common types of events: message events, time events, transaction events and composite events. At present our active DB implementation only supports message events and transaction events. We have, however, put in mechanisms for the support of composite events but as yet have not implemented any composite event types. This is something that we feel is important. Time events have not yet been considered in GemStone (we understand neither Kotz-Dittrich nor Kappel has implemented them). Again, this is something we would like to examine. Presently our rule inheritance mechanism inherits and overloads rules in a manner similar to TriGS (by using dictionaries) but this mechanism would have to be updated to incorporate the fact that composite events are also now going to be present and subject to inheritance (and possibly overloading).

We would also like, if possible, (and again like TriGS) to find some way of simulating nested transactions, as GemStone does not support them. At present the way we circumvent this is to check if a rule has returned a special symbol and if so we leave the triggering method (i.e. abort it). The problem here, though, is that if a rule causes the abort of the triggering method it does not also cause the undoing of the effects of all rules which have fired previous to the one which requests the abort, and this means that it is possible to have some rules fire when there is no cause (since the triggering method has aborted). Perhaps a simple way of overcoming this problem would be to consider integrity rules separately, since then all rules which might cause the method to abort could be fired first to ensure that no rules with side effects are fired until we are sure that the method is going to go ahead.

6.2 Future Work

Obviously, the most important future work is the implementation of the design tools that were our original aim. To restate the different types of tool we identified, we are interested in:

- design tools to help create the rule base; and
- explanation tools to explain the working of an existing rule base.

Firstly, more work is needed in the area of debugging tools, particularly for active *object-oriented* systems, since DEAR [7] only considers the debugging of method events and composite and timed events cannot be traced. Composite event tracing could be very complex, however, as the number of events that need to occur to raise the composite event could be very large and also of different types (method events, timed events, transaction events, composite events). This means that this would not be a simple task to undertake.

Secondly, work is needed on tools for the initial creation of rule bases, as we feel from our own experience that declaring rules in the language of the database is not a particularly efficient way of doing things. For example, it can be difficult to ensure that the correct numbers of parameters are declared at each stage. Kotz-Dittrich proposes the need for an integrated environment with a rule designer, a rule browser, a rule simulator and a rule tracer [17]. We feel, however, that the designer and browser would be better combined into one item and indeed the same could be said of the rule simulator and tracer. The latter is what has been done in DEAR, as the debugger here supports both the tracing of rules (where the database is actually changed) and the simulation of rules (whereby the user can say 'what if I did....' and the results could be shown without the database being altered). The aim of any browser/designer would be to improve the ease with which events and rules are created, viewed, updated and deleted.

We also wish to investigate how the creation of certain types of rules could be made simpler. Since there are certain types of rules that follow a set pattern (e.g. integrity rules) the creation of these could be largely automatic, which would take some of the burden off the rule designer. Other types of rules that could benefit from this approach are rule couplets to lock and unlock objects before and after updates and notification rules which need to appear on the screen with some message attached.

Acknowledgement

The first author of this paper is in receipt of an EPSRC studentship which has facilitated the research reported here.

References

[1] Anwar, E., Maugis, L., Chakravarthy, S.: A New Perspective on Rule Support for Object-Oriented Databases, Proc. ACM SIGMOD (May 1993) 99-108

[2] Behrends, H.: Simulation-based Debugging of Active Databases, Tech. report TR-IS-AIS-94-02, Facbereich Informatik Universitat Oldenburg (1994)

[3] Bichler, P., Schrefl, M.: Active Object-Oriented Database Design Using Active Object/Behaviour Diagrams, Proc. 4th Intl. Workshop on Research Issues In Data Engineering - Active Database Systems (1994)

[4] Dayal, U., *et al*: The HiPAC Project: Combining Active Databases and Timing Constraints, ACM SIGMOD Record 17(1) (1988) 51-70

[5] Chakravarthy, S., Mishra, D.: SNOOP: An Expressive Event Specification Language For Active Databases, Univ. of Florida CIS Tech. Rep. 93-007 (1993)

[6] Diaz, O., Paton, N., Gray, P.: Rule Management in Object-Oriented Databases: A Uniform Approach, Proc. VLDB 17 (1991) 317-326

[7] Diaz, O., Jaime, A., Paton, N.: DEAR: a DEbugger for Active Rules in an Object-Oriented Context, Proc. 1st Intl. Workshop on Rules in Database Systems (1993)

[8] Gatziu, S., Geppert, A., Dittrich, K.R.: Integrating Active Concepts into an Object-Oriented Database System, DBFL-3 Workshop (1991)

[9] Gatziu, S., Dittrich, K.R.: SAMOS: an Active Object-Oriented Database System, IEEE Quarterly Bulletin on Data Engineering (January 1993)

[10] Gatziu, S., Dittrich, K.R.: Events in an Active Object-Oriented Database System, Proc. 1st Intl. Workshop on Rules in Database Systems (1993)

[11] Gatziu, S., Dittrich, K.R.: Detecting Composite Events in Active Database Systems Using Petri Nets, Proc. 4th Intl. Workshop on Research Issues in Data Engineering: Active Database Systems (1994)

[12] Gehani, N.H., Jagadish, H.V.: ODE as an Active Database: Constraints and Triggers, Proc. VLDB 17 (1991) 327-336

[13] Gehani, N.H., Jagadish, H.V., Shmueli, O.: Event Specification in an Active Object-Oriented Database, ACM SIGMOD (1992) 81-90

[14] Gehani, N.H., Jagadish, H.V., Shmueli, O.: Composite Event Specification in Active Databases: Model and Implementation, Proc. VLDB 18 (1992) 327-338

[15] Kappel, G., *et al*: TriGS: Making a passive object-oriented database system active, JOOP (July-August 1994) 40-51

[16] Kappel G., Rausch-Schott, S., Retschitzegger, W.: Beyond Coupling Modes - Implementing Active Concepts on Top of Commercial OODBMS, Proc. Intl. Symposium of Object-Oriented Methodologies and Systems (1994) 189-204

[17] Kotz-Dittrich, A.: Adding Active Functionality to an Object-Oriented Database System - a Layered Approach, Proc. GI Conf. Datenbanksysteme in Büro, Technik und Wissenschaft (1993) 54-73

[18] Maier, D., Stein, J.: Development of an Object-Oriented DBMS - Proc. OOPSLA (1986) 472-481

[19] Stonebraker, M.: The Integration of Rule Systems and Database Systems, IEEE Transactions on Knowledge and Data Eng., 4(5) (1992)

Rule Analysis

Improved Rule Analysis by Means of Triggering and Activation Graphs

Elena Baralis[†]   Stefano Ceri   Stefano Paraboschi

Dipartimento di Elettronica e Informazione, Politecnico di Milano
Piazza Leonardo da Vinci 32, I-20133 Milano, Italy
† Dipartimento di Automatica e Informatica, Politecnico di Torino
Corso Duca degli Abruzzi 24, I-10129 Torino, Italy
baralis@polito.it, ceri/parabosc@elet.polimi.it

Abstract. In this paper, we propose new methods for the compile-time analysis of the behavior of active rules, based on the distinction between mutual triggering and mutual activation of rules. This distinction motivates the introduction of two graphs defining rule interaction, called triggering and activation graphs respectively. Analysis techniques presented in this paper are focused on the problem of termination; results provide a systematic identification of reactive behaviors which can be guaranteed to terminate and reactive behaviors which may lead to infinite rule processing.

1 Introduction

Active rules, also called production rules or triggers, were originally introduced in the context of expert systems, and in particular languages such as *OPS5* [5]; they are now being tightly integrated to database management [16]. They follow the *event-condition-action* paradigm; a seamless integration of active rules within databases occurs by mapping events to data manipulation operations, by expressing conditions as database queries, and by including database manipulations within the activities that can be performed by actions. Thus, active rules are a vehicle for providing reactive behaviors to databases.

The potential uses of reactive behavior are very significant. Active rules are a vehicle for supporting data derivations [9], integrity maintenance [6, 7], workflow management [10], replication management [8], and so on. For instance, when active rules maintain data integrity, a user-defined transaction may cause the loss of integrity; system-defined active rules take the responsibility of reacting to the integrity violation, either by repairing it, or by rolling back the transaction. More in general, active rules may impose the so-called "business rules" to user-defined applications, thereby incorporating some domain-specific knowledge, e.g. about bonds market, retail trading, production schedules, and so on.

---

* Research presented in this paper is supported by Esprit project P6333 IDEA, and by ENEL contract "VDS 1/94: Integrity Constraint Management"

In all these cases, active rules integrate or compose their actions together with user-defined applicative actions. Therefore, rules must be defined by a "rule expert", normally the *Database Administrator*. Clearly, such specification must be robust; it is unacceptable that active rules, which express a sort of "corporate behavior and control", be themselves subject to errors. However, it may be quite difficult to specify a large collection of active rules and accurately predict their behavior, due to the variety of user-defined applications that may be presented and to the unstructured and unpredictable nature of rule processing. During rule processing, rule behavior is quite subtle; mutual triggering may occur, and rules may behave differently when considered in different orders, yielding unexpected results. For this reason, experiences in using active rules are normally very careful and conservative. Experts in the field indicate design methods and tools as the key feature for definitely warranting to active rules the important applicative role that they deserve [15].

Research along this direction has been quite extensive. In particular, it has been recognized that two important and desirable properties of rule behavior are *termination* and *confluence*. These properties are defined for a *given* rule set and an *arbitrary* user-defined application. Termination occurs when, for any user-defined application, rule processing is guaranteed to terminate, i.e., rules are guaranteed not to activate each other indefinitely. Confluence occurs when, for any user-defined application, the final database state is unique, i.e., it does not depend on the execution order of rules. Confluence is easily guaranteed by imposing a deterministic ordering of rules, e.g. by means of user-specified or system-specified priorities among rules. This paper is only concerned with termination, i.e., how to decide at compile time, by analysing the interaction among rules, whether termination can be guaranteed. Termination is indeed the key property of a rule set if we assume that each rule is individually correct.

Several approaches to rule analysis for termination have been already presented, from simple syntactic analysis [1] to complex semantic analysis [4]. A description of previous related work is postponed to Section 6. The approach presented in this paper is original, because it is based on clearly separating triggering from activation, whose precise definitions are postponed to Section 3. As we will see, both infinite triggering and infinite activation are required in order for rule processing not to terminate. While the former result is well-known, the combined analysis gives an improved and powerful rule analysis technique.

The organization of this paper is as follows. Section 2 introduces the assumptions and notations required to model active rules and knowledge bases. Section 3 presents the triggering and activation graphs. Section 4 discusses termination for knowledge bases without priorities, and Section 5 extends some of the results of Section 4 to the case of prioritized knowledge bases. Finally, Section 6 compares our approach with previous work in this field and Section 7 describes the directions of future work.

2 Assumptions and Notation

Definition 1. An **Extensional Database** is a collection of *classes* of values. Each class is *typed*; in particular, we assume the type of all classes to be a *record*, whose components are called *attributes*. Each attribute has a unique label and type.

Without loss of generality, in this paper we consider only elementary attributes; under such assumptions the above model is indeed the relational model. However, results of this paper hold for arbitrarily complex attribute types and may be trivially extended for classes of (identity-based) objects. Indeed, we choose a *neutral data representation*.

Definition 2. A **Database State** of an Extensional Database is the collection of all values belonging to its classes in the considered time point.

A *data manipulation language* supports general operations for *inserting* new values into a class, *deleting* values from a class, or *updating* the value of attributes.

Definition 3. An **Active Rule** is a triple of components:

- The *Event Set* is a set of data manipulation operations being monitored.
- The *Condition* is a predicate on the current database state
- The *Action* is a sequence of data manipulation operations.

Definition 4. A **Knowledge Base** is a pair $\langle E, R \rangle$, where E is the *Extensional database* and R is the *Active Rule Set*, i.e. the set of all the active rules defined for E.

Definition 5. A **Prioritized Knowledge Base** is a Knowledge Base $\langle E, R \rangle$ where a total order $<_p$ is defined on R.

Conventionally, if $r_i >_p r_j$ we say that r_i has higher priority than r_j.

Definition 6. The **Knowledge Base Evolution** is obtained by alternating *user-specified transitions* and *rule processing*. The entire sequence of data manipulation operations performed by user-specified transitions or by active rule processing is committed or aborted as a *transaction*; we assume the usual acid properties of transactions [11]. In the context of each transaction, each rule is *triggered* by the execution of any operation in its event set.

Rule processing is initiated by system-specific mechanisms that are outside the scope of this paper. Just to give an intuition, rules may be distinguished into *immediate* or *deferred*. Processing of immediate rules is normally initiated either immediately before or immediately after an operation, while processing of deferred rules is initiated when the user issues the `commit work` statement. In this paper we do not consider *detached rules*, which run asynchronously, i.e., in the context of separate transactions. In summary, we simply assume that rule processing is initiated by some system-specific mechanism on a well-defined set of active rules.

Definition 7. The **Rule Processing Algorithm** consists of iterating the following steps:

1. If there is no triggered rule, then exit.
2. Select one of the triggered rules, which is de-triggered.
3. Evaluate the condition of the selected rule.
4. If the condition is true, then execute the action of the selected rule.

The rule selected at point (2) is the highest priority rule with a prioritized knowledge base; it is nondeterministically selected when the knowledge base does not support rule priorities.

The above algorithm either terminates by exit from point (1), thus reaching a *quiescent* knowledge base state where no rule is triggered, or does not terminate, by repeating the above cycle forever.

Definition 8. A Knowledge Base exhibits a **Non-Terminating Behavior** iff there exists at least one transaction which produces non-terminating rule processing.

The remainder of this paper is devoted to determining whether the knowledge base may or may not exhibit a non-terminating behavior, for arbitrary user-specified transitions and for a given rule set.

3 Representation of Interactions among Rules

Definition 9. Let R be an arbitrary active rule set. The **Triggering Graph** (**TG**) is a directed graph $\{V, E\}$ where each node $v_i \in V$ corresponds to a rule $r_i \in R$. A directed arc $\langle r_j, r_k \rangle \in E$ means that the action of rule r_j generates events which trigger rule r_k.

Non-terminating behaviors require cyclic triggering of rules, and acyclicity of the triggering graph implies the absence of non-terminating behaviors. These results were given in [1], where triggering graphs were first introduced.

Definition 10. Let R be an arbitrary active rule set. The **Activation Graph** (**AG**) is a directed graph $\{V, E\}$ where each node $v_i \in V$ corresponds to a rule $r_i \in R$. A directed arc $\langle r_j, r_k \rangle \in E$, with $j \neq k$, means that the action of rule r_j may change the truth value of rule r_k's condition from **false** to **true**. An arc $\langle r_j, r_j \rangle \in E$ means that rule r_j's condition can be **true** after the execution of r_j's action.

Activation graphs are complementary to triggering graphs; indeed, acyclicity of the activation graph implies the absence of non-terminating behaviors, because non-terminating behaviors may only occur if conditions remain true after rule execution or if rules cyclicly change the truth values of conditions, so that they become true before being evaluated. However, while Triggering Graph arcs are syntactically derivable, it is very difficult to precisely determine the arcs of an Activation Graph. In some cases, arcs must be pessimistically included into the activation graph at rule analysis time, but then the actual values provided at rule execution time do not actually induce a change of condition[2]. In addition, it may be difficult – or even impossible – to infer the truth value of a condition from the imperative code of a rule's action.

Each individual rule may be self-disactivating:

Definition 11. A **Self-Disactivating Rule** is an active rule whose action's execution falsifies its condition.

When a rule r is not self-disactivating, a ring $\langle r, r \rangle$ belongs in the AG. Quite luckily, rules written for many practical applications (e.g., constraint maintenance and workflow management) are self-disactivating. Note that if no rule is self-disactivating, then the activation graph does not provide any additional information for termination analysis with respect to the triggering graph.

3.1 Example

Example 1. Figure 1 illustrates a small knowledge base. The extensional database consists of a single class C having attributes A,B,C,D,E; the type of these attributes is restricted to the set of values { 0, 1 }. The rule set consists of three rules $\{r_1, r_2, r_3\}$. Rule events are update operations to the above attributes; conditions are conjunctive selection predicates; actions are sequences of update operations, expressed as simple assignments of values to attributes; operations are applied to the entire extension of the class. This simplified syntax for rules, which enables the development of small knowledge bases for illustrative purposes, will be used throughout the paper. The TG and AG graphs corresponding to the above rules are also illustrated in Figure 1. TG arcs are represented by solid lines and AG arcs are represented by dashed lines.

4 Termination without Priorities

We now concentrate on rules without priorities, and present several results concerning their termination.

Lemma 12. *Let R be an arbitrary rule set. During the rule processing phase, any rule $r \in R$ is executed more than once only if rule r has at least one incoming arc both in the TG and in the AG.*

Proof: From Definition 7, for a rule r to be eligible for execution, (a) at least one of its triggering events must have occurred, and (b) its condition must be true. After its first execution, rule r is detriggered. Then, for it to be retriggered

---

[2] Recall that the general problem of deciding the truth value of predicates is undecidable.

r_1 $\begin{bmatrix} event : U(D) \\ condition : A = 0 \\ action : A = 1, B = 0, C = 0 \end{bmatrix}$ r_2 $\begin{bmatrix} event : U(D) \\ condition : C = 0 \\ action : C = 1, E = 1 \end{bmatrix}$

r_3 $\begin{bmatrix} event : U(E) \\ condition : B = 0 \\ action : A = 0, B = 1, D = 1 \end{bmatrix}$

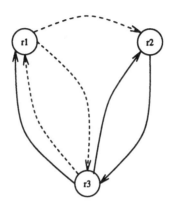

Fig. 1. A knowledge base and its triggering and activation graph

again, some rule $r' \in R$ (possibly r itself) must generate an event that retriggers r. Thus, to satisfy requirement (a), there must be an arc $\langle r', r \rangle$ in TG. After the first execution of rule r, its condition may be true if either r does not disactivate itself, or some other rule $r'' \in R$ makes r's condition true again. In either cases, an arc is present in AG: in the first case as $\langle r, r \rangle$, and in the second case as $\langle r'', r \rangle$. Thus, the presence of an incoming arc in node r in the AG is required in order for a rule to be executed more than once. □

Definition 13. Let R be an arbitrary active rule set, and TG and AG its associated triggering and activation graphs. The **Rule Reduction Algorithm** is:

    Repeat until no more eliminations are possible:
       If (no arc $\langle r', r \rangle \in TG$) or (no arc $\langle r'', r \rangle \in AG$)
          Eliminate r from the rule set R, from the TG graph, and from
       the AG graph

Definition 14. An **Irreducible Active Rule Set** IR is a subset of the active rule set R obtained by applying to R the rule reduction algorithm.

Lemma 15. *Let R be an arbitrary rule set, $S \subseteq R$ be a subset of R containing only rules that can be executed a finite number of times, and r an arbitrary rule in R but not in S with (1) incoming arcs in the triggering graph TG only from rules in S or (2) incoming arcs in the activation graph AG only from rules in S. Then, rule r can be executed only a finite number of times.*

Proof: Let rule r have incoming triggering arcs only from rules in S. Consider the worst case, in which rule r has an incoming arc in the triggering graphs from all rules $r_i \in S$. Let n be the total number of times that rules in S can be executed. Then, rule r can be executed only when a triggering event is generated, and this may happen at most once due to a transaction and n times due to the execution of rules in S. Thus, r can be executed only a finite number of times. The same holds if r has incoming arcs in AG only from rules in S: rule r can be executed only when its condition is true, and its condition can be made true only a finite number of times. □

Lemma 16. *For any user transaction, rules of a rule set R which do not belong to its irreducible active rule set IR are guaranteed of being executed a fixed number of times.*

Proof: The reduction algorithm performs a finite number of iterations, at most equal to the number of rules in R. The proof is given by induction on the iterations performed by the reduction algorithm. *Base case:* at its first iteration the reduction algorithm eliminates from R all the rules that have either no incoming arc in the TG, or no incoming arc in the AG. Thus, by Lemma 12, it eliminates all the rules that are guaranteed to be executed a finite number of times (indeed, at most once, when a user transaction both triggers and activates them). *Induction step:* let the reduction algorithm at its ith iteration yield an active rule set $R^{(i)}$, from which some rules guaranteed to execute a finite number of times are removed. We will prove that the $(i+1)^{th}$ iteration of the reduction algorithm removes from R only rules guaranteed to execute a finite number of times. At its $(i+1)^{th}$ iteration, the reduction algorithm selects for being removed all rules which have either no incoming arc in the $TG^{(i)}$, or no incoming arc in the $AG^{(i)}$. Thus, the selected rules may have been activated or triggered only by rules eliminated in previous steps of the reduction algorithm. By the induction hypothesis, those rules can be executed only a finite number of times. Then, by Lemma 15, the selected rules may be executed only a finite number of times. Thus, the $(i+1)^{th}$ iteration of the reduction algorithm removes only rules that might execute a finite number of times. □

Theorem 17. *If the active rule set R of a knowledge base is reduced to the empty set by the rule reduction algorithm, then the knowledge base cannot exhibit a non-terminating behavior.*

Proof: Let IR be the irreducible active rule set produced by the application of the reduction algorithm to the active rule set R. Suppose for the sake of a contradiction, that $IR = \emptyset$, and the knowledge base exhibits a non-terminating behavior. The number of active rules in R is finite, thus a non-terminating behavior can only be caused by infinite executions of some rule in R. As $IR = \emptyset$, by Lemma 16 all rules in R are guaranteed to execute a finite number of times, a contradiction. □

When instead the active rule set R cannot be reduced to the empty set, the knowledge base may exhibit a non-terminating behavior. Further, any rule in the irreducible rule set may be involved in some non-terminating behavior: the following theorem proves that, given the information represented by the TG and AG, the rule reduction algorithm identifies *all* the rules that can be executed an infinite number of times.

Theorem 18. *All the rules in the irreducible active rule set IR may be executed an infinite number of times.*

Proof: Let us define an arbitrary order on rules $r_1, \ldots, r_n$ in IR. We also introduce two sets, TR containing all triggered rules, and AR containing all activated rules; TR and AR evolve dynamically during the knowledge base evolution. Consider a user-defined transaction that triggers all rules in IR and makes all rule conditions true; such a transaction, although representing a worst case, is consistent with the assumptions on the TG and AG that we can use in the theorem. Then, when rule processing begins, $TR = IR$ and $AR = IR$. In absence of priority, we can assume that rules will be selected by the rule processing system in any order, and in particular in the order $r_1, r_2, ..r_n$. After each rule $r_i \in IR$ is executed, r_i is removed from TR and AR, and TR and AR are augmented with all rules with incoming (triggering or activation) arcs originating from r_i. This process repeats for all the n rules in IR. When all rules have executed, by the definition of IR there must be an arc $\langle r', r_1 \rangle$ in TG and an arc $\langle r'', r_1 \rangle$ in AG with $r', r'' \in IR$. Thus, r_1 may be again ready for execution. Analogous considerations apply for an arbitrary rule $r_i \in IR$: the sequence of rules $r_i, \ldots, r_n, r_1, \ldots, r_{i-1}$ is executed, and by the definition of IR there must be an arc $\langle r', r_i \rangle$ in TG and an arc $\langle r'', r_i \rangle$ in AG with $r', r'' \in IR$, and r_i appears in both TR and AR. Thus, any rule in IR may be cyclically reexecuted an infinite number of times. $\square$

It is possible to produce non-terminating executions with particular subsets of the irreducible rule set.

Definition 19. Let IR be an irreducible rule set. A **non-terminating rule set** is any subset S of rules in IR such that no rule of S is eliminated by applying the rule reduction algorithm to the set S itself.

Clearly, results which were proven for the irreducible rule set apply to any non-terminating rule set as well. Non-terminating rule sets constitute a lattice:

Theorem 20. *Let IR be an irreducible rule set and S' be the poset of all non-terminating rule sets S defined on IR, partially ordered by set inclusion. Assume:*

- *the empty set to be an element of S';*
- *set union as meet operation;*
- *a join operation defined as set intersection if its result is a non-terminating rule set, and as the empty set otherwise.*

Then, S' is a lattice with a null universal lower bound and set IR as universal upper bound.

Proof: Follows from the definition of lattice. □

Finally, we characterize the features of rules that may be involved in non-terminating behaviors, based on the topology of the TG and AG.

Definition 21. A rule r_j is **directly reachable** from a rule set R if there are two rules r' and r'' in R (not necessarily distinct), such that $\langle r', r_j \rangle \in AG$ and $\langle r'', r_j \rangle \in TG$; a rule r_j is **reachable** from a rule set R if it is directly reachable from R or if there are two rules r_a and r_t, both reachable from R and not necessarily distinct, such that $\langle r_a, r_j \rangle \in AG$ and $\langle r_t, r_j \rangle \in TG$.

Theorem 22. *Any non-terminating rule set includes at least a cycle in both the TG and the AG. Any rule of a non-terminating rule set is reachable from some rule set R such that elements of R belong to cycles of either the TG, or the AG, or both graphs.*

Proof: This proof follows from the structure of irreducible rule sets and is omitted. □

These results show that a correct representation of possibly non-terminating behaviors is quite difficult, since non-termination can be due to several rule sets. Each such set includes rules which contribute to cycles in the TG and/or the AG or are reachable from such cycles. Indeed, a rule analysis tool for testing termination should present the IR to the user, illustrate the TG and AG cycles within the IR, and then possibly illustrate the lattice S'. Rules participating to cycles in either the TG or the AG (even better if they participate to both of them) could be highlighted thereby suggesting to the user that their modification might be useful for guaranteeing termination.

4.1 Examples

Example 2. Consider again the example of Figure 1. The rule set is irreducible. Moreover, in TG appears a cycle involving rules $\{r_2, r_3\}$, while in AG appears a cycle involving rules $\{r_1, r_3\}$; note that the two cycles are different. Nevertheless, a non-terminating behavior may occur, involving rules $\{r_1, r_2, r_3\}$.

In fact, suppose that r_3 is triggered by the user, and next executed because its condition is true. r_3 triggers r_1 and r_2 and can make true the condition of r_1. Thus, r_1 is triggered and can be executed. This execution can make true the conditions of r_2 (which was triggered by r_1) and of r_3. r_2 is triggered and can have a true condition, so it can be executed, thus triggering r_3. But now r_3 is triggered and can have a true condition, so the cycle can restart.

Example 3. Figure 2 represents a reducible rule set. By applying the rule reduction algorithm we first remove $\{r_2\}$. When r_2 is removed, r_3 loses its incoming arc in the TG; thus, it is removed at the next iteration. Finally, we remove r_1, which does not have any incoming arc. We conclude that no non-terminating behavior is possible in this case.

$$r_1 \begin{bmatrix} event : U(F) \\ condition : A = 0 \\ action : A = 1, C = 0, D = 1 \end{bmatrix} \qquad r_2 \begin{bmatrix} event : U(D) \\ condition : B = 0 \\ action : B = 1, E = 1 \end{bmatrix}$$

$$r_3 \begin{bmatrix} event : U(E) \\ condition : C = 0 \\ action : A = 0, C = 1, F = 1 \end{bmatrix}$$

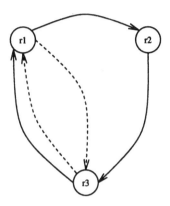

Fig. 2. A knowledge base with terminating behavior

Example 4. Figure 3 represents a reducible rule set. By applying the rule reduction algorithm we remove in the first step $\{r_1, r_5\}$, then $\{r_2, r_4\}$, and finally $\{r_3\}$.

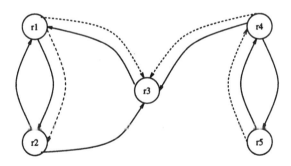

Fig. 3. A knowledge base with terminating behavior

Example 5. Figure 4 illustrates a rule system which exhibits counter-rotating cycles for TG and AG. The reduction algorithm is not able to remove any node from the graph. In fact, the system can exhibit a non-terminating behavior, if the user transaction generates a situation when a rule is triggered and has a true condition and at least another rule is either triggered or has a true condition.

$$r_1 \begin{bmatrix} event : U(F) \\ condition : A = 0 \\ action : A = 1, C = 0, D = 1 \end{bmatrix} \qquad r_2 \begin{bmatrix} event : U(D) \\ condition : B = 0 \\ action : B = 1, A = 0, E = 1 \end{bmatrix}$$

$$r_3 \begin{bmatrix} event : U(E) \\ condition : C = 0 \\ action : C = 1, B = 0, F = 1 \end{bmatrix}$$

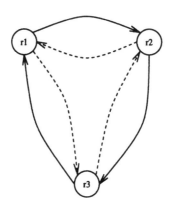

Fig. 4. A knowledge base with non-terminating behavior

Example 6. Finally, let us consider the rule set of Figure 5. Clearly, the rule set is irreducible. We can ask ourselves which rules may be executed when rule processing does not terminate. The answer to this question is given by the lattice illustrated in Figure 6, which presents in its nodes all non-terminating rule sets, i.e., all possible rule sets which may generate non-terminating sequences. The actual execution trace of a non-terminating behavior can therefore include 10 distinct patterns of cyclic rule executions, which may alternate nondeterministically in the trace.

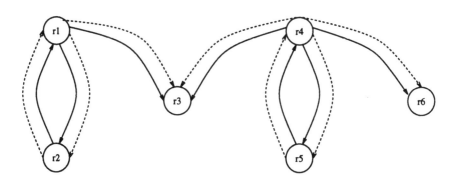

Fig. 5. A triggering and an activation graph

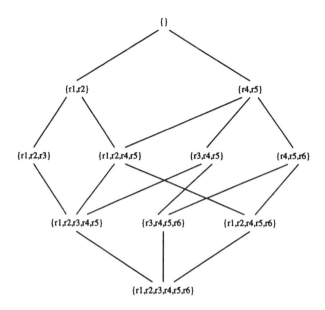

Fig. 6. A lattice for the rule system in preceding figure

5 Termination with Priorities

When rules are prioritized, some rule execution sequences are excluded by the second step of rule processing, that selects rules according to their priority. Thus, all positive results excluding non-terminating behaviors described in the previous section are confirmed; in addition, some other cases of termination can be proved.

The main idea for taking advantage of priorities is to show that certain rules are inhibited, because their activation depends on rules at lower priority than rules providing triggering. Thus, when the condition of inhibited rules is evaluated, it is false; a subsequent change of the truth value of the condition due to the execution of the activating rule has no effect, since triggering has already occurred. Without priorities, we cannot make any assumption on the execution order of rules, therefore we must pessimistically assume an ordering in which activation precedes triggering; such ordering can indeed be nondeterministically chosen by the system.

We start by further expanding the notion of reachability, that was introduced in the previous section.

Definition 23. The **reaching set** from a rule r_i to a rule r_j, $reach(r_i, r_j)$, is any subset R' of the rules R which includes r_j but not r_i, such that the following two properties hold:

1. r_j is reachable from r_i according to Definition 21 by using only the rules in the set R'.
2. The set R' is *minimal*, i.e., if we subtract any rule from R' then property (1) ceases to hold.

Intuitively, each reaching set corresponds to a set of rules which can independently cause the execution of a rule r_j given that a rule r_i has executed. Of course, there can be many distinct reaching sets for the same pair of rules: we indicate as $S_{reach}(r_i, r_j)$ a set which contains all the sets $reach(r_i, r_j)$. We can next associate to each reaching set its dominant priority as the priority of its lowest-priority rule. Such rule is the "bottleneck" in the execution of rules belonging to the set.

Definition 24. The **Dominant priority** of a reaching set, $P(reach(r_i, r_j))$, is the lowest priority associated to the rules in $reach(r_i, r_j)$.

Finally, we define inhibited rules and inhibited cycles.

Definition 25. Consider a non-terminating rule set R as defined in Definition 19; let C denote the rules belonging to a cycle of the TG. Let r_0 be a self-disactivating rule in C which is triggered by rule r_t and activated by rule r_a, with $r_t \neq r_a$ ($\langle r_t, r_0 \rangle \notin AG$, and $\langle r_a, r_0 \rangle \notin TG$). Let p_t be the lowest among the dominant priorities $P(reach(r_0, r_t))$ of all the sets $reach(r_0, r_t)$, and p_a be the highest among dominant priorities $P(reach(r_0, r_a))$ of all the sets $reach(r_0, r_a)$; then, if $p_a < p_t$ and $p_a < p(r_0)$, we say that r_0 is **Inhibited**. Cycle C is called an **Inhibited Cycle**.

The intuition behind inhibition is that r_0, a self-disactivating rule triggered by r_t, will cause the retriggering and reconsideration of r_0 before r_a can change the truth value of r_0's condition; hence, r_0's condition will be false at reconsideration, and r_0's action will not be executed.

Theorem 26. *Consider a non-terminating rule set R which includes only one cycle in the TG; if, due to priority assignment, the cycle is inhibited then non-terminating behaviors involving only the rules of R cannot occur.*

Proof: We give a sketch of this proof. Assume non-termination; then, rule r_0 which belongs to the only cycle C in TG must be executed infinitely many times. Assume it executes once. After it is executed, the condition of r_0 is false (because r_0 is self-disactivating). Given that R is a non-terminating rule set and that C is the only cycle in the TG, by Theorem 22 all rules of R are reachable from rules in C; thus, at least one set $reach(r_0, r_a)$ and one set $reach(r_0, r_t)$ exist, and after the execution of r_0 some rules must be both triggered and activated in each one of these sets; each set is sufficient to autonomously cause the triggering of either r_a or r_t.

The order in which rules are considered is driven by the rule processing algorithm of Definition 7. The condition on prioritization of the reach sets are such that the rules in $reach(r_0, r_a)$ include a dominating rule r_h which is at lower priority than any rule in any reach set in $S_{reach}(r_0, r_t)$; therefore, if the dominating rule r_h is triggered, it is not selected by step (2) of the rule processing algorithm, that will always give priority to some other triggered rule in some sets $reach(r_0, r_t)$.

Thus, if r_t is executed due to any of the independent rule sets in $S_{reach}(r_0, r_t)$, then it is executed before r_a; if it does not execute at all the cycle is anyway inhibited. Further, r_0 is also at higher priority than r_h; so after each execution of r_t, r_0 is considered prior to r_h, and its condition is certainly false whenever it is considered. Only after r_0 is last detriggered, rule r_h will be selected for consideration; this may cause several triggerings and executions of r_a (indeed, at most one execution for each independent set $reach(r_0, r_a)$ could occur), but none of these executions will be able to cause triggering of r_0; thus, rule processing eventually terminates. □

The results on cycle inhibition can be generalized removing the restrictions imposed on the uniqueness of the TG cycle.

Theorem 27. *Consider a non-terminating rule set R; if, due to priorities, all the cycles on the TG are inhibited, then non-terminating behaviors involving only the rules of R cannot occur.*

Proof: Again, we just sketch this proof, which is extremely tedious but rather straightforward. It is sufficient to partially order cycles on the basis of the priority of their dominating rule r_h introduced in Theorem 26, from the highest to the lowest priority. Then, cycles will become inhibited according to that order, after a finite number of executions of each cycle. □

Finally, we consider the universal upper bound IR.

Corollary 28. *If all the TG cycles of the irreducible set IR are inhibited due to priorities, then the corresponding knowledge base must exhibit a terminating behavior.*

Proof: An application of Theorem 27 to a particular non-terminating rule set. □

5.1 Examples

Example 7. The rule system in Figure 1 cannot exhibit non-terminating behaviors (although it was classified as a non-terminating rule set) if priorities are associated to rules such that $r_1 < r_2$ and $r_1 < r_3$. In fact, cycle $\{r_1, r_2, r_3\}$ is inhibited by rule r_2; after the first execution of r_2, r_3 executes prior to r_1 and triggers r_2; when r_2's condition is checked, it is false, so r_2 does not execute its action. Finally, r_1 executes (possibly changing the condition of r_2) and execution terminates.

Example 8. The rule system in Figure 7 contains two TG cycles: $C_1 = \{r_2, r_3, r_6\}$ and $C_2 = \{r_4, r_5, r_6\}$. If priorities are assigned so that $r_1 <_p r_2 <_p r_3 <_p r_4 <_p r_5 <_p r_6$, then the two cycles become inhibited and the system is terminating. In fact, for C_1 r_3 is a candidate node for inhibition: r_a is r_1 and r_t is r_2; $S_{reach}(r_3, r_1) = \{\{r_6, r_2, r_1\}\}$; $S_{reach}(r_3, r_2) = \{\{r_6, r_2\}\}$. Since we know that

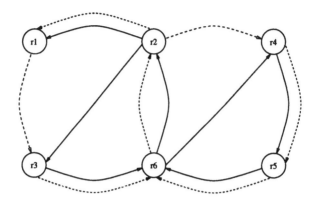

Fig. 7. A triggering and an activation graph

$max(P(reach(r_3, r_1))) < min(P(reach(r_3, r_2)))$ (i.e., $r_1 <_p r_2$), and it also happens that $max(P(reach(r_3, r_1))) < P(r_3)$, then r_3 inhibits C_1.

For C_2, r_4 is a candidate node for inhibition: r_2 and r_6 can be substituted to r_a and r_t; $S_{reach}(r_4, r_2) = \{\{r_5, r_6, r_2\}\}$; $S_{reach}(r_4, r_6) = \{\{r_5, r_6\}\}$. Since $max(P(reach(r_4, r_2))) < min(P(reach(r_4, r_6)))$ (i.e., $r_2 <_p r_5$) and it also happens that $max(P(reach(r_5, r_6))) < P(r_4)$, then r_4 inhibits C_2.

6 Related Work

Several methods have been proposed in the past to perform termination analysis, that depend on the chosen rule model. When the rule model includes events, most techniques rely on the type of triggered and generated events to detect non termination. On the other hand, if events are implicit in the rule model, then the analysis techniques rely mostly on the semantic information contained in the condition. The focus of this work is on trying to integrate, in the simplest possible way, the two different analysis techniques. In fact, we propose a method that takes into account both the explicit triggering events and the implicit events that may separately make a condition satisfied.

In [1, 7] triggering events are explicitly specified in the rule model and the proposed termination analysis technique is based on the detection of cycles in the triggering graph, built considering the type of both triggering events and events generated by the execution of rule actions. Our analysis technique complements the information contained in the triggering graph with the information contained in the activation graph, thus allowing us to discard some "false" cycles that are detected by the methods proposed in [1, 7]. Furthermore, in [1, 7] the effect of defining priorities among rules was not considered.

In the context of object-oriented database systems, a different approach to rule analysis is taken in [12]: event-condition-action rules are reduced to term rewriting systems, to which known techniques for termination analysis are applied. Proving termination requires the definition of a well-founded term ordering in the term rewriting system and seems a rather complex task even for small rule applications.

In [3, 4, 13] termination analysis is applied to rules for which events are implicit, that is, condition-action rules. The activation graph, which in [13] is called Enable-Rule graph, is used to statically predict rules behavior. This graph is generated by taking into account the complete semantics of both the rule condition and the rule action. Thus, it is similar to our activation graph, although we only consider the type of implicit events. Albeit many event-condition-action rule sets are often derived from an initial condition-action structure [7], general event-condition-action rules cannot be handled straightforwardly with this technique. The algorithm proposed in [4] to generate the activation graph can be applied in our context as well, in order to provide a more accurate determination of the activation graph arcs; results of the two papers complement nicely because [4] offers a sophisticated technique for building Activation Graphs. Analogous considerations hold for the work in [14], which proposes analysis techniques for rules with implicit event definition in the object-oriented context.

[2] proposes a different approach to the static analysis of rules behavior: a technique is described to group homogeneous rules, typically associated to a well-defined applicative objective, into modules; when modules satisfy specific behavioral or structural properties, their individual termination is guaranteed. The technique presented in [2] requires the rule programmer to autonomously guarantee the termination of rule execution inside each module, and determines the conditions under which termination of the combined execution of several rule modules is also guaranteed. This paper complements the approach of [2] because it may be applied to rule analysis *inside* each module.

7 Conclusions

This paper has indicated a new approach to termination analysis of active rules, which is based on keeping triggering and activation distinct. Several interesting results follow from the proposed rule analysis technique; it becomes possible to fully characterize the rule sets which may cause a non-terminating behavior, and indeed recognize that some rules certainly terminate even if there are cycles in the triggering graph (cfr Example 4) or in both the triggering and activation graphs (cfr Example 3), while other rules may exhibit non-terminating behaviors even if cycles in the activation and triggering graph are counter-rotating (cfr Example 5). Further, we have shown some special cases where rule priorities may inhibit cyclic behaviors (cfr Examples 7 and 8).

The proposed triggering and activation graphs may be used as a startpoint for "animating" knowledge bases, thereby obtaining simulators of active rule behaviors. The main idea is to combine arcs of activation and triggering graphs into colored Petri nets, whose firing sequences may be considered as possible execution traces of the active rules. Research on active rule animation is left for future work, which will be focused on use of these results in the context of rule design tools.

References

1. A. Aiken, J. Widom, and J. M. Hellerstein. Behavior of database production rules: Termination, confluence, and observable determinism. In M. Stonebraker, editor, *Proc. ACM SIGMOD Int'l Conf. on Management of Data*, pages 59–68, San Diego, California, May 1992.

2. E. Baralis, S. Ceri, and S. Paraboschi. Modularization techniques for active rules design. Technical Report IDEA.WP2.22P.002.01, ESPRIT Project n. 6333 IDEA, Nov. 1994.

3. E. Baralis, S. Ceri, and J. Widom. Better termination analysis for active databases. In N. W. Paton and M. H. Williams, editors, *Proc. of First Workshop on Rules in Database Systems*, WICS, pages 163–179, Edinburgh, Scotland, Aug. 1993. Springer-Verlag, Berlin.

4. E. Baralis and J. Widom. An algebraic approach to rule analysis in expert database systems. In *Proc. Twentieth Int'l Conf. on Very Large Data Bases*, pages 475–486, Santiago, Chile, Sept. 1994.

5. L. Brownston, R. Farrell, E. Kant, and N. Martin. *Programming Expert Systems in OPS5: An Introduction to Rule-Based Programming*. Addison-Wesley, 1985.

6. S. Ceri, P. Fraternali, S. Paraboschi, and L. Tanca. Automatic generation of production rules for integrity maintenance. *ACM Transactions on Database Systems*, 19(3):367–422, Sept. 1994.

7. S. Ceri and J. Widom. Deriving production rules for constraint maintenance. In D. McLeod, R. Sacks-Davis, and H. Schek, editors, *Proc. Sixteenth Int'l Conf. on Very Large Data Bases*, pages 566–577, Brisbane, Australia, Aug. 1990.

8. S. Ceri and J. Widom. Managing semantic heterogeneity with production rules and persistent queues. In R. Agrawal, S. Baker, and D. Bell, editors, *Proc. Nineteenth Int'l Conf. on Very Large Data Bases*, pages 108–119, Dublin, Ireland, Aug. 1993.

9. S. Ceri and J. Widom. Deriving incremental production rules for deductive data. *Information Systems*, 19(6):467–490, Nov. 1994.

10. U. Dayal, M. Hsu, and R. Ladin. Organizing long-running activities with triggers and transactions. In H. Garcia-Molina and H. V. Jagadish, editors, *Proc. ACM SIGMOD Int'l Conf. on Management of Data*, pages 204–214, Atlantic City, New Jersey, May 1990.

11. J. Gray and A. Reuter. *Transaction Processing Concepts and Techniques*. Morgan Kaufmann Publishers, 1993.

12. A. P. Karadimce and S. D. Urban. Conditional term rewriting as a formal basis for analysis of active database rules. In *Proc. Fourth International Workshop on Research Issues in Data Engineering RIDE-ADS '94*, Houston, Texas, Feb. 1994.

13. H. Tsai and A. M. K. Cheng. Termination analysis of OPS5 expert systems. In *Proc. of the AAAI National Conference on Artificial Intelligence*, Seattle, Washington, 1994.

14. L. van der Voort and A. Siebes. Termination and confluence of rule execution. In *Proc. of the Second International Conference on Information and Knowledge Management*, Washington DC, Nov. 1993.

15. J. Widom. Research issues in active database systems: Report from the closing panel at RIDE-ADS '94. *SIGMOD Record*, 23(3):41–43, Sept. 1994.

16. J. Widom and S. Ceri. *Active Database Systems*. Morgan-Kaufmann, San Mateo, California, Aug. 1995.

V I T A L : a Visual Tool for Analysis of Rules Behaviour in Active Databases[1]

Emmanuel Benazet , Hervé Guehl, Mokrane Bouzeghoub

Laboratoire PRiSM, Université de Versailles,
45, avenue des Etats-Unis 78035 Versailles CEDEX
Email : Emmanuel.Benazet @prism.uvsq.fr

Abstract : *Although active rules are used more and more in different IS applications, designing a coherent set of active rules is not a trivial task. Thus, it is important to provide tools to help the designer in the definition of a correct set of active rules. In this paper, we propose a toolbox which assists the designer in defining, tracing, debugging and understanding the behaviour of a set of active rules. This set of facilities is packaged in a toolbox in order to be used both during the design process, independently of any rule processor, and after the compiling process, depending on a specific rule processor. The former corresponds to a logical validation while the later corresponds to an effective validation with respect to the features of a specific DBMS (e.g. coupling modes, event interception). The toolbox includes various tools such as (i) a static analyser for a set of rules, which portrays the activation graph and its possible cycles, (ii) the step by step simulator of rule execution, (iii) a graphical interface with navigation and browsing facilities, (iv) and statistical information on the database evolution. This set of tools can be considered as a pragmatic approach to the complex problem of termination and confluence, to which the theoretical approaches have not yet provided an acceptable solution.*

1. Introduction

Conventional databases are now considered as passive storage systems in the sense that they don't react to events and don't propagate the effects of manipulation actions. They only allow to manipulate data on user requests. Active databases provide languages - based on ECA rules - which allow the definition of events, and mechanisms which automatically capture these events and trigger associated actions. When executed, these actions may, in turn, generate their own events which will initiate other actions in a cascading process. These languages and mechanisms have became more and more popular because of their ability to describe complex problems such as integrity enforcement and corrective actions, derived data maintenance, and exceptions handling. Besides their application to these technical problems inside a DBMS, active rules allow the definition of other user applications based on decision making approaches or work flows.

---

[1] This work is partly supported by the HC&M european program within the ACTNET projet, and by the PRC french program within the ACTIVE-DESIGN project.

If the active databases rule mechanisms are powerful, it is often difficult for the designer to define a coherent set of rules. Indeed, the behaviour of a set of rules can be unpredictable and often non-deterministic. Termination of the rule process is one of these problems; the cascading execution of rules may generate infinite cycles. Confluence is another complex problem; if the conflict set of rules is not ordered, many execution plans could be envisaged. Thus, a unique final result for all execution orders is not guaranteed. Beyond these theoretical problems, designers have more practical needs in visualising activation graphs of rules with their possible cycles, database states, and statistics on their use and evolution. As in any other programming languages, there is also a need for tracing, debugging and correcting rule programs.

In this paper, we propose a toolbox which assists the designer in defining, tracing, debugging and understanding the behaviour of a set of active rules. This set of facilities is packaged in a toolbox which can be used both during the design process, independent of any rule processor, and after the compiling process, dependent on a specific rule processor. The former usage corresponds to a logical validation while the later corresponds to an effective validation with respect to the features of a specific DBMS (e.g. coupling modes, event interception). The toolbox includes various tools such as (i) a static analysis of a set of rules, which portrays the activation graph and its possible cycles, (ii) the step by step simulation of rule execution, (iii) a graphical interface with navigation and browsing facilities, (iv) and statistical information on the database evolution. This set of tools can be considered as a pragmatic approach to the complex problem of termination and confluence, to which theoretical approaches have not yet provided an acceptable solution.

The remainder of this paper is organised as follows : Section 2 summarises the main issues and solution in rules definition and execution. Section 3 outlines the VITAL principles and functions. Section 4 presents an example session with the prototype.

2. Issues in Rule Definition and Execution

This section summarises the main issues in rule definition and rule execution. These issues can be organised in two categories:
* theoretical problems such as consistency, termination and confluence of a set of rules;
* practical problems such as visualising, simulating, tracing and debugging a set of rules.

In the remainder of the section, we will summarise the main features of these problems and overview some research which has addressed these problems. We also outline the desired functionalities to cope with these problems.

2.1. Theoretical issues

The theoretical issues mainly concern the termination and confluence of a set of rules. In general these problems are known as undecidable problems {2}. However, the literature identifies some restricted cases for which simple solutions can be given. Unfortunately, these restricted cases are so simple that they don't need any sophisticated theory to provide a solution; while the complex cases remain without any solution. Finally, validating a set of rules is not distinct from validating an imperative program written in a traditional programming language. In general, there is no formal process to validate such programs; however they run after a series of testing and debugging phases. Nevertheless, the work done in finding a formal solution is interesting in the way different problems are posed, and by some representation tools which are provided.

Rule termination

To study the problem of rule termination, a set of rules is represented by an "activation graph" (or triggering graph) whose nodes represent rules and edges represent the possible activation of one rule by another.

The termination problem is then posed as a problem of detecting cycles in an activation graph and studying whether the execution of these cycles end or not. If an execution graph has no cycles, then it is guaranteed to end, otherwise it is necessary to study the semantics of each cycle by observing the parts of the database on which the rules operate. Two different methods have been proposed:

- Syntactic methods are limited to cycle detection by observing the data in the rule statements (either classes, tables or attributes) on which the rules operate and the operations (events) which trigger the rules (usually insert, delete or update). The syntactic method detects potential cycles but does not identify whether they terminate or not. This decision is left to the programmer. A deeper analysis is done by taking into account the condition part of the active rules. This leads to the semantic methods, discussed hereafter.

- Semantic methods extend the syntactic methods by analysing the content of the database involved in the execution of a cycle. This deeper analysis is based on knowledge extracted from the condition part and the action part of the rules. However, this knowledge extraction is only possible in the context of the relational databases where the condition and the action parts of rules are usually represented by algebraic expressions. So it is more easy to "match" the action part of one rule and the condition part of another rule in order to check whether they invoke the same instances or not. In the following example, rules R4 and R5 address different parts of the database, so there is no risk of reproducing the same database state and cycling infinitely.

```
R4:       On action1(T1) If P Then action2(T2) where ¬Q
R5:       On action2(T2) If Q Then action1(T1) where ¬P
```

This is a simplification of what is proposed in {3} but it is sufficient to understand that the process becomes very difficult when the relational expressions become complex.

Finally, we can add that in the context of object oriented databases, this process doesn't apply because of the encapsulation of objects and the lack of standardisation of primitive operations on objects.

Rule Confluence

Confluence of a set of rules is a property which allows the rule processor to execute a conflict set in any order (in absence of priorities) and to obtain the same final database state. In fact, the rule processor can take advantage of this property to choose the best order to achieve a certain performance. In case of defined priorities between some rules, the subset of ordered rules could be considered as a unique global rule.

All the papers which address this problem agree on the assumption that to be confluent, a set of rules must first terminate. Once this condition hold, the problem of confluence is posed as a problem of rule commutation {7}.

For example, the following two rules, which are triggered by the same event, commute because the condition part of the second is independent of the action part of the first.

```
R1:   On insert(T) If T.A>a Then print(T.A)
R2:   On insert(T) If T.B=b Then T.B=b+1
```

A set of rules is confluent if all the possible pairs of rules commute. The proof for condition 1 and 2 is based on the propagation graphs proposed in {3}.

{1} provides another technique to analyse the confluence based on execution graphs. An execution graph is a directed graph whose nodes represent database states, and whose edges correspond to a rule execution. Confluence is then guaranteed if:
(i) There is not an infinite path in any of the execution graphs of the set of rules.
(ii) All the final states are the same ones. (There is only one final state).

The first condition is verified by termination analysis. The second condition cannot be verified without executing the set of rules. This execution can be simulated on a test database. However the simulation cannot be considered as a proof for confluence, but rather as a practical tool which displays possible problems.

2.2. Practical issues

Besides the theoretical problems, defining and validating a set of rules pose a number of practical problems, such as visualisation of the triggering graph, tracing of the execution graph, visualisation of the successive database states, cross referencing between the set of rules and the database schema, definition of breakpoints, filtering of events, and definition of statistics on the utilisation of rules. Designers and programmers require helpful facilities to cope with these problems. These facilities can be grouped into three categories:

High level interfaces

An active database may be defined by hundreds or thousands of rules. Managing the complexity of these rules requires the use of many interfaces and documentation tools. First, there is a need for a database schema editor to visualise the objects and relationships on which rules are or should be defined. Facilities such as templates to define rules are useful because they limit syntactic errors. To analyse the dynamic behaviour of rules, it's important to layout both the triggering graph (elaborated by a static analysis of rules) and the execution graph (elaborated by the rule processor). Browsing of these graphs allows the extraction of knowledge about, for example, the events which trigger certain rules, the operations which are executed in each rule, the attributes which are manipulated by certain rules, etc.

Interactive validation

Interactive validation is a way checking consistency of a specification by involving the designer in the final decision. This approach is usually adopted when there is no formal approach for the problem. This is generally the case of the logical consistency of a set of rules. For the rule consistency, there are different validations aspects, including the internal coherence of a given rule, the global coherence of a set of rules, and the conformance of rules with respect to the database schema definition. Internal consistency of a rule concerns the coherence of its conditions part which may contain conflicts between predicates (e.g. $age<10$ and $age>15$, or $age>15$ and $birthday>1/1/1990$.). Global inconsistency of a set of rules may concern the execution of the same action with contradictory condition parts of two distinct rules. For example: $R1$: If $age=20$ then $action1$; $R2$: If $age\neq20$ then $action1$. Obviously, in case of exception handling, the correction process could be more complex. Rules may also be inconsistent with respect to the database schema definition. The database schema may, for example, contain a domain definition [18..65] for the attribute age of an employee, while there exist some rules which refer, in their condition part, to employees having an age value of 16. These inconsistencies are generally not detected by rules parsers and compilers. Hence, it is important to detect them during the design phase or the debugging phase.

Simulation of rule execution.

Simulation of rule execution compensates the lack of formal approaches which don't solve the termination and the confluence problems. Simulation by itself is not a proof, but it allows a large number of programming errors to be detected and avoided. Simulation is also a good approach when rule execution varies from one rule processor to another; it allows a kind of portability between different active database systems. Finally the simulator allows the designer to check whether the actual actions realised by the rule processor coincide with the ones he expected. The simulation process allows us to get an abstracted view, by using several scenarios. The behaviour of the set of rules may be studied with several databases, several event management policies, and several rule execution models. But the relevance of a simulation depends heavily on the choice of the content of the test database. The richer the database content, the more pertinent is simulation.

The main difference between a debugger and a simulator is the stage during the software development at which they are used. A simulator is used before the compilation phase, a debugger is used after. Simulator are generally system independent while debuggers are system dependent. Simulators could run with different rule processors while debuggers are generally coupled to a language of the rule processor. The techniques used in both tools could be similar.

Besides the classical debuggers, two main tools, dealing with rule debugging and simulation, are proposed in the literature: DEAR {11} and ADELA {13}. DEAR has been implemented in the object-oriented database system ADAM {12} with a rule manager (EXACT {10}) that supports ECA rules. It provides facilities to keep track of activated rules and raised events, and indicates the reason for a rule firing. ADELA is a prototype that is not based on any database management system. It is a relational set-oriented rule simulator including an animated graphical interface. It shows rule activation and the effects on data. The first aim of this tool was to explain rules and to offer debugging/simulation facilities.

2.3 Toward a toolbox for analysis of rules behaviour

The fundamental problems of consistency, termination and confluence remain in active rules as well as in imperative programs. They are still complex problems, or even undecidable problems. Solutions are often given for very restricted cases which, in general, could be solved without any sophisticated theory. Programs written in classical languages (C, Pascal, ...) work in most cases. They are considered stable and often used commercially. However, their behaviour has not been formally proved. They are usually programmed using some methodology (structured programming, object-oriented programming) and then informally validated by testing. Similarly, rule programs could be informally validated by simulation and debugging, based on a parametric toolbox which provides a set of tools for visualising, browsing, simulating and debugging. This is one of the goals of the VITAL toolbox which is described in the following sections.

3. The VITAL Toolbox

VITAL is a toolbox for active rule analysis. It is part of a larger toolset environment for database design (called Kheops). Vital embodies four sets of specialised tools. The first set contains tools for the static analysis of active rules (a rule parser, an activation graph builder, and a graphics browser). It allows the user to study the static rule set behaviour (potential cycles for example) using a powerful graph browser. The second set is for rule simulation : it includes an event generator, a breakpoint manager, a trace manager, and a statistics manager. The third set of tools in the VITAL toolbox is a database simulator with DB-operators (insert, delete, update), DB-instances-generator and DB-browser. The fourth set contains tools to evaluate rules : an event captor, conditions evaluator, rules selector, rules enabler/disabler, and an action evaluator. These tools permit the complete management - event catching and testing, condition validation, action execution - of rules. All these toolsets can be used independently of each other or integrated in a global methodology for specification and validation. This toolbox can be used either during the design phase or during the compiling and testing phase. In the latter case, one can replace the simple rule evaluator by the specific rule evaluator of the target active database system.

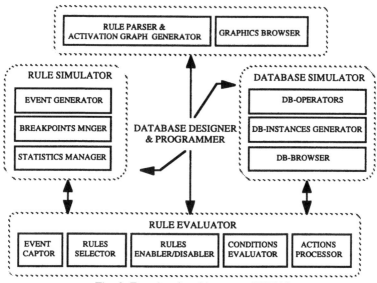

Fig. 2. Functional architecture of VITAL

3.1. Static Analysis Tools

These tools mainly parse rules and generate possible activation graphs showing the interactions between the rules.

(1) Rule Parser & Activation Graph Generator : The main goal of activation graphs {2}, {18}, {1} - is to detect termination problems using a graphical representation. They are also used to show the connectivity of the rules. The designer can thus identify and verify rules that are triggered by external events (due to user actions) and rules that are triggered by internal events (due to system actions). Note that, on the graph, the designer can see a dynamic representation of rule execution by means of a three colours code (green colour for passive rules, orange colour for triggered rules and red colour for executed rules).

(2) Graphics Browser : This tool operates on the graphical representation of the activation graph. It enables complex graphs to be managed more easily. For example, in a large graph, seeing all the potential cycles is not easy - sometimes impossible. One of the activation graph utility is precisely to detect and to show the cycles between rules. The graphics browser can graphically focus to all the cycles in the graph, it can highlight rules acting on specific data or doing specific operation.

3.2. The Rules simulator

The main role of rule simulator is to drive the rule evaluator and to provide feedback to the user. These facilities are introduced in {11} and {13}, and are summarised below:
(i) make explicit the context in which an active rule is fired (the context here is limited to the rule's event and the conflict rule set),
(ii) focus the search during the debugging process,

(iii) automatically detect inconsistencies and potentially conflicting interactions among rules,

(iv) provide an explicit view of the rules effects on data.

All these facilities are included in VITAL. Some of them are enhanced with some high level knowledge in order to obtain a better understanding of the rule set. The following paragraphs summarise the main components of the rule simulator.

Event Generator :

This tool generates external or internal events which may trigger the first rule, and initiates the simulation process. It also provides manual facilities for raising events. This provides the designer with a facility to focus on specific events which may have a specific impact on the system. He can then refine the specification of the event if necessary. Moreover, choosing the initialising event permits several execution graphs to be generated {1} allowing one to consider the confluence problem. Besides the facilities for the refinement process, the event generator supplies primitives for obtaining information on event attributes (names, raising dates, duration, etc.) and to check the event queue (in case the execution of a rule raises several events). Thus the designer may know which events are waiting to be processed and how they were raised (by a rule or by the user). To help identify which rule raises an event, the Event Generator uses a symbolic event name, for each event, which includes the name of the raising rule.

Database States Manager :

This tool keeps track of the database state after each rule execution. The history of database changes are important for observing cyclic states which may correspond to infinite cycles of rules execution. As already shown {2}, deciding whether a cycle of triggering rules is an infinite cycle or not is a complex problem (even undecidable problem in general). This needs a deep knowledge of the rules semantics. So, in a simulation approach, instead of studying infinite cycles of rules, one can detect more easily cyclic states of the database. This requires : (i) memorising states, and (ii) detecting cyclic states. Memorising states poses the problem of disk space, in the case of large rule sets applied on large databases. In the context of simulation and debugging, the database content is generally assumed to be small. Detecting cyclic states poses the problem of recognising similar states, particularly when, potential cycles which produce them are very long. Different alternatives could be used to overcome this problem. One solution is to leave the decision to the user who can visually detect repeating states. This is an easy solution to implement (because it only requires tracing database states) but doesn't provide any aid to the user. An alternative solution is to systematically inspect the database states to detect the existence of repeating states. The major drawback of this solution is its cost, related to the inspection frequency. An intermediate solution is to provide the user with a query language which helps him to check, when appropriate or when he suspects a cycle, whether a state has already occurred. This approach, which has been adopted in Vital, seems a quite good compromise between performance and an effective aid to the user. Finally database states can also be used to analyse rule confluence by validating the results of rule commutation.

Statistics Manager :

This module calculates and records statistics on the behaviour of the rule processor. Some of these statistics can be derived from the static analysis of rules (e.g. number of objects or attributes involved in a rule, number of rules triggered by a given rule, number of rules involved in a given cycle, etc.). Other statistics are obtained from the execution of a set of rules (e.g. number of tuples inserted, deleted or modified during a rule execution cycle, number of times a rule is enabled, number of times a rule is activated, etc.). This aggregated data is also used to identify infinite cycles. For example, given a potential cycle in the activation graph, one can predict the termination of the cycle if the database size manipulated in the cycle tends to decrease in a uniform way. Reciprocally, if the database size tends to increase in a uniform way, the probability of non-termination of the corresponding cycle also increases. Both things are not proofs of termination or non termination but rather strong indications for possible termination or non termination. Obviously, these statistics are significant only if the database is large enough and if the execution steps in a potential cycle are numerous. As an example of a statistic, consider the number of times a rule is executed compared to the number of times a rule is triggered. This statistic can help check the satisfiability percentage of the rules conditions. If, for example, it is close to zero, then there is potentially an error in the rule declaration. This statistic may be made more meaningful by calculating it for a couple (Rule, Event): $Ratio(R,E) = N\_Eff\_Event(R,E) / N\_Trig\_Event (R,E)$ where E is a symbolic event name, R is a rule, $N\_Eff\_Event(R,E)$ is the number of effective executions of R triggered by the occurrence of E, and $N\_Trig\_Event(R,E)$ is the number of times R was triggered by the occurrence of E. This refinement gives an indication of the likelihood that an R1 rule will launch the effective execution of an R2 rule.

Breakpoints Manager.

When simulating a complex set of rules, the designer may want to stop the execution at a particular moment to inspect the system state and the statistics. This 'breakpoint' capability can be enabled by the following six rules:
- Duration : the execution stops after a certain elapsed time.
- Rule iteration number : the execution stops after a certain number of rule executions.
- Event iteration number : the execution stops after a certain number of event raising.
- Database state : the execution stops when a certain database state is encountered.
- Event occurrence : the execution stops after a certain event has been raised.
- Rule : the execution stops before or after the execution of a certain rule.

3.3. The Database Simulator

In the database simulator, we focus on the possibility to generate a complete database instances, to apply usual operators on the data (insert, delete, update) and to query the data through a declarative query language and through browsing facilities. This set of tools supplies the minimal set of facilities a DBMS generally provides. If the toolbox is used during the programming process on a specific DBMS, the database simulator can be replaced by the specific database system.

DB-Instance-Generator :

The necessity to have a database content during the simulation process is obvious. This module helps in generating such a test database. Because the data influences rules behaviour, the choice of relevant data is crucial and difficult : which data is the best to test the rule set ? The relevance of the choice itself is even subjective. Moreover, the only way for the simulator to prove the correctness of a rule set is to use an infinite database which is obviously impossible. The discussion about sufficient and insufficient data test is far from being closed. Our approach recommends simply to define a significant sample of objects at the beginning and to proceed by an incremental approach to generate other objects when necessary. This incremental process could be done by using basic database operators.

DB-Operators :

The set of operators mainly consists of operators to add, delete and update data. These operators allow the modification of the initial testing database content in order to adapt it to a specific rule behaviour. These operators can then be used during the simulation process to insert, delete or modify specific objects which may influence the rule execution process. These operations are activated at breakpoints and their effect can be persistent or not depending on the user's need. A specific interface is provided for each kind of operator.

DB-Browser :

This tool provides the user with navigation facilities to browse through the database. It allows the user to find and visualise some database states, and to possibly modify them with the database operators. The database browser is also a practical way to search for repeating states.

3.4. The Rule Evaluator

The rule evaluator handles the rule execution, i.e. it captures events, selects candidate rules, evaluates conditions and triggers actions. At the programming level, this module can be replaced by the specific rule evaluator of the target DBMS. At the design level, this module includes:

Event Detector : This module captures events raised by rule execution (internal events) or generated by the rule simulator (external events). These events are analysed and possibly queued in order to be combined with others to form complex events.

Rule Selector : This module selects the set of rules concerned with an event. It enables these rules making them candidate rules for execution, if their corresponding conditions are satisfied. Rule priorities are taken into account by this component. The execution graph is also progressively built by this module.

Condition Evaluator : After a rule has been enabled by the rule selector, the rule execution begins by the evaluation of its conditions. If the conditions hold then the rules actions are executed. The condition part of a rule is a first order logic formula defined on the database objects.

Action Evaluator : This module executes the action of the rule if the conditions are satisfied. We consider actions as primitives and assume they correctly terminate. We limit this action part to manipulation actions such as insertion, deletion and modification.

Rule Enabler/Disabler. It might be interesting, during an activation graph analysis to study the effect on the behaviour of the system of removing a rule. This is particularly useful when we want to concentrate only on the execution of certain rule cycles. We can then disable all the rules which have no influence on the cycles termination. This allows the programmer to concentrate on the execution of each cycle.

4. Use of the VITAL Toolbox

In the previous section we defined the components of VITAL. Most of them have already been implemented. The VITAL Toolbox can be used in different ways:
(i) each of its components can be used as an independent tool which can provide facilities to specify rules, construct and layout activation graphs, detect potential cycles, generate a test database, simulate rule execution, etc.
(ii) Several components can be integrated to form a more sophisticated tool which could be used with a specific methodology.

The VITAL toolbox is intended to be used during the design phase (i.e. during the specification phase of the database schema and rules) but some of its components can also be used during the debugging and testing phase (i.e. after the compiling process of rules in a specific DBMS environment). Components of the VITAL toolbox can be modified or replaced by more specific components (e.g. a specific DBMS rule evaluator, a specific rule language syntax, etc.), provided that the standard interface with other modules is respected.

VITAL is a part of a large CASE tool environment, called KHEOPS, devoted to general database design. KHEOPS provides supports for relational database design, object-oriented database design and active database design. It allows to generate a database schema description (including data structures, constraints and rules) from high level specifications, to integrate database schemas and to validate their conformance with respect to a set of quality criteria.

The rule language used in KHEOPS [6] is a high level language which can be used to describe integrity constraints and management rules. At the formal level, integrity constraints and management rules are represented by ECA rules {8}. The general form of this rule language is the following:

```
<rule_specification> ::=
<rule_name> :-   On <event_name>  If <condition>  Then <actions> ;  |
<rule_name> :-   On <event_name>                   Then <actions> ;  |
<rule_name> :-                     If <condition>  Then <actions> ;
```

In the prototype, we limited the event section to one event and the action section to a limited list of actions : insert, delete and update actions. The condition part is any first order logic formula.

For the sake of clarity we are going to take a simple example to show how VITAL can work. This example implements, in a relational database, the statement: "*Anybody who kills someone else must stand trial, be sentenced to death and then put to death*". So we have the following tables implementing this real world :

```
PERSON(IdPerson, ..., State)
EXECUTIONER(IdExecutioner, IdExecuted)
CONDEMNED(IdCondemned)
```

The first relation contains the people and their states. The tuples we are interested in are those where the state is 'killer'. The second relation contains the chosen executioner for a person. The third relation contains the condemned people that must be put to death. The associated rules are:

```
Sentence_of_death :-
    ON modify(PERSON) {p/PERSON}{c/CONDEMNED}
    IF p.State='killer'
    THEN insert(c/IdCondemned:=p.IdPerson) and delete(p);

Put_to_death :-
    ON insert(CONDEMNED) {c/CONDEMNED}
    [p/PERSON][e/EXECUTIONER]
    IF e.IdExecutioner = c.IdCondemned
                    and e.IdExecutioner = p.IdPerson
    THEN delete(c) and update(p.State:='killer');
```

The first rule finds people who are killers, inserts them in the Condemned relation and deletes them from the Person relation. The second rule deletes the people sentenced to death in the Condemned relation and puts the executioner status to "killer" in the Person relation.

When we start the simulator, the main menu is displayed (Figure 3).

Fig. 3. Main Menu Bar

The designer can open any of the windows indicated on this menu. Selecting the Source window shows the rules studied. The activation graph (Figure 4). reveals a potential cycle between rules *Sentence_to_death* and *Put_to_death*

In the browse window (Figure 5), the tuples of relations which have been declared for automatic browsing are displayed. As we can see, the step number of the execution is written, followed by the executed rule name, the operation done on the database and its results. In our example, all the relations are declared for automatic browse.

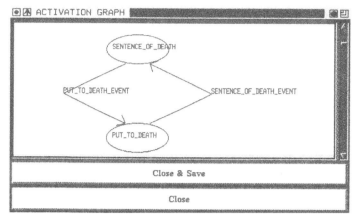

Fig. 4. Activation Graph Window

```
Step [6] : Rule 'sentence_of_death' , insert 'condemned'
     OID              | idcondemned   |
     4                | 4             |

Step [6] : Rule 'sentence_of_death' , delete 'person'
     OID              | idperson      | statu        |
     4                | 4             | killer       |

Step [7] : Rule 'put_to_death' , modifier 'person'
     OID              | idperson      | statu        |
     5                | 5             |              |

Step [7] : Rule 'put_to_death' , modifier 'person'
     OID              | idperson      | statu        |
```

| Browse | Add | Delete | Modify | Close |

Fig. 5. The Browse window

Finally, the Debug window (Figure 6) allows simulation control and displays abstracted results. During rule execution, the raised event and the rule which raises it are given. Consequences of this event raising are shown (step number execution, activated rule, if condition when verified, operations performed on data). The Debug window is connected to the Browse window through the step number. Both windows should be used simultaneously.

We must not forget that rule execution is also visible on the activation graph, offering an easy way to visualise rule behaviour. Colours of events and rules change progressively: (i) for rules: green when inactive, orange when active, red when executed ; and (ii) for events : green when not raised, orange otherwise. Contrary to the other rule debuggers or simulators which build trees following the execution, we decided to adopt this solution. The history of the execution can be analysed simply, thanks to the Debug window, or more precisely by adding the use of others windows.

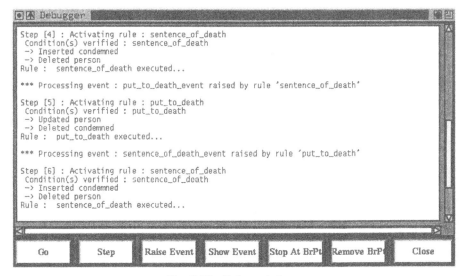

Fig. 6. The Debug window

5. Concluding Remarks

This paper has presented a pragmatic approach to static and dynamic analysis of active rules. Problems such as logical coherence, termination and confluence can be addressed using a set of tools ranging from visualisation tools to simulation of rule execution. This toolbox approach is an alternative to the theoretical approach which seems too complex for simple cases and not sophisticated enough for complex cases. However, the toolbox approach doesn't provide a formal proof for hard problem such as termination and confluence, but rather a design aid which leaves the designer free to make the final decision. The main features of our toolbox mix representation tools (e.g. activation and execution graphs) used in formal approaches, with simulation tools, and also integrate with the simulation tools, statistical information on rule behaviour. This provides a powerful decision support system which can contribute to the global quality of an active database specification.

Most of the components of the Vital toolbox are implemented, except the database state manager which is still under specification. We have focused on the modularity of our toolbox, which allows it to work with different rule syntaxes and rule evaluators. This makes the toolbox usable during the design phase, independently of any active database system, and during the debugging phase by replacing the rule syntax and the rule evaluator by those of the target DBMS.

The statistics generated can be used by the database administrator during the maintenance process to understand or interpret some misfunctioning of the rule processor. However these statistics heavily depend on the database volume, on the choice of the initial test data, and on the multiple executions of the rule processor.

Acknowledgement

We would like to thank Marc Gould for his help in making more English this paper.

References

{1}   A. Aiken, J. Widom, and J. M. Hellerstein. "Static Analysis Techniques for Predicting the Behavior of Active Database Rules".

{2}   A. Aiken, J. Widom, and J. M. Hellerstein. "behavior of Database Production Rules: Termination, Confluence, and Observable Determinism", in Proceeding of the ACM SIGMOD International Conference of Management of Data, pages 59-68, San Diego, California, June 1992..

{3}   E. Baralis, S. Ceri, and J. Widom. "Better Termination Analysis for Active Databases", in Proceedings 1st Int'l Workshop on Rules in Database Systems, pages 163-179, 1993.

{4}   H. Behrends. "Simulation-based Debugging of Active Databases", in fourth Workshop on Research issues in Data Engineering (RIDE-ADS'94), 1994.

{5}   M. Bouzeghoub, G. Gardarin, P. Valduriez. In "Objets: Du C++ à Merise Objet", Editions Eyrolles, Paris 1994.

{6}   M. Bouzeghoub, E.Métais. "Semantic Modeling of Object Oriented Databases", in Proceedings of the 17th VLDB Conference, Barcelona, Spain, 1991.

{7}   E. Baralis, J. Widom. "An algebraic Approach to Rule Analysis in Expert Database Systems", in Proceedings of the 20th VLDB Conference, Santiago, Chile, 1994.

{8}   U. Dayal & al, "The HiPAC Project : Combining Active Databases and Timing Constraints", SIGMOD Record, Vol.17, No.1, 1988

{9}   Oscar Diaz, Arturo Jaime, Norman W. Paton, Ghassan al-Qaimairi. "Supporting Dynamic Displays Using Active Rules", SIGMOD RECORD volume 23, No. 1, March 94.

{10}   O. Diaz, A. Jaime, "EXACT : an EXtensible approach to ACTive object oriented databases", 1993.

{11}   O. Diaz, A. Jaime, N. W. Paton. "DEAR : a DEbugger for Active Rules in an object oriented context", in Rules in Database Systems, pages 180-193, Springer-Verlag, 1993.

{12}   O. Diaz, N. Paton and P. Gray "Rule Management in Object Oriented Databases: A Uniform Approach", in Proc. of the 17th International Conference on VLDB, pages 317-326, Barcelona, Spain, Sept. 1991.

{13}   T. Fors, "ADELA: Animated Debugging and Explanation Of Active Database Rules", M.Sc. dissertation, Department of Computer Science, University of Skovde, Sweden, 1994.

{14}   A. P. Karadimce, and S. D. Urban. "Conditional Term Rewriting as a Formal Basis for Analysis of Active Database Rules", in fourth Workshop on Research issues in Data Engineering (RIDE-ADS'94), 1994.

{15}   B. Schneideman, "Designing the User Interface, Strategies for Effective Human-Computer Interaction", Addison Wesley Publishing Company, 1987

{16}   J. D. Ullman. Principles of Databases and Knowledge Base Systems, Volumes I-II Computer Science Press, Potomac, MD, 1988.

{17}   L. van der Voort and A. Siebes. "Termination and confluence of rule execution", in proceedings 2nd Int'l Conf. on Information and Knowledge Management, November 1993.

{18}   S. Ceri, J Widom. "Deriving production rules for constraint maintenance", in proceedings of the 16th VLDB conference Brisbane, Australia 1990.

A Visualization and Explanation Tool for Debugging ECA Rules in Active Databases *

S. Chakravarthy   Z. Tamizuddin   J. Zhou

Database Systems Research and Development Center
Computer and Information Science and Engineering Department
University of Florida, Gainesville, FL 32611
email: sharma@cis.ufl.edu

Abstract. Using ECA rules in active database systems for real-life applications involves implementing, debugging, and maintaining large numbers of rules. Experience in developing large production rule systems has amply demonstrated the need for understanding the behavior of rules especially when their execution is non-deterministic. Availability of rules in active database systems and their semantics creates additional complexity for both modeling and verifying the correctness of such systems. As part of Sentinel – an Object-Oriented Active DBMS, we have developed a visualization tool to help understand the behavior of rules defined as part of an active database application. This is especially important in active databases as rules are invoked (as a side effect) based on event occurrences (both primitive and composite) and are executed concurrently based on user-provided priority information. In this paper, we describe the rationale for the development of the tool, how it has been implemented exploiting the architecture of Sentinel, functionality of the resulting tool, and show several screen dumps to provide a feel for the information presented by the visualization tool.

1   Introduction

Using ECA rules in active database systems for real-life applications involves implementing, debugging, and maintaining large numbers of rules. Experience in developing large production rule systems has amply demonstrated the need for understanding the behavior of rules especially when their execution is non-deterministic. Availability of rules in active database systems and their semantics creates additional complexity for both modeling and verifying the correctness of such systems.

For the effective deployment of active database systems, there is a clear need for providing a debugging and explanation facility to understand the interaction – among rules, between rules and events, and between rules and database objects.

* This work is supported by the Office of Naval Research and the Navy Command, Control and Ocean Surveillance Center RDT&E Division, and by the Rome Laboratory.

Due to the event-based nature of active database systems, special attention has to be paid for making the context of rule execution explicit [DJP93]. Unlike an imperative programming environment, rules are triggered in the context of the transaction execution and hence both the order and the rules triggered vary from one transaction/application to another. Use of the nested transaction model for rule execution in Sentinel [Bad93, Tam94] provides such a context. Our graphics visualization tool (which uses Motif) displays transaction and rule execution by using directed graphs to indicate both the context (i.e., transactions/composite events) and the execution of (cascading) rules. The same mechanism will be used for run-time as well as post-execution visualization of event definition, detection, and rule execution. In both modes, we provide interactive facilities (e.g., click on a rule to display the objects used, chain of rules it is part of, rules that it has signaled) for obtaining a detailed understanding of rule execution.

The model of the traditional debuggers (of conventional programming languages) is not adequate for debugging rules in active database systems. The emphasis in traditional debuggers is on low level details such as program variables, subroutines, pointer referencing/dereferencing. The rationale behind the rule debugger is to help understand the interaction – among rules, between rules and events as well as between rules and the database objects (including the objects held by a transaction/subtransaction). This is in contrast with the conventional debugging of programs. The interaction among rules refers to such details as nested triggering of rules, the events which cause the rule to fire or the context in which the rules are fired. The rules also affect the state of the database by way of modifying database objects and as a consequence acquiring locks. The rule debugger shows the rule-database interaction in terms of the locks acquired/released and the transactions in which the rules fire. The debugger is not meant to replace a conventional debugging tool (e.g., xdb), but to provide a tool at a higher level of abstraction to cater to ECA rule design, implementation, testing, and debugging.

The rest of the paper is structured as follows. Section 2 discusses the Sentinel architecture to briefly describe rule execution context and the functional modules introduced to make Open OODB active. Section 3 elaborates on the design of the visualization and explanation tool. Section 4 describes the implementation aspects. In section 5 we show several screen dumps produced by the tool at different stages of a sample application execution. Section 6 contains conclusions.

2 Sentinel Architecture

In this section, we briefly discuss the overall architecture of Sentinel [CM94, AMC93, Bad93, CKAK94, CKTB95, Tam94] and its functional modules. The Sentinel architecture shown in Figure 1 extends the passive Open OODB system [WBT92, Ins93]. The Open OODB toolkit uses Exodus as the storage manager and supports persistence of C++ objects. Concurrency control and recovery for the top level transactions are provided by the Exodus storage manager. Nested transactions are supported in the client address space and a separate lock table is maintained by Sentinel. This essentially gives a two level transaction management (top level transaction concurrency is provided by Exodus at the server and the nested transaction concurrency is provided by Sentinel for each client). There is no recovery at the nested subtransaction level. The Sentinel architecture allows the execution of subtransactions that are *not* necessarily rules. A full C++ pre-processor is used for extending the user class definitions as well as application code. To make Open OODB active, the following extensions were made.

- ECA rules can be incorporated either as part of the class definition or as part of the application code. This allows the specification of class level and instance level definition of rules and events. Additional (Open OODB has its own pre-processor) Sentinel pre-processors were written to preprocess and translate the event and rule definitions into appropriate C++ code for event detection and rule execution.
- Detection of primitive events [CKAK94] was incorporated by adding Notify (a method call to the event detector class) into the wrapper method of the Open OODB. The wrapper method permits us to invoke a notification when an event occurs and conveys it to the composite event detector.

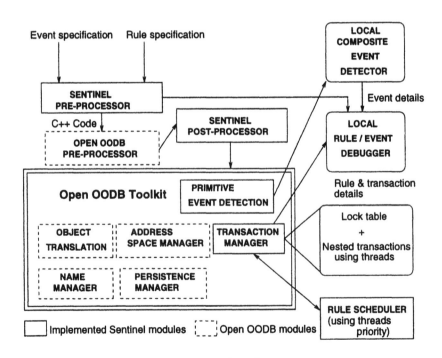

Fig. 1. Sentinel Architecture

- To detect composite events a composite event detector [CM94, CKAK94] has been implemented. Each Open OODB application has a composite event detector. The event detector is implemented as a class and we have a single instance of this class per application. This is shown in Figure 1 as the local composite event detector. Also there is a clean separation between event detection and application execution.
- To support rule execution, we have extended the skeletal transaction manager of the Open OODB to a full-fledged transaction manager supporting the nested transaction model. The design of this transaction manager was described in [Bad93] and implemented on a previous version of Open OODB (Zeitgeist). The nested transaction manager has been redesigned and implemented for Sentinel [Tam94]. It is beyond the scope of this paper to describe the implementation of the nested transaction manager.
- As shown in the Sentinel architecture we have designed and implemented a Rule visualization/debugger module to provide feedback about event detection and rule execution. We discuss the design and implementation of the visualization tool in the next section.

3   Design of the Visualization and Explanation Tool

In a conventional imperative program debugging environment, the factors considered are variables, subroutine calls, exceptions (stack overflows), pointer referencing/dereferencing etc. The user knows the context in which to debug the program. For example, the instructions of a program are executed in a fixed sequence given by the programmer. If there is an error such as an overflow, nonexistent pointer dereferencing etc, then the program fails and with the help of the debugger the user can locate where the error has occurred. The debugger aids the user in this process by furnishing low-level details, such as the line number of the program where the error occurred, variables accessed.

When we consider debugging in the context of an active database system, we need to take into account several factors:

- **Database component:** The database operations are performed on database objects. The database operations are carried out in well defined atomic units called transactions. In order to ensure atomicity and the correctness of the operations, locking is used according to the concurrency control mechanism used. Hence to get a complete picture of what is happening in a database system we need to take into account transactions, database objects and locks held (especially when there are concurrent transactions).
- **Rule and event interaction:** The active functionality of a database management system adds another dimension to the process of debugging. We have to consider the interactions among rules, between rules and events and between rules and database objects. When event(s) are raised appropriate rule(s) are triggered. A rule may raise an event which may cause some other

rule to fire. Hence we may have a nested execution of rules. An event may trigger several rules simultaneously. The rule and database objects interaction is in terms of locks acquired/released on objects in the process of rule execution.

We used the following rationale for obtaining the features of a rule debugger for an active object-oriented database management system:

- The rule debugger should concentrate on the high level details such as rule-event interaction, interaction among rules, and interaction of rules with database objects, rather than the low-level details typically provided in a programming environment.
- The debugger should show the execution of rules graphically preserving the triggering order, current status, and other relevant details. This is particularly useful when there is a nested execution of rules.
- In addition to the rule trace, the context (i.e., the events raised, whether the event was raised from within a rule or the top level transaction) should be shown.
- The debugger should allow the user to monitor specific rules/events of interest. This is useful in applications having a large number of rules.
- Finally, it should be possible to visualize application execution either at run-time or after the execution of an application for the analysis of rule execution. This should be accomplished without having to change either the architecture of Sentinel or the visualization tool.

The architecture for the visualization tool is dictated by the architecture for event detection in Sentinel. The functional architecture of the Visualization tool is as shown in the Figure 2.

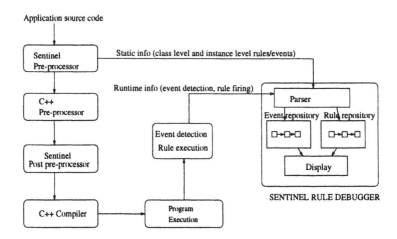

Fig. 2. Functional Modules

As illustrated in Figure 1, the visualization tool communicates with the local event detector and the rule manager of each application. Since the local event detector detects the occurrence of an event and notifies the appropriate rule to be fired and is aware of the event object and the rule object ids, the runtime information about the event occurrence and rule execution is obtained from the local event detector. From the rule manager we get the transaction ids of the subtransactions within which the rules are executed.

We have designed and implemented the visualization tool to monitor rules and events within an application. We have adopted a *problem oriented* and *coupled approach* to debugging. Since we have adopted a coupled approach, the debugger and the active database system need to communicate. The way communication is achieved *for post-execution debugging* is via log files. The log files contain information regarding rule/event definitions, rule/event object id's, the actual occurrence and firings of events and rules, respectively, and other transaction related information. From the rule/event definition we can infer which rule subscribes to which event and hence rule-event interactions. The transaction related information gives the rule-database interactions. The information in the log files is obtained by the pre-processor, event detector, and the rule manager. The visualization tool then reads these files to obtain the trace of event occurrences and rule execution. It is important to note that, currently, there is no runtime visualization done by the visualization tool. We say that runtime visualization is achieved when the visualization tool shows the occurrence of events and rule firings as and when they happen. If this were to be achieved then the communication between the visualization tool and the database system has to be done in real-time using sockets or named pipes. However, currently the visualization tool gathers information from the log files already created by the application execution and simulates runtime visualization. It makes only a single pass on the log files to obtain the relevant information and build in-memory data structures used by the visualization tool.

The input to the debugger consists of:

− The class level and the instance level rule and event definitions: This information is supplied by the user in the application program using the event [CM94] and rule definition [CKAK94] language. Since we have incorporated the event and rule definition language as extensions of C++ language, we preprocess the definitions. During this process, the preprocessor gathers this static information in the form of a file to the visualization tool.
− The event detection information: This is the runtime information obtained on the occurrence of events and the creation of event objects. This information is obtained at two points in the execution of the application program. First, when the event objects are created, the event name and the event object oid is given to the rule debugger. This information is used later by the rule debugger to associate the event object oids with their user supplied names. As mentioned previously the object id information is particularly useful in the case of composite events. Finally when the event is actually raised it is

notified to the rule debugger by the event detector.

- Finally, the rule firing information is furnished to the visualization tool in the same way as the event detection information. The rule object identifiers and the user supplied rule names are associated when the rule objects are created. In addition to the rule firing information, the transaction in which rules where fired, the locks acquired/released on database objects are also furnished. This helps the rule debugger to associate the rules in the transactions in which they were fired and also the objects which were accessed in the process of rule execution.

All the information mentioned above is furnished to the visualization tool in the form of two files. One of the files contains the static information on class and instance level events and rules. The second file contains the runtime information on event and rule object oids, the occurrence and firing of rules and the transaction and object access information.

4 Implementation of the Visualization Tool

We have implemented a visualization tool for active DBMS in an object-oriented context. The rule manager supports the event-condition-action paradigm as mentioned before. Apart from tracing the execution of rules, the visualization tool also keeps track of the events (both primitive and composite). As mentioned in [DJP93], the tracing of events gives important hints to the user. The event-rule cycle allows the user to not only to know which rules are fired but also which event(s) caused the rule(s) to fire. The occurrence of the events sets the context for the rule execution.

As mentioned earlier the input to the visualization tool is in the form of two files. One of the files furnishes static information in terms of the definition of events and rules, which rule subscribes to which event. This file is in fact generated by the preprocessor of Sentinel. The second file is generated at runtime and it furnishes information regarding event occurrences and rule execution. The first part of this file contains event object names with their object ids and rule objects and rule ids. This information is generated when the event and rule objects are created at runtime.

The visualization tool parser reads the static information and stores the event and rule information in the event repository and rule repository respectively. The event and the rule repositories are linked list structures. With the help of this static information the user can see structure of an event/rule, which rule has subscribed to which event, individual instance and class level rules. The rule debugger requires the following information with respect to an event: name, classname with which the event is associated if it is a class level event, type (primitive or composite), signature of the method on which the event is defined along with the event modifier whether it is raised before or after the invocation of the method and event expression if it is composite. The rule debugger requires the following information with respect to a rule: name, classname if it is class level, signature of the methods implementing the condition and action, context for which the rule is fired, coupling mode, trigger mode and priority.

The visualization tool takes in the above static and runtime information and parses it, then creates two tree-like data structures for events and transactions. In the event tree, primitive events are leaf nodes and composite events are seen as parent nodes of their components. The event tree grows from primitive events to the root, which is a composite event. The data structure which captures the nested execution of rules is an n-ary tree. The root node represents the top-level transaction of the application. When this transaction triggers a rule and since rules are executed as subtransactions, the child node of the top-level transaction represents the rule fired. This node in turn could trigger another rule and it is represented as the child node (subtransaction) and so on. The transaction tree grows in a top-down way: it starts from the top-level transaction and spans to the descendents. Presently the transaction tree nodes represent only rules. The events which cause these rules to fire are shown in a separate tree and are linked to the transaction nodes to indicate the firing of a rule by an event (primitive or composite).

5 Functionality of the Tool

The visualization tool's interface and functionality has been designed to provide as much information as possible in an uncluttered manner. Some information (e.g., event and rule detection and execution) is provided as part of the visualization whereas other information (e.g., objects held by a rule/subtransaction) is provided on a demand basis.

The user interface window consists of the following parts:

1. Predefined event information. All events defined in an application are arranged as a list inside a scrolled window. When an item is chosen by a mouse click, a dialog window pops up showing event type, name, method and when for primitive events and description of component events for composite events.
2. All predefined rules and their details including name, condition, action, priority, coupling mode, context, associated event are arranged in scrolled window in the same way as event information pane.
3. A group of push buttons provide various functions supported by the tool.
   HELP: on-line help.
   TRACE: run trace of rule execution.
   SELECT/ADD: select a subset of rules to monitor.
   CLEAR SELECT: delete the selection of rule subset.
   CONTMODE: select the continuous tracing mode.
   STEPMODE: select the step tracing mode.
   CLEAR GRAPH: clear the drawing-area windows.
   QUIT: exit from the program.

4. Event/rule visualization window. During a trace, the upper half of this drawing-area window shows the event tree, with leaf nodes (primitive events) on the top. Composite events link with their component nodes through straight lines. Initially, since no event has been detected/raised, all nodes are in the color of grey.

   The lower half of the drawing-area displays rule execution tree, which demonstrates the nested nature of transactions. Each node stands for a subtransaction. Different colors are used for the three states of subtransactions: green for running, yellow for suspended and red for committed. Whenever a rule is fired a line connecting the transaction node of current rule and the triggering event is shown, and the color of the triggering event is changed to brown. The program can detect the type of display device automatically and use appropriate colors to represent different states of subtransactions. When monochrome display is used, an empty box drawn with dashed lines would represent a suspended subtransaction node, while a box with solid lines stands for a running node and a box filled in black corresponds to a committed subtransaction. This is demonstrated in the screen dumps at the end of this paper.

5. Execution console window. A drawing-area (extreme right) displaying execution information in plain text. The information includes all transaction/subtransactions with their ID, events that are raised and rules that are fired. This window records the event detection, subtransaction and rule firing sequence. This window can be scrolled to look the textual trace of execution. Colors differentiate various items displayed to make it more readable.

6   Visualization Using the Tool

The tool currently works as a post-execution visualization tool. In other words, after the execution of the application (successfully or otherwise), this tool can be invoked for observing the execution of rules, transactions, and subtransactions. The tool uses the information collected both at the pre-processing of the application and the actual execution of the application to graphically display primitive events, composite events, their detection, rules, and their execution as sub-transactions. Additional information on applications objects (e.g., events, rules, and database objects) can be obtained by an explicit action by the user. Below, we show a sequence of displays (or screen dumps) highlighting on the information provided to the user.

Figure 3 shows the output of a step-mode trace before any event is raised. It shows a display consisting of all the primitive and composite events specified (the event graph with event expressions shown graphically) in the application. In the event graph, there are 4 primitive events and 2 complex events. Lines connecting events show the composition of a composite event. It also shows that

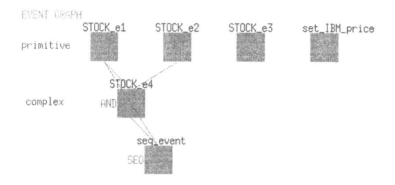

Fig. 3. Starting display of the Visualization Tool

a top level transaction 1 and a subtransaction (not a rule) 100 has started. The colors of the event nodes indicate that no event has been detected.

Figure 4 shows the state of the same application when event stock_e4 is raised and rule R1 is triggered. It also shows the dialog when button R1 (for the rule R1 that has been fired) is pressed. The text pane contains a description on the triggered rule.

Figure 5 shows the display after the trace is completed. In the event graph, nodes that are shown in black represent events that were raised during the trace. In the rule graph all transaction nodes are filled in black because they are all committed. Lines connecting pairs of event/rule nodes indicate the relationship between triggering events and fired rules.

The above displays have been drawn from a simple stock market application consisting of a few events (both primitive and composite), rules, and subtransactions for exercising the functionality of the visualization tool.

7 Conclusions

In this paper, we have presented an overall architecture of a visualization tool especially tuned for the requirements of an active database system. We have also detailed the design and implementation of the visualization tool. The debugger currently supports visualization of rules as post-execution analysis. We have adopted an problem oriented approach to debugging of rules. In addition to merely showing the trace of rules the debugger also furnishes the context-(events) in which the rules are fired. Additional information on most of the objects of interest (event, rule, transaction) can be obtained by the user.

Currently the visualization tool supports only post-execution analysis of rule execution. Our next step is to support runtime visualization as well. We also plan on incorporating static analysis tools as part of the visualization toolkit

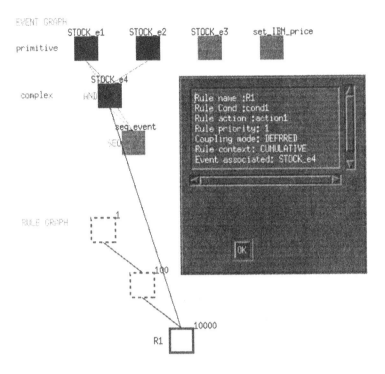

Fig. 4. Display of the Visualization Tool after Stock_e4 is raised

so that runtime execution can be compared with static analysis. Both static analyzers for checking the termination, confluence, and observable determinism characteristics [AWH92] and debuggers (or visualization tool) for observing the run time behavior are extremely useful. In addition to rule execution, the composite event detection in various parameter contexts will also require feedback for ascertaining the correctness of parameter context used. Ideally (i.e., for the long term), it would be useful to have a visualization tool to which you can *specify* your expected behavior and the tool provides a visual feedback on how the actual execution differs from the specification and offers guidance for correction.

Thus far we have seen that all rules and events produced are shown by the visualization tool. This can become quite inconvenient for the user if he/she is dealing with large number of rules. Potentially we can identify two ways of pruning the tree: the user can either choose the rules or events he wants to monitor. This is possible in our case since events and rules are objects and more over there is a one to one correspondence between rules and transactions. When the tree is pruned in this way the child node may not be an immediate subtransaction of the parent node, but rather a descendant of the parent transaction.

Interactive debugging is another feature that we plan on adding in the next version. The user should be able to selectively enable and disable a subset of

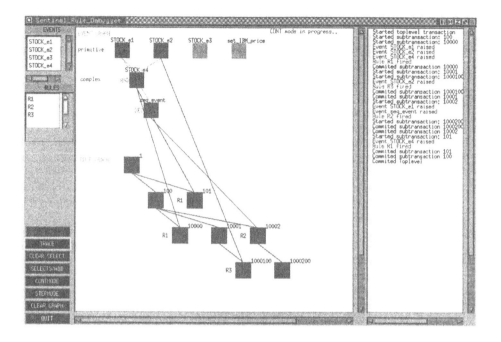

Fig. 5. Display after rule execution finishes

events and rules for debugging purposes (in the run time debugging mode). This entails some changes to the Sentinel architecture to be able to stop and take into account user requests at run time.

Visualization tool is a first step towards the use of reactive capability for simulation applications. In simulation applications, the mechanism used typically for debugging is itself the front-end (or user interface). The availability of customizable visualization tool will help use the system for simulation applications, such as threat analysis, slow-motion execution of various situations.

References

[AMC93] E. Anwar, L. Maugis, and S. Chakravarthy. A New Perspective on Rule Support for Object-Oriented Databases. In *Proceedings, International Conference on Management of Data*, pages 99–108, Washington, D.C., May 1993.

[AWH92] A. Aiken, J. Widom, and J. M. Hellerstein. Behavior of Database Production Rules: Termination, Confluence, and Observable Determinism. In *Proceedings, International Conference on Management of Data*, pages 59–68, May 1992.

[Bad93] R. Badani. Nested Transactions for Concurrent Execution of Rules: Design and Implementation. Master's thesis, Database Systems R&D Center, CIS Department, University of Florida, Gainesville, FL 32611, October 1993.

[Cha91]   S. Chakravarthy. Active Database Management Systems: Requirements, State-Of-The-Art, and an Evaluation. In H. Kangassalo, editor, *Entity-Relationship Approach: The Core of Conceptual Modeling*, pages 461–473. Elsevier Science Publishers, North-Holland, 1991.

[CKAK94] S. Chakravarthy, V. Krishnaprasad, E. Anwar, and S.-K. Kim. Composite Events for Active Databases: Semantics, Contexts, and Detection. In *Proceedings, International Conference on Very Large Data Bases*, pages 606–617, August 1994.

[CKTB95] S. Chakravarthy, V. Krishnaprasad, Z. Tamizuddin, and R. Badani. ECA Rule Integration into an OODBMS: Architecture and Implementation. In *Proceedings, International Conference on Data Engineering*, Feb. 1995.

[CM94]   S. Chakravarthy and D. Mishra. Snoop: An Expressive Event Specification Language for Active Databases. *Data and Knowledge Engineering*, 14(10):1–26, October 1994.

[DJP93]   O. Diaz, A. Jaime, and N. W. Paton. Dear: A debugger for active rules in an object-oriented context. In *Proc. of the 1st International Conference on Rules in Database Systems*, September 1993.

[Ins93]   Texas Instruments. Open OODB Toolkit, Release 0.2 (Alpha) Document, September 1993.

[Tam94]   Z. Tamizuddin. Rule Execution and Visualization in Active OODBMS. Master's thesis, Database Systems R&D Center, CIS Department, University of Florida, Gainesville, FL 32611, May 1994.

[WBT92]   D. Wells, J. A. Blakeley, and C. W. Thompson. Architecture of an Open Object-Oriented Database Management System. *IEEE Computer*, 25(10):74–81, October 1992.

Deductive Databases

Strategies for Parallel Linear Recursive Query Processing

Thomas Zurek[1] and Peter Thanisch[1]

Department of Computer Science, Edinburgh University, United Kingdom

Abstract. Query optimization for sequential execution of non-recursive queries has reached a high level of sophistication in commercial DBMS. The successful application of *parallel* processing for the evaluation of *recursive* queries will require a query optimizer of comparable sophistication. The groundwork for creating this new breed of query optimizer will consist of a combination of theoretical insight and empirical investigation. Restricting our attention to *linear* recursive queries, we illustrate this process by developing a family of query processing strategies and, through experiments on a parallel computer, obtaining the basic information needed for an optimizer's heuristics.

1 Introduction

Two trends in database technology, namely parallel computing and the introduction of recursion into query languages, have made the task of query optimization much harder. Parallel computing has added an extra dimension to the optimization problem because the optimizer may have to decide on the computational resources to be allocated to each database operation and it may also have to decide on which *sets* of operations may be executed concurrently.

There are good theoretical and practical grounds for believing that recursive queries may be harder to optimize. Intuitively, a non-recursive SQL-query can be represented, for optimization purposes, as an algebraic expression with a fixed number of join operations, whereas a recursive query may, in general, require a data dependent number of join operations and/or additional operations, such as transitive closures, which may be even more computationally expensive than join operations.

Much research has been published on the subjects of exploiting parallel computing in query processing, e.g. in [11], [3], [21], and techniques and operators for recursive query processing, e.g. in [2], [9], [10], [15], [16], [17],[20], [23] and many others. Furthermore some research has also examined the application of parallel computing to recursive query processing [7].

In order to bring this work into the mainstream of commercial DBMS query processing, it is necessary to develop an appropriate query optimizer. The difficulty of this class of optimization problem means that such an optimizer is

---

[0] Part of this research was sponsored by TRACS, an EC-funded project at EPCC, Edinburgh.

likely to be driven by heuristics. The parameters for such heuristics may have to be obtained from observing the performance of the algorithmic technique on the target parallel computer. We illustrate this process in the case of *linear* recursive queries.

After some outlining comments about linear recursion – probably the most common class of recursion in queries [5] [10] [23] – section 2 concludes with an example of a linear recursive query which is sufficiently general to show the basic properties of two processing techniques, namely *bottom-up evaluation* (section 3) and *transitive closure evaluation* (section 4).

The transitive closure evaluation is a parallelization of the technique presented by Jagadish *et. al.* in [10]. Both techniques are subsumed in the generation matrix model of section 5 which defines a 'gameboard' allowing several simple operations to move over the board i.e. to process a query. The model provides a framework for analyzing processing strategies and for involving several efficiency issues such as parallelism and optimization features. The cost model presented in section 6 identifies the most important parameters that affect query processing performance or, in terms of the model, the costs of a move. In section 7 we give performance results obtained from an experimental implementation on a Connection Machine CM-200. Results are given for varying over three parameters:

- the length of the longest path in the underlying database relation (section 7.1),
- the number of transitive closures to be computed (section 7.2) and
- the data skew in the source and destination attributes (section 7.3).

Finally the paper is concluded in section 8.

2 Linear Recursion

In this paper, we are concerned with queries to relational databases where the user wants to interpret some of the data as a graph structure. In its simplest form, there will be a pair of columns in a table in which the entries are interpreted as the names of graph vertices and, for each tuple in the table, the sub-tuple corresponding to this pair of columns represents an arc in the graph.

Suppose that we have a table, *Flights*, with four columns, *Airline*, *Flight*, *From* and *To*. Suppose that we want to know if it is possible to travel between two particular cities. Consider the following query[1]:

---

[1] These are *Datalog equations* [18]. Throughout this paper we rather prefer describing the queries by using relational algebra operators to make the reader aware of the operations that are involved in query processing although the resulting expressions are in 'Datalog style', i.e. we use Datalog-like notations like $P(X, Y, Z)$ and refer to attributes in the relation P by variables X, Y, Z. This also simplifies the notation of a join as the join conditions can be easily derived by matching the variables. Therefore we just denote a join by $\bowtie$ without giving the conditions explicitly. This notation is a hybrid of relational algebra and logic programming notation.

Using relational algebra expressions suggests that the techniques proposed in this paper can be applied to a wide range of query languages and not only to Datalog.

Example 1. Accessibility.

$$C(X, Z) = Flights(A, F, X, Z).$$
$$C(X, Z) = C(X, Y) \bowtie Flights(A, F, Y, Z).$$

This program is a representation of a simple graph connectivity problem which may be computed by a transitive closure operation. A well-known observation is that such a computation cannot be represented by an algebraic expression in which the operators are drawn from the traditional repertoire of relational algebra [4]. Of course, this observation is only important if one needs to manipulate algebraic expressions. A transitive closure computation could be performed by repeated joins, although the number of such join operations would be data-dependent.

Suppose that an awkward customer insists that for each flight in his/her journey, the airline must be the same, but it does not matter which airline is used. The following Datalog program provides the answer to this version of the accessibility problem.

Example 2. Accessibility by the Same Airline.

$$CA(A, X, Z) = Flights(A, F, X, Z).$$
$$CA(A, X, Z) = CA(A, X, Y) \bowtie Flights(A, F, Y, Z).$$

The Datalog program in example 2 can also be computed using a transitive closure operator. However, this process is not as straightforward as in example 1. We have a choice between (1) executing one transitive closure operation for each airline and (2) constructing a much larger graph in which the names of the vertices are formed from a pair (A, X), where A is the name of an airline and X is the name of a city.

If we give a logic programming style of representation to our queries, then we can say that a query is *linear recursive* if there is at most one subgoal of any rule that is mutually recursive with the head. Several authors have noted that linear recursive queries may be evaluated efficiently by using special-purpose evaluation techniques that cannot be applied to the more general class of recursive queries. Several such techniques are discussed in Ullman [19].

Not all queries can be expressed as linear recursive queries. The reader might refer to Afrati and Cosmadakis [1] for examples of queries that cannot be computed by any linear recursive Datalog program.

In this paper, we parallelize the strategy outlined in Jagadish *et al.* [10] for using it in a parallel computing environment. This enables us to avoid the large graph structure described by Ullman [19], replacing it with a collection of smaller transitive closure operations which may be computed in parallel.

Consider the linear recursive query in example 3, below. Sections 3 and 4 will then present two strategies for evaluating this query. Although such an example cannot claim to cover every aspect of query processing we rather prefer this way to give the reader the basic ideas behind the processing model that is presented in section 5 of the paper. Apart from that we can claim that the following example is sufficiently general to emphasize the important issues of linear recursive query processing as the linear recursive rule is in, what Jagadish *et al.* call, the *canonical form for transitive closure*. *Every* linear recursive rule can be transformed into this form. This form is essential for applying the transitive closure technique of section 4 but it is *not* necessary for the naive bottom-up evaluation presented in section 3.

Example 3.

$$P(X_1, X_2, Z) = E(X_1, X_2, Z). \tag{1}$$
$$P(X_1, X_2, Z) = P(X_1, X_2, Y) \bowtie Q(X_1, Y, Z). \tag{2}$$

We will refer to (1) as the *exit rule* or *exit equation* and to (2) as the *linear recursive rule/equation* of the query. For our purposes we can assume X_1, X_2, Y, Z to be single arguments but there is no problem to consider them as lists or ordered sets[2] of arguments.

3 Bottom-Up Evaluation

As is well known, a linear recursive query may be evaluated 'bottom-up', i.e. starting with the initial relation given by the exit rule further tuples are added by applying the linear recursive rule until no more new tuples are added. We will describe this process using the example 3.

For the purpose of a bottom-up evaluation the rules (1) and (2) are used in the following way:

1. The initial tuples are given by the exit rule (1). These tuples are said to be of *generation* P_0 so

$$P_0(X_1, X_2, Z) = E(X_1, X_2, Z).$$

---

[2] which implies that there are no repeated arguments. This assumption is no restriction because repeated arguments can be easily projected out from the canonical form and replicated after the essential query processing steps have been performed. The interested reader might refer to [10].

2. Further tuples are added by sequential applications of equation (2) to produce the generations P_1, P_2, ... :

$$P_{i+1}(X_1, X_2, Z) = P_i(X_1, X_2, Y) \bowtie Q(X_1, Y, Z).$$

Therefore a bottom-up evaluation produces the generations P_i of tuples in a sequential order starting with the initial relation E as P_0 and joining Q in each step. Finally the resulting relation P of the query is obtained by

$$P = \bigcup_{i \geq 0} P_i = \bigcup_{i=0}^{M} P_i \text{ such that } P_j \subseteq \bigcup_{i=0}^{M} P_i \text{ for all } j > M \qquad (3)$$

which means that all P_j with $j > M$ do not contribute any new tuple to P. The existence of such an M is guaranteed [18] [19]. When we refer to M in this paper then M is considered to be the smallest number such that (3) holds.

The notion of representing the resulting relation as a set of generations of tuples is quite useful. Note that a generation is a set of tuples that were generated in the same way and generations do not have to be disjoint as some tuples might be derived in several ways. The union of all generations represents the result of the query. In figures in this paper, the set of tuples in a generation shall be represented graphically as a square.

A bottom-up evaluation can then be considered as producing a chain of generations, up to generation M, as in figure 1 where we get generation P_{i+1} by applying the linear recursive rule (or equation) to generation P_i.

We note that a bottom-up evaluation requires M join operations where M depends on the characteristics of the underlying data relations.

$$P_3(X_1, X_2, Z) = P_2(X_1, X_2, Z) \bowtie Q(X_1, Y, Z)$$

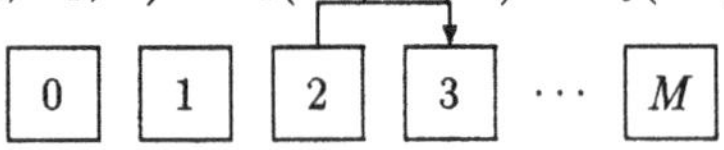

Fig. 1. Graphical representation of a bottom-up evaluation producing a chain of tuple-generations.

4 Transitive Closure Evaluation

The example of section 3 shows that evaluating linear recursive queries can be done by computing a number of equi-joins involving the relation Q. If we look at the Datalog equations to compute a generation P_i we can see that the chain of joins on Q represents computing a kind of transitive closure:

$$P_i(X_1, X_2, Z) = E(X_1, X_2, Y_i) \bowtie Q(X_1, Y_i, Y_{i-1}) \bowtie \cdots \bowtie Q(X_1, Y_1, Z)$$
$$= E(X_1, X_2, Y_i) \bowtie Q^i(X_1, Y_i, Z)$$

with

$$Q^i(X_1, Y_i, Z) = Q(X_1, Y_i, Y_{i-1}) \bowtie Q(X_1, Y_{i-1}, Y_{i-2}) \bowtie \cdots \bowtie Q(X_1, Y_1, Z)$$

In fact if we had all the Q^i's for $i = 1, \ldots, M$ we could easily compute the result P:

$$P = \bigcup_{i=0}^{M} P_i = E \cup \bigcup_{i=1}^{M} P_i = E \cup (E \bowtie \bigcup_{i=1}^{M} Q^i)$$

We note that the union of the $Q^i(X, Y, Z)$ seems to be a transitive closure with Y as the source and Z the destination attribute. The problem is that there is also the X attribute so we can only combine tuples (X, Y, Z) with equal X-values. This results in transitive closures for every single value of attribute X: Let $\{a_1, \ldots, a_T\}$ be the values of the X attribute in $Q(X, Y, Z)$ and

$$Q_{a_j}(Y, Z) = \pi_{Y,Z}(\sigma_{X=a_j}(Q(X, Y, Z)))$$

The Q_{a_j}'s are the relations comprising the set of (Y, Z) subtuples of $Q(X, Y, Z)$ that are associated with the X-value a_j. So we can compute the union of the Q^i's by computing the transitive closures of the Q_{a_j}'s and the result P of the query can be obtained by

$$P = E \cup E \bowtie \bigcup_{i \geq 1} Q^i = E \cup (E \bowtie \bigcup_{j=1}^{T}(\{a_j\} \times Q_{a_j}^+))$$

where $Q_{a_j}^+$ denotes the transitive closure of Q_{a_j}.

Essentially the processing technique shown in this example can be applied to *every* linear recursive query although there exist linear recursive queries that must be transformed into the canonical form of the query in the example so that the transitive closure technique can be applied [10]. We avoid presenting the transformations and the processing algorithm in detail. The reader might refer to [10] or [24].

To show in which way the resulting relation P of a query is computed using the transitive closure technique we will present the essential steps and give a graphical representation of the method in section 5:

1. The substitution graph of the linear recursive rule of the query is analyzed and two characteristic parameters g and d are obtained. [24] provides more details on how to get the optimal values for g and d.

2. Let r be the linear recursive rule. We let r^d denote d applications of r and refer to r^d as the *d-step rule*. r^d is itself linear recursive. [10] shows that a linear recursive query using generation P_g as the initial relation and having r^d as the linear recursive rule[3] can be processed in the way shown in the example.

3. $P_1, \ldots, P_g$ are computed by applying the linear recursive rule, r, g times to the initial relation $E = P_0$.

4. The d-step query involving r^d as the linear recursive rule and using P_g as the initial relation is evaluated by computing T transitive closures as shown in the example above. The resulting relation $\bar{P}$ of the d-step query is the union of the generations P_{g+id} (for all $i \geq 0$).

5. Finally the (original) linear recursive rule r is applied $(d-1)$ times to $\bar{P}$ to get the generations $P_{g+id+1}, \ldots, P_{g+(i+1)d-1}$ for $i \geq 0$.

6. The resulting relation P of the (original) query is the union of the generations computed in steps 3., 4. and 5.

5 The Generation Matrix Model

5.1 Generation Matrix

Figure 2 shows the generations P_i that form the result P of a linear recursive query. The matrix has d columns and a number of rows depending on the depth of the transitive closure[4]. Thus the number of rows is a data-dependent parameter whereas d is query-dependent.

Basically computing the result of a linear recursive query means computing the generations of its underlying generation matrix. We will now show graphically in which way these generations can be computed: we start in the top left corner as the generation P_0 (square 0) is given by the exit rule. Our goal is to proceed to every square (i.e. to compute every generation) in the matrix. Various operations are allowed that correspond to moves from one square to another:

(R) moving to the next generation to the right (i.e. computing P_{i+1} from P_i) means applying the linear recursive rule r to P_i,

(R2) moving two generations to the right (i.e. computing P_{i+2} from P_i) means applying the linear recursive rule r twice or applying the 2-step rule, r^2, once to P_i,

(Rd) moving to the generation below (i.e. computing P_{i+d} from P_i) means applying the linear recursive d-step rule, r^d, to P_i,

(TC) covering, or moving to, all generations of a column means applying the transitive closure technique using the d-step rule r^d. This move can only be executed if we have already reached or passed P_g.

---

[3] We will refer to this query as the *d-step query*.

[4] i.e. the length of the longest path in the directed graph that is defined by the underlying relation.

Finally we can apply (R), (R2) and (Rd) simultaneously to a group of generations (squares) to reach their respective neighbours, i.e. applying a join to several generations like in

$$P_{k+1} \cup P_{l+1} = (P_k \cup P_l) \bowtie Q \tag{4}$$

A summary of the moves is given in table 1.

move	corresponding operation	costs
(R)	$P_{i+1} = P_i \bowtie Q$	1 join per move
(R2)	$P_{i+2} = P_i \bowtie Q \bowtie Q$	1 join per move
		1 join for building $Q \bowtie Q$ (once)
(Rd)	$P_{i+d} = P_i \bowtie \underbrace{Q \bowtie \cdots \bowtie Q}_{Q^d}$	1 join per move
		$(d-1)$ joins for building Q^d (once)
(TC)	$Q_{a_j}^+$, for $j = 1, \ldots, T$	T selection operations to build the Q_{a_j}'s
		T transitive closures

Table 1. Moves, corresponding operations & costs

Obviously we could also generate moves (R3) or (R4) to move three or four generations to the right by deriving the 3-step rule and the 4-step rule. These (Rx) moves do not appear to be of any practical use as they 'jump' over squares that have to be visited anyway but we should allow the general possibility of creating and applying such moves. Actually we will only use the (R) and the (TC) move.

Several strategies/routes of 'running through the matrix' can be considered. The strategy described in section 4 (see steps 3., 4. and 5.) is the following; see also figure 3:

(a) Starting at square 0 perform right-moves (R) until you reach square g – this corresponds to step 3.
(b) Move down the column of square g – this corresponds to step 4 or a (TC) move.
(c) Perform $(d-1)$ right moves (R) from all squares of the respective column of square g simultaneously to get to the remaining squares. – this corresponds to step 5.

The simple bottom-up strategy corresponds to a series of (R) moves starting in the bottom-left square.

5.2 Parallel Aspects

The generation matrix model of section 5.1 provides a framework for analyzing several strategies to process a linear recursive query. The moves (R) and (TC) may be combined in several ways for query evaluation. Considerations of sequential strategies dwell upon whether to apply the (TC) move or to go rather for an ordinary bottom-up evaluation, i.e. applying (R) moves. This is a crucial point and we can open the ground for a wide range of new processing strategies by involving parallelism. Parallel issues in the evaluation process are:

Data parallel moves: (4) gives already an example in which an (R) move can be applied to several portions of data (e.g. several generations) in parallel. This is called data parallelism as the same instructions are executed on different items of data. In this case data parallelism is possible because there are no constraints in between the portions of data. E.g. generations do not have to be disjoint and can be built independently from one another. This means that (R) moves – and the same applies to (TC) moves – can be performed simultaneously on several generations, e.g. as shown in (4).

Different moves in parallel: The (R) and (TC) moves do not interfere with each other so (R) and (TC) moves can be executed in parallel even on the same portion of data, i.e. (R) or (TC) can be applied whenever possible and regardless of whether there is already another activity going on.

Parallelizing the (R) move: Clearly the (R) move can be parallelized internally. As we have already seen it consists mainly of a join operation[5]. Therefore efforts should be mainly concentrated on implementing one or more appropriate[6] parallel join algorithms.

Parallelizing the (TC) move: The same ideas that have applied to the (R) move can be used for the (TC) move. The dominant operation in this case is clearly the transitive closure. There are several well investigated parallel transitive closure algorithms based on boolean matrix multiplications, the Warshall constraints or hash-join techniques. Furthermore there are techniques regarding the characteristics of parallel computers, e.g. [3], [6], [8].

6 Choosing a Strategy

Usually a database management system (DBMS) incorporates a query optimizing module that decides on the best way to process the query. Given the generation matrix model and the moves and the parallel issues of sections 5.1 and 5.2, a variety of strategies to move through the generation matrix, i.e. of processing a query, can be considered. Naturally it would be nice to find out a way to determine the optimal, i.e. the fastest or cheapest, strategy in advance.

We can consider a strategy to be a sequence of stages that are consecutively executed. In the simplest, i.e. sequential, case a stage consists of a single move; in the more complex, parallel case a stage consists of several moves that are executed in parallel.

---

[5] Projection and selection operations may also be involved but can be neglected regarding the performance issues that are dominated by the join operation

[6] E.g. regarding the underlying machine's architecture.

The costs of a strategy are the sum of the costs of all its stages and the costs of a stage are the costs of the most expensive move in a stage. The problem of calculating the strategy costs is therefore reduced to the problem of identifying the move costs.

Although the dimensions of the matrix and the values of d and g are parameters that influence the performance we may neglect them as they are the same for each of the competing strategies to process the query so these parameters are not of any use to distinguish between the strategies. We can therefore concentrate on the costs of the moves.

Table 1 shows that the costs of a move are not constant and depend parameters like T or on the size of the relations involved in a join operation. Therefore predicting the costs of a strategy is not straightforward. Basically we can concentrate on the following issues:

1. on the efficiency of a right-move (R), i.e. essentially the efficiency of the underlying join operations as one right-move is in fact executing one join operation, which is dominated by
   (a) the size of the databases relations involved in the join and
   (b) the data skew, i.e. whether the data values are distributed uniformly or not
2. on the efficiency of the (TC) move; this is dictated by
   (a) the number T of transitive closures[7] for computing the generations of the column in which square g is located,
   (b) the sizes of the underlying graph structures and
   (c) the lengths of the longest paths in the graphs.

The sizes of intermediate join relations and the sizes of the underlying graph structures cannot be predicted easily [13]. Therefore we will follow a heuristic approach. The following section will present the costs for (R) and (TC) moves obtained by experiments on a Connection Machine CM-200. We give these results to prove the dependency of these costs on the lengths of the longest paths, on the number T of transitive closures and on data skew and to show in which way a query optimizer can use these parameters to choose the most appropriate strategy.

7 Move Costs

We now present the performance results for (R) and (TC) moves. These results were obtained from several sequences of experiments run on a Connection Machine CM-200. The CM-200 has an SIMD architecture using 16384 processors. It is an inherently data parallel machine which allows us to exploit all but the second of the parallel issues mentioned in section 5.2.

The dependency of the move costs on three parameters are shown:

---

[7] Actually T is also a skew parameter as it immediately depends on the number of values appearing in a certain attribute or set of attributes.

- the length L of the longest path in the underlying graph,
- the number T of values occurring in the attribute(s) that are common to every literal in a linear recursive rule[8],
- the data skew amongst the source and destination attributes of the transitive closure(s).

The bottom-up and the transitive closure strategies were implemented using a data parallel hash join [14] [11] which is sensitive to data skew and a simple and data-skew-insensitive join algorithm [24]. The transitive closure algorithm used in the tests is based on parallel boolean matrix multiplications. This proved to be the most efficient [24].

The times given in the experiments are CM *elapsed* times in seconds and incorporate the times for interaction with the secondary storage.

7.1 Varying L

The query used in these experiments is the most simple for computing the transitive closure $P(X, Z)$ of a relation $Q(X, Z)$:

$$P(X, Z) = Q(X, Z).$$
$$P(X, Z) = P(X, Y) \bowtie Q(Y, Z).$$

The underlying graph structure[9] of Q was a number of binary trees each of them having a depth not larger than L. L was varied over the range of $\{2, 3, \ldots, 10\}$. The size of Q was 1000 tuples in each experiment. Thes results for performing one (R) and one (TC) move are shown in figures 4 and 5 respectively.

Figure 4 shows that the average costs for an (R) move are cheaper for higher values of L. This is due to the fact that for low L values the average join result is larger than for high L values. This is reasonable as small L values force the data to be 'denser' i.e. to be connected by short paths. Therefore a larger number of nodes can be reached by combining two pathes (i.e. computing a join) that are already known.

The costs of a (TC) move are clearly dominated by the number of matrix multiplications to be performed. This number is given by $\lceil \log_2 L \rceil$ which causes the 'stair effect' in figure 5.

Figure 6 shows the overall performance of the two strategies in the experiments. The transitive closure performs better than the bottom-up strategy for higher values of L as it increases logarithmically with a linearly increasing L whereas the bottom-up strategy grows linearly. There exists a crossoverpoint which is can be used by an optimizer to decide on the more efficient strategy. The exact location of the crossover naturally depends on hardware and implementation issues.

---

[8] see for example the X_1 attribute in the linear recursive rule (2).

[9] A relation $Q(X, Z)$ can be considered as the set of edges of the graph, i.e. a tuple $(a, b) \in Q$ denotes that there is an edge from node a to node b. The values for attributes X and Z define the set of nodes of the graph.

7.2 Varying T

In these experiments the query (1), (2) of section 2 was used:

$$P(X_1, X_2, Z) = Q(X_1, X_2, Z).$$
$$P(X_1, X_2, Z) = P(X_1, X_2, Y) \bowtie Q(X_1, Y, Z).$$

The underlying graph structure of Q were a number of simple pathes each one not longer than 10, i.e. L was set to 10 in each experiment. The number T of values of the attribute X_1 in $Q(X_1, X_2, Z)$ was varied over the range of $\{10, 20, \ldots, 100\}$; the size of Q was 1000 tuples.

Actually the parameter T characterizes a kind of redistribution skew of the X_1 attribute [22] which is relevant for parallel implementations of relational algebra operators. They often use hash functions depending on the data values of a particular attribute to spread the data over a number of processors. This implies that an increasing number of distinct values results in the data being distributed over a larger number of processors. This applies for the hash join algorithm we used in the experiments of figure 7; additionally the results for the simple parallel join are given. The latter algorithm is not sensitive to effects of redistribution skew.

Figure 7 shows the costs of a single (R) move using the hash join and the simple join respectively. The hash join is influenced by the redistribution skew and performs worse than the simple join for small values of T. Both join algorithms suffer from linearly increasing join results for T being increased but the hash join overcompensates this effect by achieving a better data distribution for large T values.

Figure 8 gives the costs for a (TC) move. The costs rise nearly linearly with increasing T values. This is due to the fact that T is the number of transitive closures that have to be computed in each case. The costs of each transitive closure is nearly constant although the underlying graph is larger for a smaller T. Nevertheless they remain constant in this case due to specific Connection Machine programming characteristics.

Finally figure 9 shows the overall performance of the transitive closure and the bottom-up strategies. As in the case of L in section 7.1 the remarkable fact is the existence of a crossover. Again, the exact location depends on implementation and architectural characteristics and must be obtained experimentally. But the experiments prove again that it is worth to have an optimizer to decide on the most efficient strategy (including a decision on the most appropriate join algorithm).

7.3 Varying the Data Skew

The query used in these experiments is the same as in section 7.1.

The underlying graph structure of Q was a number of DAGs (acyclic directed graphs). The size of $Q(X, Y)$ was set to 1000 tuples and each of the attributes held 333 distinct values $0,1,\ldots,332$ so redistribution skew was fixed. The values of the X and Y attributes were Zipf-distributed [12] with

$$x_i = \frac{c}{i^\theta}$$

to be the probability of value i in the X attribute where

$$c = \frac{1}{H_{333}^{(\theta)}} \quad \text{and} \quad H_{333}^{(\theta)} = \sum_{k=1}^{333} \frac{1}{k^\theta}$$

So in these experiments the tuple placement skew [22] was varied rather than the redistribution skew, i.e. we varied over the frequency of the values rather than the number of distinct values. The probability y_i of value i in the Y attribute was set to $y_i = x_{333-i-1}$ which results in contrary distribution. Having the values distributed in this way allows to generate a sequence of relations Q synthetically such that $x < y$ for every $(x, y) \in Q(X, Y)$ which guarantees acyclicity.

The resulting DAGs had different lengths of their respective longest paths so the depth of the recursion was fixed to 4 in all experiments to avoid the results being influenced by that parameter.

Figure also shows the effect of varying the parameter θ: a small θ value means less skewed data and results in an increased overlap of the values which implies larger join results for $Q(X, Y) \bowtie Q(Y, Z)$.

Figure 10 presents the costs for an (R) move depending on the skew parameter θ. The hash join benefits from low θ values as they imply a better distribution amongst the 333 processors that are involved in the computation. Both join algorithms benefit from decreasing join results for an increasing data skew. This is due to the effect that the overlap decreases with in a θ increasing.

The result shown in figure 11 show that the (TC) move is not affected by data skew. This is caused by the fact that the boolean matrix multiplication technique was used for computing the transitive closure. There are several other parallel transitive closure algorithms which are based on hash techniques, and which are therefore sensitive to skew effects.

Figure 12 gives the overall performance results for the strategies and summarizes the issues that were already discussed. [22] denotes changing join result sizes as another type of skew, namely the join product skew. Following this interpretation and stating that every join algorithm naturally depends on the size of the join result we can conclude from figure 12 that the bottom-up strategy is very sensitive to skew effects (either tuple placement or join product skew) whereas the transitive closure strategy can be implemented such that is nearly[10] unaffected by data skew.

---

[10] Naturally transforming the boolean matrix into the final result – a database relation – is also influenced by the number of resulting tuples that have to be generated. Figure 12 proves that this effect is not significant.

8 Conclusions

After outlining the problems of linear recursion in section 2 we presented *two* evaluation techniques in sections 3 and 4 which were integrated in *one* query processing model in section 5. The generation matrix model suits as an abstract representation for a query optimizer because it provides a small set of simple operators which can be combined to create several strategies to process a query. It also pays attention to the fact that linear recursive queries have to be processed – regarding performance and computer resources – by computing a *data-dependent* number of transitive closures. This data-dependancy cannot be expressed in relational algebra with an additional transitive closure operator[11].

In section 7 performance results were given for an implementation of the processing model on a data parallel architecture. The results prove that it is worth to consider parameters like the lengths of the longest path, the number of transitive closures and data skew for choosing the appropriate strategy for processing a particular query. Information about these parameters can be stored in the database catalog and are available before a query is processed.

References

1. F. Afrati and Cosmadakis. Expressiveness of restricted recursive queries. In *Proc. 21st Annual ACM Symp. on Theory of Computing*, pages 113–126, New York, 1989. ACM.

2. R. Agrawal. Alpha: An Extension of Relational Algebra to Express a Class of Recursive Queries. In *Proc. IEEE 3rd Intern. Conf. Data Eng., Los Angeles, CA*, February 1987.

3. R. Agrawal and H.V. Jagadish. Multiprocessor Transitive Closure Algorithms. In *Proc. Intern. Symposium on Databases*, pages 56–66, 1988.

4. A.V. Aho and J.D. Ullman. Universality of data retrieval languages. In *Proc. Sixth ACM Symp. on Princ. of Programming Languages*, pages 110–120, New York, 1979. ACM.

5. F. Bancilhon and R. Ramakrishnan. An Amateur's Introduction to Recursive Query Processing Strategies. In *Proc. ACM SIGMOD 1986 Conf. on Management of Data*, pages 16–52, May 1986.

6. F. Cacace, S. Ceri, and M.A.W. Houtsma. An Overview of Parallel Strategies for Transitive Closure on Algebraic Machines. In P. America, editor, *Parallel Database Systems: PRISMA Workshop, Proc.*, pages 44–62, Noordwijk, The Netherlands, September 1990. Springer. LNCS 503.

7. S.R. Cohen and O. Wolfson. Why a Single Parallelization Strategy is not Enough in Knowledge Bases. In *PODS 89*, pages 200–216, 1989.

8. S. Dar and R. Ramakrishnan. A Performance Study of Transitive Closure Algorithms. In *ACM SIGMOD*, pages 454–465, 1994.

---

[11] although we remind that – in theory – every linear recursion can be replaced by computing the transitive closure of one, possibly very large graph [19] [10]. This can be expressed by relational algebra including an additional transitive closure operator.

9. Y.E. Ioannidis and E. Wong. Towards an Algebraic Theory of Recursion. *Journal of the ACM*, 38(2):329–381, April 1991.

10. H.V. Jagadish, R. Agrawal, and L. Ness. A Study of Transitive Closure As a Recursion Mechanism. In *Proc. ACM SIGMOD 1987 Conf. on Management of Data*, pages 331–344, 1987.

11. M. Kitsuregawa and K. Matsumoto. Massively Parallel Relational Database Processing on the Connection Machine CM-2. In *Annual Report of Kitsuregawa Lab.* University of Tokyo, 1991.

12. D.E. Knuth. *The Art of Computer Programming – Sorting and Searching*, volume 3. Addison-Wesley, 1973.

13. R.J. Lipton and J.F. Naughton. Estimating the Size of Generalized Transitive Closures. In *Proc. 15th Intern. Conf. on VLDB*, pages 165–171, 1989.

14. E.M. Minty. An Algorithm for a Data Parallel Hash Join on the Connection Machine. Technical Note EPCC-TN93-02, Edinburgh Parallel Computing Centre (EPCC), March 1993.

15. J.F. Naughton. One-Sided Recursions. In *Proc. 6th ACM Symp. on Principles of Database Systems*, pages 340–348, 1987.

16. J.F. Naughton, R. Ramakrishnan, Y. Sagiv, and J.D. Ullman. Efficient Evaluation of Right-, Left-, and Multi-linear rules. *SIGMOD Record*, 18(2):235–242, June 1989.

17. Y. Sagiv. Optimizing Datalog Programs. In J. Minker, editor, *Deductive Databases and Logic Programming*. Morgan-Kaufman, 1988.

18. J.D. Ullman. *Database and Knowledge-Base Systems*, volume 1. Computer Science Press, 1988.

19. J.D. Ullman. *Database and Knowledge-Base Systems*, volume 2. Computer Science Press, 1989.

20. P. Valduriez and H. Boral. Evaluation of Recursive Queries Using Join Indices. In *Proc. 1st Intern. Conf. on Expert Database Systems*, pages 197–208, April 1986.

21. P. Valduriez and S. Khoshafian. Transitive Closure of Transitively Closed Relations. In *Proc. 2nd Intern. Conf. on Expert Database Systems*, pages 377–400, April 1988.

22. C.B. Walton, A.G. Dale, and R.M. Jenevein. A Taxonomy and Performance Model of Data Skew Effects in Parallel Joins. In G. M. Lohman, A. Sernadas, and R. Camps, editors, *Proc. 17th Intern. Conf. on VLDB*, pages 537–548. Morgan Kaufman San Mateo, September 1991.

23. C. Youn, H.-J. Kim, Henschen L.J., and J. Han. Classification and Compilation of Linear Recursive Queries in Deductive Databases. *IEEE Trans. on Knowledge and Data Engineering*, pages 52–67, February 1992.

24. Th. Zurek and P. Thanisch. Processing Linear Recursive Database Queries on the Connection Machine. Technical Report EPCC-TR93-05, Edinburgh Parallel Computing Centre (EPCC), 1993.

Fig. 2. Generation matrix

Fig. 3. Transitive closure strategy of moving through the generation matrix

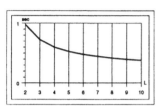

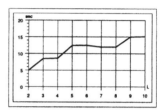

Fig. 4. Costs of one (R) move depending on the length L of the longest path; a hash join algorithm was used.

Fig. 5. Costs of a (TC) move depending on the length L of the longest path.

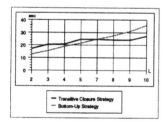

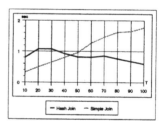

Fig. 6. Overall performance of the strategies depending on L

Fig. 7. Costs of one (R) move depending on the number T of values in the X_1 attribute of $Q(X_1, X_2, Z)$ for a parallel hash join and a simple data parallel join.

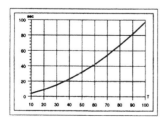

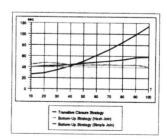

Fig. 8. Costs of one (TC) move depending on the number T of values in the X_1 attribute of $Q(X_1, X_2, Z)$.

Fig. 9. Overall performance of the strategies depending on T

229

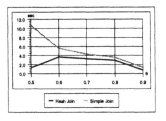

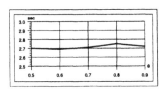

Fig. 10. Costs of one (R) move depending on the skew parameter θ for the parallel hash join and a simple data parallel join.

Fig. 11. Costs of a (TC) move depending on the skew parameter θ.

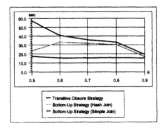

Fig. 12. Overall performance of the strategies depending on θ

Planning Complex Updates to Satisfy Constraint Rules Using a Constraint Logic Search Engine

Suzanne M. Embury and Peter M.D. Gray

Department of Computing Science, King's College,
University of Aberdeen, Aberdeen, Scotland, AB9 2UE
E-Mail: {sme|pgray}@csd.abdn.ac.uk
URL: http://www.csd.abdn.ac.uk/~pfdm

Abstract. In scientific and design applications, updates typically require the creation of a set of database objects, which together form a complex structure exhibiting some desired property or semantics. To support this kind of data manipulation, we have extended the Daplex data manipulation language with constructs to express constraints over the creation of sets of objects. Complex update descriptions are combined with semantic and structural constraints from the database schema, and are compiled into CHIP programs which search for an update that will meet the given constraints. The resulting system uses an efficient search technique, and avoids the problems of "knock-on" actions found in more traditional approaches using triggers.

1 Introduction

The emergence of the semantic [12] and object oriented [1] data models has largely alleviated the problems of representing the structural complexity found in design and scientific domains. The new challenge which these application areas present to database implementors is how to represent and preserve the complex behavioural semantics they demand. P/FDM [10] is an implementation of Shipman's Functional Data Model [20] in Prolog, which aims to provide both structural and semantic support for such applications. The principal data manipulation language (DML) is Daplex [20], a functional-style language combining a rich set of constructs for describing predicates on database classes with navigation via function composition. In our implementation, Daplex programs are compiled into Prolog clauses, which contain calls to the database access primitives. A recent extension allows users to state semantic integrity constraints in Daplex, which are then compiled into Prolog rules that can enforce them [7, 6].

P/FDM's ability to model complex data has been demonstrated by its use in the storage of three-dimensional protein structure data [11] and data for use in the modelling of hydrocarbon reservoirs [17]. Daplex in particular has stood up well to use in the protein domain, and has proved itself able to express all the *ad hoc* and often very complicated queries that have been posed by protein biochemists. However, where Daplex and, in fact, the majority of DMLs are less suitable, is in the expression of the *complex updates* found in these domains. In the protein database, for example, updates involve the selection of a set of protein fragments which must be combined to form a complete protein with the appropriate atomic connectivity; or the placement of atoms within a partially completed protein model so that no atoms intersect. The difficulty with updates of this kind is that each individual state change has consequences for the overall update that are complex and difficult to foresee. For example, the placement of an atom at one three-dimensional position within a protein model may mean that no legal positioning exists for some atoms placed later, whereas a different placement for the first atom may allow a complete model to be built. In fact, in updates of this kind, the user is not really concerned with the exact attribute values assigned to objects (for example, the exact three-dimensional coordinates of the atoms), provided that the resulting structure has the properties required of the solution (such as having the correct atomic connectivities and no steric overlap between atoms).

In a conventional DML the burden of finding a set of attribute or relationship values that will preserve the real-world semantics in the updated database is left to the user. Even an integrity checking mechanism can only offer partial help, by informing the user when their requested update would violate the semantics. Nor would a repair mechanism based on ECA-rules help, since the interaction of attribute values is too complex, and the number of alternative but incorrect solutions too high for individual rules to be able to analyse and correct. What is really required is some mechanism by which the user can specify the constraints that the complete update must satisfy, so that the DBMS can use this information to plan the sequence of low-level updates that will achieve them, and thus avoid repeated triggering of rules and the problems of knock-on actions. In other words, a more declarative approach to the specification of updates is required.

In view of this, we have extended the Daplex language with a new construct for describing an important class of database updates declaratively. The extended language allows the creation of sets of (possibly related) database objects so that the resulting database state satisfies some given constraints. This class covers most of the updates encountered so far in the protein database which could not be expressed using the unextended version of Daplex [4].

The extension consists of a new construct which specifies non-deterministic choice of attribute values for new objects, according to a set of given constraints. The compiler then generates a set of rules describing the search process that will simulate the non-determinism, by testing different combinations of attribute values against the given constraints. Since this class of programs are essentially constrained search problems (CSPs), we use a constraint logic programming language (CHIP [24]) as our underlying search engine. However, programs expressed in the extended Daplex language are different from CSP's in general in that the constraints are expressed in terms of object identifiers and their database relationships; and the solution that is generated must not only be internally consistent, but must also satisfy the problem constraints relative to the existing database objects. Not only this, but the solution must also conform to the structural constraints imposed by the data model, and the semantic integrity constraints imposed by the application schema! All this makes for a very complex code generation process, but it is complexity that can be handled more thoroughly and safely by the DBMS than by the user—the DBMS will not forget to include all the relevant integrity constraints, for example, whereas a fallible human user might.

The type of non-deterministic choice implemented by our extended language is *angelic non-determinism* [21]. This is a form of non-determinism in which the choice of each variable or attribute value is made so that the complete set of values satisfies the given constraints. We therefore refer to the new language as Angelic Daplex (or Daplexfor short), in order to differentiate it from the deterministic, ordinary mortal version of Daplex. This paper describes the Daplexlanguage (Sect. 2), and the underlying CHIP search strategy by which solutions are located (Sect. 3). We discuss the means by which structural and semantic constraints are maintained by the DBMS (Sect. 4). Finally, we discuss similar language features provided by other systems (Sect. 5) and conclude.

2 The Angelic Daplex Language

Programs in the Daplex language consist of two basic sections: the "loops" part, which gives a declarative description of a set of database values, and the "actions" part, which iterates over this set applying the specified operations to each combination of loop values. Consider the following schema and query:

```
create private module chessdb
declare queen ->> entity
declare column(queen) -> integer
declare row(queen) -> integer
key_of queen is column, row;

for each c in {1 to 8}
   for the q in queen such that column(q) = c
print('Queen placed at position (', c, ',', row(q), ')');
```

The effect of this program is to print out the positions of the queen objects in the solution to the 8-Queens problem stored in the database. The loop beginning with the keywords "for each" evaluates the set of integers $\{1, 2, 3, \ldots, 8\}$, and for each element of this set the inner loop, beginning with the keywords "for the", evaluates the singleton set described by "q in queen such that column(q) = c". Once these sets have been evaluated, the actions of the program are executed, with the loop variables being substituted for the appropriate loop set elements.

This division of data manipulation programs into the side-effect free "loops" and the state-changing "actions" is important in Daplex as it clearly defines which parts of the program may be treated functionally (i.e. as referentially-transparent expressions) and which may not [4]. It allows us to limit the restrictions on program transformations caused by the (necessary) introduction of the notion of state into the language.

The Daplexlanguage extends the standard Daplex language with a new loop construct for describing the non-deterministic creation of database objects. The new loop has the syntax:

```
for a new <var> in <class> such that <predicate>
```

which can be read informally as requesting the creation of a new instance of <class> whose identifier is bound to the variable <var> and whose attributes have values such that the constraints specified in <predicate> are satisfied. We can use the new loop construct, for example, to describe the creation of a solution to the 8-Queens problem as instances of the database class queen:

```
program queens is
for each c in {1 to 8}
  for a new q in queen such that
      column(q) = c and row(q) in {1 to 8} and
      no q1 in queen has (q1 <> q and (
        column(q1) = column(q) or row(q1) = row(q) or
        abs(row(q1) - row(q)) = abs(column(q1) - column(q))))
print('Queen placed at ', column(q), row(q));
```

This program requests the creation of a new queen instance for each column value, with a row position selected so that no other queen is attacking the newly created queen. Notice how we have used the new loop construct, which describes the creation of a single new instance, to create a set of instances by nesting it within an ordinary "for each" loop. In this respect, the "for a new" loop behaves like any ordinary Daplex loop, in that it may be nested within an arbitrary number of other loops. It is even possible to nest "for a new" loops within other "for a new" loops, thus making the creation of one instance contingent upon the successful creation of another set of instances.

There are two other points to note about the queens program. The first is that the constraints on the attribute values of the new queen instances are specified in terms of the complete solution, and must be satisfied with respect to the instances that have yet to be created as well as those new instances that have already been dealt with—this is the non-determinism at work! Additionally, the constraints are specified over the existing database objects, as well as over the solution objects—thus the set of queen objects referred to in the quantified expression (no q1 in queen has ...) notionally includes all the queen instances existing prior to the execution of the program, and all the queen instances that have been and will be created by it.

The second point to note is that the entire loops set is evaluated, and a valid solution created in the database, before any of the actions at the end of the loops are executed, such as printing values from the solution, or making further (deterministic) updates. This means that our nqueens program prints only the details of the queen instances that exist in the final solution, and the existence of any incomplete solutions that were investigated during the search for a full solution is completely hidden from the user. This is another advantage of the non-deterministic approach to the specification of this kind of problem: not only is the problem description more concise, but the details of the underlying search mechanism used are completely hidden from the user of the language.

2.1 The Semantics of D̊aplex

Although the extension from Daplex to D̊aplexrequires only one simple syntactic addition, we might reasonably expect the change in the semantics of the language, i.e. from deterministic to non-deterministic searching, to be more extensive. After all, we have apparently introduced an update command into the declarative, side-effect free "loops" part of an D̊aplexprogram. In fact, this is not the case, and the change in the semantics is less significant than might at first be thought. The semantics of a deterministic Daplex program [5] are equivalent to a ZF-expression [18], which describes a set of tuples of values, where each tuple represents one of the combination of values produced by the loops. For example, the loops part of the example query given earlier is equivalent to:

```
[ (c, q) | c <- [1..8]; q <- queen; column(q) = c ]
```

The generators and restrictions describing each individual loop set are simply added to the body of the ZF-expression one after another to describe the full set of loop value tuples. Once this set has been evaluated, the actions of the program are executed once for each element (i.e. each tuple) of the set.

The semantics of the loops of an D̊aplexprogram are also based on ZF-expressions, in an idiom corresponding to the "list of successes" technique for describing constrained search problems of this kind functionally [25]. The only difference between the standard Daplex loops and the non-deterministic "for a new" loop is that the former contribute existing database values to the loops set, while the latter contributes a set of tuples describing the attribute values of the new instances required to satisfy the given constraints in the database. Thus, the evaluation of the loops of the program does not involve any data update—merely a search for data values that will combine to form a solution.

We do require, however, that the actions phase of the program is executed in the context of the newly discovered solution. This allows the user to relate the solution objects to existing database objects, as well as just displaying the details of the solution. All the actions are executed subject to the normal integrity checking mechanism, applied in the context of the new objects. If, however, any action fails, it fails individually and does not undo the earlier object creation. This is in line with the semantics of standard Daplex actions. The evaluation of an D̊aplexprogram, then, is divided into the following distinct phases:

1. evaluate the loops set, to find a solution to the constrained search problem described by the program loops,
2. create the solution in the database, using the information generated by the evaluation of the loops, and
3. execute the actions, subject to normal integrity checking in the context of the committed solution.

We will refer to these three phases as the *loops* phase, the *commit* phase and the *actions* phase respectively.

The first implementation of a compiler for Ďaplex[4] was based on standard backtracking search—an obvious choice given that our target language is Prolog. Moreover, the equivalence of programs involving non-deterministic choice and backtracking search algorithms has long been known [8]. In order to implement this search strategy, we moved the updates from the commit phase into the loops phase, so that the state of the search at any point was represented by the current state of the database. However, in order to ensure that invalid partial solutions were not allowed to exist in the database, we used special versions of the update primitives that undid themselves on backtracking. This approach has two significant advantages. The first is that, since both the current solution and the existing data are represented as ordinary database objects, the process of generating code to check the constraints on the trial solutions becomes a simple matter of generating code to check the constraints over the entire database— something which the standard Daplex compiler is already capable of doing. The second advantage is that, because we are using the ordinary database primitives to create the new solution objects, we are automatically ensuring that the solution that is eventually formed meets the structural and semantic constraints of the data model and the schema, since these checks are built-in to the update primitives themselves.

Unfortunately, the backtracking approach also has a significant disadvantage in that it does not give us a very efficient form of search. Backtracking search is prone to the behaviour known as *thrashing* (see [24], p. 21), and, in our case, the problem was exacerbated by the fact that each exploration of a candidate solution required not only some variable instantiations but also several database updates, possibly requiring complex constraint checks over large parts of the database. Even the process of backtracking involved the deletion of data from the database. The obvious solution, therefore, was to move to a more intelligent form of underlying search. Given that our system operated in a logic programming environment, the most obvious choice for an alternative search engine was a constraint logic programming language, such as CHIP [24].

3 The Combined Prolog/Chip Search Architecture

3.1 A Brief Introduction to CHIP

The CHIP (Constraint Handling in Prolog) language, in common with other CLP languages, extends standard Prolog with two new inference rules for providing forward checking and lookahead search strategies in addition to the standard backtracking search mechanism. CHIP provides facilities for solving CSPs over the Boolean, rational arithmetic and finite domains. It is the finite domain solver that we use as the search engine for our Ďaplexlanguage.

A CHIP program can be separated into two distinct phases: the *constraint posting* phase, in which variables are allocated domains and constraints are applied to reduce those domains, and the *labelling* (or *searching*) phase, in which values are selected from the reduced domains in an attempt to find a combination of values that will satisfy all the constraints.

Before the constraints can be posted, domains must be specified using the special "::" operator. For example, the following CHIP goal says that the variable X may take any of the values from 5 to 10 inclusive: X :: 5..10. This declares X to be a *domain variable* (as opposed to an ordinary Prolog variable) which may be used in constraint solving. The constraints on the values of the finite domain variables are then posted using the special CHIP operators #=, #\=, #>, #>=, #< and #=<. E.g. X #>= 6. Note that no value is chosen for X as a result of this goal, but the domain of X is reduced to the set of values from 6 to 10 inclusive.

CHIP also provides more specialised constraints, e.g. alldifferent(L) which specifies that each of the domain variables given in its argument list L must have a unique value. Another important constraint is the element/3 predicate, e.g.

```
element(X, [5, 10, 15, 15, 20, 25], Y).
```

Here, X and Y are domain variables, with the additional constraint that Y has the value of the Xth element of the given list. The domain of X is now reduced to those values between 1 and 6. Given the earlier constraints on X, the only value which meets these criteria is 6, which implies that the only possible value for Y is 25. As we shall see, the element/3 constraint is particularly important in the generation of CHIP code from Daplex, as it allows us to turn a Prolog variable such as Y into a CHIP variable with a domain given by an element/3 constraint.

At the end of the *constraint posting* phase, CHIP will have derived reduced domains for each of the variables. If, however, during the constraint posting process, the domain of some variable is reduced to the empty set, then the constraints given are too restrictive and no solution exists.

Next comes the *labelling* phase in which values are selected from the domain of each variable, in an attempt to find an assignment of values to all the variables that meets the given constraints. The simplest way to do this is to use the indomain(Var) predicate, which instantiates its argument variable with some value from its domain. Values are selected for variables one at a time, and the consequences of each selection are immediately propagated to the domains of the remaining (unlabelled) variables. If at any point during the labelling phase, the domain of some variable is found to have been reduced to the empty set, then the currently selected set of values is not part of a complete solution. In this case, the system must backtrack and try some other selection.

3.2 The DBMS's View of the Search Process

Since the role of CHIP in the search process is confined to searching for the set of loop variable values that meet the problem constraints, we must also generate some Prolog code to (i) initiate the searching process, (ii) turn the results of that process into actual database objects and (iii) execute the actions in the context of the new data. The first step is to initialise the link from the DBMS (i.e. Prolog) to CHIP, and to assert the CHIP code that describes the search process. This link, called ChipLink [15], uses remote procedure calls to allow two-way communication between the P/FDM and CHIP processes (which may be running on different processors). It allows P/FDM to call CHIP goals and to receive data back as a result of those goals, and it allows CHIP to execute Prolog code fragments containing embedded database calls in order to receive data from the database.

The CHIP code is represented as a list of terms (chip_clause(Head, Body)) each of which represent a clause of the form (Head :- Body). Once each of these clauses has been defined within CHIP's clause base, the searching process is initiated by a call to the execute_chip/2 primitive. This routine takes the CHIP goal that is to be executed as its first argument (i.e. the name of the top level routine just asserted), and a variable which will be instantiated with the results of the search process, as its second argument. If no solution to the constraint problem can be found then the atom no_solutions is returned. We must check for this and report our failure to the user. Otherwise, the result variable is instantiated to a nested list structure containing the values for the loop variables and the tuples describing the new objects to be created. For example, a result list describing a solution to the 4-Queens problem might be:

```
[ [1, queen(queen(56), column(1), row(2))],
  [2, queen(queen(57), column(2), row(4))],
  [3, queen(queen(58), column(3), row(1))],
  [4, queen(queen(59), column(4), row(3))] ]
```

Each tuple represents the creation of a new queen instance with the given column and row values. The first argument of the tuple is a temporary identifier that is used to distinguish it from the other queen instances generated in the solution. This identifier is required to handle non-deterministic searching over database relationships. It has no meaning outside the results list and has no relationship to the identifier of the database object that will be created from the tuple.

The commitment process requires a straightforward pass over the results list, with a call to the relevant update primitive for each tuple that is encountered. As a by-product of this operation, a list of "real" loop variable values is created, in which the new instance tuples are replaced with the identifiers of their corresponding disk objects. For example, if commitment of the above 4-Queens solution results in the creation of four new queen objects with identifiers queen(8), queen(9), queen(10) and queen(11), then the "real" loop values will be:

```
[[1, queen(8)], [2, queen(9)], [3, queen(10)], [4, queen(11)]]
```

representing pairs of values located by the program for the loop variables c (the column positions) and q (the identifiers of the new queen instances) respectively. The actions of the program are executed against these loop values exactly as they would be for those generated from a standard Daplex program.

3.3   CHIP's View of the Search Process

In our architecture, the task of the CHIP search engine is to construct a fully instantiated results list which satisfies the given constraints. Since the structure of this list is determined by the nested loop structure of the original Daplexprogram, the structure of the CHIP code which will create it follows the same pattern.

We generate two recursive routines for each "for" loop, one which creates a list of partially-instantiated results and posts the constraints among the variables within it, and the other which labels these result variables. Each of these routines recurses along the list of variable values generated by the preceding "for" loop, and for each such value generates (or labels) the set of loop variable values described by the "for" loop from which it was compiled. This set is then passed to the routine representing the next nested "for" loop for it to recurse over in turn. These points are illustrated by the CHIP clauses given in the appendix, which were produced by our compiler from the N-Queens example program.

Since the nqueens program contains two loops, we generate four procedures: two to post the constraints described by the loops and two to perform the labelling. The constraint posting routine generated for the first "for" loop has a slightly different structure from the others, as it forms the top level routine which is invoked by the DBMS to start the search process. It begins by generating the set of loop variable values for the loops it represents, and passes it to the routine which posts the constraints for the next loop. This procedure returns the partially instantiated result list as its last argument, which is then passed to the top-level labelling routine for completion. If both the constraint posting and the labelling routines succeed then we can return the completed results list to Prolog. Otherwise we return the atom no_solutions.

In order to generate the constraint posting and labelling code we must examine the constraints placed on each attribute and decide whether any searching is required to find an acceptable value for it, or whether the constraints uniquely determine its value. In the nqueens program, for example, the value of the column attribute is uniquely defined by the variable c and can therefore be assigned immediately. The value of the row attribute, on the other hand, is given as one of a set of possible values. It is therefore modelled as a domain variable. For each attribute that must be modelled in this way, we select one constraint to give us the initial domain which will be allocated to it, and consider the rest as conventional constraints. From the nqueens program we select the constraint that "row(q) in {1 to n}" as the generator for the initial domain. The skeleton code which creates and initialises a domain variable DVar is:

```
findall(V, generator_for_constraint(V), Vs),
convert_to_domain(Vs, Domain),
element(_, Domain, DVar)
```

This fragment collects the set of possible values described by the selected constraint, and converts them into a list of integer values, suitable for use as a CHIP domain. The code for the generator is obtained by using the standard Daplex compiler to turn the constraint into Prolog.

A crucial part of our search strategy is to avoid copying all of the database into CHIP memory before constraint solving. Instead, we retrieve only those values which are required to construct domains, and retrieve extra data as it is required by the constraint checks. In order to do, this we separate the remaining constraints into two types: those which may be posted immediately and those which cannot be posted until after labelling. Any constraint which involves database retrieval combined with domain variables must be postponed until after labelling when the domain variables involved have been given a concrete value. This is illustrated by the check that queen objects are not attacked by other database queens—we wait until we have allocated a position to a new queen before we check that it is not attacked by any queen object already existing in the database. This constraint also illustrates the extra difficulty of code generating constraint checks when the current candidate solution is represented as domain variables in memory, in a different form from the pre-existing data, stored as objects in the database. We must effectively generate two pieces of code to check each constraint, one to check that it is satisfied relative to the candidate solution, and another to check its validity relative to the original database objects.

4 Preserving Structural and Semantic Integrity in CHIP

Although the use of CHIP as a search engine does improve on our original backtracking strategy, we unfortunately lose out on the two advantages of the simpler approach, and must pay the price for this in the increased complexity of code generation. Where previously we generated one recursive predicate per Daplex "for" loop, we must now generate two predicates—one for constraint posting and one for labelling; where we used to have one type of variable, we now have two (domain variables and ordinary variables) with different operators for comparing them; where we used to check all constraints in one place, we must now divide them between the posting and labelling routines; and where we used to generate one piece of code per constraint, we now generate one for the domain variables and one for the database objects.

However, these measures will only ensure that the solution found satisfies the constraints given in the original problem description. They will not guarantee to find a solution that is also structurally and semantically valid. Under the architecture described above, we would not discover that there was any problem with the solution found by CHIP until we had returned the control to the DBMS and were trying to create the solution objects in the database—at which point it is clearly too late to ask CHIP to find another solution. Even if the architecture allowed further solutions to be returned from CHIP on request, we would have an inefficient form of search equivalent to a generate-and-test strategy. Ideally, we would like CHIP to be aware of these extra constraints on the problem and to be able to use them in a more generative fashion in the search for a solution.

In order to do this, we must explicitly include the relevant structural and semantic constraints into the CHIP program in the same manner as the problem constraints specified by the user. In fact, we can do this very easily using the existing Daplex→CHIP compiler by adding these extra constraints to the original problem description and then compiling it in the usual way. For example, if we wish to maintain the structural data model constraint that keys must be unique within object classes when generating solutions to the nqueens problem, we can add the following constraint to the "for a new" loop predicate:

```
no q2 in queen has (q2 <> q and key_of(q2) = key_of(q));
```

(In fact, this constraint is already subsumed by the original problem constraints but the compiler has as yet no way of knowing this.) Similarly, if we have the semantic constraint that row and column positions must be positive integers, specified in the Daplex constraint language as:

```
constrain each q1 in queen
to have row(q1) > 0 and column(q1) > 0;
```

then we must extend the nqueens program with the predicate:

```
row(q) > 0 and column(q) > 0
```

The expanded nqueens program can then be submitted to the compiler described above to produce CHIP code that will search for a solution meeting all the required constraints, whether structural, semantic or problem-specific in origin.

We are currently extending our compiler to automatically include constraints of this kind into Daplexprograms. In fact, of course, we do not include these new constraints into the text description of the Daplexas shown above, but instead modify the internal representation of the program. We have already demonstrated the feasibility of this approach in our original Daplex→Prolog compiler, which has the ability to include relevant integrity constraints into the program to prevent the exploration of some invalid branches of the search space [4]. Apart from making the code generation process simpler, this technique has the added advantage that the new constraints are available for use as domain generators, should they be suitable. However, the disadvantage is that we may not generate such efficient code as we could if the Daplex→CHIP compiler was able to take advantage of its knowledge of the form of these constraints (making more use of high-level constraints such as alldifferent/1, for example).

5 Related Work

Constraint handling techniques have only recently been recognised as having any value in the area of DMLs, and most of the work in this area so far has centred on the introduction of constraints into deductive databases, One of the earliest examples was the *or-type* [13], which allows database attributes to be specified as a disjunction of possible values, rather than as a single, known value. This construct is useful in design and planning applications, in which the user describes the resources that are available for problem-solving using *or-types*, and then queries the data to discover whether certain constraints can be met by selecting combinations of values for each *or-type*. An example of this kind of hypothetical query might be "does an allocation of classes to teachers exist, in which no teacher takes more than three classes per week?" Such queries, expressed in a version of Datalog, can be evaluated using standard SLD-resolution [14]. Other work [22] has used an adaptation of the Magic Sets approach to evaluate queries involving parametrised constraints. Although our own language does not currently allow hypothetical queries of this kind, it could easily be modified to do so, simply by removing the commit-phase of the evaluation, and restricting the actions to print statements describing the solution found.

These systems, however, are concerned with answering queries, rather than with using constraints to build solutions in the database. The *LCDB* system (Linear Constraint DataBase) [2] uses a variant of SQL in order to describe the creation of new relations which contain tuples satisfying a given set of linear arithmetic constraints. The main contribution of this system is that it recognises that both constraint handling and database access techniques must be combined, in order to solve constraint problems over large data sets in practical time-scales. Their own evaluation strategy consequently combines novel indexing techniques with constraint reasoning.

The *LCDB* language, however, is not as expressive as D̊aplex, since it is restricted to linear arithmetic constraints, whereas D̊aplexcan handle constraints expressed over string-valued attributes, and even over database relationships. Also, an individual LCDB program is only able to describe the construction of a single relation, although this is less of a restriction than might first be thought since the resulting relation need not be completely defined and may contain its own constraints. Thus, such a relation can be used to create additional relations.

All the above systems are tuple-based, rather than object-based; none of them uses a semantic data model. Thus, none of them address the issues of combining the problem constraints explicitly specified by the user, with the structural and semantic constraints implied by the data model and schema, as discussed in Sect. 4. This is partly because they are based on the relational data model, which imposes practically no structural constraints anyway. Moreover, the relational model does not cope well with the complex data structures found in the kind of application areas for which constraint handling is most important. It is vital, therefore, that we learn how to combine constraint solvers with more complex data models.

6 Conclusions and Future Directions

The extension of Daplex to D̊aplexintroduces notions of non-deterministic choice and constraint satisfaction into a high-level DML. The result allows users to describe both data retrieval and data creation in a declarative fashion, simply by stating the constraints on the data that must be retrieved or created. The DBMS then assumes the responsibility for selecting the most appropriate execution strategy for the individual problem in hand, whether this is a failure-driven iteration, a recursive backtracking search or forward-checking search in CHIP. The DBMS also ensures that all relevant structural and semantic integrity constraints are preserved by any state changes. As we have seen, the code generation required by the DBMS in order to perform these duties is complex, but not impossibly so. This has been helped by the fact that our target languages, Prolog and CHIP, are themselves relatively high-level and declarative. We have also been able to reuse much of the existing compiler for Daplex, with all its knowledge of standard database optimisation techniques, in the implementation of the Daplex→CHIP compiler. Thus we can generate efficient code for constraint checks over both the solution objects and the pre-existing database objects.

The form of the generated CHIP code described in this paper represents the simplest, most naive translation from Daplexthat retains the required semantics, and as such it does not take advantage of all the efficiency gains offered by CHIP. The next stage in our work, therefore, will involve the extension of the compiler with the intelligence required to produce more efficient CHIP code. The most obvious immediate improvement will be to move the constraint checks on the partial CHIP solution from the labelling phase to the constraint posting phase, where possible, to allow more domain pruning before the search process begins. We may also find that more efficient code for checking the structural constraints can be generated by including them directly into the CHIP code, rather than including them at the Daplex code level. More interestingly, we hope also to be able to recognise the situations in which the special built-in constraints of CHIP (such as `alldifferent/1` and `element/3`) can be used. In particular, we would like to be able to apply the *global* (or higher-order) constraints, such as the `cumulative`, `diffn` and `cycle` constraints, which have proven key to CHIP's success in solving large, real-world problems.

In the longer term, our aim is to make use of the facilities for automatically generating CHIP code described above to generate CLP descriptions of transaction repair problems [9]. Transaction repair is the process of automatically generating a sequence of update operations that will restore validity to a database at the end of a transaction in which integrity constraints have been violated. Previous approaches to this problem have been based on active rules [23] and deductive rules [16]. In the former approach rules are generated which fire when a particular integrity constraint is found to have been violated, and whose action is to make some update to restore consistency relative to that constraint. However, since each rule is aware of only one constraint, there can be problems with *anomalous rule behaviour* (to use the terminology of [23]) in which two or more rules undo each other's updates in an attempt to satisfy two or more violated constraints. The deductive rule approach does not suffer in this way, since it is able to consider all violated constraints in the search for repair updates. However, as Moerkotte and Lockemann point out [16], it suffers from performance problems, which reduce its usefulness in practice. We believe that our own approach of making database constraints amenable to processing by a constraint logic search engine will overcome these performance problems, and allow transaction repair to become a practical tool for database users.

Acknowledgements

Suzanne Embury is supported by the EPSRC. The authors are members of the ACT-NET network, supported by the EU. We would also like to acknowledge the work of Scott Leishman at Aberdeen in implementing the ChipLink system.

A CHIP Code Generated for the 8-Queens Example

```
nqueens1 :-
    initialise_domain_keys,
    ( findall(A, int_set(1, 8, A), B),
      nqueens2_posting(B, C),
      nqueens1_labelling(C, C) - >
      retractall(domain_pairs(D, E)),
      chip_result(C)
    ; retractall(domain_pairs(F, G)),
      chip_result(no_solutions)
    ).


nqueens2_posting([], []).

nqueens2_posting([A|B], [[A,C]|D]) :-
    E = A,
    findall(F, (int_set(1,8,G), F=G), H),
    H \== [], I = H,
    length(I, J),
    K :: 1..J,
    element(K, I, L),
    generate_dummy_identifier(queen, M),
    C = [queen(M, row(L), column(E))],
    nqueens2_posting(B, D).


nqueens1_labelling([], A).

nqueens1_labelling([[A, B]|C], D) :-
    nqueens2_labelling(B, A, D),
    nqueens1_labelling(C, D).
```

```
nqueens2_labelling([], A, B).

nqueens2_labelling([[A]|B], C, D) :-
    A = queen(E, row(F), column(G)),
    indomain(F),
    check_constraints(
        queen(H, row(I), column(J)),
        ( H=E
        ; J \== G,
          I #\= F,
          K is I - F,
          getfnval(abs, [K], L),
          M is J - G,
          getfnval(abs, [M], N),
          L \== N
        ),D),
    \+ ( getentity(queen,O),
         O \== E,
         ( getfnval(column, [O], P),
           P = G
         ; getfnval(row, [O], Q),
           Q = F
         ; getfnval(row, [O], R),
           K is R - F,
           getfnval(abs, [K], L),
           getfnval(column, [O], S),
           M is S - G,
           getfnval(abs, [M], N),
           L = N
         )),
    nqueens2_labelling(B, C, D).
```

References

1. M. Atkinson, F. Bancilhon, D. DeWitt, K. Dittrich, D. Maier, and S. Zdonik. The Object-Oriented Database System Manifesto. In W. Kim, J.-M. Nicolas, and S. Nishio, eds., *Proc. DOOD'89* pp. 223–240, Kyoto. North Holland (1990).
2. A. Brodsky, J. Jaffar, and M.J. Maher. Toward Practical Constraint Databases. In R. Agrawal, S. Baker, and D. Bell, eds., *Proc. of the 19th VLDB Conf.*, pages 567–580, Dublin, 1993. Morgan Kaufmann Publishers, Inc.

3. C. Delobel, M. Kifer, and Y. Masunaga, editors. *Second Int. Conf. on Deductive and Object-Oriented Databases*, Munich, December 1991. Springer-Verlag.

4. S.M. Embury. *Constraint-Based Updates in a Functional Data Model Database.* PhD thesis, University of Aberdeen, King's College, Aberdeen, Scotland, July 1994.

5. S.M. Embury. A Formal Semantics for the Daplex Language. Technical Report AUCS/TR9504, University of Aberdeen, March 1995.

6. S.M. Embury and P.M.D. Gray. Compiling a Declarative, High-Level Language for Semantic Integrity Constraints. In R. Meersman and L. Mark, eds., *Proc. of 6th IFIP Conf. on Data Semantics*, Atlanta, May 1995. Chapman and Hall.

7. S.M. Embury, P.M.D. Gray, and N.D. Bassiliades. Constraint Maintenance Using Generated Methods in the P/FDM Object-Oriented Database. In [19], p. 364–381.

8. R.W. Floyd. Nondeterministic Algorithms. *JACM*, 14(4):636–644, October 1967.

9. P. Fraternali and S. Paraboschi. A Review of Repair Techniques for Integrity Maintenance. In [19], pages 332–346.

10. P.M.D. Gray, K.G. Kulkarni, and N.W. Paton. *Object-Oriented Databases: a Semantic Data Model Approach.* Prentice Hall Series in Computer Science, 1992.

11. P.M.D. Gray, N.W. Paton, G.J.L. Kemp, and J.E. Fothergill. An Object-Oriented Database for Protein Structure Analysis. *Protein Engineering*, 3:235–243, 1990.

12. R. Hull and R. King. Semantic Data Modelling: Survey, Applications and Research Issues. *ACM Computing Surveys*, 19(3):201–260, September 1987.

13. T. Imielinski, S. Naqvi, and K. Vadaparty. Incomplete Objects — a Data Model for Design and Planning Applications. In J. Clifford and R. King, editors, *SIGMOD 91 Conf.*, pages 288–297, Denver, Colorado, May 1991. ACM Press.

14. T. Imielinski, S. Naqvi, and K. Vadaparty. Querying Design and Planning Databases. In Delobel et al. [3], pages 524–545.

15. S. Leishman. ChipLink User Manual. Technical report, University of Aberdeen, Dept. of Computing Science, King's College, Aberdeen, U.K., 1995.

16. G. Moerkotte and P.C. Lockemann. Reactive Consistency Control in Deductive Databases. *ACM TODS*, 16(4):670–702, December 1991.

17. J. Owens. *Using Object-Oriented Databases to Model Hydrocarbon Reservoirs.* PhD thesis, University of Aberdeen, King's College, Aberdeen, Scotland, 1995.

18. N.W. Paton and P.M.D. Gray. Optimising and Executing Daplex Queries Using Prolog. *The Computer Journal*, 33:547–555, 1990.

19. N.W. Paton and M.H. Williams, editors. *Proc. of 1st Int. Workshop on Rules in Database Systems (RIDS '93)*, Edinburgh, August 1993. Springer-Verlag.

20. D.W. Shipman. The Functional Data Model and the Data Language DAPLEX. *ACM Transactions on Database Systems*, 6(1):140–173, March 1981.

21. H. Söndergaard and P. Sestoft. Non-Determinism in Functional Languages. *The Computer Journal*, 35(5):514–523, 1992.

22. P.J. Stuckey and S. Sudarshan. Compiling Query Constraints. In *Proc. of ACM PODS*, pages 56–67, Minneapolis, USA, May 1994.

23. S.D. Urban, A.P. Karadimce, and R.B. Nannapaneni. The Implementation and Evaluation of Integrity Maintenance Rules in an Object-Oriented Database. In *8th Int. Conf. on Data Engineering*, pages 565–572, Phoenix, Arizona, 1992. IEEE.

24. P. Van Hentenryck. *Constraint Satisfaction in Logic Programming.* MIT Press, 1989.

25. P. Wadler. How to Replace Failure by a List of Successes. In J.-P. Jouannaud, editor, *Proc. of the IFIP Int. Conf. on Functional Prog. Langs. and Computer Arch.*, LNCS , Vol. 201, p. 113–128, Nancy, France, Sept. 1985. Springer-Verlag.

Constant Propagation Versus Join Reordering in Datalog

Mariano P. Consens[1], Alberto O. Mendelzon[2],
Dimitra Vista[2], and Peter T. Wood[3*]

[1] Dep. of Computer Science, Univ. of Waterloo, Waterloo, Canada N2L 3G1
[2] Computer Systems Research Institute, Univ. of Toronto, Toronto, Canada M5S 1A1
[3] Dep. of Computer Science, Univ. of Cape Town, Rondebosch 7700, South Africa

Abstract. Constant propagation and join reordering are two standard optimization techniques used for Datalog programs. These techniques have typically been studied independently of one another. However, in order to achieve constant propagation it is sometimes necessary to impose a certain join ordering on a given program. In the worst case this ordering may result in efficiencies which overcome the benefit of constant propagation. Thus the goal of constant propagation should not necessarily be pursued to the exclusion of all else. We study this problem in the context of GraphLog, a visual language whose queries are graphical notations which are translated into Datalog. We study two translation schemes from GraphLog to Datalog, one which always achieves constant propagation and another which does not. We show that each translation can significantly outperform the other. We demonstrate this by both measuring execution times using actual application data, and by providing analytical formulae to explain the trade-off between constant propagation and join reordering.

1 Introduction

Two topics of research in the area of query evaluation for recursive Datalog rules have been constant propagation and join ordering. In the former, given a recursive Datalog program with a constant in the query, the goal is to propagate the constant from the query down to the base (EDB) relations in order to reduce the number of tuples computed by the program. In the latter, the goal is to order the joins in the bodies of rules in such a way as to minimize the size of intermediate results.

Up to now, the topics of constant propagation and join ordering have been pursued independently. In addition, ordering of joins has been restricted to consideration of one rule at a time. Of course, if a program is nonrecursive, it can be translated to relational algebra (say), after which conventional approaches to join ordering can be applied. In the case of recursive programs, however, we know

---

[*] Most of this work was done while the author was on sabbatical at the University of Toronto.

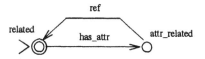

Fig. 1. The automaton M corresponding to (has_attr · ref)*

of no work on global rewriting of a program in order to improve the ordering of joins.

In this paper, we investigate the interaction of constant propagation and join ordering in recursive Datalog programs. We restrict our attention to a class of queries which correspond to path computations on graph databases as specified by regular expressions. These are the queries which can be computed by the Hy+ database visualization system developed at the University of Toronto [4]. We show that, if we insist on propagating constants to EDB relations, then certain join orderings are precluded. One of these orderings may be more efficient than that imposed by constant propagation. We provide cost formulas and heuristics to guide a choice among the alternative strategies.

Example 1. Consider a graph G representing schema information for an object database. The nodes of G represent class names and attribute names. There are two types of edges: **has_attr** relates a class name with an attribute name which is a property of the class, and **ref** relates an attribute name to a class name when the attribute is a reference (relationship) attribute. These edges can be represented by two binary relations **has_attr(class, attr)** and **ref(attr, class)**. We say that classes c_1 and c_2 are *related* if c_1 has an attribute which references c_2 either directly or indirectly. We can represent this relationship using the regular expression $R = $ (**has_attr · ref**)* (where · represents concatenation and * represents reflexive transitive closure).

If we construct a Datalog program based on the parse tree of R, we obtain the program P_1:

```
related(ClassX, ClassX).
related(ClassX, ClassY) ← related(ClassX, ClassZ),
                          directly_related(ClassZ, ClassY).
directly_related(ClassX, ClassY) ← has_attr(ClassX, Attr),
                                    ref(Attr, ClassY).
?- related(ClassX, ClassY).
```

Here the concatenation in R is represented by the **directly_related** predicate. The two rules for **related** compute the closure.

On the other hand, we can first construct a nondeterministic finite automaton (NFA) M for recognizing strings in the language denoted by R. The NFA M has two states: **related**, which is both the initial and final state, and **attr_related**. Figure 1 shows M. Each state of M corresponds to a derived predicate: **related** is the relation of interest, and **attr_related** is an intermediate relation. The intuition behind the automaton representation is the following: the initial state, **related**, at start, knows that any class is related to itself. Then, alternatively examining a **has_attr** and **ref** fact, more **related** facts are produced, until no more facts can be thus derived. We use the NFA M to produce P_2.

```
related(ClassX, ClassX).
attr_related(ClassX, Attr) ← related(ClassX, ClassY),
                             has_attr(ClassY, Attr).
related(ClassX, ClassY) ← attr_related(ClassX, Attr),
                          ref(Attr, ClassY).
?- related(ClassX, ClassY).
```

The bottom-up evaluation of the rules of P_2 mimics the breadth-first traversal of graph G starting from all class nodes, and alternatively following **has_attr** and **ref** edges. The rules are obtained from M as follows. The first rule comes from the fact that **related** is the initial state of M. The next two rules are derived from transitions from **related** to **attr_related** (labelled **has_attr**) and from **attr_related** to **related** (labelled **ref**), respectively. The query comes from the fact that **related** is the final state of M.

The above two translations from regular expressions to Datalog are implemented in the GraphLog query language [5, 7] provided by the Hy$^+$ system. We call the former the *closure* translation, because it computes closures of EDB or IDB relations, and the latter the *nfa* translation. Datalog programs are passed by Hy$^+$ to the CORAL deductive database system for evaluation [12]. Which translation should be adopted is one of the issues explored in this paper.

Consider the bottom-up evaluation of P_1. If we abbreviate **has_attr** by h and **ref** by r, then the sequence of joins performed during the evaluation is

$$(h \bowtie r)$$

$$(h \bowtie r) \bowtie (h \bowtie r)$$

$$((h \bowtie r) \bowtie (h \bowtie r)) \bowtie (h \bowtie r)$$

$$\vdots$$

Now consider the bottom-up evaluation of P_2. The sequence of joins is:

$$(h \bowtie r)$$

$$((h \bowtie r) \bowtie h)$$

$$(((h \bowtie r) \bowtie h) \bowtie r)$$

$$\vdots$$

Note that both translations produce left-linear programs. Right-linear versions of each would produce other join orderings.

Now assume that we are interested only in those classes related to the particular class called **object**. One crucial difference between the two translations is that the *nfa* translation admits the propagation of constants to base relations using the technique of factoring [11], while the *closure* translation does not. For program P_1 from the *closure* translation, we simply substitute object for ClassX in the query clause and apply the magic sets transformation [2].

The *nfa* translation modifies P_2 as follows:

```
class_related_to_object(object).
attr_related_to_object(Attr) ← class_related_to_object(Class),
                              has_attr(Class, Attr).
class_related_to_object(Class) ← attr_related_to_object(Attr),
                                ref(Attr, Class).
related(object, Class) ← class_related_to_object(Class).
?- related(object, Class).
```

The above program corresponds to traversing graph G starting at the node representing the class object. This ability to perform constant propagation might lead one to conclude that the *nfa* translation would always be preferable to the *closure* translation when constants appear in a GraphLog query. This is not the case, however. The reason is that the join ordering imposed by the *nfa* translation may be particularly expensive. The different ordering adopted by the *closure* translation may overcome the initial loss in performance due to a constant not being propagated, outperforming the *nfa* translation after one or two iterations of the fixed point computation.

The remainder of the paper is organized as follows. In the next section, we use regular expressions, which are a fundamental component of GraphLog, to introduce the two translation schemes: the *closure* translation in Section 2.1, and the *nfa* translation in Section 2.2. An example from the application of performance tuning during software development is presented in Section 3, which also reports on some performance results which suggest that the *nfa* scheme is always better. This conclusion is refuted in Section 4 where we show through further empirical results as well as analytical formulae that each translation can outperform the other. Concluding remarks are found in Section 5.

2 Translating Regular Queries to Datalog

In this section, we describe the regular queries which form a fundamental part of the GraphLog query language as well as their translation to Datalog. Two translations are described: the first is the *closure* translation, which defines the semantics of GraphLog; the second is the *nfa* translation. Section 3 and 4 presents both experimental and analytical comparisons between the two methods.

Since for the purposes of this paper we do not require a number of features of GraphLog, we simplify the following description accordingly. For a complete description of the language, the reader is referred to [3].

In GraphLog, a *term* is either a constant or a variable (once again, more general terms are in fact allowed). An *edge label* is an expression generated by the following grammar, where p is a predicate:

$$E \rightarrow E|E; \; E \cdot E; \; -E; \; (E); \; E^+; \; E^*; \; p; \; \neg p$$

This is essentially a grammar for regular expressions, with "|" representing alternation, "." concatenation, "−" inversion (a traversal from head to tail, rather than tail to head), "¬" negation (the absence of a path), "+" transitive closure, and "∗" reflexive transitive closure.

Database instances are directed graphs whose nodes are labelled with ground terms and whose edges are labelled with predicates. Database instances of the object-oriented or relational model can easily be visualized as graphs. For example, an edge labelled p from a node labelled T_1 to a node labelled T_2, corresponds to tuple (T_1, T_2) of relation p in the relational model.

Queries are directed graphs whose nodes are labelled by terms and each edge is labelled by an edge label. The query graph represents a pattern; the query evaluator searches the database graph for all occurrences of that pattern.

A query must have one *distinguished* edge, labelled by a positive literal. The meaning of a query is to define the predicate in this distinguished literal in terms of the rest of the pattern. The semantics of queries is given by a translation to stratified Datalog. Each query graph G translates to a rule with the label of the distinguished edge in the head, and as many literals in the body as there are non-distinguished edges in G. If an edge is labelled with a regular expression, additional rules to define its predicate are necessary.

2.1 The Closure Translation

Suppose between nodes labelled X and Y, there is an edge labelled p, where X, Y are terms and p is a predicate. We will denote this by $p(X, Y)$. In fact, the meaning of such an edge is given by the Datalog fact $p(X, Y)$.

Given a GraphLog query Q with non-distinguished edges $p_1, \ldots, p_n$, where p_i is from node labelled X_{i-1} to node labelled X_i, and with distinguished edge p from node labelled X_{j_1} to node labelled X_{j_2}, the translation for Q contains the following rule that defines the predicate p:

$$p(X_{j_1}, X_{j_2}) \leftarrow l_1(X_0, X_1), l_2(X_1, X_2), \ldots, l_n(X_{n-1}, X_n).$$

where $l_i(X_{i-1}, X_i)$ is $p_i(X_{i-1}, X_i)$, if the edge is positive, $\neg p_i(X_{i-1}, X_i)$, if the edge is negated, or it is defined recursively on the structure of the label according to the following algorithm (assuming that the edge is from a node labelled X to one labelled Y):

- *Inversion*: Label $-e$ corresponds to the literal $e(Y, X)$.
- *Concatenation*: Label $e_1 \cdot e_2$ corresponds to the rule

$$conc(X, Y) \leftarrow e_1(X, Z), e_2(Z, Y).$$

- *Alternation*: Label $e_1 | e_2$ corresponds to the rules

$$alter(X, Y) \leftarrow e_1(X, Y).$$
$$alter(X, Y) \leftarrow e_2(X, Y).$$

- *Closure*: Label e^+ corresponds to the rules

$$tc\_e(X,Y) \leftarrow e(X,Y).$$
$$tc\_e(X,Y) \leftarrow tc\_e(X,Z), e(Z,Y).$$

- *Kleene closure*: Label e^* corresponds to the rules

$$kleene\_e(X,X).$$
$$kleene\_e(X,Y) \leftarrow kleene\_e(X,Z), e(Z,Y).$$

Note that the rules for the two forms of closure above are left-linear. The choice between left- and right-linear rules is another which could be made by the query language optimizer; for simplicity and consistency, we will use left-linear rules throughout. The reader is referred back to program P_1 of Example 1 for an example of the output of the *closure* translation.

GraphLog users are allowed to label nodes with (single) constants. The *closure* translation of such a query to Datalog will result in a program containing a single constant in the query goal, whereupon the rewriting techniques such as magic sets [2], factoring [11] and context rewriting [10] become applicable. We assume that readers are familiar with each of these.

CORAL provides an annotation for controlling evaluation called **@factoring**. This applies the context rewriting transformation of [10]. We will use the term *factoring* in the same way as in [11] to mean the reduction in the number of arguments in recursive predicates. Context rewriting does not do this, so to avoid confusion we will refer to the CORAL annotation as *context rewriting*.

There are at least two limitations of context rewriting. Firstly, it is not applicable to all programs generated from GraphLog queries. Secondly, context rewriting may be an order of magnitude less efficient than a true factoring transformation. The original factoring transformation applies to a very restricted class of programs [11]. However, it was shown in [13, 14] that the factoring transformation can be applied to any program generated by an alternative translation from (single-edge) GraphLog queries to Datalog. A simplified version of this translation is presented below; for a complete version, the reader is referred to [13].

2.2 The NFA Translation

Rather than a translation based on the structure of the regular expression R in the GraphLog query, in this subsection we describe a translation based on a nondeterministic finite automaton (NFA) constructed from R. We assume the reader is familiar with the definition of a nondeterministic finite automaton [9]. Given NFA M, the language $L(M)$ *accepted* by M is the set of all strings accepted by M.

We assume that we are given a single edge from a GraphLog query. The edge is labelled with an arbitrary regular expression R. The first step in the translation is·to construct an NFA M from R. The transitions in M are labelled with predicates from R. The second step is to generate a Datalog program P

from M. This uses the standard technique of generating a regular grammar from an NFA, and yields a regular chain program.

The details of the translation from regular expression R to program P are as follows:

1. Construct an NFA M which accepts the language $L(R)$, as described, for example, in [9].
2. For each transition t in M from p to q labelled with e, generate a Datalog rule as follows:

$$q(X, Y) \leftarrow p(X, Z), e(Z, Y).$$

If, instead, t is labelled with $-e$, generate:

$$q(X, Y) \leftarrow p(X, Z), e(Y, Z).$$

3. For the initial state s_0 of M, generate the fact $s_0(X, X).$, and for each final state f of M, generate a rule

$$s(X, Y) \leftarrow f(X, Y).$$

where s is the distinguished (query) predicate.

Note, once again, that left-linear rules are produced by the above translation.

When one of the nodes v in the GraphLog query is labelled with a constant, we modify the translation as follows. If v is the head node, we first reverse the automaton M, also performing the inversion of each term labelling a transition in M. Now we modify steps (2) and (3) above by deleting all occurrences of X from the rules generated in (2), and replacing $s_0(X, X).$ by $s_0(c).$ in (3), where c is the node constant in the GraphLog query. Also in (3) for each final state we generate $s(c, X) : -f(Y)$. We have thus successfully propagated the constant to the EDB predicates and reduced the number of arguments in all the IDB predicates.

We refer back to the program P_2 of Example 1. When comparing P_2 to P_1 (the output of the *closure* translation), there are two differences to note. Firstly, the recursion in the *nfa* translation is in terms of mutually recursive rules, while that in the *closure* translation is in terms of the closure of an IDB predicate. This results in different join orderings being chosen by the two translations. Secondly, when a constant is present, the *nfa* translation factors the recursive predicates and propagates `object` into the program.

These two differences, join ordering and constant propagation, provide the principal explanations for the performance results presented in the following two sections.

3 Application-Based Performance Comparisons

In this section we describe the differences in performance stemming from the two different translations in an application of performance tuning during software development (described in detail in [3, 6]). In this setting, we regard the code as a set of functions that call each other. The code is partitioned into *sections*, which are load modules. Each section consists of a set of functions and a set of overlay *areas* that are arranged in *series* in memory. An area consists of a set of sections that are arranged in *parallel* in memory.

The data of interest are generated by a linker and are represented by these sets of facts: section_function(S,F) denotes that section S contains function F; section_area(S,A) that section S contains area A; area_section(A,S) that area A contains section S; and, calls(F1,F2) that function F1 calls function F2. The database comprises about 180K bytes, with the number of tuples as follows: calls (4593), section_function (995), section_area (31), and area_section (107).

When the program is executed, the root section is loaded and remains resident in memory until termination. All other sections are loaded on demand, and the loader guarantees that all ancestors of a section in the section-area tree are in memory whenever the section is. In order to retain acceptable performance, the loader must keep track of when it is actually necessary to reload a section.

We look at two relations in this database: overwrites and smashable_caller.

overwrites

When a section is loaded it may *overwrite* other sections. For example, parallel sections in the same overlay area overwrite each other. We say that section S1 overwrites section S2 if there exist two distinct sections, SP1 and SP2, at the top level of the same area A, such that SP1 (resp. SP2) is an ancestor of S1 (resp. S2) or is S1 (resp. S2) itself.

The definition of overwrites has a *common sub-expression*: the relation that associates a given section A with a section S1 that A contains. We define the auxiliary relation aux(A,SP1,S1) whenever area A directly contains SP1, and SP1 is either S1 or an ancestor of S1. In other words, aux corresponds to the regular expression area_section · (section_area · area_section)*. The predicate overwrites is then defined as:

```
overwrites(S1,S2) ←
        aux(A,SP1,S1),
        aux(A,SP2,S2),
        not SP1 = SP2.
```

We can use either the *closure* or the *nfa* translation for the definition of aux. Moreover, in the presence of constants, we can project out the A argument of the aux predicate, and push the constant as far as possible (in both schemes). For example, if we are interested in overwrites within the deskArea area, the *closure* translation of the aux predicate is (A argument dropped):

```
aux(SP1,S1) ← area_section(deskArea,SP1), kl_compo(SP1,S1).
kl_compo(SP1,SP1).
kl_compo(SP1,S1) ← kl_compo(SP1,X), compo(X,S1).
compo(X,Y) ← section_area(X,Z), area_section(Z,Y).
```

while the *nfa* translation is:

```
p(SP1) ← area_section(deskArea,SP1).
q(SP1,X) ← p(SP1), section_area(SP1,X).
r(SP1,S1) ← q(SP1,X), area_section(X,S1).
q(SP1,X) ← r(SP1,S1), section_area(S1,X).

aux(SP1,SP1) ← p(SP1).
aux(SP1,S1) ← r(SP1,S1).
```

Note that the *nfa* translation is not able to factor all IDB predicates since both variables of the closure are required as join attributes in the rule for **overwrites** above. Nevertheless, as shown in Figure 2, the *nfa* translation performs slightly better than the *closure* translation. An explanation of the improvement in the absence of constants is postponed to Section 4.

smashable_caller

When a function call returns, the loader checks that the section being returned to is still in memory, and if not, reloads it. Recall that while any function is executing, its section and all of its ancestors in the section area tree will be in memory. We say that a section S2 is a *smashable caller* of function F1 if S2 contains a function F2 that calls F1 and S2 is not an ancestor in the section area tree of the section S1 that contains F1. Section S2 is potentially smashable because it is not guaranteed to be in memory while F1 is executing.

The Datalog definition of **smashable_caller** is

```
smashable_caller(S2, F1) ←
        section_function(S2, F2),
        calls(F2, F1),
        section_function(S1, F1),
        not kl_compo(S1, S2).
```

where **kl_compo** is the (Kleene) closure of the relation among sections in the section area tree. The *closure* definition for it is as follows:

```
kl_compo(X, X).
kl_compo(X, Y) ← kl_compo(X, Z), compo(Z, Y).
compo(X, Y) ← section_area(X, Z), area_section(Z, Y).
```

Assume now that S1 is bound to the constant **initSect**. In the *closure* translation, all occurrences of S1 in the rule for **smashable_caller** are replaced with **initSect**; the rules for **kl_compo** are unchanged. In contrast, the *nfa* definition yields the following:

```
p(initSect).
q(Temp) ← p(S1), section_area(S1, Temp).
p(S2) ← q(Temp), area_section(Temp, S2).
kl_compo1(S2) ← p(S2).
```

Query	Constant	Which Constant	Output	Closure	Nfa
overwrites	–	–	6 684	6.08	**4.84**
overwrites	√	deskArea	352	0.87	**0.49**
smashable_caller	–	–	2001	21.73	**2.91**
smashable_caller	√	initSect	95	0.58	**0.19**

Fig. 2. Performance results on computing **overwrites, and smashable_caller**

Predicates p and q correspond to the two states of an NFA for the regular expression (**section_area** · **area_section**)*. State p is both the initial and final state.

Note that, in the presence of the constant, the *nfa* translation is able to factor **kl_compo**. This explains why it outperforms the *closure* translation on this example. It should be noted that **area_section** and **section_area** are small relations, so the performance difference is not that great. By increasing the size of these relations, the performance differential can be made arbitrarily large.

One reason for the relatively large difference in performance in the absence of constants is that CORAL uses ordered search for the evaluation of negated subgoals [12]. This also precludes the use of context rewriting when constants are present.

Figure 2 is a summary of our performance results (all times indicate the user cpu time in seconds and are averaged over a number of runs on a lightly loaded Sun Sparc10). As indicated, each query was run with and without a constant labelling one of the nodes in order to compare the effects of constant propagation. The column labelled "output" indicates the number of tuples in the answer of the query. The programs produced by the *closure* translation were run with the default rewriting scheme of CORAL, namely supplementary magic sets. Those produced by the *nfa* translation were run with no rewriting.

The results in Figure 2 suggest that the *nfa* translation always outperforms the *closure* translation. However, it is easy to find other examples where the *closure* translation runs faster than the *nfa* translation for queries with or without constants. We explore this in the next section.

4 Performance Analysis

Previous results on comparing performance costs induced by different evaluation strategies or optimization methods seem to suggest that an overriding factor is the presence or absence of constants in the query [1, 8]. In this section, we demonstrate both analytically and experimentally that the choice of which translation is preferable is *not* guided by the presence or absence of constants. It is guided only by the shape of the graph, that is, the join selectivity of the relations involved.

Query	Constant	Output	Closure	Nfa
(section_function.calls.(-section_function))$^+$	–	10 713	**14.41**	217.77
(function_call.section_call)$^{+4}$	–	14 224	120.12	**7.19**
(section_call.function_call)$^+$	$\checkmark$	4	**0.16**	0.24
(section_function.calls.(-calls).(-section_function))$^+$	$\checkmark$	104	46.52	**2.87**

Fig. 3. More experimental results on the overlay database

We focus on expressions involving the closure of a concatenation. The reason for this is that the two translations give rise to different join orderings for this class of expressions, while producing identical programs for other classes. The concatenation of a with b, $a \cdot b$, is the join of a and b, $a \bowtie b$, with the join attributes projected out. We will denote the concatenation as simply ab.

4.1 In the Absence of Constants

Suppose that the relation to be computed is the transitive closure of ab, that is, $(ab)^+$. The program of the *closure* translation computes ab and then joins every intermediate result $(ab)^i$ with ab in order to compute the next intermediate result $(ab)^{i+1}$. The program of the *nfa* translation, on the other hand, first joins $(ab)^i$ with a, and then the result, $(ab)^i a$, with b to get $(ab)^{i+1}$. Note that the *nfa* program requires twice as many semi-naive iterations, and therefore twice as many actual joins, as the *closure* program. The point is that the actual joins that are needed for the *nfa* program may be *cheaper*.

The algebraic expression that expresses the cost of evaluating the *closure* program is

$$\text{cost}(a \bowtie b) + \sum_{i=1}^{l-1} \text{cost}((ab)^i \bowtie ab)$$

while that for the *nfa* program is

$$\text{cost}(a \bowtie b) + \sum_{i=1}^{l-1} \left(\text{cost}((ab)^i \bowtie a) + \text{cost}((ab)^i a \bowtie b) \right)$$

where l is the maximum length of computed paths.

Case 1: Where Closure Beats Nfa If the cost of joining $(ab)^i$ with ab is smaller than the cost of first joining $(ab)^i$ with a and then joining the result with b for each i, then the *closure* translation is better than the *nfa* translation. If the condition holds in the first iteration, and we assume some uniformity of the property across iterations, then it likely holds in subsequent iterations. So,

---

[4] Only a subset of the database is considered.

checking the condition for $i = 1$ provides a heuristic for choosing between the two translations in the absence of constants.

For illustrative purposes, we use the simplest measure for the cost of computing a join below, namely, the product of the sizes of its operand relations. Our motivation for this is that using a more sophisticated and accurate measure does not alter which of the translations is the more efficient in each of the cases we consider.

Figure 3 shows the results on further experiments on the database of Section 3. The following table computes the costs for $i = 1$, first for the *closure* translation, then for the *nfa* translation corresponding to the first row of Figure 3.

relation	no. of tuples	cost
section_function	995	
calls	4592	
r = section_function ⋈ calls ⋈ (-section_function)	511	
r ⋈ r	1993	2.6×10^5
total for *closure* in 2nd iteration ($i = 1$)		2.6×10^5
s = r ⋈ section_function	37220	5.1×10^5
t = s ⋈ calls	28432	1.7×10^8
t ⋈ (-section_function)	1993	2.8×10^7
total for *nfa* in 2nd iteration ($i = 1$)		1.9×10^8

Clearly, it is more beneficial to produce the join once and then use it repeatedly. This explains why the *closure* translation for this program requires only 14.41 sec while the *nfa* translation requires 217.77 sec. Note that the numbers in the **cost** column above are derived by multiplying the sizes of the operand relations in the corresponding join. Hence, the first number is $511 * 511 = 2,6 * 10^5$.

Case 2: Where Nfa Beats Closure If the cost of joining $(ab)^i$ with ab is greater than the cost of joining $(ab)^i$ first with a and then with b, then it is likely that the *nfa* translation is better than the *closure* translation.

As an example consider the program that corresponds to the second row of Figure 3.

relation	no. of tuples	cost
function_call	115	
section_call	139	
r = function_call ⋈ section_call	13376	
r ⋈ r	14098	1.8×10^8
total for *closure* in 2nd iteration ($i = 1$)		1.8×10^8
s = r ⋈ function_call	212	1.5×10^6
s ⋈ section_call	14098	2.9×10^4
total for *nfa* in 2nd iteration ($i = 1$)		1.5×10^6

Two new relations are used in this example: function_call(F, S) which is true if F calls a function in section S; and, section_call(S, F) which is true if a function in section S calls F. The comparative costs for $i = 1$ are given above. Clearly, in this case the *nfa* translation is more efficient (cf. Figure 3), 7.19 sec vs 120.12 sec. The same reasoning explains why the *nfa* translation outperforms the *closure* translation on the examples in Section 3.

4.2 In the Presence of Constants

Suppose now that we request the transitive closure of ab starting from a given constant, say c. Let us denote the computed relation by $\pi_c((ab)^+)$. The program of the *closure* translation first computes the whole of ab and then projects it on c. Subsequently, it joins each $\pi_c(ab)^i$ with ab in order to compute $\pi_c(ab)^{i+1}$. The program of the *nfa* translation, on the other hand, first projects a on c (to get $\pi_c(a)$) and then joins it with b. Then, it joins each $\pi_c(ab)^i$ with a and the result, $\pi_c(ab)^i a$, with b to get $\pi_c(ab)^{i+1}$.

Note that the *nfa* program requires twice as many semi-naive iterations, and therefore twice as many actual joins, as the *closure* program. Also, note the difference with the case of no constants. Given the initial constant to start the computation from, the *nfa* program never in fact computes the whole join ab. The initial step in the computation is $a \bowtie b$, for the *closure* program, but, $\pi_c(a) \bowtie b$, for the *nfa* program. The algebraic expression that expresses the cost of the *closure* program is

$$\text{cost}(a \bowtie b) + \sum_{i=1}^{l-1} \text{cost}(\pi_c(ab)^i \bowtie ab)$$

while that for the *nfa* program is

$$\text{cost}(\pi_c(a) \bowtie b) + \sum_{i=1}^{l-1} \left(\text{cost}(\pi_c(ab)^i \bowtie a) + \text{cost}(\pi_c(ab)^i a \bowtie b) \right)$$

where l is the maximum length of computed paths.

If we hope to devise a heuristic for choosing between the two methods, as in the previous case, we have to consider the following two factors. The first is the initial cost of computing $a \bowtie b$, for the *closure* program; the *nfa* program computes initially just $\pi_c(a) \bowtie b$. The second factor is, as before, to compare the cost of joining $\pi_c(ab)^i$ with ab to the cost of joining first with a and then with b.

Case 1: Where Closure Beats Nfa Consider the program corresponding to the third row of the Figure 3. We consider the cost for the case $i = 1$ below.

It is clear that joining with **section_call** expands the size of the intermediate relation by so much that after a few iterations (in fact in no more than two iterations) the total cost paid by the *nfa* program exceeds the initial cost of the *closure* program, and the *closure* program performs better overall.

relation	no. of tuples	cost
section_call	568	
function_call	928	
r = section_call $\bowtie$ function_call	16	5.2×10^5
s = $\pi_{specialSect}(r)$	4	16
$s \bowtie r$	4	64
total for *closure* after 2nd iteration		5.2×10^5
v = $\pi_{specialSect}$(section_call)	324	
s = $v \bowtie$ function_call	4	3.0×10^5
t = $s \bowtie$ section_call	423	2.2×10^3
$t \bowtie$ function_call	4	3.9×10^5
total for *nfa* after 2nd iteration		5.7×10^5

Case 2: Where Nfa Beats Closure Finally, consider the two translations for the program that gives better performance to the *nfa* program, the last row of Figure 3.

relation	no. of tuples	cost
section_function	995	
calls	4592	
r = section_function $\bowtie$ calls $\bowtie$ (-calls) $\quad$ $\bowtie$ (-section_function)	5878	2.1×10^{13}
s = $\pi_{scanselSect}(r)$	92	5.8×10^3
$s \bowtie r$	102	5.4×10^5
total for *closure* after 2nd iteration		2.1×10^{13}
$t1$ = $\pi_{scanselSect}$(section_function)	13	
$v1$ = $t1 \bowtie$ calls	44	5.9×10^4
$u1$ = $v1 \bowtie$ (-calls)	417	2.0×10^5
$w1$ = $u1 \bowtie$ (-section_function)	92	4.1×10^5
$t2$ = $w1 \bowtie$ section_function	934	9.1×10^4
$v2$ = $t2 \bowtie$ calls	917	4.2×10^6
$u2$ = $v2 \bowtie$ (-calls)	743	4.2×10^6
$u2 \bowtie$ (-section_function)	102	7.4×10^5
total for *nfa* after 2nd iteration		9.9×10^6

It is clear that the initial cost of computing the complete join in the *closure* program results in its poor performance. Hence constant propagation is to be favored in this case.

5 Conclusions

In this paper we have compared the relative merits of constant propagation and join reordering as optimization methods for Datalog programs. This has been investigated using two different translations from the visual language GraphLog to Datalog. Our motivation is that visual presentation and querying of data will not be adopted by practitioners unless usefulness is matched by efficiency.

The *nfa* translation permits the propagation of constants in a query to the base relations, while the *closure* translation does not. Common wisdom suggests that this should favour the *nfa* translation in the presence of constants. We showed, however, that this is not the case. Given a query representing the closure of a concatenation of relations, the two translations produce programs which result in different join orderings being chosen during evaluation. This difference can override the benefit of constant propagation, thereby making it undesirable in some circumstances.

Recently it has been shown that the original factoring translation of [11] can be correctly applied to closure programs [15]. In addition, after further optimizations, a closure program generated from regular expression R is transformed into precisely the program generated by the *nfa* translation for R [15]. The results of the present paper indicate, however, that this transformation may not always be desirable.

References

1. F. Bancilhon and R. Ramakrishnan. An Amateur's Introduction to Recursive Query Processing Strategies. In *SIGMOD*, pages 16–52, 1986.
2. C. Beeri and R. Ramakrishnan. On the Power of Magic. In *PODS*, pages 269–283, 1987.
3. M.P. Consens. *Creating and Filtering Structural Data Visualizations using Hygraph Patterns*. PhD thesis, Department of Computer Science, University of Toronto, February 1994. (Available as Technical Report CSRI-302).
4. M.P. Consens, F.Ch. Eigler, M.Z. Hasan, A.O. Mendelzon, E.G. Noik, A.G. Ryman, and D. Vista. Architecture and Applications of the Hy^+ Visualization System. *IBM Systems Journal*, 33(3):458–476, 1994.
5. M.P. Consens and A.O. Mendelzon. GraphLog: A Visual Formalism for Real Life Recursion. In *PODS*, pages 404–416, 1990.
6. M.P. Consens, A.O. Mendelzon, and A. Ryman. Visualizing and Querying Software Structures. In *ICSE '92*, pages 138–156, 1992.
7. M.P. Consens, A.O. Mendelzon, and D. Vista. Deductive Database Support for Data Visualization. In *EDBT*, pages 45–58, 1994.
8. J. Han and H. Lu. Some Performance Results on Recursive Query Processing in Relational Database Systems. In *ICDE*, pages 533–539, 1986.
9. J.E. Hopcroft and J.D. Ullman. *Introduction to Automata Theory, Languages, and Computation*. Addison-Wesley, 1979.
10. D. Kemp, K. Ramamohanarao, and Z. Somogyi. Right-, Left-, and Multi-Linear Rule Transformations that Maintain Context Information. In *VLDB*, pages 380–391, 1990.
11. J.F. Naughton, R. Ramakrishnan, Y. Sagiv, and J.D. Ullman. Argument Reduction by Factoring. In *VLDB*, pages 173–182, 1989.
12. R. Ramakrishnan, D. Srivastava, S. Sudarshan, and P. Seshadri. Implementation of the CORAL Deductive Database System. In *SIGMOD*, pages 167–176, 1993.
13. D. Vista and P.T. Wood. Efficient Evaluation of Visual Queries Using Deductive Databases. In R. Ramakrishnan, editor, *Applications of Logic Databases*, pages 143–161. Kluwer Academic Publishers, Boston, 1995.
14. P.T. Wood. Factoring Augmented Regular Chain Programs. In *VLDB*, pages 255–263, 1990.
15. P.T. Wood. Magic Factoring of Closure Programs. In *PODS*, pages 174–183, 1995.

Compilation and Simplification of Temporal Integrity Constraints

Dimitris Plexousakis*

Dept. of Computer Science, University of Toronto
Toronto, Ont M5S 1A4, Canada
E-mail: dp@ai.toronto.edu

Abstract. The paper presents a novel compilation scheme for temporal integrity constraints and deductive rules expressed in an interval-based first-order temporal logic. Compilation builds a dependence graph with simplified forms of the constraints and rules. This permits the compile-time simplification of the formulae that have to be verified at run-time, as well as the precomputation of potential implicit updates. We show how simplified forms can be obtained with respect to transactions made up of arbitrary sequences of basic updates. Additional optimization steps exploit the organization of simplified forms in dependence graphs.

1 Introduction

The maintenance of semantic integrity is recognized as a cornerstone issue for the development of data bases and knowledge bases alike [11], [27], [18]. Integrity constraints express application dependent semantics that are not built into the data structures used to represent knowledge. Additionally, they constitute a means for controlling the quality of information stored in knowledge repositories.

Despite the extensive research conducted during the last decade, semantic integrity enforcement has yet to become a practical technology. This is due to the lack of efficient methods for checking the satisfaction of general integrity constraints. Commercial database management systems provide automatic enforcement of limited types of integrity constraints, such as keys and referential integrity constraints, if at all. Moreover, the vast majority of research results on semantic integrity maintenance concern *static* integrity constraints, whereas only relatively few papers have dealt with the enforcement of *dynamic* constraints.

The need for modeling evolving domains has given rise to challenging research issues relating to the incorporation of time in knowledge bases. The by now well established notions of *static* and *transitional integrity* [19], [9] must be generalized to that of *temporal integrity*. The problem of ensuring that the correctness criteria expressed by integrity constraints will not be violated, now has an additional dimension, namely that of monitoring time-dependent properties. Such properties arise naturally in dynamic domains. For instance, a common task of power plant monitoring systems is to enforce the requirement that values

---

* Current Address: Department of Computing and Information Sciences, Kansas State University, Manhattan, KS 66506-2302, USA

of certain parameters fluctuate in limited ways in certain time periods. Financial and trading applications need to preserve constraints on the time-varying characteristics of the objects involved, e.g. stock prices over time [6].

Temporal databases [26] and their extensions [2], [20] need robust mechanisms for ensuring that time-dependent properties do not become violated due to the evolution of the database or the passage of time. The properties that need to be ensured may refer to arbitrarily many states, past or future, of the database. Thus, the verification of integrity constraints may involve reasoning in multiple states. The complexity of verifying temporal integrity constraints is substantially higher than that of verifying properties that refer to a single state only or to pairs of consecutive states.

So far, the research community has dealt with the problem of maintaining semantic integrity in contexts such as relational, deductive or object-oriented databases [4], [5], [13]. On the other hand, research in temporal databases has almost exclusively adopted a relational model [15], [7], [12], [25]. Work on temporal deductive databases has mainly dealt with the problem of finitely representing infinite temporal properties [14] and with the evaluation of temporal logic programs [2]. This paper proposes an efficient method for enforcing temporal integrity constraints in a structurally object-oriented framework and in the presence of temporal deductive rules.

First-Order Temporal Logic (FOTL) [10] and several of its variants or subsets have been the most popular formalisms for expressing temporal constraints. Deontic variants of Dynamic Logic [28] have also been proposed for the expression of dynamic and deontic properties. We use a reified temporal logic based on time intervals for the expression of constraints and rules.

Integrity constraint verification consists of determining whether all integrity constraints are satisfied in the state resulting after an update. The expressive power of the assertion language, the anticipated large numbers of constraints and rules, and the inherent complexity of deduction in first-order (temporal) logic constitute major impediments to constraint verification. Constraint simplification methods attempt to derive simpler forms of the constraints that have to be verified when updates occur. Simplification methods can be classified as *run-time* or *compile-time* depending on whether simplification takes place at update time or at knowledge base definition time. Naive constraint verification methods check all integrity constraints after every update. *Incremental* methods, however, restrict attention to only a subset of all constraints, namely those affected by a particular update type. They are based on the premise that the knowledge base is known not to violate any constraint at the state in which an update takes place. This knowledge can be exploited for the simplification of temporal formulae, as well as for the minimization of the amount of historical information that needs to be examined for constraint verification.

This paper proposes such an incremental compile-time simplification method for temporal constraints and rules. The basic approach was described in [20]. Here we focus on enhancements of the method with respect to the treatment of temporal constraints for arbitrary transactions. Specifically, we propose compile-time simplifications to the formulæ expressing temporal constraints and rules. The simplified forms that suffice to be evaluated at run-time, when arbitrary transactions are issued, are organized in the form of a dependence graph, a structure that captures their logical and temporal interdependence. Furthermore, additional optimization steps aiming at minimizing the validity intervals over which satisfaction of temporal constraints has to be verified, are proposed.

The remainder of this paper is organized as follows. Section 2 introduces the assertion language used for expressing temporal constraints and rules. Section 3 presents the generation of simplified forms with respect to arbitrary transactions. Section 4 discusses dependence graphs and additional temporal simplification steps that are applied to the compiled formulæ. Section 5 summarizes the contributions of this paper. Proofs of theorems can be found in [22].

2 Assertion Language

The representational framework of Telos [17] is a generalization of graph-theoretic data structures used in semantic networks, semantic data models and object-oriented representations. Telos treats attributes as first-class citizens, supports a powerful classification mechanism which enhances extensibility and offers special representational and inferential mechanisms for temporal knowledge. Telos has a formal semantics based on a possible-worlds model [21]. This section presents the features of Telos that are relevant to the processing of constraints and rules.

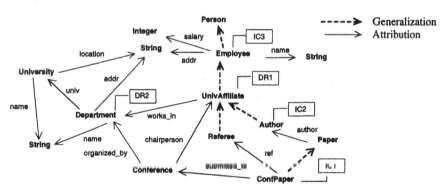

Fig. 1. An example Telos knowledge base

2.1 Structural Component

A Telos knowledge base consists of structured objects built out of two kinds of primitive units, *individuals* and *attributes*. Individuals are intended to represent entities (concrete ones such as John, or abstract ones such as Person), while attributes represent binary relationships between entities or other relationships. Individuals and attributes are referred to by a common term – *proposition*. As in object models, Telos propositions have their own internal identifiers. Propositions are organized along three dimensions, referred to in the literature as *attribution*, *classification* and *generalization* [3].

Structured objects consist of collections of (possibly multi-valued) attributes that have a common proposition as a source, thus adding a simple form of *aggregation*. Each proposition is an instance of one or more generic propositions called *classes* – thus giving rise to a classification hierarchy. Propositions are classified into *tokens* – propositions having no instances and intended to represent concrete entities in the domain of discourse, *simple classes* – propositions having only tokens as instances, *meta classes* – having only simple classes as instances, *metametaclasses*, and so on. Orthogonally to the classification dimension, classes can be organized in terms of *generalization* or isA hierarchies. The attribute mechanism is also used for attaching assertions to Telos objects. Figure 1 shows an example Telos knowledge base in the form of a labeled directed graph.

2.2 Temporal Knowledge

Every Telos proposition has an associated *history* time and a *belief* time. The history time of a proposition represents the lifetime of a proposition in the application domain (i.e., the lifetime of an entity or a relationship). A proposition's belief time, on the other hand, refers to the time when the proposition is believed by the knowledge base, i.e., the interval between the moment the proposition is added to and that when it is removed from the knowledge base.[2] Both history and belief time are represented by means of time *intervals*. The model of time adopted is a modification of Allen's framework [1]. The temporal relations equal, meet, before, after, during, start, end together with their inverses are used to characterize the possible positions of two intervals on a (non-branching) time line. Temporal relationships participate in the expression of deductive rules and integrity constraints in the assertion language. Disjunction of temporal relationships is disallowed in order to facilitate temporal reasoning. The class Time denotes the class of time intervals. We assume that time is linear, discrete and unbounded. The model also includes temporal constants (dates and times), semi-infinite time intervals, the special interval Alltime and the special interval variable systime denoting the current clock time.

2.3 The Assertional Component

The assertion language is a many-sorted first-order language with equality. The language includes a sort for each built-in or user-defined class. We identify one sort for time intervals. The terms of the language include variables and constants, including conventional dates. The atomic formulae of the assertion language include the predicates instanceOf(), isA(), att() for an attribute *att*, the temporal predicates and their inverses. The predicate[3] instanceOf(x,y,t) means that x is an instance of y for the time period t. Similarly, isA(x y,t)

---

[2] The terms *history* and *belief* time correspond to the more popular terms of *valid* and *transaction* time respectively.

[3] For the purposes of this paper we will assume that only historical time appears in assertions. Belief time can be treated in a similar manner, as shown in [20].

means that x is a specialization of y for time t. Finally, $att(x\ y,t)$ denotes that y is a value of the attribute att of x for t. For terms x and y and evaluable predicate θ, $x\ \theta\ y$ is an atomic formula with the obvious meaning.

Well-formed formulae (wffs) of the assertion language are formed by using logical connectives and restricted quantification. Restricted quantification is of the form $\forall\ x/C$ and $\exists\ x/C$ for a Telos class C. We conjecture that the assertion language we use is at least as expressive as FOTL [23].

Integrity constraints are expressed as rectified[4] closed wffs of the assertion language. An integrity constraint can have one of the following two forms:
$$I \equiv \forall x_1/\mathsf{C}_1 \ldots \forall x_k/\mathsf{C}_k F, \quad \text{or} \quad I \equiv \exists x_1/\mathsf{C}_1 \ldots \exists x_k/\mathsf{C}_k\ F$$
where F is any wff whose quantified subformulae are of the above forms and in which the variables $x_1, \ldots, x_k$ occur free. Each C_i is a Telos class and the meaning of each restricted quantification is that the variable bound by the quantifier ranges over the extension of the class. Any constraint in this form is *range-restricted*.[5] The quantifications $\forall x/C\ F$ and $\exists x/C\ F$ are short forms for:
$$\forall x\ \forall t\ \mathtt{instanceOf}(x, \mathsf{C}, t) \wedge \mathtt{instanceOf}(t, \mathtt{Time}, \mathtt{Alltime}) \Rightarrow F\ \text{ and,}$$
$$\exists x\ \exists t\ \mathtt{instanceOf}(x, \mathsf{C}, t) \wedge \mathtt{instanceOf}(t, \mathtt{Time}, \mathtt{Alltime}) \wedge F$$
respectively. The introduction of temporal variables and their restricting literals is necessary since all atomic formulae have a temporal component.

Example 1. Referring to figure 1, the following formula expresses the constraint that *"no author of a conference paper can be a referee for it"*.
$$\forall p/\mathtt{ConfPaper}\ \forall x/\mathtt{Author}\ \forall r/\mathtt{Referee}\ \forall t/\mathtt{Time}$$
$$(author(p, x, t) \wedge referee(p, r, t) \Rightarrow (r \neq x))\ (\text{at } 1993..*)$$
The above constraint is an example of a *static* constraint. The canonical example of a *dynamic* integrity constraint, expressing the property that *"an employee's salary should never decrease"*, can be expressed by the formula:
$$\forall p/\mathtt{Employee}\ \forall s, s'/\mathtt{Integer}\ \forall t_1, t_2/\mathtt{Time}$$
$$(salary(p, s, t_1) \wedge salary(p, s', t_2) \wedge \mathtt{before}(t_1, t_2) \Rightarrow (s \leq s'))\ (\text{at } 02/01/93..*)$$

The general form of deductive rules in the assertion language is:
$$DR \equiv \forall x_1/\mathsf{C}_1 \ldots \forall x_n/\mathsf{C}_n\ (F \Rightarrow A)$$
where F is subject to the same restrictions as above and A is an atomic formula. Rules are assumed to be *stratified* [16]. Constraints and rules are associated with history and belief time intervals. If no such association appears explicitly with their definition, both intervals are assumed to be equal to (systime..*).

Example 2. Consider the rule *"A university affiliate works in the department that has the same address as she does"*, expressed as the formula:
$$\forall u/\mathtt{UnivAffiliate}\ \forall d/\mathtt{Department}\ \forall s, s'/\mathtt{Address}\ \forall t/\mathtt{Time}$$
$$(address(u, s, t) \wedge (D\_addr(d, s', t) \wedge (s = s') \Rightarrow works\_in(u, d, t))\ (\text{at } 1993..*)$$

---

[4] A formula is rectified if no two quantifiers introduce the same variable [4].
[5] This class of constraints is equivalent to both the *restricted quantification form* of [4] and the *range form* of [13].

2.4 Satisfaction of Temporal Assertions

A Telos knowledge base, KB, comprises a set of propositions, KB_P, defining the validity of predicates over (history) time intervals, as well as a set, KB_R, of deductive rules and a set, KB_I, of integrity constraints.

Definition 1. An *object variable substitution* σ is a function mapping a variable x_i of sort S_i to an instance of the corresponding Telos class C_i so that $\texttt{instanceOf}(\sigma(x_i), C_i, t) \in KB_P$ for some interval t.

Definition 2. Let I denote the set of time intervals with integer endpoints. A *temporal variable substitution* τ is a function mapping a temporal variable t of sort **Time** to an interval in I.

Definition 3 (*Satisfaction of Temporal Formulae*). For a base predicate[6] P, object substitution σ and temporal substitution τ

- If P is ground, then $(KB, \sigma, \tau) \models P$ if and only if (iff) $P \in KB_P$.
- $(KB, \sigma, \tau) \models P(x, t)$ iff there exists an interval t' such that $((\tau(t) \text{ during } \tau(t'))$ and $(KB, \sigma, \tau) \models P(\sigma(x), \tau(t'))$.
- $(KB, \sigma, \tau) \models \neg P(x, t)$ iff there does not exist an interval t' containing t such that $(KB, \sigma, \tau) \models P(\sigma(x), \tau(t'))$.
- If Q is also a base predicate, then $(KB, \sigma, \tau) \models P(x, t_1) \vee Q(x, t_2)$ iff $(KB, \sigma, \tau) \models P(x, t_1)$ or $(KB, \sigma, \tau) \models Q(x, t_2)$.
- $(KB, \sigma, \tau) \models \forall x/C \ P(x, t)$ iff $(KB, \sigma[x/d], \tau) \models P(x, t)$ for all d such that $\texttt{instanceOf}(d, C, T)$ for some interval T contained in $\tau(t)$. $\sigma[x/d]$ is the substitution that differs from σ only in the binding d for x.
- $(KB, \sigma, \tau) \models \forall t/\texttt{Time} \ P(x, t)$ iff $\forall T \in I \ (KB, \sigma, \tau[t/T]) \models P(x, t)$.

If P is a derivable predicate defined by a set of deductive rules with bodies $R_1, \ldots, R_k$ and respective time intervals $T_1, \ldots, T_k$, then

- $(KB, \sigma, \tau) \models P(x, t)$ iff $(KB, \sigma, \tau) \models \bigvee_{i=1}^{k} R_i \wedge (t \text{ during } T)$, where T is the intersection of the intervals T_i.

Now we are in a position to define the satisfaction of temporal integrity constraints. We will use the notation $C \ [at \ T]$ to denote an integrity constraint C associated with the history time interval T.

Definition 4 (*Satisfaction of Temporal Integrity Constraints*). If the temporal variables $t_1, \ldots, t_k$ occur in the constraint C, then $(KB, \sigma, \tau) \models C \ [at \ T]$ iff $(KB, \sigma, \tau) \models C'$, where $C' \equiv C \wedge \bigwedge_{i=1}^{k}(t_i \text{ during } T)$.

The above definition shows that the semantics of integrity constraints is taken into account in the definition of the notion of satisfaction. It would not make sense to evaluate an integrity constraint outside its validity interval. We do not define the respective notions for the bitemporal case, where both history and belief time are present, since their definitions follow similar lines.

---

[6] The satisfaction of the basic temporal predicates is defined as in [1].

3 Compilation and Simplification

Our approach builds on the method proposed in [4], which was adapted to an object-oriented setting in [13]. It extends the latter by the treatment of temporal constraints and by the introduction of an efficient compilation scheme that allows us optimize the computation of implicit updates and to perform additional simplifications. The efficiency of the method stems from the separation of the task of constraint maintenance in two separate phases: a *compilation* phase, performed at schema definition time and an *evaluation* phase performed at knowledge base update time. During compilation, constraints and relevant rules are compiled into simplified forms whose evaluation can be triggered by the occurrence of affecting updates. Compilation and simplification apply uniformly to integrity constraints and the bodies of their relevant deductive rules. It exploits the assumptions that, first, the knowledge base is known to satisfy its constraints prior to an update and, second, that the types of updates can be anticipated.

In [20], we presented a compilation method that produced simplified forms of constraints and rules with respect to a single affecting update. We extend the method to treat dynamic constraints in a special manner and to take into account multiple updates. The notions of *affecting updates, transactions* and *literal dependence* are defined first.

Definition 5. An *update* is an instantiated literal whose sign determines whether it is an insertion or a deletion. A *transaction* is an arbitrary sequence of updates.

We will henceforth assume that constraints are written in disjunctive normal form (DNF). A constraint in DNF is affected by an update only when a "tuple" is inserted into the extension of a literal occurring negatively in the constraint, or when a "tuple" is deleted from the extension of a literal occurring positively in the constraint. The definition of *relevance* found in [13] is not sufficient in the presence of time. Definition 6 provides sufficient conditions for "relevance" of a constraint to an update, by considering the relationship of the history time intervals participating in the literals of the constraint and the update.

Definition 6. An update $U(\_, \_, t)$ is an *affecting update* for a constraint C [at T] iff there exists a literal $L(\_, \_, \_)$ in C such that L unifies with the complement of U and the intersection, $t * T$, of intervals t and T is non-empty. A transaction $X = [U_1, \ldots, U_m]$ is called an *affecting transaction* for a constraint C [at T] iff at least one of $U_1, \ldots, U_m$ is an affecting update for the constraint.

During compilation, along with each integrity constraint, deductive rules that may contribute to the constraint's evaluation will be compiled. These are rules whose conclusion literal unifies with literals of the constraint. In this case, it is said that the constraint *directly depends* on the deductive rules. A constraint cannot directly depend on a rule whose conclusion literal does not match any of the constraint's literals. It can however depend on a rule whose conclusion literal matches a condition literal of a rule on which the constraint depends. We define the notions of *dependence* and *direct dependence* along the lines of [13].

Definition 7. A literal L *directly depends* on a literal K iff there exists a rule of the form $\forall x_1/C_1 \ldots \forall x_n/C_n$ $(F \Rightarrow A)$ such that, there exists a literal in F unifying with K with most general unifier θ and $A\theta = L$. A literal L *transitively depends* (or, simply, depends) on literal K iff it directly depends on K, or depends on a literal M that directly depends on K.

Hence, a constraint C depends on a rule R if a literal in the constraint depends on the rule's conclusion literal. Similarly, a rule R_1 depends on a rule R_2 if R_1's body contains a literal that depends on R_2's conclusion literal. These relationships define a *dependence graph* for a set of rules and constraints. A dependence graph represents how implicitly derived facts can affect the integrity of the knowledge base. Dependence graphs are discussed in section 4.

The key issue in compilation is to associate every constraint or rule body with the updates that may affect its evaluation. Compilation produces a *parameterized simplified structure* (PSS) for each such literal. This form contains a simplified form of the constraint or rule that suffices to be evaluated when an affecting update on the literal occurs at run time. Note that, for every occurrence of a literal in a constraint or rule, there is only one update that may affect the constraint or rule. Since the only updates possible are insertions and deletions in the extensions of literals, a literal occurrence can only be affected by one of the two operations.

3.1 Compile-time Simplification

We first list the rules for generating a PSS simplified form for each update and then show how to obtain the simplified form for a transaction given the simplified forms for individual updates. The analysis of the soundness and completeness of the rules can be found in [22]. Note that we cannot possibly derive the simplified forms with respect to all possible transactions that may affect a given constraint due to the exponential number of such transactions.

Definition 8. Given a temporal constraint C [*at* T] expressed in DNF and a literal L occurring positively (negatively) in C, the *parameterized simplified structure* of C with respect to L is a quintuple $(L, Params, CC, T, SF)$, where, $Params$ is the list of instantiation variables[6] of L, CC is the concerned class[7] of L, T is the history time interval of the constraint, and SF is the simplified form of the constraint that suffices to be evaluated when a deletion from (insertion to) L takes place. SF is derived as follows:

1. The quantifiers binding instantiation variables are dropped. Variables become parameters.

---

[6] Instantiation variables are $\forall$-quantified variables that are not in the scope of a $\exists$.

[7] The *Concerned Class* [13], [20] for a literal L is the most specialized class CC such that, inserting or deleting an instance of CC can affect the truth of L and the time intervals of L and CC are unifiable. The compile-time derivation of concerned classes of literals is discussed in [20].

2. The temporal variables are constrained with respect to the history time of the constraint: a temporal predicate of the form (t_i during T) is conjoined with C for every temporal variable t_i that occurs in C.

3. The literal into (from) whose extension a tuple is inserted (deleted) is substituted by the **True** (**False**) and absorption rules of first-order logic are applied. If a literal occurs more than once with different history time intervals, then select for replacement the literal with the greatest right endpoint.

4. Temporal simplification rules are applied if applicable.

A comment on the treatment of dynamic constraints in step 3 is in order. Dynamic constraints are distinguished from static constraints by the presence of explicit temporal constraints on the history time variables. Since they express properties depending on two or more knowledge base states, some literals will occur more than once in their expression. Step 3 replaces the literal with the time interval extending to the future of the rest of the intervals in the other literal occurrences. This is done because the constraint must be verifiable using the history of the knowledge base up to the present state. Determining which literal to replace can be done by comparison of the intervals if their endpoints are known, or by reasoning by cases based on the temporal relationship of the time intervals of the literals. Lemma 9 expresses the above property.

Lemma 9. *Let C be the constraint $(\neg L(\overline{x}, t_1) \vee \neg L(\overline{y}, t_2) \vee \neg(t_1 \ r \ t_2) \vee R)$ [at T], where R is a temporal formula in DNF that does not mention any L literal and r is a temporal relation. Given that C is known not to be violated in the state prior to the occurrence of an affecting update on L, C's satisfaction can be determined in the state after the update iff the satisfaction of $\overline{C}$ can be determined, where $\overline{C}$ is the formula obtained from C as follows: if r is* **before, during, overlaps, meets, starts** *or* **finishes,** *then the literal $\neg L(\overline{y}, t_2)$ is substituted with a Boolean constant and the variables y, t_2 become instantiated. If r is* **after, contains, overlapped-by, met-by, started-by** *or* **finished-by,** *then the literal $\neg L(\overline{x}, t_1)$ is substituted with a Boolean constant and the variables x, t_1 become instantiated. If r is* **equal,** *any of the literals can be substituted.*

Example 3. Applying steps 1-4 to the dynamic constraint of example 1 will generate the following simplified form (capitalised variables denote parameters):

$\forall s / $**Integer** $\forall t_1 / $**TimeInterval** $(salary(P, s, t_1) \wedge (t_1$ **during** $02/01/1993..*)$
$\wedge \ (t_1$ **before** $T_2) \Rightarrow (s \leq S'))$

In this example, the literal $salary(p, s', t_2)$ of the original constraint was replaced because of the relationship (t_1 **before** t_2) between t_1, t_2.

The last step in the generation of simplified forms is temporal simplification. The objective is to simplify a conjunction of temporal relationships into a single temporal relationship. Hence, the number of subformulae to be evaluated at runtime is reduced. Temporal simplification replaces a conjunction (t **during** i_1) $\wedge$ ($t \ r_1 \ i_2$), where i_1 and i_2 are known time intervals, with a temporal relationship r, such that ($t \ r \ i$) is satisfied iff the original conjunction is satisfied. The interval i is a function of the intervals i_1 and i_2. The fact that the intervals i_1 and i_2

are known permits us to derive a relationship r_2 that is true of (i_1 and i_2). The expression that is simplified is the conjunction (t **during** i_1)$\wedge$(t r_1 i_2)$\wedge$(i_1 r_2 i_2). It is not always possible to derive a single definite relation r that has the above property. For some combinations of temporal relationships, r is a disjunction of temporal relationships. In those cases, and for the sake of completeness, we do not replace the original expression by the equivalent disjunction. Temporal simplification can be performed efficiently as shown in [20]: only a table lookup is needed for any of the 169 possible combinations of relations r_1 and r_2. In the case that the negation of a temporal relationship appears in r_1, one can only suggest a weaker condition r, which if satisfied guarantees that the original conjunction is satisfied.

The following theorem expresses the soundness of the simplification.

Theorem 10. *A constraint C, known not to be violated in the state prior to the occurrence of an affecting update, is violated in the state resulting from the update if the formula produced after applying the simplification steps 1-4 is.*

3.2 Generating Simplified Forms for Transactions

We now turn to the derivation of simplified forms of constraints with respect to arbitrary transactions. This derivation takes place at run-time when the actual transaction is specified, but uses the simplified forms that were generated with respect to the individual updates at compile-time.

As far as the integrity of a knowledge base is concerned, transactions are considered to be atomic. Hence, the effect of a transaction made up of any subset of the affecting updates for a particular integrity constraint is the same independently of the order in which the updates occur in the transaction. [8] This is easy to see, if we consider that it is known that the constraint is not violated in the state prior to the transaction's execution and we apply the simplification steps for all updates occurring in the transaction simultaneously. The above observation allows us to use the simplified forms generated for individual updates in order to derive one simplified form that suffices to be evaluated in order to verify the satisfaction of a constraint with respect to a transaction containing an arbitrary sequence of the individual updates.

Definition 11. Let $X = [U_1, \ldots, U_m]$ be a transaction affecting constraint C, and let i be the index of the first U_i in X that affects C. Let X' be the sequence of updates in X that follow U_i and affect C. Then, the simplified form of C with respect to X, is obtained by applying all updates in X' simultaneously to the PSS $(L, Params, CC, T, SF)$ of C that is such that L is unifiable with U_i.

The resulting formulae can be considerably simpler than the ones produced if only individual updates are considered. The following is a simple example showing the simplification of a constraint with respect to a transaction. We are using first-order predicate calculus notation for ease of exposition.

---

[8] Of course, the order of updates is important for producing the result intended by the transaction specifier.

Example 4. Consider the constraint $\forall \overline{x}, \overline{y}(P(\overline{x}) \wedge \neg Q(\overline{x}, \overline{y})) \vee (R(\overline{x}, \overline{y}) \wedge \neg P(\overline{x})) \vee S(\overline{x}, \overline{y})$ and the transaction $X = [\neg P(\overline{X}), \neg R(\overline{X}, \overline{Y})]$. If the updates were treated independently, two formulae would need to be verified, namely $\forall \overline{y}(R(\overline{X}, \overline{y}) \vee S(\overline{X}, y))$ and $(P(\overline{X}) \wedge \neg Q(\overline{X}, \overline{Y})) \vee S(\overline{X}, \overline{Y})$. This should be contrasted with the formula $S(\overline{X}, \overline{Y})$ that is the simplified form of C that suffices to be verified when C is simplified with respect to X.

The following theorem establishes the soundness of the simplification method with respect to transactions. Its proof uses the result of theorem 10.

Theorem 12. *A temporal constraint C, known not to be violated in the state prior to the execution of an affecting transaction, is violated in the state resulting from the transaction's execution if the formula produced after applying the simplification steps of definition 11 is.*

4 Dependence Graphs

In this section we examine the organization of the simplified forms of rules and constraints into *dependence graphs* and the optimization potentials that this scheme provides.

4.1 Graph Construction and Properties

The definitions of direct and transitive dependence define a directed graph representing how literals, implicitly derived from deductive rules, can affect the integrity of the knowledge base. The graph nodes are the PSSs of rules and constraints. Edges denote dependence of constraints/rules on rules.

Definition 13. The dependence graph of a knowledge base KB is defined as $G(KB) = (V, E)$, where V comprises one node for each PSS of an integrity constraint or deductive rule of KB. $V = V_I \cup V_R$, where V_I and V_R are the sets of nodes corresponding to to integrity constraints (KB_I) and deductive rules (KB_R) respectively. $E = \{(v_i, v_j) | v_i \in V_R, v_j \in V_I \text{ and } v_j \text{ directly depends on } v_i\} \cup [(v_i, v_j) | v_i, v_j \subset V_R \text{ and } v_i \text{ directly depends on } v_j]$.

A dependence graph may contain cycles among deductive rule nodes. This happens in the case that the knowledge base contains mutually recursive rules. As shown in [22], the graph is free of trivial cycles and may contain cycles of length at most equal to the number of deductive rules participating in the same recursive scheme. The number of nodes in the dependence graph is in the order of the number of literals occurring in rule and constraint bodies, since one node is created for each compiled form. The number of edges in the graph can be at most equal to twice the number of rules in KB_R since there exists an edge between compiled forms of a rule and a constraint only if the rule's head unifies with the constraint's literal or a literal in another rule's body. For an average number of literals per constraint or rule greater than 2, the dependence graph

of a knowledge base is sparse. The dependence graph is constructed once when
the knowledge base is compiled and is updated incrementally when new rules
or constraints are inserted or deleted. Below we list some of the properties that
the above compilation scheme enjoys and which contribute to the efficiency of
integrity constraint checking. These properties are elaborated on in [20] and
[22], where performance results with randomly generated dependence graphs are
presented. These results attest to the efficiency of the compilation scheme.

A dependence graph reflects both the logical and temporal interdependence
of rules and constraints. Following paths from rules to constraints in the graph
permits us to derive potential implicit updates caused by explicit ones. The set
of implicit updates can be precomputed at the time of graph construction by
computing the graph's transitive closure. At evaluation time, node reachability
information does not have to be recomputed. The actual updates can be obtained
by instantiating the potential updates and evaluating the rule bodies in which
they occur, starting with the ones matching the update's literal and following
the order in which the implicit updates were computed. The dependence graph
structure is incrementally modifiable to accommodate insertions/deletions of
rules and constraints without having to recompile the entire graph. [22] presents
algorithms for efficiently maintaining the graph's transitive closure.

4.2 Optimizations

We now present additional optimizations that take into account the temporal
properties of constraints and rules. They take place after the graph's construction
and aim at producing more efficiently evaluable temporal formulae.

Algorithm: *Minimize Intervals* (G, S)
begin
       For every node $v \in S$ {
           $Temp := \emptyset$
           For every node $u \in V_R$ such that $(u, v) \in E$ {
                $u.T := (v.T * u.T)$
                $newSF := u.SF \wedge \bigwedge_{t_i \in qtv(u.SF)}(t_i \ during \ u.T)$
                $u.SF := temp\_simp(newSF)$
                $Temp := Temp \cup \{u\}$ }
       } $S := Temp$
       Minimize Intervals (G, S)
end

Fig. 2. Interval Minimization

The first optimization step replaces the temporal intervals of the PSSs that
comprise the graph nodes by smaller intervals. Algorithm *Minimize Intervals* (see
figure 2) is applied after the construction of the dependence graph is complete
and whenever the dependence graph structure is modified by the insertion of a
new constraint or rule. The algorithm starts with an initial set of nodes and, for
every node v in this initial set, it replaces the history time intervals of each of its

incident nodes with the time interval that results from computing the intersection of the time interval of v with that of its incident node. The algorithm proceeds in a breadth-first fashion until no more replacements can take place. In this manner, the validity time intervals of the formulae whose satisfaction has to be determined at run-time are minimized. Since the history time intervals of the constraints and rules are used to constrain the temporal variables of their respective expressions, the minimized intervals must be used in their place. As was shown in section 3.1, the time intervals originally associated with a rule or constraint are factored-in the rule or constraint expression using a **during** relationship that captures the semantics of temporal validity. When the minimized interval of a PSS is computed, the new interval must also be factored into the simplified form. The **during** relationship that introduced the original interval in the temporal formula expressing the constraint or rule may not appear explicitly due to simplification step 4 that replaces conjunctions of temporal relationships by a new relationship. Hence, a new **during** relationship introducing the minimized interval must be conjoined with the simplified form. Additional simplifications may be carried out if applicable. In the presentation of the algorithm we assume that each node is represented as a PSS and we use the "." (dot) operator to refer to its components. The call to *temp_simp* symbolizes the application of step 4 of definition 8. The function *qtv* returns the quantified temporal variables of a simplified form.

Initially, the algorithm is applied to a dependence graph G with the set of nodes V_I corresponding to simplified forms of integrity constraints as the set of source nodes S. When G is modified by the insertion of a new integrity constraint, the set of source nodes is the set comprising the PSSs of the new constraint. If a new rule is inserted, then the set of source nodes is the set of successor nodes of all the PSSs of the newly inserted rule. Note that we do not need to apply the algorithm for the case of deletions of constraints or rules since deletion can only disconnect graph nodes. Since a dependence graph may be cyclic, special attention must be paid to the graph's strongly connected components which can be identified at compile time. The algorithm can be easily modified to take the graph's strongly connected components into account.

We argue that the optimization steps presented above can yield considerable savings in evaluating simplified forms at run-time by minimizing the intervals over which the evaluation of formulae must take place and by, possibly, carrying out additional temporal simplifications. The transformations carried out preserve the satisfaction of constraints since only the simplified forms of their relevant rules are modified. Moreover, the derivation of the actual implicit updates becomes simpler since the formulae that have to be verified have been simplified. Lemma 14 and theorem 15 establish the correctness of the algorithm.

Lemma 14. *Let SF be the simplified form of a rule whose associated time interval is restricted by algorithm* Minimize Intervals *and let SF' be the new simplified form. Then, $KB \models (SF \Rightarrow SF')$.*

Theorem 15. *Algorithm* Minimize Intervals *is correct: if the violation of a constraint C can be determined using the dependence graph G, then it can also be determined using the graph resulting from applying* Minimize Intervals *to G.*

5 Conclusions and Outlook

This paper presented a simplification method applying uniformly to temporal integrity constraints and deductive rules in large Telos knowledge bases. The proposed techniques focus on simplifying formulae as much as possible at schema definition time and aim at yielding acceptable performance at update time. During compilation integrity constraints and deductive rules are simplified with respect to the anticipated types of updates and organized in a graph structure that permits the efficient derivation of implicit updates. This structure is incrementally modifiable for accommodating dynamic changes to the rule and constraint set. Moreover, additional optimizations on the formulae expressing the simplified forms generated at compile-time were proposed. These optimizations minimize the temporal intervals over which the validity of formulae has to be checked in order for their satisfaction to be verified at update-time. They exploit the semantics of constraint satisfaction and the organization of simplified forms in the dependence graph structure. Similar simplification steps can be performed when constraints contain belief time, in addition to history time [23].

Another contribution is the simplification of temporal formulae with respect to arbitrary transactions. The simplified formulae produced by the compile-time simplification method are used in order to derive a single formula that suffices to be verified at update-time when a transaction takes place. Hence, a single formula incorporating the affecting updates of an arbitrary transaction needs only to be verified as opposed to a number of more complex formulae incorporating only individual updates.

Current research focuses on devising historical knowledge minimization techniques for integrity constraints, in the lines of [7], and [24] but in the richer context of knowledge bases introduced in this paper. The reuse and adaptation of proofs of temporal formulae satisfaction over dependence graphs is investigated. Last, but not least, the derivation of incrementally evaluable formulae as simplified forms of constraints expressed in the interval based assertion language is examined. Incrementally evaluable formulae lend themselves to an implementation using an active rule model, as, e.g., in [12], [8] and [25].

References

1. J. Allen. Maintaining Knowledge about Temporal Intervals. *Communications of the ACM*, 26(11):832–843, November 1983.
2. M. Baudinet, J. Chomicki, and P. Wolper. Temporal Deductive Databases. In Tansel, A. et al., editor, *Temporal Databases*. Benjamin Cummings, 1993.
3. M. Brodie, J. Mylopoulos, and J. Schmidt, editors. *On Conceptual Modeling: Perspectives from AI, Databases and Programming Languages*. Springer Verlag, 1984.
4. F. Bry, H. Decker, and R. Manthey. A Uniform Approach to Constraint Satisfaction and Constraint Satisfiability in Deductive Databases. In *Proceedings of the Int. Conference on Extedning Data Base Technology*, pages 488–505, 1988.
5. S. Ceri and J. Widom. Deriving Production Rules for Constraint Maintenance. In *VLDB-90*, pages 566–577, 1990.

6. R. Chandra and A. Segev. Managing Temporal Financial Data in an Extensible Database. In *VLDB-93*, pages 302–313, 1993.

7. J. Chomicki. History-less Checking of Dynamic Integrity Constraints. In *8th Int. Conference on Data Engineering*, pages 557–564, Phoenix,AZ, 1992.

8. J. Chomicki and D. Toman. Implementing Integrity Constraints Using an Active DBMS. In *Proceedings, RIDE-94 Active Database Systems*, pages 87–95, 1994.

9. H. Ehrich, U. Lipeck, and M. Gogolla. Specification, Semantics and Enforcement of Dynamic Database Constraints. In *VLDB-84*, pages 301–308, 1984.

10. E. A. Emerson. Temporal and Modal Logic. In J. van Leeuwen, editor, *Handbook of Theoretical Computer Science*, pages 996–1072. MIT Press, 1990.

11. J. Florentin. Consistency Auditing of Databases. *Computer Journal*, 17(1):52–58, 1974.

12. M. Gertz and U. Lipeck. Deriving Integrity Maintaining Triggers from Transition Graphs. In *9th Int. Conference on Data Engineering*, pages 22–29, 1993.

13. M. Jeusfeld and M. Jarke. From Relational to Object-Oriented Integrity Simplification. In *Proceedings of DOOD-91*, pages 460–477, 1991.

14. F. Kabanza, J-M. Stevenne, and P. Wolper. Handling Infinite Temporal Data. In *PODS-90*, pages 392–403, 1990.

15. C.H. Kung. On Verification of Database Temporal Constraints. In *SIGMOD-85*, pages 169–179, 1985.

16. J. Lloyd and R. Topor. A Basis for Deductive Database Systems. *Journal of Logic Programming*, 2:93–109, 1985.

17. J. Mylopoulos, A. Borgida, M. Jarke, and M. Koubarakis. Telos: A Language for Representing Knowledge in Information Systems. *ACM TOIS*, 8(4):325–362, 1990.

18. J. Mylopoulos, V. Chaudhri, D. Plexousakis, A. Shrufi, and T. Topaloglou. Building Knowledge Base Management Systems. *The VLDB Journal*, 1995. To appear.

19. J.-M. Nicolas. Logic for Improving Integrity Checking in Relational Databases. *Acta Informatica*, 18:227–253, 1982.

20. D. Plexousakis. Integrity Constraint and Rule Maintenance in Temporal Deductive Knowledge Bases. In *VLDB-93*, pages 146–157, 1993.

21. D. Plexousakis. Semantical and Ontological Considerations in Telos: a Lanugage for Knowledge Representation. *Computational Intelligence*, 9(1):41–72, 1993.

22. D. Plexousakis. Integrity Maintenance in a Telos based KBMS, 1994. Submitted to IEEE-TKDE.

23. D. Plexousakis. *On the Efficient Enforcement of Integrity Constraints in Temporal Deductive Knowledge Bases*. PhD thesis, 1995. Forthcoming.

24. G. Saake and U. Lipeck. Foundations of Temporal Integrity Monitoring In C. Roland, editor, *Temporal Aspects in Information Systems*, pages 235–249. 1988.

25. A.P. Sitsla and O. Wolfson. Temporal Conditions and Integrity Constraints in Active Database Systens. In *SIGMOD-95*, pages 269–280, 1995.

26. A. et al. Tansel. *Temporal Databases, Theory Design and Implementation*. Benjamin/Cummings, 1993.

27. J. Ullman. *Fundamentals of Database and Knowledge-base Systems*, volume 1. Computer Science Press, 1988.

28. R. Wieringa, J-J. Meyer, and H. Weigand. Specifying Dynamic and Deontic Integrity Constraints. *Data and Knowledge Engineering*, 4:157–189, 1989.

Implementation and Benchmarking of Active Database Systems

An Active Component for a Parallel Database Kernel

M.L. Kersten

CWI, Kruislaan 413, 1098 SJ Amsterdam
{mk@cwi.nl}

Abstract. The Monet parallel database server is an experimentation platform for a variety of datamodels and novel applications. In this paper we describe its active behavior based on the notion of trigger abstractions and an event notification scheme. Trigger abstractions can be used to construct intricate trigger instance networks. The events notified in the DBMS kernel threads flow into a shared event pool. The trigger-event-monitor watches this pool for event combinations to enable trigger firing. We illustrate how these concepts can be used by a rule compiler and describe a performance metric to guide the search for an efficient architectural solution.

1 Introduction

Recent years have shown an increased research interest in active database support [15]. The stream of publications find their origin in the area of rule-based programming [7], i.e. rule processing, and transaction management [14]. The former looks for better ways of rule processing in knowledge intensive applications. The latter aims at simplified transaction management of complex business environments through database triggers [14]. Rules and triggers are the declarative and procedural ends of active behavior which require comparable measures for their implementation.

Generic solutions to both dimensions are sought in the design and implementation of active databases, i.e. a database system that responds to events generated internal or external to the system by activation of a routine. Event-Condition-Action rules form the key procedural concept for specifying active behavior and the approaches taken primarily differ in their choice of abstractions for the components involved. The Event, Condition, and Action components are either explicitly used in the interface language or hidden behind a declarative façade and derived by a rule compiler. A classification of systems against several dimensions is given in [11, 13].

The main contributions of this paper are twofold. First, we present an overview of trigger implementation in Monet, a parallel DBMS kernel under development since 1993 [2]. [1] It complements earlier approaches in aiming for a re-targetable active kernel in a truly parallel setting. We strongly believe that rule-based

---

[1] The work is in part sponsored by Stichting Informatica Onderzoek Nederland (SION) and European Union (Pythagoras EU 7091).

systems should be built around an optimizing compiler that can exploit the model/language semantics. Such a compiler relies on triggers that can be efficiently implemented within a database kernel. The Monet extension presented is geared towards providing this functionality. It is designed around a minimal set of orthogonal concepts, primarily dealing with event streams, trigger abstractions and their management in a parallel setting.

Active behavior is modelled as procedures, whose bodies are (repeatedly) executed when their event condition holds. A trigger admission policy detects (and rejects) trigger instances whose firing state can not be reached. This leads to early warning of 'useless' active triggers and aids the design of active applications. Furthermore, the DBMS primitives for queue management supports all coupling modes at any level of precision required, such as parallel execution of the actions. Together they provide the building blocks for code generation by a rule compiler.

Second, we demonstrate the performance of our prototype implementation using a benchmark core. This benchmark is our driving force for finding efficient implementation techniques. The results obtained form a reference point for quantitative comparison with other systems.

The remainder of this paper is organized as follows. Section 2 provides an architectural overview of the Monet DB kernel and choices mode for active behavior. Section 3 describes the event and trigger model. Applicability of the model is presented in Section 4 and the performance metric is presented in Section 5. An outlook on future research activities concludes the paper.

2 Architectural Overview.

In section 2.1 we give an overview of the Monet system architecture [2]. [2] The design considerations for inclusion of active behavior are sumarized in Section 2.2. A more detailed description is given in the remainder of this paper.

2.1 Monet Architecture

Monet is a customizable database system developed at CWI and University of Amsterdam, intended to be used as the database back-end for widely varying application domains. It is designed to get maximum database performance out of today's workstations and multiprocessor systems. It has already achieved considerable success in supporting a Data Mining application [8], and work is well under way in a project where it is used in a high-end GIS application. Monet is a type- and algebra-extensible database system and employs shared memory parallelism of SGIs and SUNs. The distributed store version based on [1] is under development and targeted at an IBM SP1 multiprocessor.

The principal assumptions and ideas to achieve Monet's design goals are:

---

[2] For more details on Monet and related projects, see
http://www.cwi.nl/cwi/projects/monet.html

- *Use large main memories* Monet makes aggressive use of main memory by assuming that the database hot-set fits into main memory. All its primitive database operations work primarily on main memory structures, no hybrid (memory-disk) algorithms are used. For large data sets it fully exploits the virtual memory manager capabilities of the underlying operating system.
- *Decomposed storage model with deltas.* Monet uses a simple data model based on Binary Association Tables (BATs). This allows for flexible object-representation using the Decomposed Storage Model (DSM)[10]. This vertical decomposition also helps partitioning the database such that the tables fit easier in main memory. Moreover, the BATs come with a *delta* facility, providing access to all elements added (**alpha**) and deleted (**delta**) since transaction begin.
- *Extensible interface.* The Monet Interface Language (MIL) provides for an execution-level binary table algebra and a complete set of imperative programming constructs. Furthermore, the Monet Extension Language (MEL) permits extension of the core functionality through abstract data types and user-defined commands. Such extensions can be dynamically added to a running server.

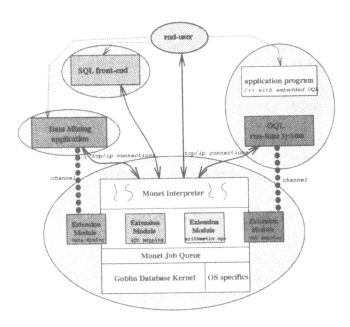

Fig. 1. The Monet Architecture

Figure 1 shows the Monet Interpreter as a multi threaded process, connected to its clients via TCP/IP links. The basic interaction is through the Monet Interface Language (MIL), a simple C-like scripting language. Applications typically accompany themselves by a specific extension module, which provides the extra functionality needed. Extension modules provide operations ranging from arithmetic operations on BATs, geometric library for GIS, to statistical routines for data mining.

2.2 Options for Active Behavior

An active database management system is build around *events*, *event detectors*, a *trigger definition language*, and a *trigger-event-monitor* (TEM). Events are the smallest pieces of information emitted from a system to 'trigger' active behavior upon detection by a trigger-event-monitor. In designing an architecture for a wide spectrum of active models it is mandatory to take the following considerations into account:

- to differentiate enough DBMS kernel events;
- to avoid excessive overhead in their detection;
- to avoid a complex analysis to determine the eligible ECA-rule(s);
- to aim for a simple and open execution model;
- to provide hooks and tools for debugging and performance assessment.

These considerations have been taken into account during system design and experimentation. The baseline has been to consider active behavior a well-identified layer around the physical database and its algebraic engine. This way experimentation with different data and execution models becomes feasible. To set the stage, a short overview of the Monet active behavior is given first.

Event notification Active behavior starts with explicit notification of an event at some point in the system code. Therefore, event detectors are hardwired at specific places in the system kernel, while user-defined events are raised explicitly by user-supplied code. For example, NAOS [3] and SAMOS [5] uses a compiled approach where methods are wrapped by event notification code. This gives the compiler designer and user precise control over the granularity required.

In the Monet architecture there are two obvious places for event notification. Either notification takes place within the database kernel routines or within the MIL interpreter. The former leads to fine-grained event detection with the disadvantage of processing overhead due to generating events under all circumstances. Attachment routines to the storage manipulation operations (e.g. Starburst) only marginally improve the situation, because checking for such attachments consumes recognizable time in a main-memory oriented DBMS.

We have chosen for an flexible approach where event notification is coupled with the operations known by the MIL interpreter. Depending on the mapping from MIL operation to kernel operation this results in fine- or coarse- grain event notification. Furthermore, the extensibility of Monet permits the user to refine any MIL operation to provide a different event notification policy.

Event properties An event comes with properties to identify its environment such that a decision can be made on the old- and new- value of the objects affected or the table with net-effects. In SAMOS the event structure contains the time of the occurrence, the enclosing transaction identifier, and user responsible for its initiation. The event records are represented by persistent objects in the server, which makes them accessible to an object browser.

The Starburst system takes a hybrid approach. Each triggering event places a parameterized procedure call on the prepare-to-commit queue through its attachment mechanism. Moreover, the transaction log keeps track of the net-effect of successive transitions. The log, however, is difficult to analyse with the standard tools offered.

Our approach is to store all event properties within the database. An object identifier is used to re-locate these properties later on. Furthermore, the primitive data structures are set up such that old- and new- values can always be obtained; independent of active behavior. A consequence of our Spartan approach is a potentially higher workload on the kernel, because more query interactions are required to determine the outcome of the condition part. The benefit is a clear distinction between event handling and database activities.

Trigger definitions A trigger defined in a front-end language, such as SQL or rule-language, can be either translated into Monet Interface Language (MIL) constructs or a Monet Extension Language (MEL) module. We have opted for the former, i.e. provision for trigger concept within MIL, because it supports ease of experimentation at a slight overhead in execution speed.

Monet trigger definitions are abstractions, much like procedures. A trigger definition consists of a formal parameter list, an event expression and an action part. The action part is a sequential or parallel MIL statement block. Since MIL is a computationally complete programming language, its provides for a rich environment to construct and experiment with different active applications.

The alternative is to use the Monet Extension Language which supports dynamic linkage of arbitrary C-code with the system kernel. Although extremely powerful, this interface is not meant for casual users without experience in C-programming or limited understanding of the Monet internals. Yet, if need arises, the trigger can be (hand-) compiled to remove interpretation overhead and go for speed.

Trigger execution model Trigger execution encompasses decisions on two issues: identification of fireable triggers and the effect on the process thread raising the event(s). A naive approach is to store the event in the pool and let a separate monitor process inspect the pool repeatedly for eligible combinations. Although this increases parallelism (given multiple CPUs), it also leads to many process switches and dependency on the process priority scheme. Instead, we have chosen for a direct call of the TEM whenever an event is raised. The pool is then inspected and trigger instances are scheduled for execution accordingly. The event is stored in the event_pool otherwise.

The execution model of trigger, i.e. what happens with the thread of control causing the event, differs considerably between systems. Many models differentiate between immediate and deferred execution. In SAMOS the event may cause instances to be executed immediately, effectively suspending the main thread of control. In Starburst the event leads to a delayed procedure call. Once executed at the transaction boundary, they block the main thread of control until active behavior has come to rest[3]. Both solutions are influenced by the system architecture and impose limitations on the active behavior that can be modelled.

We assume that most event expressions are rather simple and that deferred execution semantics can be modelled in the rule language (compiler) using immediate mode of execution and availability of low-level queue management operations. Therefore, all instances raised by an event are scheduled for parallel execution and the main thread of control awaits their termination. Deferred mode can be realized using an event that blocks instances from firing until the transaction boundary is reached. Detached mode is obtained by using the Monet primitives to install (and activate) MIL commands and their dependencies in the request queue explicitly.

In the next section we summarize the events and triggers semantics for Monet. Their formalization is beyond the scope of this paper. The architectural overview of the components involved is shown in Figure 2.

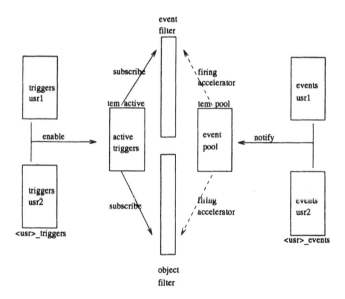

Fig. 2. The active components data structures

---

[3] attachment procedures can be used to realize immediate actions.

3 Monet Event Model

Events are classified into primitive -, time -, and abstract- events. They are identified by a unique symbolic name and an internal event number administered in a user-readable Monet table.

Primitive events detectors are 'hardwired' into the Monet kernel. In particular, all built-in MIL commands raise an event upon entry and return from their body. Since event detection is the potential source of performance degradation, their event numbers are fixed at compilation time to avoid table lookups. Their symbolic name is a concatenation of the command name and *Entry* or *Exit*. They can be used within the MIL scripts.

Time events are generated within the kernel using the clock interrupt mechanism of the underlying operating system. An event can be raised relative to the current time with a granularity of about 10 ms. Absolute timer events go off at a specific date and time provided the system is running at that moment.

Abstract events are introduced by the user using an **event** $<id>$ command; they can be subsequently used like any other event. The abstract event should be uniquely identifiable by its name within the context of the user session. Unlike primitive and time events, an abstract event is explicitly raised using the **notify** command in user code.

An event record carries as little data as possible. It merely designates a state change. The event record contains the internal event number and possibly a single atomic value. For example, upon deletion of an entry from a table C the MIL interpreter executes the command **notify** *(C, deleteExit)*. What has been deleted is not part of the event record, but part of the database state itself. The trigger body can use the command C.**delta** to extract this information from the database.

The events of interest are collected in a single global event pool, called *tem_pool*, represented by a user-readable table. An event is added if-and-only-if it passes a hash-based subscription filter, i.e. there is at least on trigger instance with expressed interest. Otherwise the event is considered useless and ignored. The event pool is discarded when the server is stopped.

4 Monet Trigger Model

A trigger is processed in three staged. First, it is defined and administered in a user-specific trigger table. Second, an instantiation is created to watch for the events to occur. Third, the body is scheduled for execution when the events appear in the event pool. These phases are described in more detail below.

Trigger definitions The trigger definition is aligned with the procedural abstraction mechanism of the Monet interface language to provide for templates of active behavior. A trigger definition consists of a header (**trigger** *name(arg....)*), an event expression (**on** *term, ...*) , and an action. The header is a list of formal arguments to specialize event expression and their action. The action is a MIL statement block.

The event expression is a conjunctive boolean expression over event terms. A term obeys the format N or $O.N$ where O denotes a variable and N an event name. Both O and N may be a formal parameter. A term is optionally negated with $\sim$ to require absence of the designated event in the pool. The conjunction and negation operators provides the computational power to model first-order formulas over event pools. Disjunctions merely require expression normalization and replication of the trigger action to obtain a trigger family.

A rationale for this approach is that we expect most triggers to use the objects mentioned in the event expression. Then a disjunctive expression would often imply further analysis within the body to determine what action to be taken. The user then better separates the trigger bodies and encapsulate the common part in a separate routine. Such transformations can be hidden from the user with an ECA or rule compiler.

Trigger definitions are stored in the table $<usr>\_triggers$. It is initialized with the triggers defined by the database administrator in the database prelude file.

For example, the trigger below defines a cascading insert from any table S into D. The term $S.insertExit$ becomes true when the command **notify**($insertExit,S$) has been executed by the Monet interpreter. The second term illustrates event negation; it prohibits execution of the trigger body when an error has also occurred. It is raised by the command **notify**($errorExit$). Finally, an instance is created to propagate updates on the employee table to a back-up table.

```
trigger cascade(D, S)
on S.insertExit, ~errorExit
{
  T:= S.alpha();
  if(T.count > 0) D.insert(T);
}
cascade(emp,empBackup);
```

Trigger enabling A trigger becomes enabled by 'calling' it using actual arguments to look after specific event combinations. This 'call' is handled by the Trigger Event Monitor, which enters it into a table of active trigger instances *tem_active*. The instance remains there until it becomes disabled using the **disable** command.

A novelty is to use an admission policy, which determines for each 'call' whether the state of the event pool on which it is to fire can be reached at all. Otherwise, the 'call' is rejected as being not satisfiable. Likewise, a 'call' is refused if it implicitly disables existing triggers. The admission policy routine can be refined by the user.

For example, consider the event expressions "**on** A,$\sim$B" and "**on** B,$\sim$A", i.e. a trigger instance fires whenever the A or B event appears exclusively. Furthermore, assume that the event pool is analysed after each event occurrence. Then extension with the rule "on A,B" becomes meaningless, because this state can not be reached.

Trigger firing Each trigger instance behaves like a procedure call (with its own scope of control) whose body is (re-)scheduled for execution when its event expression is satisfied by the event pool. The fireable instances are selected upon arrival of the each event and all their actions are scheduled for execution. This leads to an immediate E-A coupling mode. The user can subsequently switch to decoupling mode explicit scheduling the main part of the action separately. using the MIL request queue management primitives.

In line with all Monet operations, the trigger body emits the signals <trigger>*Entry* and <trigger>*Exit*. The object associated with the event is the first argument of the trigger call. They can be used to serialize execution of different triggers and to differentiate among events.

For example, assume that after the cascade operation a statistics table should also be updated. This scheduling order is achieved by the event term that the trigger instance *cascade* has finished. The parameter D binds with the object of interest. Note that the original events causing *cascade* to fire have already been removed from the pool.

```
trigger statistics(D)
on D.cascadeExit
{
  statcnt.replace(D,D.count);
  statavg.replace(D,D.average);
}
statistics(empBackup);
```

5 Higher Order Semantics.

The trigger mechanism described is the target language for compiling more complex ECA-rules. In this section we illustrate how enriched models can be compiled into these primitives using three prototypical examples: incremental query evaluation for rule processing, history information to control trigger activation, and transaction management.

Incremental conditions Active models permit arbitrary (existential) queries to control their execution where the query has access to a) the current state; b) the current state and transition information; and c) the current state, transition information, and transaction parameters. The Monet active component supports a) only, because limited information is retained about the context in an event record. Therefore, the ECA-rule compiler should generate code to support the other dimensions.

Simple state transition information is already maintained by the underlying BAT implementation. The proposed additions and deletions since the transaction start can be obtained using the commands **alpha** and **delta**, respectively. This feature can be used to maintain a discrimination network [7].

This discrimination network can be produced by an ECA compiler front-end, which produces triggers to collect and propagate information through the network based on the update events. An illustrative and complete algorithm is described in [4], which optimizes incremental query processing by balancing storage and re-construction cost for TREAT and A-TREAT networks.

Here we focus on their mapping to trigger definitions and instances. To illustrate we derive the triggers for the simplified rule A(x,a),B(x,b) → C(x,c). This rule requires two inserted-memory nodes (n1, n2) and a single beta-memory node (p1). The former is captured by the *amemory* trigger skeleton below. It reacts to an insertion event. The body requests the elements inserted, selects those of interest (>=C), and inserts the result into N. Similar, *bmemory* reacts to insertions on precisely one operand. It determines the x-values to be propagated to N using a semi-join over the delta of C1. The BAT-loop operation finally updates the container N. Two instantiations are needed to cope with all possible update combinations. Note that the TREAT network components merely require two trigger abstraction, while the actual network can be built out of their instantiation.

```
trigger amemory(C, Container, Value)
on Container.insertExit
{ C.insert(Container.alpha.select(Value));}


trigger bmemory(N,C1,C2)
on C1.insertExit
{
  Z := semijoin(C2,C1.alpha));
  Z @ batloop() { N.insert($1,"c");}
}
```

```
n1 := new(int,str); # create the place holders
n2 := new(int,str);
t1 := amemory(n1, A,"a"); # propagation triggers
t2 := amemory(n2, B,"b");
p1 := new(int,str); # join place holder
bmemory(p1, n1, n2); # propagation triggers
bmemory(p1, n2, n1);
```

Delayed notification The second enrichment considered here is an event history mechanism. The Monet kernel does not maintain an event history, because its semantic is highly dependent on the envisioned application domain. Instead, these policies are better compiled into trigger families using database objects for state administration. In particular, it supports triggers that fire after a specific number of events have been received. The Monet trigger abstraction capturing this semantics is shown below. It counts the events and generates a new event when the high- water mark is reached. The counter is a variable local to the trigger instance and reset immediately.

```
trigger count(E, C, N, EventNew)
on E
{ if (C >= N) { notify(EventNew); C := 0; }
else C := C +1;
}
countExit(errorExit, 0, 3,fatal);
```

Transaction coupling modes Many systems couple trigger activation and their scope of control to the transaction responsible for satisfying their event and query condition. The basis for transaction-based triggers is to support the concept at the user interface, i.e. clients indicate the transaction **begin, abort**, and **commit** explicitly. A built-in event makes them visible to the trigger monitor, but it also requires the transactions primitives to cooperate with the TEM. For example, the commit operation in the kernel should wait for the last transaction event to be handled.

The Monet solution is based on two properties. First, postponement of the trigger firing to transaction commit simply requires a test for the *commitEntry* or *commitExit* event to appear in the pool. This effectively means that they occur as terms in (all) the event expressions. Second, the event pool is a user-readable structure and applications can postpone continuation unto a **wait** *event expression* over it becomes satisfied. This way synchronization of parallel actions can be realized.

6   A Performance Metric

The performance of the active component has been measured to isolate the bottlenecks in our architecture as early as possible. Performance depends on the following factors: raw database processing, event detection, event analysis, and trigger instantiation and activation [6]. Although each issue can be analysed in isolation by simulation and analytical modelling, we have implemented a fully functional trigger system and measured the combined effect. This way, we avoid early bias by the perceived performance gains of sophisticated algorithms that do not significantly contribute to the total system responsiveness.

Our experiments have been chosen such that re-implementation on other active database system is feasible. Yet, the implementation makes heavy use of the database structures and kernel operations. A low-level profiler has been used to squeeze the last cpu cycles.

The evaluation platform consists of a Silicon Graphics Indigo 2 workstation with R4400 processor running at 200 Mhz, 1 Mbyte secondary cache and 256 Mb of memory. The performance experiments have been conducted with the Software Testpilot[9], a performance assessment tool developed at CWI.

The Countdown experiment The first experiment determines the baseline for active behavior, namely handling a single (abstract) event and subsequent firing of a single trigger. To deal with the granularity of the system clock, the experiment is modelled as a trigger loop where a variable is decremented until it becomes zero. The condensed Monet code for the abstraction and creation of an instance of 100 cycles is shown below. The loop is started using an explicit notification of the abstract event *down*.

The performance results are shown in Figure 3 with all times measured in milliseconds wall-clock time. The definition and instantiation consumes about 3 ms., which is spent on parsing and compilation to an internal format. The cycle time is largely determined by the cost to schedule the trigger body and its subsequent interpretation. Each cycle takes less than 0.2 ms. Detailed analysis showed that the actual cost to be attributed to active behavior is less than 0.05ms. Initial runs helped us in detecting bad resource management, which lead to non-linear behavior.

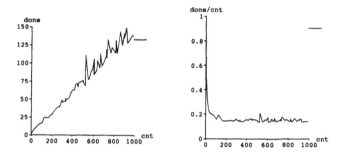

Fig. 3. The Countdown experiment

```
trigger countdown(N)
on down
{   if ( cnt < N ) {
    cnt := cnt+1;
    notify(down);
} }
cnt := 0;
countdown(100);
notify(down);
```

The Dominoes Experiment The second experiment is an analogy of a domino game. The game consists of two phases: setting up the dominoes and pushing the first such that one after the other they fall. The simulated dominoes are trigger instances whose sole action involves raising an event for the next stone.

The purpose of this experiment is to determine whether the implementation can quickly isolate a firable instance. It has been used to assess the effectiveness of the hash-filter against our preliminary linear event expression evaluator.

The Monet code for both phases is shown below. The trigger *dominoes* enables a trigger for each stone which takes a constant time of about 0.4 ms /stone. As shown in Figure 4 the cycle time is also constant (ca. 0.22 ms), because there is exactly one event for each trigger instance. It proved that our hashfilter implementation was effective over the range studied.

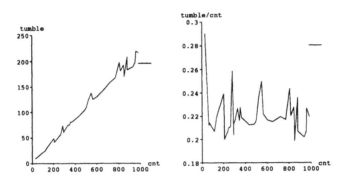

Fig. 4. The Dominoes experiment

```
trigger stone(N)
on N.tumble
{   notify(N+1, tumble); }
trigger dominoes(N)
on setupDomino
{   if ( cnt < N ) {
  cnt := cnt + 1;
  stone(cnt);
  notify(setupDomino);
} }
dominoes(100);
notify(0, tumble);
```

The Pyramid Experiment To increase both the number of trigger instances and the number of events awaiting in the pool for consumption we designed the pyramid experiment. In the construction phase a simple binary tree of trigger instances is constructed, such that each element awaits for a private de-blocking event and an event generated by its parent. The private event is immediately raised, such that after pyramid construction there are as many events in the pool as there are active triggers. The second event encodes the level of the trigger in the pyramid. The destruction phase then merely involves tumbles the root, which subsequently fires all triggers in the next layer. This leads to a quickly increasing workload of trigger actions.

This experiment can be used to demonstrate degradation due to excessive loads on the system kernel and its ability to handle them in parallel. Furthermore, the effectiveness of the accelerator constructs are tested. The Monet trigger abstractions used to build a Pyramid are shown below. The results of this experiment - without optimizations- is given in Figure 5.

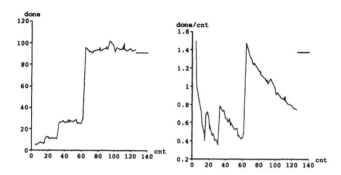

Fig. 5. The Pyramid experiment

```
event destruct, fall;
trigger stone(N,D) on D.fall, N.destruct{
  notify(D/2,destruct);
}
proc pyramid;
proc pyramid(N,D) := {
  stone(N,D);
  if( D> 0) {
    pyramid(N+D,D/2);
    pyramid(N-D,D/2);
    notify(D, destruct);
  }
}
pyramid(4,2);
notify(4,fall);
```

7 Summary

We have described the core-implementation for active behavior in Monet, a parallel DBMS kernel. The key concept exploited is to align active behavior with procedural abstraction, i.e. trigger abstractions. Trigger enabling then aligns with 'calling' the abstraction. Thereafter the trigger action becomes scheduled for (parallel) execution whenever the event expression can be satisfied. This conceptual coupling of trigger instances with procedure bodies and its 'indirect invocation' through events proved a simple and effective means to model a wide-range of examples.

A metric has been defined to test progress of the implementation and to provide a guidance to the ECA compiler writers. The performance figures show that Monet can efficiently support coarse grain active behavior. We intend to further study the impact of parallel triggers. In particular would we like to know the granularity of the trigger actions to exploit the parallelism offered by the kernel implementation.

References

1. C.A. van den Berg and M.L. Kersten. *An analysis of a dynamic query optimisation scheme for different data distributions.* In J.Freytag, D. Maier, and G.Vossen, editors, *Advances in Query Processing*, pp. 449-470. Morgan-Kaufmann, 1994.
2. P. Boncz, M.L Kersten *A Impressionist Sketch of the Monet Database System* Basque workshop in Database Systems, June 1995.
3. C. Collet, T. Coupaye, T. Svensen, *NAOS: Efficient and Modular Reactive Capabilities in an Object-Oriented Database System*, Proc. 20th Int. Conf. on Very Large Databases, Chile, September 1994.
4. F. Fabret, M. Regnier, E. Simon, *An Adaptive Algorithm for Incremental Evaluation of Production Rules in Databases*, Proc. VLDB 19, Dublin, Ireland, Aug. 1993, pp.455-466.
5. S. Gatziu, K.R. Dittrich, *Detecting Composite Events in an Active Database System Using Petri Nets*, Proc. Workshop on Rules in Database Systems, Edinburgh, UK, September 1993, Springer-Verlag.
6. A. Geppert, S. Gatziu, and K.R. Dittrich, *Performance Evaluation of an Active Database Management System: OO7 Meets the BEAST*, Institut für Informatik der Universität Zürich, Nov. 1994
7. E. Hanson, *Rule Condition Testing and Action Execution in Ariel*, Proc. ACM SIGMOD, San Diego, June 1992, pp. 49-58.
8. M. Holsheimer, M.L. Kersten, A. Siebes, *Data Surveyor: Searching the Nuggets in Parallel*, Chapter 4 in Knowledge Discovery in Databases 2 editor Piatetsky-Shapiro and Frawley, MIT Press, Menlo Park, California,1995.
9. M.L. Kersten, F. Kwakkel, *Design and Implementation of a DBMS Performance Assessment Tool* Proceedings DEXA'93, Praag, Sept 1993, pp. 265-276.
10. S. Khoshafian, G. Copeland, T. Jadodits, H. Boral, P. Valduriez (1987) *A Query Processing Strategy for the Decomposed Storage Model*, In Proceedings of the IEEE Data Engineering Conference, pages 636-643.
11. N.W. Paton, O. Diaz, M.H. Willims, J. Campin, A. Din and A. Jaime, *Dimensions of Active behaviour*, Proc. Workshop on Rules in Database Systems, Edinburgh, UK, September 1993, Springer-Verlag.
12. A. Shatdal, C. Kant, J.N. Naughton, *Cache Conscious Algorithms for Relational Query Processing*, Proc. 20th VLDB, Santiago, Chili, 1994, pp. 510-521.
13. J. Widom, *Deductive and Active Databases: Two paradigms or Ends of a Spectrum*, Proc. Workshop on Rules in Database Systems, Edingburgh, UK, September 1993, Springer-Verlag.
14. J. Widom, R,J, Cochrance, B.G. Lindsay, *Implementing Set-Oriented Production Rules as an Extension to Starburst*, Proc. 17th Int Conf. on Very Large Databases, Barcelona, Spain, September 1991.
15. J. Widom, S.Chakravarthy, *Research issues in data Engineering*, proc. RIDE'94, Houston, Texas, Feb 14-15, 1994.

Using Delta Relations to Optimize Condition Evaluation in Active Databases*

Elena Baralis[1] and Jennifer Widom[2]

[1] Politecnico di Torino - Torino, Italy
baralis@polito.it
[2] Stanford University - Stanford, USA
widom@cs.stanford.edu

Abstract. We give a method for improving the efficiency of condition evaluation during rule processing in active database systems. The method derives, from a rule condition, two new conditions that can be used in place of the original condition when a previous value (true or false) of the original condition is known. The derived conditions are generally more efficient to evaluate than the original condition because they are *incremental*—they replace references to entire database relations by references to *delta relations*, which typically are much smaller. Delta relations are accessible to rule conditions in almost all current active database systems, making this optimization broadly applicable. We describe an attribute grammar based approach that we have used to implement our condition rewriting technique.

1 Introduction

Active database systems allow users to specify *event-condition-action* rules that are processed automatically by the database system in response to data manipulation by users and applications. A rule's *event* specifies what causes the rule to become triggered; typical (simple) triggering events are data modification or data retrieval. A rule's *condition* is a further qualification of a triggered rule, usually expressed as a predicate or query over the database. A rule's *action* is performed when the rule is triggered and its condition is true; actions usually are sequences of arbitrary database commands. Most current active database systems, both research prototypes and commercial systems, use this rule paradigm; see [19].

Rule processing in active database systems usually consists of an iterative cycle in which: (1) a triggered rule is selected; (2) the rule's condition is evaluated; (3) if the condition is true the rule's action is executed. In this paper we give a method for optimizing step (2) in this cycle for active databases that use the relational model.[3] Our method is based on the following two assumptions:

---

* This work was partially performed while the authors were at the IBM Almaden Research Center, San Jose, CA. At Stanford this work was supported by the Anderson Faculty Scholar Fund and by equipment grants from Digital Equipment Corporation and IBM Corporation.

[3] Adapting the method to active OODB's is planned for further work; see Section 6.

1. During the rule processing cycle, the rule processor may be aware of the previous value of a rule's condition (true or false), either because the rule was evaluated earlier during rule processing, or because the rule is enforcing an integrity constraint that was consistent at the beginning of the transaction.

2. The rule language permits references to *delta relations*, which contain the data that was modified in a relation since the last time the rule was evaluated or since the beginning of the transaction.[4]

Although these assumptions may appear strong, we note that many of the prominent relational active database systems do satisfy the assumptions, including *A-RDL* [15], *Ariel* [9], *Heraclitus* [8], and *Starburst* [20]. Furthermore, for those active database systems that do not exactly satisfy this paradigm, e.g., *Postgres* [17], relatively straightforward modifications of our method should be applicable.

Given a rule r with condition C, our method statically derives from C two "optimized" conditions, $PT(C)$ (the *Previously True* condition) and $PF(C)$ (the *Previously False* condition). When rule r is selected at run time, if it is known that r's condition was previously true, then $PT(C)$ is evaluated instead of C. Similarly, if it is known that r's condition was previously false, then $PF(C)$ is evaluated instead of C. $PT(C)$ and $PF(C)$ reference delta relations where C references entire relations, so $PT(C)$ and $PF(C)$ are likely to be much more efficient to evaluate than C.

For generality (and for ease in proving correctness) we present our method using a rule condition language based on relational algebra. The adaptation of our method for a condition language based on SQL or Quel is straightforward. We also specify our method as an attribute grammar; this allows a direct implementation of the method using a compiler-generator such as YACC [10].

1.1 Previous Related Work

There is a clear connection between our work and the well-studied problem of *incremental evaluation*, especially as addressed in [12, 13, 16]. [13] proposes an incremental optimization technique for rule conditions, with similar goals to ours. However, rule conditions are restricted to Select-Project-Join (SPJ) expressions, and all relations are required to have user-accessible tuple identifiers. In contrast, our rule conditions are more general than SPJ expressions (see Section 3), and user-level tuple identifiers are not required. [12] proposes a set of transformations that compute incremental changes to arbitrary relational expressions. Although the methods in [12] do apply to (a small variation on) the problem we consider, the application itself is not direct and is rather difficult to understand. Furthermore, the method in [12] sometimes determines that there have been additions to and deletions from an expression when in fact the net effect of the changes is null. This produces an unnecessary reevaluation of the relational expression,

---

[4] We assume that delta relations can be accessed efficiently, since in most systems delta relations are stored or indexed in main memory. We also assume that delta relations typically are much smaller than the corresponding entire relations.

while our method correctly detects that there has been no change. [16] presents a "partial differentiation" technique to derive incremental rule conditions. Like [12], the approach in [16] may produce a superset of the actual changes; in [16] an extra "filtering" step is introduced to eliminate the extra changes. In all three of [12, 13, 16], update modifications are modeled as deletions followed by insertions. We handle update modifications directly, which in some cases produces more efficient incremental expressions than those in [12, 13, 16], particularly when only certain attributes are updated (see our γ transformation in Section 4). Note also that our attribute grammar specification is a unique approach that leads directly to an implementation.

In [14], a classification is given of techniques to optimize the performance of transaction execution when transactions include active rules. One of the suggested techniques is to detect in advance when a rule will have no effect on the database because the rule's condition is guaranteed to be false. This optimization is more effective than ours when it is applicable, but it applies only in very special cases, and it requires compile-time analysis of transaction code, which our method does not.

Some active database systems use methods based on *Rete* or *TREAT* networks [18] for efficient condition evaluation, e.g., [7, 9]. Unfortunately, these methods apply only to rule languages where references to a relation R implicitly reference delta relations for R, and to rule conditions that are restricted to SPJ expressions. We consider more general conditions, and we determine those scenarios in which R can be replaced by its delta relations. Commercial active rule languages appear to be following our model, so our techniques should be applicable in very practical settings.

Finally, note that in [6] we suggest techniques similar to those we present here, but only a very restricted case is described. In this paper we elaborate the suggestions of [6] in a general context.

1.2 Outline of the Paper

In Section 2 we give a more rigorous description of active database rule processing and we formalize the notion of delta relations. In Section 3 we define our condition specification language and we provide some examples. Section 4 is the core technical section: it contains our method for rule condition rewriting and several examples of the method. Section 5 specifies an implementation of the method using an attribute grammar. Finally, Section 6 concludes and proposes improvements and extensions to our technique.

2 Rule Processing and Delta Relations

Consider an active database system in which a set of event-condition-action rules are defined as described in Section 1. Suppose further that a set of user or application modifications are performed on the database, then rule processing is invoked. The pseudo-code in Figure 1 describes the general behavior of the

```
S = initial DB state
user or application modifications
S' = new DB state
repeat until no rules are triggered:
    select a triggered rule r
    evaluate r's condition based on S' and delta relations
    if true, execute r's action based on S' and delta relations
    S' = new DB state
```

Fig. 1. Active database system behavior

system. Note that issues such as the "granularity" of rule processing (i.e., when rule processing is invoked relative to triggering events) and the method for selecting among multiple triggered rules do not affect our method. Furthermore, our method also applies to rule languages in which triggering events are implicit rather than explicit, e.g., [9, 14, 15, 16].

When a rule's condition is evaluated and its action is executed, this occurs with respect to a database *transition*, i.e., the changes that have occurred since some previous database state. We consider a semantics in which each rule uses the transition since that rule was last selected, or since the original state (state S in Figure 1) if the rule has not yet been selected during rule processing. While this is the semantics taken by many active database systems, systems with slightly different semantics may require corresponding modifications to our method.

Delta relations encapsulate the changes that have occurred during a rule's transition, and they may be referenced in a rule's condition and action. For each relation R we assume four delta relations:

- *inserted*(R) contains the tuples inserted into R during the transition.
- *deleted*(R) contains the tuples deleted from R during the transition.
- *old-updated*(R) contains the pre-transition values of the tuples modified in R during the transition.
- *new-updated*(R) contains the current (i.e., new) values of the tuples modified in R during the transition.

In addition, *new-updated* and *old-updated* may be restricted to sets of attributes. Let $A_1, \ldots, A_n$ be attributes of relation R. Then:

- *old-updated*($R, \{A_1, \ldots, A_n\}$) contains the pre-transition values of the tuples in R for which at least one of $A_1, \ldots, A_n$ was modified during the transition.
- *new-updated*($R, \{A_1, \ldots, A_n\}$) contains the current values of the tuples in R for which at least one of $A_1, \ldots, A_n$ was modified during the transition.

Typically, delta relations reflect the *net effect* of database modifications; that is, they contain only the net result of successive actions over the same tuple.

This concept of net effect is used widely, e.g., [9, 15, 21], so we assume it here. Note that one implication of using net effects is that *inserted(R)*, *deleted(R)*, *old-updated(R)*, and *new-updated(R)* are disjoint.

We introduce four abbreviations that are used throughout the remainder of the paper:

(1) $\Delta^+(R) = inserted(R) \cup new\text{-}updated(R)$

(2) $\Delta^-(R) = deleted(R) \cup old\text{-}updated(R)$

(3) $\Delta^+(R, \{A_1, \ldots, A_n\}) = inserted(R) \cup new\text{-}updated(R, \{A_1, \ldots, A_n\})$

(4) $\Delta^-(R, \{A_1, \ldots, A_n\}) = deleted(R) \cup old\text{-}updated(R, \{A_1, \ldots, A_n\})$

Note that in (3) and (4), if the attribute list is empty, then Δ^+ and Δ^- degenerate to *inserted(R)* and *deleted(R)*. We informally refer to (both versions of) Δ^+ and Δ^- as *incremental* and *decremental changes*, respectively.

Sometimes our optimized conditions require access to the "old" value of a relation, i.e., the relation's pre-transition value. We denote the old value of a relation R as R^O. While some active database rule languages provide a feature for accessing R^O directly, others do not. However, R^O always can be derived from the current value of R and R's delta relations, based on the equivalence:

$$R^O = (R - \Delta^+(R)) \cup \Delta^-(R)$$

3 Condition Language

In active database rule languages, conditions are sometimes expressed as predicates and sometimes as queries, where in the latter case usually the interpretation is that the condition is true iff the query produces a non-empty result. It can easily be shown that the two representations are equivalent [2]; we represent conditions as predicates. The grammar of our condition language is given in Figure 2. The language is powerful enough to describe any condition expressible in relational algebra or calculus extended with aggregate functions, with the exception of duplicates and ordering conditions.

In the grammar's productions, terminal symbol R stands for a relation name and R.A for an attribute of relation R. The meaning of the language is mostly self-explanatory. Condition $\exists(Rexp)$ is satisfied iff relational expression *Rexp* produces one or more tuples, while condition $\neg\exists(Rexp)$ is satisfied iff *Rexp* produces no tuples. We assume a set semantics, i.e., no duplicates. Note the following points:

- Although not included in the grammar explicitly, joins can be expressed using cross-product and selection.
- A selection that is a boolean combination of comparisons can be expressed in our language by using the following equivalences:

$$\sigma_{c_1 \wedge c_2} Rexp = \sigma_{c_1}(\sigma_{c_2} Rexp)$$
$$\sigma_{c_1 \vee c_2} Rexp = \sigma_{c_1} Rexp \cup \sigma_{c_2} Rexp$$

$$
\begin{array}{ll}
Cond & ::= \exists(Rexp) \mid \neg\exists(Rexp) \\
& \mid Cond_1 \wedge Cond_2 \mid Cond_1 \vee Cond_2 \mid (Cond) \\
Rexp & ::= \mathsf{R} \mid Rexp_1 \cup Rexp_2 \\
& \mid Rexp_1 \times Rexp_2 \mid Rexp - SimpleRexp \\
& \mid \sigma_{Compare}Rexp \mid \pi_{AList}Rexp \\
& \mid Aggr(Attr_1[, Attr_2])Rexp \mid (Rexp) \\
SimpleRexp & ::= \mathsf{R} \mid SimpleRexp_1 \cup SimpleRexp_2 \\
& \mid SimpleRexp_1 \times SimpleRexp_2 \mid \sigma_{Compare}SimpleRexp \\
& \mid \pi_{AList}SimpleRexp \mid (SimpleRexp) \\
Compare & ::= Term_1 \; Op \; Term_2 \\
Term & ::= Attr \mid \mathsf{Const} \\
Op & ::= > \mid < \mid \leq \mid \geq \mid = \mid \neq \\
Aggr & ::= \mathsf{sum} \mid \mathsf{avg} \mid \mathsf{min} \mid \mathsf{max} \mid \mathsf{count} \\
AList & ::= Attr_1, \ldots, Attr_n \\
Attr & ::= \mathsf{R.A}
\end{array}
$$

Fig. 2. Condition language syntax

- Negation of selection predicates can be expressed by repeatedly applying De-Morgan's laws and then negating the innermost comparisons (i.e., $\leq$ becomes $>$, $=$ becomes $\neq$, etc.).
- *Terms* may be arithmetic expressions over attributes and constants without affecting our method, although for simplicity we have omitted this feature from our grammar.
- The *Aggr* operation is for handling the aggregate functions sum, avg, min, etc. It extends a given relational expression with a new attribute containing the computed value of the aggregate function. The function is computed over the attribute $Attr_1$ and grouping may optionally be performed by specifying the $Attr_2$ attribute; see [4] for a detailed description of this construct.
- "Simple relational expressions" (*SimpleRexp*) are introduced to restrict the expressions that may appear as the second operand of a difference. The need for this restriction is explained in Section 4.[5]
- Most active database rule languages permit explicit references to delta relations in rule conditions. Therefore, technically we should include *Rexp* productions for *inserted* (R), *deleted* (R), etc. in our grammar. However, since there is no need to attempt optimization for these references, for clarity and simplicity we omit them from the grammar; adding them is trivial.

3.1 Examples

We give two examples of conditions expressed in our language, which are adapted from a case study in [3, 6] involving an electrical power distribution network;

---

[5] This restriction does not reduce the expressive power of our condition language with respect to relational algebra; see [2].

these examples use the two relations WIRE(wire-id,from,to,voltage) and TUBE(tube-id,from,to,protected), which we abbreviate as W and T, respectively.

Example 3.1: Informally: Some unprotected tube contains a high voltage ($> 5k$) wire. In our condition language:

$$\exists(\sigma_{W.<from,to>=T.<from,to>}(\sigma_{W.voltage>5k}W \times \sigma_{T.protected=false}T))$$

where $\sigma_{W.<from,to>=T.<from,to>}$ is an abbreviation for $\sigma_{W.from=T.from}\sigma_{W.to=T.to}$.

Example 3.2: Informally: Some tube contains no wires. More precisely, there is some tube such that no wire has the same from and to attributes. In our condition language:

$$\exists(T - \pi_{schema(T)}(\sigma_{T.<from,to>=W.<from,to>}(T \times W)))$$

where we use schema(T) as an abbreviation for a list of all the attributes of T.

4 Derivation of Optimized Conditions

Let C be a condition expressed using the language of Section 3. Suppose we want to evaluate C with respect to a database state S' and the transition from some previous database state S. Further suppose that the result of C in state S is known, i.e., C was either true or false in S.[6] In this case we use one of two optimized conditions in place of C:

- $PF(C)$ (PF for "Previously False") is chosen when the outcome of the previous evaluation of C was false.
- $PT(C)$ (PT for "Previously True") is chosen when the outcome of the previous evaluation of C was true.

In general, $PF(C)$ only provides a useful optimization for conditions with existential quantifications ($\exists$) and disjunction, while $PT(C)$ only provides a useful optimization for conditions with negative existential quantification ($\neg\exists$) and conjunction. Intuitively, this is for the following reasons. When the condition was previously false, an existential quantification tells us that no data satisfied the relational expression. Hence we can check if data now satisfies the relational expression by checking changed data only. However, suppose we have a negative existential quantification. Then, since the condition was previously false, some data did previously satisfy the relational expression. In this case it is impossible to tell, by examining changed data only, whether the relational expression is now empty. If a previously false condition contains disjuncts, then we know that all

---

[6] Recall from Figure 1 that this information is available whenever C's rule has been selected previously or the value of C was known in the initial state before user modifications.

C	$PF(C)$	$PT(C)$
$\exists(Rexp)$	$\exists(\vartheta(Rexp))$	$\exists(Rexp)$
$\neg\exists(Rexp)$	$\neg\exists(Rexp)$	$\neg\exists(\vartheta(Rexp))$
$Cond_1 \wedge Cond_2$	$Cond_1 \wedge Cond_2$	$PT(Cond_1) \wedge PT(Cond_2)$
$Cond_1 \vee Cond_2$	$PF(Cond_1) \vee PF(Cond_2)$	$Cond_1 \vee Cond_2$
$(Cond)$	$(PF(Cond))$	$(PT(Cond))$

Table 1. The PF and PT optimized conditions

disjuncts were false and we can optimize each one based on that knowledge. However, if the condition contains conjuncts, then we don't know which conjuncts were previously false, and optimization is impossible. The same argument, in converse, holds for previously true conditions.[7]

In $PF(C)$ and $PT(C)$, each reference to a relation R is replaced by one of its corresponding incremental or decremental changes, $\Delta^+(R)$ or $\Delta^-(R)$, whenever possible. We define $PF(C)$ and $PT(C)$ by means of transformation rules based on the structure of C according to the grammar of Figure 2. The rules are given in Tables 1, 2, and 3; the rules are applied inductively to derive $PF(C)$ and $PT(C)$ for an arbitrarily complex condition. The correctness of these rules is shown in [2]. We now provide more intuition for the rules, including an explanation for certain details of Tables 1, 2, and 3.

$Rexp$	$\vartheta(Rexp)$
R	$\Delta^+(R)$
$Rexp_1 \cup Rexp_2$	$\vartheta(Rexp_1) \cup \vartheta(Rexp_2)$
$Rexp_1 \times Rexp_2$	$(\vartheta(Rexp_1) \times Rexp_2) \cup (Rexp_1 \times \vartheta(Rexp_2))$
$Rexp_1 - SimpleRexp_2$	$(\vartheta(Rexp_1) - SimpleRexp_2) \cup (Rexp_1 \cap \vartheta'(SimpleRexp_2))$
$\sigma_{Compare} Rexp$	$\sigma_{Compare}(\vartheta(Rexp))$
$\pi_{AList} Rexp$	$\pi_{AList}(\vartheta(Rexp))$
$Aggr(Attr_1[, Attr_2])Rexp$	$Aggr(Attr_1[, Attr_2])Rexp$
$(Rexp)$	$(\vartheta(Rexp))$

Table 2. The ϑ transformation for relational expressions

In Table 1, the rules for $PF(C)$ and $PT(C)$ use a transformation ϑ, which is applied to relational expressions. Table 2 contains the transformation rules for

---

[7] Certainly we might do somewhat better here, e.g., keep track of which conjuncts/disjuncts were previously true/false, keep track of which data previously satisfied the condition, or handle certain special cases. We plan to investigate these improvements as future work.

$Simple\,Rexp$	$\vartheta'(Simple\,Rexp)$
R	$\Delta^-(R)$
$SR_1 \cup SR_2$	$(\vartheta'(SR_1) - SR_2) \cup (\vartheta'(SR_2) - SR_1)$
$SR_1 \times SR_2$	$(\vartheta'(SR_1) \times SR_2^O) \cup (SR_1^O \times \vartheta'(SR_2))$
$\sigma_{Compare} SR$	$\sigma_{Compare}(\vartheta'(SR))$
$\pi_{AList} SR$	$\pi_{AList}(\vartheta'(SR)) - \pi_{AList} SR$
(SR)	$(\vartheta'(SR))$

Table 3. The ϑ' transformation for simple relational expressions

ϑ applied to an arbitrary relational expression $Rexp$, while Table 3 contains an additional transformation ϑ' applied to an arbitrary simple relational expression $Simple\,Rexp$. (Recall that simple relational expressions are those relational expressions that can appear as the second operand of a difference. Hence, ϑ' is applied in the fourth line of Table 2.) Intuitively, ϑ applied to a relational expression $Rexp$ produces an optimized expression $Rexp'$ that computes the incremental changes to $Rexp$. When ϑ is applied to an expression with the difference operation, decremental changes to the second operand cause incremental changes to the entire expression. Hence, ϑ' is a "negated" version of ϑ that computes these decremental changes. Decremental changes can be computed only on *monotonic* relational expressions. This explains our introduction of simple relational expressions: simple relational expressions exclude difference and aggregate operators, which are non-monotonic.

Observe the following points:

- For convenience, we use $\cap$ in ϑ applied to $Rexp_1 - Simple\,Rexp_2$. Expression $Rexp_1 \cap Rexp_2$ is equivalent to $Rexp_1 \times Rexp_2$ with a selection condition equating all corresponding attributes and appropriate projection.
- The computation of an aggregate function over a relational expression always requires the entire relational expression result (not just an incremental portion), thus aggregate expressions cannot be optimized in the general case. However, conditions containing aggregate function expressions as operands still may be optimized in their other operands.
- Note that in ϑ, the treatment of projection and union are substantially simpler than in general incremental query evaluation such as [12].
- ϑ' on cartesian products refers to "old" relational expression SR^O. Here we are using SR^O as an abbreviation for SR with all relation names R replaced by R^O, denoting the old value of R. (Recall that if old relations are not directly accessible, they can be derived from delta relations as described in Section 2.)
- For ϑ' applied to projections, if the attribute list $AList$ contains a key for the expression SR (as is often the case), then our formula can be simplified to $\pi_{AList}(\vartheta'(SR))$.

While we expect the sizes of $\Delta^+(R)$ and $\Delta^-(R)$ in $PF(C)$ and $PT(C)$ to be small (much smaller than R), we can further reduce the sizes of $\Delta^+(R)$ and $\Delta^-(R)$ by ignoring all updates to attributes that do not influence the outcome of the condition. Let R' denote a specific reference to relation R in a condition C. We compute the *relevant attribute set* $\rho(R',C)$, where $\rho(R',C)$ is the set of all attributes in R whose updates can affect the outcome of condition C with respect to reference R'. Let $Rexp(R')$ be any relational expression (or simple relational expression) in C containing the reference R'. For each attribute A_i of R, $A_i \in \rho(R',C)$ iff:

1. A_i appears in a selection comparison over $Rexp(R')$ (predicate *Compare* in $\sigma_{Compare}$), or
2. A_i is used for aggregate computation or grouping on $Rexp(R')$ ($Attr_1$ or $Attr_2$ in $Aggr$ operation), or
3. there is a union or difference applied to $Rexp(R')$.

Thus, given an original condition C and optimized condition C' (either $PF(C)$ or $PT(C)$), we further optimize C' as $\gamma(C')$, where γ replaces every reference $\Delta^+(R')$ or $\Delta^-(R')$ in C' by $\Delta^+(R', \rho(R',C))$ or $\Delta^-(R', \rho(R',C))$. This additional optimization has not been suggested previously (to the best of our knowledge); it can be very effective in practice, as shown by the examples in the next section.

The proof of correctness of the $PF(C)$ and $PT(C)$ transformations is given by Theorem 1. Due to space constraints, the proof is omitted; it appears in [2].

Theorem 1: Let C denote any condition specified using the language of Figure 2. Then:

(a) If C was false in state S, C is true in state S' iff $PF(C)$ is true in state S'.
(b) If C was true in state S, C is true in state S' iff $PT(C)$ is true in state S'. □

4.1 Examples

We show the optimized conditions for the two examples introduced in Section 3.1.

Example 4.1: Some unprotected tube contains a high voltage ($> 5k$) wire. In our condition language:

$$C = \exists(\sigma_{W.<from,to>=T.<from,to>}(\sigma_{W.voltage>5k}W \times \sigma_{T.protected=false}T))$$

The optimized conditions are:

$$PF(C) = \exists(\sigma_{join}(\sigma_{volt}incr\text{-}W \times \sigma_{unprot}T) \cup (\sigma_{volt}W \times \sigma_{unprot}incr\text{-}T)))$$
$$PT(C) = C$$

where *join* is $W. < from, to > = T. < from, to >$, *volt* is $W.voltage > 5k$, *unprot* is $T.protected = false$, *incr-W* is $\Delta^+(W, \{voltage, from, to\})$, and *incr-T* is $\Delta^+(T, \{from, to, protected\})$. Note that this same example could not be optimized using the method presented in [6].

Example 4.2: Some tube contains no wires. In our condition language:

$$C = \exists(T - \pi_{schema(T)}(\sigma_{T. < from, to > = W. < from, to >}(T \times W)))$$

Since this example has a difference operator, transformation ϑ' is used as well as ϑ. Recall that W^0 and T^0 refer to the pre-transition (old) states of W and T, respectively. Note also that here delta relations cannot be restricted to updates on specific attributes (because of the difference operator), and that we are applying the simplified formula for ϑ' applied to projections since the projected attributes form a key. The optimized conditions are:

$$PF(C) = \exists((\Delta^+(T) - \pi_t(\sigma_j(T \times W))) \cup (T \cap \pi_t(\sigma_j((\Delta^-(T) \times W^0) \cup (T^0 \times \Delta^-(W))))))$$
$$PT(C) = C$$

where t is $schema(T)$, and j is $T. < from, to > = W. < from, to >$. As in Example 4.1, this condition could not be optimized using the method in [6].

Numerous additional examples can be found in [2].

5 Attribute Grammar Implementation

Now we address the issue of implementing our approach. Suppose a new rule r with condition C is added to the database (or an existing rule's condition is to be optimized). The following steps are followed:

1. C is translated into our condition language.
2. The optimized conditions $PF(C)$ and $PT(C)$ are generated.
3. $PF(C)$ and $PT(C)$ are translated back to the rule's condition language.[8]
4. At run-time, whenever possible, the evaluation of C is replaced by the evaluation of $PF(C)$ or $PT(C)$.

Note that steps 1–3 are *static*: they are performed only once, when rule r is first defined. At run-time, the system evaluates an optimized condition (step 4) just as it would have evaluated the original condition.

We consider in detail the implementation of step 2. The ϑ and γ transformations can be computed during the parsing of a condition to yield the optimized conditions. Thus, we have chosen to implement the derivation of optimized conditions using an *attribute grammar*. In an attribute grammar, each symbol is

---

[8] Note from Section 4 that our process is highly unlikely to yield constructs in $PF(C)$ and $PT(C)$ that are not available in the language used to specify the original rule condition.

1. $Cond ::= \exists(Rexp)$
   $Rexp.\gamma := \emptyset$
   $Cond.PF := \exists(Rexp.\vartheta)$
   $Cond.PT := \exists(Rexp.E)$
   $Cond.C := \exists(Rexp.E)$

2. $\quad | \quad \neg\exists(Rexp)$
   $Rexp.\gamma := \emptyset$
   $Cond.PF := \neg\exists(Rexp.E)$
   $Cond.PT := \neg\exists(Rexp.\vartheta)$
   $Cond.C := \neg\exists(Rexp.E)$

3. $\quad | \quad Cond_1 \wedge Cond_2$
   $Cond.PF := Cond_1.C \wedge Cond_2.C$
   $Cond.PT := Cond_1.PT \wedge Cond_2.PT$
   $Cond.C := Cond_1.C \wedge Cond_2.C$

4. $\quad | \quad Cond_1 \vee Cond_2$
   $Cond.PF := Cond_1.PF \vee Cond_2.PF$
   $Cond.PT := Cond_1.C \vee Cond_2.C$
   $Cond.C := Cond_1.C \vee Cond_2.C$

5. $\quad | \quad (Cond_1)$
   $Cond.PF := (Cond_1.PF)$
   $Cond.PT := (Cond_1.PT)$
   $Cond.C := (Cond_1.C)$

Fig. 3. Attribute grammar for the *Cond* production

allowed to have a fixed number of associated values, called attributes, and each grammar production has a set of attribute evaluation rules. Attributes can be used to pass information up a syntax tree: these are called *synthesized attributes*, and the evaluation rules associated with each production describe how the attributes' left-hand-side (LHS) values are computed from their right-hand-side (RHS) values. If instead the information flows down the syntax tree, these are called *inherited attributes*, and their evaluation rules describe how RHS attribute values are computed as a function of LHS values. For a more detailed description of attribute grammars refer to [1].

Our attribute grammar computes the ϑ and γ transformations at the same time. At the end of the parsing process, the grammar produces the optimized conditions $PF(C)$ and $PT(C)$ as attributes. The grammar uses one inherited attribute (γ) and eight synthesized attributes (ϑ, ϑ', PF, PT, A, C, E, EO), as follows:

- The ϑ and ϑ' synthesized attributes implement the ϑ and ϑ' transformations. At any time during the parsing process, attribute ϑ for a relational expression *Rexp* contains ϑ applied to *Rexp*. Attribute ϑ' is similarly defined for simple relational expressions.
- The PF and PT synthesized attributes are used to build the complete optimized condition, using as building blocks the optimized conditions provided

6. $Rexp ::=$ R

$R.\gamma := \pi_{\text{schema}(R)}(\text{Rexp}.\gamma)$

$\text{Rexp}.\vartheta := \Delta^+(R, \{R.\gamma\})$

$\text{Rexp}.E := R$

7. $\quad | \quad Rexp_1 \cup Rexp_2$

$\text{Rexp}_1.\gamma := \text{All}(\text{Rexp}_1)$

$\text{Rexp}_2.\gamma := \text{All}(\text{Rexp}_2)$

$\text{Rexp}.\vartheta := \text{Rexp}_1.\vartheta \cup \text{Rexp}_2.\vartheta$

$\text{Rexp}.E := \text{Rexp}_1.E \cup \text{Rexp}_2.E$

8. $\quad | \quad Rexp_1 \times Rexp_2$

$\text{Rexp}_1.\gamma := \text{Rexp}.\gamma$

$\text{Rexp}_2.\gamma := \text{Rexp}.\gamma$

$\text{Rexp}.\vartheta := (\text{Rexp}_1.\vartheta \times \text{Rexp}_2.E) \cup (\text{Rexp}_1.E \times \text{Rexp}_2.\vartheta)$

$\text{Rexp}.E := \text{Rexp}_1.E \times \text{Rexp}_2.E$

9. $\quad | \quad Rexp_1 - SimpleRexp_2$

$\text{Rexp}_1.\gamma := \text{All}(\text{Rexp}_1)$

$\text{SimpleRexp}_2.\gamma := \text{All}(\text{SimpleRexp}_2)$

$\text{Rexp}.\vartheta := (\text{Rexp}_1.\vartheta - \text{SimpleRexp}_2.E) \cup (\text{Rexp}_1.E \cap \text{SimpleRexp}_2.\vartheta')$

$\text{Rexp}.E := \text{Rexp}_1.E - \text{SimpleRexp}_2.E$

10. $\quad | \quad \sigma_{Compare} Rexp_1$

$\text{Rexp}_1.\gamma := \text{Rexp}.\gamma \oplus \text{Compare}.A$

$\text{Rexp}.\vartheta := \sigma_{\text{Compare}}(\text{Rexp}_1.\vartheta)$

$\text{Rexp}.E := \sigma_{\text{Compare}}(\text{Rexp}_1.E)$

11. $\quad | \quad \pi_{AList} Rexp_1$

$\text{Rexp}_1.\gamma := \text{Rexp}.\gamma$

$\text{Rexp}.\vartheta := \pi_{\text{AList}}(\text{Rexp}_1.\vartheta)$

$\text{Rexp}.E := \pi_{\text{AList}}(\text{Rexp}_1.E)$

12. $\quad | \quad Aggr(Attr_1 [, Attr_2]) Rexp_1$

$\text{Rexp}_1.\gamma := \text{Rexp}.\gamma \oplus \text{Attr}_1.A \oplus \text{Attr}_2.A$

$\text{Rexp}.\vartheta := \text{Aggr}(\text{Attr}_1, \text{Attr}_2)\text{Rexp}_1.E$

$\text{Rexp}.E := \text{Aggr}(\text{Attr}_1, \text{Attr}_2)\text{Rexp}_1.E$

13. $\quad | \quad (Rexp_1)$

$\text{Rexp}_1.\gamma := \text{Rexp}.\gamma$

$\text{Rexp}.\vartheta := (\text{Rexp}_1.\vartheta)$

$\text{Rexp}.E := (\text{Rexp}_1.E)$

Fig. 4. Attribute grammar for the *Rexp* production

by the ϑ attribute. At the end of the parsing process, these attributes contain the optimized conditions $PF(C)$ and $PT(C)$, respectively.

- The γ inherited attribute allows us to progressively build top-down the relevant attribute set ($\rho(R, C)$ from Section 4), by adding the attributes involved in all predicates and aggregate functions while descending the parse tree. When the relation terminal symbol is reached (R), the reduced delta relation is defined using the relevant attribute set contained in the γ attribute.

14. $SRexp ::= R$

$\qquad R.\gamma := \pi_{schema(R)}(SRexp.\gamma)$

$\qquad SRexp.\vartheta' := \Delta^-(R, \{R.\gamma\})$

$\qquad SRexp.E := R$

$\qquad SRexp.EO := R^0$

15. $\qquad | \quad SRexp_1 \cup SRexp_2$

$\qquad SRexp_1.\gamma := All(SRexp_1)$

$\qquad SRexp_2.\gamma := All(SRexp_2)$

$\qquad SRexp.\vartheta' := (SRexp_1.\vartheta' - SRexp_2.E) \cup (SRexp_2.\vartheta' - SRexp_1.E)$

$\qquad SRexp.E := SRexp_1.E \cup SRexp_2.E$

$\qquad SRexp.EO := SRexp_1.EO \cup SRexp_2.EO$

16. $\qquad | \quad SRexp_1 \times SRexp_2$

$\qquad SRexp_1.\gamma := SRexp.\gamma$

$\qquad SRexp_2.\gamma := SRexp.\gamma$

$\qquad SRexp.\vartheta' := (SRexp_1.\vartheta' \times SRexp_2.EO) \cup (SRexp_1.EO \times SRexp_2.\vartheta')$

$\qquad SRexp.E := SRexp_1.E \times SRexp_2.E$

$\qquad SRexp.EO := SRexp_1.EO \times SRexp_2.EO$

17. $\qquad | \quad \sigma_{Compare}SRexp_1$

$\qquad SRexp_1.\gamma := SRexp.\gamma \oplus Compare.A$

$\qquad SRexp.\vartheta' := \sigma_{Compare}(SRexp_1.\vartheta')$

$\qquad SRexp.E := \sigma_{Compare}(SRexp_1.E)$

$\qquad SRexp.EO := \sigma_{Compare}(SRexp_1.EO)$

18. $\qquad | \quad \pi_{AList}SRexp_1$

$\qquad SRexp_1.\gamma := SRexp.\gamma$

$\qquad SRexp.\vartheta' := \pi_{AList}(SRexp_1.\vartheta') - \pi_{AList}(SRexp_1.E)$

$\qquad SRexp.E := \pi_{AList}(SRexp_1.E)$

$\qquad SRexp.EO := \pi_{AList}(SRexp_1.EO)$

19. $\qquad | \quad (SRexp_1)$

$\qquad SRexp_1.\gamma := SRexp.\gamma$

$\qquad SRexp.\vartheta' := (SRexp_1.\vartheta')$

$\qquad SRexp.E := (SRexp_1.E)$

$\qquad SRexp.EO := (SRexp_1.EO)$

Fig. 5. Attribute grammar for the *SimpleRexp* production

- The A, C, E, and EO synthesized attributes are needed to aid the propagation process. Attribute A allows us to extract from a predicate or aggregate definition the list of relevant attributes. Attributes C, E, and EO propagate up the parse tree the definition of the original condition, and the current and old relational expressions, so that they are available each time they are required in the definition of $PF(C)$, $PT(C)$, ϑ, and ϑ'.

In Figures 3, 4, and 5, the attribute grammars for the *Cond*, *Rexp*, and *SimpleRexp* productions are given, while the remaining productions are given in Figure 6. The renaming of tokens appearing in both the LHS and RHS productions, although not necessary, improves the readability of the grammar. The $\oplus$

20. $Compare ::= Term_1\ Op\ Term_2$
   $Compare.A := Term_1.A \oplus Term_2.A$

21. $Term \quad ::= Attr$
   $Term.A := Attr.A$

22. $\quad\quad\quad | \quad Const$
   $Term.A := \emptyset$

23. $Op \quad\quad ::= > | < | \le | \ge | = | ! =$

24. $Aggr \quad ::= sum | avg | min | max | count$

25. $AList \quad ::= Attr_1, \ldots, Attr_n$

26. $Attr \quad\quad ::= R.a$
   $Attr.A := R.a$

Fig. 6. Attribute grammar for the remaining productions

operator performs list concatenation; it is used to build attribute lists. Note that not every production needs to compute every attribute, since different attributes have different scopes; for details see [1].

We have built a prototype condition rewriter using the parser-generator tools *LEX* [11] and *YACC* [10]. We would like to incorporate our condition rewriting facility into an active database rule system, most likely Starburst [20]. This should be relatively straightforward: Delta relations as used in this paper are directly available in Starburst. The Starburst SQL-based condition language easily translates to and from our condition language. We can generate the optimized conditions and store them with the original condition in the Starburst *Rule Catalog* [20]. It is then sufficient to add to the run-time rule processor the logic for: (a) storing a previous outcome of condition evaluation for each rule, and (b) choosing an optimized condition for evaluation in place of the original condition whenever possible. Based on the implementation architecture of the Starburst Rule System [20], both of these tasks can be performed easily and efficiently.

6 Conclusions and Future Work

We have described a method for improving the condition evaluation phase of active database rule processing. Our method is based on rule conditions expressed in an extension of relational algebra; this provides both a logical formulation and a framework that can apply to multiple rule languages. We have also specified an implementation of our approach based on an attribute grammar.

As future work we plan to:

- Improve our handling of aggregate functions.
- Extend our condition language to more succinctly express certain constructs, so that we can improve our rewriting for these constructs (e.g., negative subqueries, which are now expressed as relational difference).

- Handle special cases where $PF(C)$ and $PT(C)$ can optimize conditions currently not optimized (recall Section 4).
- Consider similar methods in the context of deductive and object-oriented active database systems (e.g., we hope to use these methods in the *IDEA* project [5], where they should apply in a straightforward way).
- Investigate query optimization strategies that exploit references to very small relations, such as the delta relations used in our optimized conditions.
- Implement our method in the Starburst Rule System and experiment with its practical effectiveness under a variety of database and rule processing loads.

Although we believe that our optimized conditions will be much cheaper to evaluate in most scenarios, there may be some cases in which the original condition is cheaper. Our optimized conditions generally have a more complex structure than the original conditions (i.e., a larger number of subconditions), and there may be some run-time situations in which delta relations are not significantly smaller than their corresponding complete relations. Hence, to address this issue, we plan to develop and exploit an appropriate cost model. The cost model will be based on, e.g., the cardinality of the referenced relations versus their delta relations, and the selectivity of predicates appearing in the condition. The cost model then can be used to predict whether or not it will actually be beneficial to evaluate an optimized condition in place of the original condition.

References

1. A. Aho, R. Sethi, and J. Ullman. *Compilers: principles, techniques, and tools.* Addison-Wesley, Reading, Massachusetts, 1986.
2. E. Baralis. *An Algebraic Approach to the Analysis and Optimization of Active Database Rules.* PhD thesis, Politecnico di Torino, Torino, Italy, Feb. 1994.
3. E. Baralis, S. Ceri, G. Monteleone, and S. Paraboschi. An intelligent database system application: The design of EMS. In *Proc. of the First Int. Conf. on Applications of Databases,* LNCS 851, Vadstena, Sweden, June 1994. Springer-Verlag.
4. S. Ceri and G. Gottlob. Translating SQL into relational algebra: Optimization, semantics, and equivalence of SQL queries. *IEEE Trans. Softw. Eng.*, 11(4):324–345, Apr. 1985.
5. S. Ceri and R. Manthey. Consolidated specification of Chimera, the conceptual interface of Idea. Technical Report IDEA.DD.2P.004, Politecnico di Milano, Milan, Italy, June 1993.
6. S. Ceri and J. Widom. Deriving production rules for constraint maintenance. In *Proc. of the Sixteenth Int. Conf. on Very Large Data Bases,* pages 566–577, Brisbane, Australia, Aug. 1990.
7. F. Fabret, M. Regnier, and E. Simon. An adaptive algorithm for incremental evaluation of production rules in databases. In *Proc. of the Nineteenth Int. Conf. on Very Large Data Bases,* pages 455–466, Dublin, Ireland, Aug. 1993.
8. S. Ghandeharizadeh, R. Hull, D. Jacobs, et al. On implementing a language for specifying active database execution models. In *Proc. of the Nineteenth Int. Conf. on Very Large Data Bases,* Dublin, Ireland, Aug. 1993.

9. E. Hanson. Rule condition testing and action execution in Ariel. In *Proceedings of the ACM SIGMOD Int. Conf. on Management of Data*, pages 49–58, San Diego, California, June 1992.

10. S. Johnson. YACC — yet another compiler compiler. Technical Report CSTR 32, Bell Laboratories, Murray Hill, New Jersey, 1975.

11. M. Lesk. LEX — a lexical analyzer generator. Technical Report CSTR 39, Bell Laboratories, Murray Hill, New Jersey, 1975.

12. X. Qian and G. Wiederhold. Incremental recomputation of active relational expressions. *IEEE Trans. on Knowledge and Data Eng.*, 3(3):337–341, Sept. 1991.

13. A. Rosenthal, S. Chakravarthy, B. Blaustein, and J. Blakeley. Situation monitoring for active databases. In *Proc. of the Fifteenth Int. Conf. on Very Large Data Bases*, pages 455–464, Amsterdam, The Netherlands, Aug. 1989.

14. E. Simon, F. Fabret, F. Llirbat, and D. Tombroff. Triggers and transactions: Performance issues. In *Proc. of the PUC Rio DB Workshop on New Database Research Challenges*, pages 53–64, Rio de Janeiro, Brazil, Sept. 1994.

15. E. Simon, J. Kiernan, and C. de Maindreville. Implementing high level active rules on top of a relational DBMS. In *Proc. of the Eighteenth Int. Conf. on Very Large Data Bases*, pages 315–326, Vancouver, British Columbia, Aug. 1992.

16. M. Sköld and T. Risch. Compiling active object-oriented relational rule conditions into partially differentiated relations. Technical Report LiTH-IDA-R-94-10, Linköping University, Linköping, Sweden, Mar. 1994.

17. M. Stonebraker, A. Jhingran, J. Goh, and S. Potamianos. On rules, procedures, caching and views in data base systems. In *Proc. of the ACM SIGMOD Int. Conf. on Management of Data*, pages 281–290, Atlantic City, New Jersey, May 1990.

18. Y.-W. Wang and E. Hanson. A performance comparison of the Rete and TREAT algorithms for testing database rule conditions. In *Proc. of the Eighth Int. Conf. on Data Engineering*, Phoenix, Arizona, Feb. 1992.

19. J. Widom and S. Ceri. *Active Database Systems: Triggers and Rules for Advanced Database Processing*. Morgan Kaufmann, San Francisco, California, 1995.

20. J. Widom, R. Cochrane, and B. Lindsay. Implementing set-oriented production rules as an extension to Starburst. In *Proc. of the Seventeenth Int. Conf. on Very Large Data Bases*, pages 275–285, Barcelona, Spain, Sept. 1991.

21. J. Widom and S. Finkelstein. Set-oriented production rules in relational database systems. In *Proc. of the ACM SIGMOD Int. Conf. on Management of Data*, pages 259–270, Atlantic City, New Jersey, May 1990.

A Designer's Benchmark for Active Database Management Systems: 007 Meets the BEAST

Andreas Geppert, Stella Gatziu, Klaus R. Dittrich
Institut für Informatik, Universität Zürich[1]

Abstract: A benchmark for active database management systems is described. We are particularly interested in performance tests that help to identify performant and inefficient components. Active functionality that is relevant with respect to performance is identified, and a series of tests is designed that measure the efficiency of the performance-critical components. Results obtained from running the benchmark for a concrete system are presented.

Keywords: active database systems, benchmarks, object-oriented database systems

1 Introduction

Active database management systems (ADBMSs) [e.g., 2, 9] have recently found great interest as a topic of database research, and restricted ADBMS-functionality is already offered by some products [e.g., 19]. An ADBMS implements "reactive behavior" since it is able to detect situations in the database and beyond and to perform corresponding actions specified by the user. Applications using reactive behavior are freed from performing "polling" in order to detect interesting situations. ADBMSs release such applications from encoding (possibly redundantly) situation detection and reactions.

As for any system, ADBMSs should implement their functionality *efficiently*. In fact, the evolution of ADBMSs is currently in a state where performance arguments play a crucial role, both from an application as well as from a system point of view:

- ADBMS researchers have developed different techniques for tasks of an ADBMS such as composite event detection [e.g., 11, 15], and it is thus interesting to compare these approaches with respect to performance.
- Different architectural approaches have been developed and need to be compared. For instance, the layered architecture for ADBMSs is often claimed to be less efficient than an integrated ADBMS [3].
- Authors have claimed that an ADBMS outperforms polling in applications [8], which has still to be proven by appropriate measurements.

Nevertheless, figures describing the performance of ADBMSs are not yet available. Moreover, it is so far still unclear what the relevant *performance measures* of an ADBMS might be, and an approach how to methodically measure the (in)efficiency of ADBMSs has not yet been proposed.

The objective of this paper is to describe a benchmark for (object-oriented) ADBMSs. Such a benchmark would be useful for at least three purposes:

- potential users can run it to compare the performance of multiple ADBMSs,

---

1. Authors' address: Institut für Informatik, Universität Zürich, Winterthurerstr. 190, CH-8057 Zurich, Switzerland. Fax: +41-1-363 0035, Email: {geppert I gatziu I dittrich}@ifi.unizh.ch

- ADBMS designers can run it to identify performance weaknesses of their system in comparison to others, and
- it can be used to compare the performance of an ADBMS with that of a passive DBMS, where the active behavior is encoded manually in the applications.

The BEAST[2] benchmark focuses on the second point, i.e., our intention is that of designers that want to assess their system. BEAST tests the *active* functionality of DBMSs, since appropriate benchmarks for passive DBMSs have already been developed [e.g., 4, 5, 14]. Furthermore, we concentrate on *object-oriented* ADBMSs, since —although we focus on the active part— the underlying data model influences ADBMS performance. Even passive object-oriented and relational systems are intended for different application domains. Thus, one type of system would be at a disadvantage when BEAST is used to compare relational and object-oriented ADBMSs.

BEAST considers relevant aspects of an ADBMS that need particularly efficient implementation:

- event detection,
- rule management, especially rule retrieval, and
- rule execution.

For each component, we define a group of tests that serve to measure its performance. We have used these tests to measure the performance of the ADBMS SAMOS [10]. Further ADBMSs will be tested in the near future.

The remainder of this paper is organized as follows. The next section gives a short introduction of ADBMSs, as far as necessary to comprehend the benchmark. Section 3 describes the benchmark, and section 4 presents benchmark results for SAMOS. Section 5 concludes the paper.

2 Active Database Management Systems

In order to make the benchmark better understandable, we give a short introduction of ADBMSs. An ADBMS is a DBMS that in addition to its regular features supports the specification and implementation of reactive behavior. Most ADBMSs support event-condition-action rules (ECA-rules) for specifying reactive behavior. An event is an implicitly or explicitly defined point in time and specifies when the rule has to be executed. Events can be *simple* (e.g., data item updates, message sending, transaction begin and commit, time events, abstract events[3], etc.) or *composite* (e.g., sequence, disjunction, negation, repeated occurrence, etc.). Current systems support rather different kinds of events. The condition is either a boolean function or a database query. If the condition evaluates to true (or returns a non-empty result), the action is executed. An action is typically written in the data manipulation language (DML) of the ADBMS, and can include the sending of messages in the case of object-oriented ADBMSs.

The *execution model* of an ADBMS specifies how rules are actually executed. It determines how condition evaluations and action executions are realized in terms of the transaction model. The *coupling mode* of a rule specifies when the condition or ac-

---

2. BEnchmark for Active database SysTems

3. *Abstract events* (or *external events*) are events that are not detected by the ADBMS, but that have to be signalled explicitly by the application or the user.

tion parts of a rule are executed with respect to the transaction that triggered the event. Popular coupling modes are *immediate* (directly after the event occurred), *deferred* (at the end of the triggering transaction, but before commit), or *decoupled* (in a separate, independent transaction). In this paper, we assume that the coupling modes for conditions relate condition evaluation to the triggering event, and that the coupling mode for actions relate action execution to condition evaluation. Finally, the execution model also defines how to process multiple rules that are all triggered by the same event. One possibility is to let the user specify (partial) orders, e.g., by means of *rule priorities*.

3   BEAST: A Benchmark for ADBMSs

In this section, we first identify relevant requirements and design decisions and then describe the BEAST benchmark for ADBMSs. We use the steps proposed in [16] as a reference model of how to proceed in benchmark design.

1. Definition of goals and the tested system. For any performance measurement the goals must be defined beforehand. The goal of BEAST is to measure the execution time of the services offered by an ADBMS. We currently assume a single-user ADBMS.

2. Definition of services. There is only one tested service: active behavior. For this service, BEAST proposes a collection of *tests*, each of which focuses on a specific subtask of active behavior. The selection of goals and services should be fair, i.e., it should not favor specific systems. BEAST tests the features that are common to most current ADBMSs, and does not stress special features that are available only for a few systems. The proposed tests are described in detail in section 3.1.

3. Selection of metrics. The performance measure we have chosen for BEAST is *response time*. Since BEAST has no access to internal interfaces of a tested ADBMS, we cannot precisely measure the performance of active behavior subtasks. Thus, BEAST tests invoke active behavior, which always performs several phases such as rule execution. Response time is then defined as the time interval that starts directly before event occurrences and ends directly after rule execution (i.e., when the control returns to the application)[4].

4. Selection of factors. *Factors* are parameters that influence performance. Typical factors for passive DBMS are buffer size, database size, etc. Below we identify additional factors for ADBMS performance measurement (e.g., number of defined rules).

5. Workload definition. Workload definition is a prime task in developing a benchmark. In BEAST, the workload is defined such that basic ADBMS functionality can be tested. Note that BEAST does not propose a typical application, since (1) the possible application domains are rather different and (2) knowledge on how to use ADBMSs for real life applications is still evolving. BEAST does not propose a typical application and test its performance, but determines relevant functionalities and their performance.

---

4. Exceptions to this definition are necessary for coupling modes other than immediate (see below).

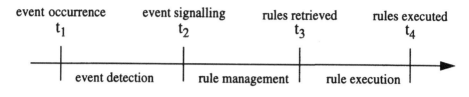

Figure 1. Phases of Active Behavior

3.1 Benchmark Design

BEAST is based on the 007 benchmark [4]. It uses the schema of 007 as well as the corresponding databases (i.e., programs to create and fill databases). One reason for re-using parts of 007 is to easily obtain a schema and database. Moreover, for a given object-oriented ADBMS, BEAST and 007 together allow to measure the performance of the active and the passive parts of a system, respectively.

BEAST considers three components where performance is crucial:

- event detection,
- rule management, and
- rule execution.

We have selected these components since they implement the three phases that comprise active behavior (see Fig. 1). They are thus contained in most ADBMS-architectures [3, 6, 13, 17].

After an event occurs, it must be *detected*, i.e., ADBMS components must realize (or be notified) that the event has happened. At the end of the event detection phase, the event is *signalled*[5]. The second phase (rule management) starts as soon as the event has been signalled and determines whether (and which) rules must be executed. Internal information must be consulted that links event descriptions with rule definitions. In the simplest case (the immediate coupling mode), rule management is directly followed by the rule execution phase (starting at t_3). In this phase, the triggered rules are executed. Each of the three phases is relevant with respect to performance.

Event detection is realized by the components that recognize the occurrence of specific events of interest. Two subtasks of event detection affect performance: detection of primitive and of composite events. In general, we expect that performance is better when the set of signalled primitive events can be small (i.e., only events that have rules attached or that contribute in composite events are actually signalled). Second, composite event detection can be realized in several ways that may have different performance characteristics.

Rule management also affects the performance of an ADBMS. Rule management refers to the storage and retrieval of rules and to the modification of the rulebase. After a primitive event has been signalled, the ADBMS determines whether it is used in ECA-rules and/or whether it participates in a composite event. Since information on rules must be retrieved after the signalling of a triggering event, efficient identification and retrieval of corresponding rules is crucial for ADBMS performance.

---

5. In general the precise point in time when an event occurred is not known. In BEAST tests, however, we enforce event occurrence and thus know this point in time.

Rule execution refers to the identification of condition and action parts that have to be executed after event occurrences as well as the execution of these parts. In particular, it is interesting how efficiently the various coupling modes are implemented and how efficiently multiple rules triggered by the same event can be executed.

BEAST tests each component with a series of tests. The result of running BEAST is therefore a collection of figures instead of a single figure for each ADBMS. Note that we cannot test the performance of each component directly, due to lacking access to internal interfaces of an ADBMS. Thus, most BEAST tests specify one or more rules that are triggered when executing the test, i.e., the test actually causes the event occurrence. In order to stress performance of single phases, we keep all other phases as small as possible. For instance, a rule testing event detection performance simply defines the condition to be `false`, such that condition evaluation is cheap and the action is not executed.

We elaborate on each group of tests subsequently. Tested functionality is described, and possible interpretations are given. The rule schema can be found in Appendix A. Note that the tests are not always enumerated consecutively, since some of the ones described in [12] have been omitted in this paper.

Tests for Event Detection

For event detection tests, BEAST focuses on the time it takes to detect an event. Both, the detection of primitive and composite events are tested.

Tests for Primitive Event Detection: BEAST contains five tests for primitive detection:
1. detection of value modification (ED-01),
2. detection of message sending (ED-02),
3. detection of transaction events (ED-03),
4. detection of a *set* of different primitive events (ED-04),

We illustrate the execution of tests with the test ED-02. The first operation of this test is to record the actual time. The next operation causes the event in question to occur. In this case, a message is sent. Note that in this way we know the point in time of event occurrence. The ADBMS subsequently detects the event, determines attached rules, and executes them. It then returns control to the test program. Finally, the test program again records the time and computes the required CPU time.

The first three tests measure detection of single events. The corresponding rules for all tests have a false condition and an empty action in order to restrict the measured time to event detection, as far as possible. Coupling modes for action and condition parts are `immediate`. Another possible kind of primitive event would be *time events*, but technically no meaningful way for measuring their detection exists.

The test ED-04 runs a transaction that raises multiple abstract events and measures the time needed for this transaction to execute. Directly afterwards, the same transaction is executed again. Information about each raised event is required and thus must be retrieved twice. Buffering of event information can decrease the time needed for the second event occurrence and rule retrieval. Thus, a system that applies buffering for event and rule information might outperform others that do not cache this information.

Tests for Composite Event Detection: Composite event detection typically starts after a (primitive or other composite) event has been detected. The event detector then checks whether the occurred event participates in a composite event. This is generally possible in two ways. In the first alternative, the ADBMS records each event occurrence, determines whether it can participate in a composite event, and checks whether other participating events have already occurred. The second alternative is to perform detection of composite events in a stepwise manner, e.g., by means of automata [15] or Petri nets [11]. Of course, the different approaches may have different performance characteristics and therefore need to be compared with respect to efficiency. This is accomplished through tests ED-06 through ED-11.

In order to stress the time needed for composite event detection, we use abstract events in the definitions of composite events wherever possible. Using abstract events enables more accurate measurements, since only the time for event signalling is required and primitive event *detection* is not necessary. In order to measure the entire composite event detection process (even for stepwise detection), the tests raise the component events directly one after the other. Thus, the measured time includes all steps of composite event detection.

BEAST contains six tests for the detection of composite events:
1. detection of a sequence of primitive events (ED-06)
2. detection of the non-occurrence of an event within a transaction (negative event, ED-07),
3. detection of the repeated occurrence of a primitive event (ED-08),
4. detection of a sequence of events that are in turn composite (ED-09),
5. detection of a conjunction of method events for the same receiver object (ED-10),
6. detection of a conjunction of events raised by the same transaction (ED-11).

The motivation for these tests is as follows. The first three ones test constructors offered by most ADBMSs (given they support composite events at all) and/or are likely to be required by many applications. The fourth one tests an arbitrary complex expression. The last two ones test event restrictions, which are also expected to be quite typical for ADBMS-applications (e.g., it is not sufficient to detect an arbitrary sequence of two specific component events, but in addition specific conditions must hold).

We are interested in the time it takes to detect the events, and therefore conditions, actions, and coupling modes are kept as simple as possible. Tests ED-06 through ED-08 measure event detection for common composite event constructors. Test ED-09 considers one specific constructor applied to events that are in turn composite. Finally, the last two tests measure the performance of event detection when the events of interest are further restricted by event parameters.

Tests for Rule Management

The second group of tests considers *rule management*. It is based on the observation that an ADBMS has to store and retrieve the definition and implementation of rules, be it in the database, as external code linked to the code of the ADBMS, or as interpreted code. Apparently, the time it takes to retrieve rules influences ADBMS performance. Rule management tests measure rule retrieval time, but they do not consider *rule definition* and *rule storage*. These services are executed rather seldom, and therefore their efficient implementation is less important.

The test RM-1 raises an abstract event, evaluates a `false` condition, and therefore does not execute any action. The three parts are kept such simple in order to restrict the measured time to the rule retrieval time as far as possible.

Tests for Rule Execution

The tests for rule execution are subdivided into two groups: one for the execution of single rules, and one for the execution of multiple rules. The first subgroup of tests determines how fast rules can be executed. The execution of a single rule consists of loading the code for conditions and actions and of processing or interpreting these code fragments. Again, different approaches exist for linking and processing condition and action parts, and can be compared by means of the tests in this group.

Different strategies can also be applied for executing multiple rules all triggered by the same event (e.g., concurrent or parallel execution). The performance characteristics of these approaches are tested by the second subgroup.

For the execution of single rules, we consider one rule with different coupling modes. The coupling mode of the condition is always `immediate`. The coupling modes of the actions are `immediate`, `deferred`, and `decoupled`, respectively. The intention of these tests is to measure the overhead needed for storing the fact that the action still needs to be executed at the end of the transaction (`deferred`), as well as the overhead necessary to start a new transaction in the `decoupled` mode. In order to stress these aspects of rule execution, we use an abstract event in order to avoid event detection, and use a simple `true` condition and an empty action. Note that the performance of condition evaluation and action execution is not of interest, because it is determined by the "passive" part of the DBMS.

The second group of tests for rule execution considers multiple rules. The first test (RE-04) uses four rules all triggered by the same event. Conditions and actions are more complex than in the previous tests, in order to better be able to observe effects of optimization of condition evaluation (ED-04) and concurrency (ED-05). All rules have the same conditions. An ADBMS that recognizes equality of conditions (e.g., if it is able to optimize sets of conditions) will perform better than a non-optimizing ADBMS. All rules have the coupling modes (`immediate`, `immediate`). A total ordering is defined for the four rules. In addition to the rule execution, this test measures the overhead obtained through enforcing the ordering of the rules.

The second test in this group (RE-05) again considers four rules all triggered by the same event. However, no ordering is given. An ADBMS that is able to process conditions and actions in parallel or at least concurrently will thus perform better in this test. This test uses the same conditions and actions as test RE-04, such that both tests can be used to observe the impact of orderings on performance.

Factors and Modes

A crucial step when designing a benchmark is the proper identification of *factors* [16], i.e., parameters that influence performance measurements. Several parameters of a database can have an impact on the performance of an ADBMS. In addition to the database parameters relevant for benchmarking a passive DBMS (e.g., buffer size, page size, number of instances stored in the database), these include:

- the number of defined events,

- the fraction of composite events, and
- the number of defined rules.

The time to detect events is ideally constant, i.e., independent of the number of defined events. However, especially for composite events it may be the case that a large number of events slows down the event detection process for single events. Furthermore, an ADBMS needs to store and retrieve internal information on event definitions during (or after) event detection. Apparently, a large number of event definitions can increase the time needed to retrieve event information. It is thus interesting to investigate for each tested ADBMS how large response times are when the number of events increases. We therefore include the number of defined events as a factor.

The second factor (fraction of composite events) determines how many of the events are composite ones. We specify this number in terms of the nesting depth of composite events, i.e., how often composite event constructors are applied recursively. A nesting depth of 0 means that there will not be any composite events, and a nesting depth of 1 specifies that always two primitive events will form one composition. Generally speaking, a nesting depth of n means that n+1 primitive events will be used to form n composite events.

Furthermore, the total number of rules defined by a concrete database is relevant for performance. Recall that rule information has to be retrieved before rule execution. While a small number of rules can be entirely loaded into main memory without problems when the ADBMS starts execution, this is no longer possible if the rulebase is large. In the latter case, rules must be selectively loaded into main memory from secondary storage upon rule execution. It is thus an important question how efficient an ADBMS can handle large sets of rules, and how the system behaves when the number of rules grows larger. For example, an ADBMS that stores rules as objects can make use of the clustering and indexing mechanisms already offered by the passive part of the DBMS. Note also that some tests consider buffering of rule and event information.

For the three factors, we choose three possible values for a small, a medium, and a large rulebase (see Table 1). Tests for larger rulebases are easily possible, since the values of all factors can be specified as parameters of the rulebase creation program.

parameter	rulebase size		
	small	medium	large
#events	50	250	500
nesting depth	2	3	4
#rules	50	250	500

Table 1. Parameter Values for Different Rulebase Sizes

Many rules and events will actually not be used by the benchmark, i.e., their execution is not measured. However, they are important in order to increase the load of the ADBMS as well as the data/rulebase size. These "dummies" therefore yield information whether the ADBMS is able to handle large sets of rules with a performance comparable to small numbers of rules.

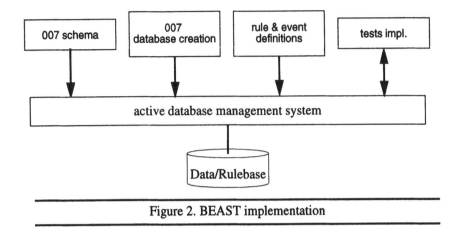

Figure 2. BEAST implementation

3.2 Benchmark Implementation

The implementation of BEAST for an ADBMS consists of the following parts (Fig. 2):
- the 007 schema and database creation programs,
- event and rule definition through the rule definition language of the ADBMS,
- specific new classes for the benchmark tests (e.g., response time measuring).

In order to run the benchmark for a concrete ADBMS, the 007 schema and the database creation programs must be adapted to the data model of the ADBMS. The next step consists of specifying and compiling the ECA-rules. Finally, the desired tests are executed. Each test computes the CPU-time the operating system process has spent for the test execution (due to the fact that the process is subject to operating system scheduling, process-specific CPU-time can be a fraction of the total elapsed time). Each test is executed separately in order to avoid "cross-test" buffering effects.

It is not necessary to execute all tests for each ADBMS. Alternatively, a designer can choose the tests where results are interesting, and can easily configure and instantiate the benchmark for his/her needs.

4 Benchmark Application

We have run the benchmark on our home-grown ADBMS SAMOS [10, 13]. SAMOS offers a rich collection of event definition facilities and uses Petri nets for composite event detection [11]. We therefore are especially interested in the performance of the Petri net approach and how well SAMOS scales for medium and large rulebases.

4.1 Benchmark Results

This section presents the results of running the benchmark on SAMOS. We also discuss differences to earlier measurements [12]. Each test has been run multiple times for the same database/rulebase size. Arithmetic means, standard deviations, and confidence intervals have been computed. Table 2 shows means and confidence intervals for a 90% confidence level (i.e., the mean of all possible executions of a test is within the interval with 90% confidence [16]). All results refer to CPU time in milliseconds.

Test	Parameter	Configuration (Rulebase Size)			
		empty (1)	small (2)	medium (3)	large (4)
ED-02	mean	147	253	450	840
	conf. interval	[137, 157]	[245, 261]	[434, 466]	[825, 855]
ED-04	mean	685	905	1438	1634
	conf. interval	[665, 705]	[893, 917]	[1420, 1460]	[1613,1655]
	mean	573	740	1039	940
	conf. interval	[556, 590]	[733, 747]	[1026, 1051]	[932,948]
ED-06	mean	395	500	680	1066
	conf. interval	[385, 405]	[491, 509]	[658, 702]	[1055,1088]
ED-08	mean	836	1000	1529	1724
	conf. interval	[817, 855]	[984, 1017]	[1502, 1556]	[1710,1738]
ED-09	mean	819	973	1478	1639
	conf. interval	[804, 835]	[958, 989]	[1437, 1519]	[1617,1649]
ED-11	mean	357	469	800	1076
	conf. interval	[343, 372]	[451, 486]	[787, 813]	[1053,1099]
RM-01	mean	154	256	438	179
	conf. interval	[147, 163]	[247, 265]	[424, 452]	[168, 191]
RE-01	mean	157	200	562	203
	conf. interval	[150, 165]	[194, 208]	[545, 580]	[193, 214]
RE-02	mean	157	205	506	197
	conf. interval	[151, 163]	[197, 214]	[492, 522]	[188, 205]
RE-04	mean	325	353	660	1072
	conf. interval	[319, 332]	[346, 360]	[642, 678]	[1056,1088]

Table 2. BEAST Results for SAMOS

The tests have been run on a SUN- SparcServer 4/690 server under SUNOS 4.1.3. Each test has been compared with four different configurations that vary in the number of dummy events and rules (cf. Table 1): (1) no dummy events/rules, (2) 50 dummy events, (3) 250 dummy events, and (4) 500 dummy events. Accordingly, we use the small (1 and 2), the medium (3) and large (4) 007 databases.

Results for Event Detection Tests

The test for primitive event detection (ED-02) shows a dependency on the rulebase size (concretely, the total number of defined events). Ideally, we would expect that ED-

02 is independent of the rulebase size, or at least that the slope of the increase is much smaller than in the shown results. The reason for the increase is that event objects must be retrieved. SAMOS currently unfortunately scans the entire extension of event definitions upon event signalling in order to find appropriate event objects, and applies string comparisons for determining these objects. In the future, we will replace the event name as a parameter of event signalling by integer constants, and will also use indexes (B-tree or hashing) for the retrieval of event objects.

ED-04 contains two sequences of event occurrences (ED-04a and ED-04b). It can be observed that the second sequence requires much less time than the first one, i.e., there is a buffering effect of event objects. Moreover, in comparison to ED-02 much more event objects must be retrieved, but measured times are only twice as large (for large rulebases). We therefore conclude that the expensive actions in ED-02 (and elsewhere) are not the retrievals of *single* event objects, but querying the entire *event extension*. Therefore, in ED-04, there is not only a buffering effect between the two event signalling sequences, but also within each of them.

The tests for composite event detection also show a strong dependency on the rulebase size. However, we have achieved dramatic improvements in comparison to previous tests [12]. The previous version of SAMOS used queries (joins) for traversing the Petri Net. In a re-designed version of the Petri Net component, pointers have been used, so that the joins are replaced by pointer traversals. In this way, e.g., , times for ED-08 have decreased from 4814 to 1724, and ED-09 from 5350 to 1639 ms (large rulebase).

Nevertheless, the absolute figures of composite event detection tests are still high, and we would expect nearly constant behavior. Similar to the case of test ED-02, the increase is due to the use of queries for determining information on (composite) events, since upon primitive event signalling the entire extension of events needs to be scanned. Once the primitive event object is found, associated composite events are found through pointer traversals. We are therefore also interested in the impact of indexing of primitive event objects on composite event detection performance.

For most tests the time required for the detection of the component events is also interesting. The reason to measure the detection of component events is twofold:
- since component events typically do not occur directly one after the other, the component detection time tells how much an application is slowed down whenever a participating event occurs.
- for system designers, it is interesting to see where composite event detection spends which fraction of the total time.

It turns out that for most constructors the detection of the second component event requires much more time than the detection of the first. This is only partially due to the fact that the second time also includes rule retrieval and rule execution. After the detection of the second component event, the composite event must be signalled, and (in SAMOS) event parameters must be determined for the composite event. These additional actions obviously are responsible for the larger required time for the second participating event.

Results for Rule Management Tests

Rule retrieval time also depends on the rulebase size (RM-01). Again, the increase is due to the inefficient querying of the event extension. Once the event object has been found, corresponding rule objects can be retrieved via pointer traversals, which has only marginal effects on the response time. Similar to the tests RE-01 and RE-02, the figures for RM-01 show a peak for the medium rulebase. Execution times become smaller for the large rulebase. We have currently no explanation for this strange behavior, but suppose that object placement, buffering, and indexing of extensions by the underlying OODBMS are responsible for this behavior.

Results for Rule Execution Tests

Three tests have been performed for rule execution: test RE-03 and RE-05 have been omitted since decoupled rules and priorities are not yet implemented in SAMOS. The rule execution tests show that rule execution time is also dependent on the rule/database size. Test RE-04 (in comparison to ED-02) shows that rule execution is quite cheap in comparison to event detection. ED-02 performs one condition evaluation and no action execution, while RE-04 evaluates four conditions and executes four actions, but response time of RE-04 is approx. 25% higher than that of ED-02. Hence, retrieval of event information from the extension of event objects is **the** dominating factor in the current implementation of SAMOS.

Discussion of Results

Although we have not yet enough comparative figures for other systems, we feel that management of events, their retrieval, and event detection (particularly of composite events) is not yet acceptable from a performance point of view.

We have drawn two major observations from the results. First, the storage and retrieval of events must be significantly improved. The facilities offered by ObjectStore for physical storage (indexing and clustering) will be better used.

Secondly, we have observed strange effects for some tests and different rulebases (execution times are sometimes smaller for larger rulebases). Apparently, ObjectStore internals are responsible for this behavior, and more investigations using performance analysis tools [e.g., 18] are necessary in order to understand these effects. On the other hand, these tests show that response time *can* be decreased, and the challenge is to enforce such improvements deliberately. Hence, the tests show possibilities for ADBMS tuning, which is a topic of our current work.

More figures are necessary in order to assess the performance of composite event detection. It would be nice to have performance figures for applications that require reactive behavior but are implemented on top of a passive DBMS. It then might (or might not) turn out that — though time spent for composite event detection is large — it is still smaller than the time needed to perform equivalent tasks in a passive system. Note further that usually the total time needed to detect composite events is not spent in one piece, but typically is required in slices distributed among multiple executions of applications.

5 Conclusion and Future Work

We have presented a benchmark for active object-oriented database management systems, and have tested the ADBMS SAMOS with this benchmark.

As designers, we are particularly interested in identifying inefficient components. In this respect, we have seen that the most complex SAMOS component — composite event detection — is also the most expensive one (by orders of magnitude), and that management and retrieval of event information is not yet tolerable. These components are the ones most worthwhile to be optimized and tuned.

In order to definitely assess the performance of SAMOS, we need comparative figures for other systems. We have measured the performance of ACOOD [1], and will run BEAST on NAOS [7] and possibly other systems in the near future. Further systems will be tested as soon as they are available for us.

BEAST currently tests ADBMSs in single-user mode, while results may be quite different when multi-user mode is considered as well. Especially, it is interesting whether performance of composite event detection depends on the rulebase and the number of concurrently active transactions. However, finding the right "transaction mix" is a problem. We are currently investigating concurrency on composite event detectors, however in an analytical way.

6 Acknowledgments

We gratefully acknowledge the discussions with Dimitris Tombros on the BEAST benchmark and the work of Hans Fritschi on the SAMOS implementation.

7 References

1. M. Berndtsson, B. Lings: *On Developing Reactive Object-Oriented Databases.* Bulletin of the TC on Data Engineering 15:1-4, 1992.
2. A.P. Buchmann: *Active Object Systems.* In A. Dogac, T.M. Ozsu, A. Biliris, T. Sellis (eds): Advances in Object-Oriented Database Systems. Computer and System Sciences Vol 130, Springer, 1994.
3. A.P. Buchmann, J. Zimmermann, J.A. Blakeley, D.L. Wells: *REACH: A Tightly Integrated Active OODBMS.* Proc. 11th Intl. Conf. on Data Engineering, Taipei, Taiwan, March 1995.
4. M.J. Carey, D.J. DeWitt, J.F. Naughton: *The 007 Benchmark.* Proc. ACM SIGMOD Intl. Conf. on Management of Data, Washington, DC, May 1993.
5. R.G.G. Cattell, J. Skeen: *Object Operations Benchmark.* ACM ToDS 17:1, 1992.
6. S. Chakravarthy, V. Krishnaprasad, Z. Tamizuddin, R.H. Badani: *ECA Rule Integration into an OODBMS: Architecture and Implementation.* Proc. 11th Intl. Conf. on Data Engineering, Taipei, Taiwan, March 1995.
7. C. Collet, T. Coupaye, T. Svensen: *NAOS: Efficient and Modular Reactive Capabilities in an Object-Oriented Database System.* Proc. 20th Intl. Conf. on Very Large Data Bases, Santiago, Chile, September 1994.
8. U. Dayal: *Active Database Management Systems.* Proc. 3rd Int. Conf. on Data and Knowledge Bases, Jerusalem, 1988.
9. U. Dayal, E. Hanson, J. Widom: *Active Database Systems.* W. Kim (ed): Modern

Database Systems. ACM Press / Addison Wesley, 1995.

10. S. Gatziu: *Events in an Active Object-Oriented Database System.* Doctoral Dissertation, University of Zurich, 1994. Published by Verlag Dr. Kovac, Hamburg, Germany, 1995.

11. S. Gatziu, K.R. Dittrich: *Detecting Composite Events in an Active Database Systems Using Petri Nets.* Proc. of the 4th Intl. Workshop on Research Issues in Data Engineering: Active Database Systems, Houston, February 1994.

12. A. Geppert, S. Gatziu, K.R. Dittrich: *A Designer's Benchmark for Active Database Management Systems: 007 Meets the BEAST.* Technical Report 94.18, Computer Science Department, University of Zurich, November 1994.

13. A. Geppert, S. Gatziu, K.R. Dittrich: *Architecture and Implementation of an Active Object-Oriented Database Management System: the Layered Approach.* Technical Report, Institut fuer Informatik, Universitaet Zuerich, 1995.

14. J. Gray (ed): *The Benchmark Handbook for Database and Transaction Processing Systems.* 2nd ed., Morgan Kaufmann Publishers, 1993.

15. N.H. Gehani, H.V. Jagadish, O. Shmueli: *Composite Event Specification in Active Databases: Model & Implementation.* Proc. 18th Conf. on Very Large Data Bases (VLDB), Vancouver, British Columbia, Canada, August 1992.

16. R. Jain: *The Art of Computer Systems Performance Analysis. Techniques for Experimental Design, Measurement, Simulation, and Modeling.* Wiley 1991.

17. D.R. McCarthy, U. Dayal: *The Architecture of an Active Data Base Management System.* Proc. ACM SIGMOD Intl. Conf. on Management of Data, Portland, Oregon, May/June 1989.

18. *Quantify User's Guide.* Pure Software Inc., 1992.

19. Sybase Inc.: *SYBASE - Data Server.* Berkeley, CA, 1988.

Appendix A The BEAST Rule Schema

The rule schema is given in pseudo-syntax in Table 3. The first four columns of this table are self-explanatory. The column "CM" specifies the coupling mode of the rule, and "P" defines priorities. For event definitions, we use the following conventions:

- properties of objects are referred to through the dot notation,
- transaction events are represented as "BOT" and "EOT", followed by the name of the transaction whose begin or commit has to be detected,
- the prefixes "Ev.." is used for abstract events,
- ";" is the event constructor for sequences,
- "&" is the event constructor for conjunctions,
- "|" is the event constructor for disjunctions,
- "!" is the event constructor for negative events (the within clause is used to express the time interval in which the event should not occur),
- times is the event constructor for repeated occurrence,
- oid that is used in the tests RE-04 and RE-05 is an event parameter representing an instance of class Document,
- DoNothing, searchString, replaceText, setAuthor, and setDate are methods of 007 classes, and
- GenerateAtomicPart is the name of a transaction program.

Test	Event	Condition	Action	CM	P
ED-01	update (AtomicPart.docId)	FALSE		i/i	—
ED-02	before AtomicPart.doNothing				
ED-03	EOT GenerateAtomicPart				
ED-04	EvED-04i (i=1..10)				
ED-06	EvED-061 ; EvED-062				
ED-07	! EvED-07	FALSE		i/i	—
ED-07	within (BOT GenerateAtomicPart , EOT GenerateAtomicPart)				
ED-08	times (EvED-08, 10)				
ED-09	times (EvED-091, 3);(EvED-092 | EvED-093);EvED-094				
ED-10	Module.doNothing & Module.setDate: same_object				
ED-11	update (AtomicPart.x) & update (AtomicPart.y): same_transaction				
RM-01	EvRM-01	TRUE			
RE-01	EvRE-01			i/def.	
RE-02	EvRE-02			i/dec.	
RE-03	EvRE-03				
RE-04	EvRE-04	oid->searchString ("I am") > 0	cout << "doc contains word I am"	i/i	1
			oid.replaceText("I am", "This is")		2
			oid->setAuthor()		3
			oid->setDate()		4
RE-05	EvRE-05	oid->searchString ("I am") > 0	cout << "doc contains word I am"		1
			oid.replaceText("I am", "This is")		2
			oid->setAuthor()		3
			oid->setDate()		4

Table 3. The BEAST Rule Schema

Cooperative System Support

Realization of Cooperative Agents Using an Active Object-Oriented Database Management System

Andreas Geppert   Markus Kradolfer   Dimitrios Tombros

Institut für Informatik, Universität Zürich
Winterthurerstr. 190, CH-8057 Zürich, Switzerland
Email: {geppert|kradolfer|tombros}@ifi.unizh.ch

Abstract: Cooperative, process-oriented environments (CPEs) are systems whose behavior is defined in terms of process models. We show how CPEs are realized through brokers, which are a special form of software agents[1] used to model participating entities in CPEs. A broker can represent a human participant, an existing software tool, or a part of the environment infrastructure. In our approach, we implement brokers on top of the active object-oriented database management system (ADBMS) SAMOS. Particularly, we use the facilities of SAMOS for implementing communication/cooperation between and control of brokers in CPEs. Our approach allows the construction of flexible, extensible systems and the definition of the behavior of participating entities local to brokers, avoiding the need for a centralized process engine.

Keywords: active database systems, software processes, workflows, agent control

1   Introduction and Motivation

Research in cooperative process-oriented environments is currently a very active topic. Example types of CPEs are process-centered software development environments (PCDEs) [9] and workflow management systems (WFMSs) [13, 23]. Regardless of whether software processes can actually be treated as a special case of workflows, as for example stated in [19], PCDEs and WFMSs have in common the notion of process. Both support the computer-based modeling and execution of processes[2], whereby a process has the following characteristics:

- it is a possibly long-lasting activity,
- it consists of several sub-activities (steps or tasks),
- the execution of these sub-activities can be constrained (e.g., through execution order, predicates on input or output data, or timing constraints), and
- it may involve both human beings and tools.

Multiple processes may have to be modeled and executed in the same environment, and different CPEs may comprise different component systems (e.g., tools). Thus, it is not feasible to define one concrete, fixed CPE. Instead, a CPE framework is required

---

1. We use the term "agent" in the sense of "processing entity" as it is used in the workflow literature [e.g., 6]. Brokers represent software agents [12]. Both terms should not be confused with the concept as it is used in AI.
2. Subsequently, the term "process" subsumes "workflow" and "software process".

that can be customized to specific requirements. Such a framework has to satisfy the following criteria:
- it should support modeling of the structure and execution semantics of processes,
- it should support the execution (enactment) of processes and thus:
  - provide *communication* between agents,
  - *coordinate* the various agents (humans and — possibly external — tools) according to the process model, and
  - *control* the process state and progress. Depending on the process state (and the desired process semantics), the CPE must react appropriately.

Most PCDEs or WFMSs support coordination and control through a *process engine* (synonymously, task manager, activity manager). This component is central to the system and guides processes, while most other components (agents) are more or less passive, i.e., they can act only as far as allowed or explicitly requested by the process engine. The problem with such a process engine is its complexity, especially if *process evolution* should be supported, too. The complexity of a centralized process engine stems from the fact that it has to keep all information on the possibly dynamically changing capabilities of participating agents and on the state of process execution. Moreover, process engines do hardly support an architectural view integrating services, software agents, and process logic.

We propose *brokers* and *services* as constructs for building CPEs. They provide a service-oriented view of the environment and are used to model both, the static architecture and the behavioral aspects of CPEs (i.e., the process model). Brokers are able to detect situations in which they have to react automatically, so that control and coordination can be decentralized and distributed among the components of the CPE. Such situations are often more complex than simple service requests. For instance, a broker must be able to realize the fact that two alternative tasks have both failed, or that a specific deadline is only one week away, and so on. We show that such powerful brokers can be implemented on top of an advanced ADBMS supporting composite events. The advantage of using this implementation platform is that we can keep the description of agent behavior and process control information local to the participating agents instead of having a centralized process engine interpreting a process program responsible for the tasks of agent coordination and cooperation.

The remainder of this paper is organized as follows. In the next section, we describe the broker/services model. In section 3 we show how brokers and services are used for the realization of CPEs. Section 4 introduces the ADBMS SAMOS and shows how it is used to implement brokers. Section 5 presents an example, section 6 briefly surveys related work, and section 7 concludes the paper.

2 The Broker/Services Model

In this section, we introduce the *broker/services model* we use to describe the structure of a system, its behavior, and architectural constraints. By "system" we mean an environment that consists of several agents (applications, environment infrastructure components, human users). In order to obtain an integrated architecture, these agents are represented by *brokers*. Due to reasons which become apparent later, the ADBMS SAMOS [10, 16] is always part of the environment infrastructure. We further assume that agents offer *services* to their potential clients, and that the system behavior is defined by a *process model* determining under which circumstances a specific service can or must be provided.

Our model uses an object-oriented approach to system construction, extended with the possibility to define reactive behavior of the participating objects[3]. In addition to the concepts introduced above, we use *responsibilities* to relate services with the broker(s) responsible for their provision. A CPE-architecture is then defined as a collection of brokers operating in various roles, responsible for providing services and able to monitor complex events and react according to predefined ways. The services provided by brokers can refer to the manipulation of data or to the control and coordination of other brokers. Below, we describe these concepts in more detail. Fig. 1 contains a textual specification of the key concepts of the model. Note that the process model will be encoded within broker definitions; an example thereof is presented in section 5.

2.1 Services

Services model the functionality of system components. The totality of services provided by components represents the functionality of the entire system. The use of services allows a view of the environment abstracting from concrete implementations. A specific service is provided by one or more brokers (see below) and can be requested by various client brokers. It is specified by a service signature consisting of the service name, its parameters, the possible replies and exceptions its request may cause.

2.2 Brokers

Brokers represent agents, responsible for the provision of system services. In order to model varying degrees of integration in the CPE, we distinguish between three kinds of brokers: *internal, external,* and *interface* brokers. Internal and interface brokers are described by their state, the services they are *responsible* for providing, and their reaction to predefined events. External brokers represent agents whose "implementation"

```
BROKER broker_name: broker_kind        SERVICE service_name
    STATE   {state_name: type}              PARAMETERS {param_name: type}
    RULES   {RULE rule_name                 REPLIES:
            ON event                            {reply_name, {para_name: type}}
            IF condition                    EXCEPTIONS {exception_name}
            DO action
            [PRECEDENCE rule_name_list]}
    ROLES
            STATE {state_name: type}
            RULES { //as above }

            RESPONSIBILITY service_name: broker_name
```

Figure 1. Key Concepts of the Broker/Services Model .

---

3. The term "reactive behavior" describes the capability of objects to autonomously execute various actions in response to the occurrence of predefined situations (not just method calls).

is not known (e.g., humans). The state of a broker consists of typed instance variables which can be either *sub-brokers* or passive objects. Passive objects can be used to represent data manipulated by a broker, thus providing a mapping to a common data model for all participating agents. Brokers which have sub-brokers are called *composite*. Sub-brokers of internal and interface brokers can only be internal or interface brokers themselves.

Internal brokers represent proprietary CPE components. Interface brokers implement the behavior of proprietary CPE components interacting with human beings and external tools. A typical example is a session manager representing the human user interface to the system. External brokers are blackboxes for which the internal state and service implementations do not have to (but can) be defined. They model the behavior of human users and external tools, and can request services from other external brokers as well as from interface brokers.

Brokers and their sub-brokers form a hierarchy with a predefined visibility of service requests. This allows the definition of different behavior according to the organizational context of a request.

2.3 Roles

Roles specify the responsibilities of brokers in various situational and organizational contexts. The concept of roles is used to model for example the fact that the same agent (e.g. a person), may have different responsibilities in different organizational sub-groups. Roles are used in a slightly different sense to the conventional in workflow modeling, where they define a grouping of capabilities [6] usually associated with a functional objective in an organization. An example of this definition of a role is to "be a manager" and thus every person who is a manager plays this role. In our case however, roles denote the responsibilities a concrete broker (human or non-human) has in a (sub)organization at some point during its lifetime. Thus roles can only be defined as part of a broker definition. Each role specification consists of a set of event-condition-action-rules (ECA-rules) and state variables. There may however be state variables and ECA-rules common to all roles of a broker (i.e. role-independent).

2.4 ECA-Rules

ECA-rules define the reaction of brokers (within the context of a role) to specified external events of various types. They have a unique name and consist of an event clause, a condition clause, and an action part. It is possible that more than one rule reacts to the same event within one broker (role).

The events to which brokers react can occur for example due to a sequence of broker actions within a process, or when specific points in time are reached. In order to describe events occurring during the operation of a CPE, we use various *event types*. Our model uses the following *primitive event types*:

- *Service provision events* are explicitly raised by brokers through special (parametrized) operations. These include the events generated by service requests and their subsequent replies. The events have parameters corresponding to those needed by the specific operations.

- *Time events* occur when a particular point in time is reached. They are specified either absolutely (by giving a clock-time), relatively to another event, or as periodic events.
- *Value events* are related to the modification of an object value. This allows among others the monitoring of (database) object states. Such events are defined for update operations on object attributes and take place before or after the operation that updates the value of the object is performed.
- *Method events* are bound to the execution point of a specific passive object method. Their occurrence point is specified as being just before or immediately after (i.e. directly before the method returns to its caller) method execution.

Note that the last two event types can only refer to passive (database) objects.

Time intervals can be defined in order to limit the period in which an event occurrence is of interest and should be monitored. Such *monitoring intervals* specify a — possibly implicitly defined — time interval in which an event has to occur in order to be considered as relevant. The monitoring intervals are a part of the event definition.

In order to adequately model reactive broker behavior in more complex situations (e.g. within the context of process control, see below) we introduce *composite events*. Composite events are defined by combining component events — possibly recursively — through the following constructors:

- *conjunction*: occurs when both component events have occurred,
- *disjunction*: occurs when one of the two components has occurred,
- *sequence*: occurs when the component events have occurred in the specified order,
- *negation* of an event: occurs when the component event has not occurred within a specified time interval,
- *times*: occurs when the component event has occurred a specified number of times within a certain time interval,
- *closure*: occurs when the component event has occurred at least once within a specified time interval, but is signalled only once regardless how often the component event actually occurred.

While monitoring intervals are mandatory in the last three cases, they are optional in the first three ones.

Conditions are expressed over the state of brokers and guard the execution of the action part. In the action part of the broker role ECA-rules, various operations (e.g. service requests and replies), or calls to methods of broker-specific passive components may be performed in order to implement services. Due to space economy, these are only exemplified in section 5.

A partial ordering of rule execution can be defined by using a precedence clause. A precedence order has to be defined in case the action part of a rule affects the condition part of another one, therefore influencing rule execution semantics.

3 Modeling Process-Oriented Environments With Brokers

3.1 Requirements

A CPE framework should meet the following requirements:

- it should be customizable in an *abstract* and *declarative* way, to the functional and operational requirements of specific organizations and projects using the developed CPE,
- it should support different, but *integrated views* of the functionality it offers,
- it should support *communication* between participating agents of the various sorts,
- it should support *coordination* between participating agents of the various sorts,
- it should be able to *control* participating agents wherever possible and necessary.

Naturally, the process-oriented view describing tasks, their structure, and related constraints is important in a CPE. The process-oriented view describes the "process logic" since it defines the "how" of a process model. We additionally require that a CPE provides activity-oriented and agent-oriented views as well. The first one focuses on the activities performed by the CPE agents and the services used for the realization of the CPE functionality, while the latter one additionally supports the assignment of tasks to concrete agents.

An integrated, abstract view is thus needed. Generally, it can be the case that CPE components are implemented on different platforms using even different data stores. It must still be possible to have a level providing a uniform view of the entire CPE, i.e., heterogeneous component systems should be integrated into a coherent environment. Given that components may be heterogeneous but still have to interoperate, communication cannot simply be realized through message passing. Appropriate mechanisms for communication between agents have to be provided at a higher level of abstraction.

The same holds for coordination: it will seldom be the case that agents are completely independent from each other. Usually some of them will have to cooperate to various degrees in order to fulfill the overall task. In other words, the CPE should provide a mechanism that allows agents to be coordinated according to the process model.

Ultimately, agents must be controlled during process execution. The CPE must provide a mechanism for the enforcement of required constraints, the prevention of inconsistent process states and transitions, and the automatic reaction to such situations.

The first steps in customizing a CPE are the following:

- identify the processes to be modeled,
- determine the required tasks,
- determine agents that are responsible for specific tasks in one of the processes.

Clearly, a methodical approach for these steps is required. Nevertheless, we assume that this analysis has already been performed, and subsequently describe how brokers are used for the customization of a CPE.

3.2 Integrated Software Architecture and Different Views

Given the three steps mentioned above, the next step consists of determining the appropriate (static) software architecture. By software architecture, we mean

- a collection of brokers representing agents or internal components,
- a set of services, where each service either represents a task of a process or an internal service,
- a set of responsibilities assigning services to brokers.

Any agent in a CPE — be it a proprietary component, an external tool, or a human — is represented by a broker. On its top level, the CPE is integrated since all brokers interact via service requests and replies. Depending on the concrete agent, we typically know more or less about how the corresponding broker implements its services. For a proprietary component, we will know all implementation details. For external tools, we know their interface and the (operational) semantics of their operations. For humans, we know their responsibilities but do not (need to) have precise knowledge of how they do their work. This variety is captured through the specialization of brokers into the three subclasses of brokers mentioned above (internal, external, and interface brokers).

As mentioned before internal brokers represent proprietary components and interface brokers are used to represent external tools by providing a tool wrapping mechanism. The service implementation is actually a shell mapping service requests to the interface of the tool, collecting the tool output, and eventually returning the results. External brokers represent blackbox agents such as humans for which only service signatures are known.

3.3 Modeling Process Control

Control means enforcing constraints, including task dependencies and constraints on data items accessed and manipulated by some task of the process. The following kinds of task dependencies can be distinguished [21]:

- execution dependencies,
- data or value dependencies, and
- temporal dependencies.

Execution dependencies are defined through execution states of tasks. An execution dependency can for example state that upon termination of a task, another one has to be started. Data or value dependencies of tasks are expressed through the output values of other tasks or values which are accessed by arbitrary systems. A data or value dependency can for example state that task A has to be executed if task B terminates with an output value below a certain threshold. Temporal dependencies define arbitrary timing constraints on tasks like "task B has to be started within 6 weeks after the termination of task A".

In the broker/services model, we can model the above dependencies by using ECA-rules. We can additionally model their combinations by using logical operators like conjunction, disjunction and negation on events. For example the execution dependencies "and-join" (e.g. only after a set of tasks has terminated, another (set of) task(s) must be started) and "or-join" (e.g. only when a certain number out of multiple (parallel) tasks has been terminated (successfully), another one can or must be started) described in [23] can be defined.

For example, assume that an execution dependency refers to previously executed tasks T_i ($1 \leq i \leq n$) whose termination is indicated through raising reply events including an optional list of parameters. Let the dependency require task T to be executed. Then the mapping of dependencies to composite events is as follows:

- an and-join is mapped to an event conjunction ($\wedge$)
- an or-join is mapped to an event disjunction ($\vee$),
- deadline dependencies are mapped to time events or events constrained by monitoring intervals.

Furthermore value or data dependencies are mapped to a parametrized event and a parameter test in a condition. Examples of these mappings are presented in Table 1.

Dependency	ECA-Rule defined for broker		
	Event	Condition	Action
data or value	reply of T1, including parameter p	if p	request T
execution (sequence)	reply of T_i	-	request T
execution (and-join)	$\wedge_i$ reply of T_i	-	request T
execution (or-join)	$\vee_i$ reply of T_i	-	request T
temporal (deadline)	! ($\wedge_i$ reply of T_i) within interval	-	notification etc.

Table 1. Examples of ECA-Rules for Modeling Task Dependencies

Current PCDEs or WFMSs typically implement control in some kind of process engine, which then keeps track of the process state. Some also use ADBMSs for control [e.g., 6, 17], which however are typically not able to detect complex situations (and therefore the process engine is nevertheless needed).

In our model, control can be completely performed by brokers on top of the ADBMS. Thus, control information is distributed among brokers and less centralized than in current systems. In addition, localized control leads to a more rigorous client/ server approach. Apparently, some of the process engine's task are pushed into the ADBMS, which we see as an advantage in terms of using standard base components wherever possible and striving for a "minimality of concepts".

4 Implementation of Brokers

In this section, we introduce SAMOS and then show how it is used for the implementation of brokers.

4.1 SAMOS, an Active Object-Oriented DBMS

In addition to passive data modeling facilities, SAMOS supports the specification (and implementation) of reactive behavior by means of ECA-rules (henceforth called SAMOS ECA-rules).

Events can be primitive or composite. Primitive events can in turn be of one of the following kinds:
- *message sending event*: occurs at the beginning or the end of a method execution,
- *value event*: occurs before or after the value of an object is modified,
- *transaction event*: occurs before or after a transaction operation (begin, commit, or abort transaction),
- *time event*: occurs at a specific point in time (absolute time event), periodically after a specified interval (periodical time events), or as soon as a specified time interval following another event occurrence has elapsed (relative time events), and
- *abstract event*: "occurs" when explicitly signalled by a user or application.

SAMOS allows the definition and detection of composite events specified with the following event constructors: conjunction, disjunction, negation, sequence, closure, and times. For a definition of the semantics of these constructors, see [11].

Upon event detection, the condition is checked. If it holds, the action is executed, otherwise the execution of the rule terminates. Both conditions and actions must be given in the data manipulation language (DML) of the underlying ooDBMS Object-Store. For details of rule execution, which are less relevant in this context, see [16].

4.2 Implementation of Brokers Using SAMOS

For the implementation of brokers we strive to map the concepts present in the brokers to the functionality provided by SAMOS. We avoid however the extension of SAMOS functionality in order to abstract from a specific implementation platform. The concepts of interest in the mapping process are brokers and their responsibilities, passive broker components, services, replies and ECA-rules describing the reactive broker behavior. The underlying ADBMS (in this case SAMOS) is used to manage and detect events relevant to the brokers, to manage the rules describing broker behavior and to implement coordination and communication mechanisms for individual brokers.

Similar to SAMOS' approach to represent events and rules as objects [11, 16], we model brokers as instances of a class broker (Figure 2). Each broker contains a non-empty set of role objects. Among the methods of the role class are predefined operations with which brokers in a role can request services from other brokers (at the same level or subbrokers) or reply to incoming service requests. References to the rules describing the broker behavior in a role are also stored in order for example to locate the relevant rules when this behavior is modified.

Passive broker components can be of different types and are instances of children of a generic component class. They are referenced in an attribute of each broker instance (Set<Comp*>) and are declared such that brokers can call their methods.

During the mapping process ECA-rules defining the reaction of a broker b in a role r to a service request s are transformed to SAMOS ECA-rules as described below. Suppose we have two brokers b1 and b2 with b1 being responsible to provide s1

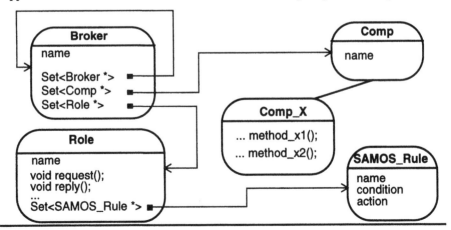

Figure 2. Brokers and components

when in the role r1. Suppose further that in order to provide s1, b1 requests the service s2 provided by b2 (in role r5) by sending a message m1 to its component c. This situation is defined as follows:

```
b1.r1                          and            b2.r5
    RULE rule1                                     RULE rule2
    ON    s1                                       ON    s2
    DO    request(s2)                              DO    c->m1()
```

Based on the broker ECA-rules SAMOS ECA-rules are generated taking into account the implicit responsibilities of each broker as expressed in the above rules. We thus have the following SAMOS statements:

```
DEFINE EVENT s1            DEFINE EVENT s2
DEFINE RULE rule1    and   DEFINE RULE rule2
ON    s1                   ON    s2
DO    b1->r1.request(s2)   DO    b2->c->m1()
```

In the action part of the SAMOS ECA-rule we can have either calls to predefined broker (role) operations, or calls to methods of the passive components of the broker for which the rule is generated. Responsibilities are used when transforming broker rules to SAMOS ECA-rules in order to associate services to the roles or components that provide them. Service requests are modeled as SAMOS abstract events and are signalled by the request operations performed by brokers which send the *raise_event* message to the rule manager with the service name as parameter.

Relationships between brokers (e.g. precedence in responding to a service request, or "exactly one" agent execution semantics) are also taken into account when transforming their rules into SAMOS ECA-rules. Such transformations may introduce priorities in rule execution or mutually exclusively executing rules.

5 An Example

In this section, we present an example workflow. An example from the software process domain can be found in [22]. Consider the processing of a health insurance claim (HIC) as shown in the activity diagram in Figure 3. Once the HIC is received, a human agent creates an electronic dossier containing the diagnosis, the treatments, and costs (from the HIC), and if an insurance policy exists, a reference to the entry in the insurance company database (activity A1). An automatic agent controls whether there is a valid insurance policy for this HIC (A2). Activity A3 controls whether the total cost is less than a certain amount (e.g. 300 Francs). In that case the HIC is directly forwarded to an automatic agent which prepares a check, prints it and notifies a clerk (A4). Otherwise, further controls are performed in parallel by automatic and human agents. One is whether some of the treatments are contained in a blacklist in which case their coverage will be denied (A5). Activity A6 performed by an external rule-based system controls whether the (combined) treatment actually suits the diagnosis, and A7 checks for compatibility of the diagnosis and treatment, with respect to the patient's history. If one of these controls fails, an entry is made in the customer history, a notification of the rejection is printed (A8) and a clerk is informed. Otherwise, a payment check is printed and a clerk is again notified. Ultimately, a law specifies that the insurance com-

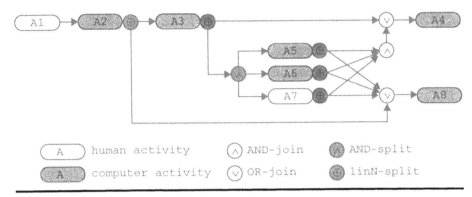

Figure 3. Sample Workflow

pany must react (either positively or negatively) at the latest after six weeks. For our example we assume that if no rejection decision has been made within six weeks from the dossier creation the claim is automatically accepted. Note that the activity diagram does not show the transitions in case the HIC is accepted due to having reached the time limit as shown in rule accept2 below.

Parts of the broker definitions responsible for these activities are shown below in order to show a possible implementation of activity sequencing constraints (see Table 1) of the workflow described. We assume the following (incomplete) type definition for HIC dossiers:

```
TYPE HIC_DOSSIER
        amount : AMOUNT
        creation_date : DATE
        state : HIC_STATE {Rejected, Accepted, InProcess}
        insurance_policy : INSURANCE_POLICY_REF
        ...
```

A *sequence* is defined in the following two rules describing the reaction of the broker responsible for the activity A3 (Broker_C) to the successful completion of A2 by Broker_B. Note that depending on the outcome of A3 either activity A4 will take place or other checks will be performed in activities A5, A6, and A7 (1-in-N split):

```
BROKER Policy_Checker: INTERNAL
// reaction to the request to check the claim validity
RULE  check1
ON    check_hic(hic_dossier: HIC_DOSSIER)
IF    NOT (hic_dossier.insurance_policy == NULL)
DO    reply(policy_valid, check_hic, hic_dossier)
...
BROKER Amount_Checker: INTERNAL
// reaction to a reply that the HIC refers to a valid policy
RULE  valid1
ON    policy_valid(hic_dossier: HIC_DOSSIER)
IF    hic_dossier.amount =< 300
DO    hic_dossier.state = Accepted
```

```
        reply(amount_small, check_hic, hic_dossier)
// reaction to a reply that the HIC refers to a valid policy
RULE  valid2
ON    policy_valid(hic_dossier: HIC_DOSSIER)
IF    hic_dossier.amount > 300
DO    reply(amount_large, check_hic, hic_dossier)
...
```

An *AND-join* is exemplified in the rule accept1 of an internal broker (e.g. Broker_D) when the checks made in activities A5, A6, and A7 are all positive the claim can be accepted:

```
// reaction to positive results from various checks
RULE accept1
ON    not_blacklisted(hic_dossier_1: HIC_DOSSIER) AND compatible_treatment
      (hic_dossier_2: HIC_DOSSIER) AND compatible_history(hic_dossier_3:
      HIC_DOSSIER)
IF    hic_dossier_1 == hic_dossier_2 == hic_dossier_3
DO    hic_dossier.state = Accepted
      reply(hic_accept, check_hic,hic_dossier_1)
```

An *OR-join* is exemplified in the rule print1 of a printer interface broker which describes the activities performed upon acceptance of the claim:

```
// reaction to acceptance of the claim
RULE print1
ON    amount_small(hic_dossier: HIC_DOSSIER) OR
      hic_accepted(hic_dossier: HIC_DOSSIER)
DO    printer->printCheck(hic_dossier) // call method of printer component
      request(notify_clerk, print_location)
```

A *deadline* is defined with the rule accept2 of the Broker_D stating that if no rejection of the HIC has been made within 6 weeks the claim will be accepted:

```
// acceptance of claim if deadline has been reached and it has not been rejected
RULE accept2
ON    NOT(reject_hic(hic_dossier: HIC_DOSSIER, reason: REASON))
      IN [hic_dossier.creationdate + 6 weeks]
IF    hic_dossier.state == InProcess// set in A1 and since not changed
DO    hic_dossier.state = Accepted
      reply(hic_accept, check_hic, hic_dossier)
```

Service Name	Parameters	Replies
check_hic	hic_dossier: HIC_DOSSIER	policy_valid, reject_hic, amount_large, amount_small, hic_accept, not_blacklisted, compatible_treatment, compatible_history
notify_clerk	print_location: PRINTER_NAME	

Table 2. Services and replies used in the example workflow

6 Related Work

Both WFMSs and PCDEs use some kind of "process engine" for process enactment [e.g., 6, 17]. It has been investigated for both kinds of systems how active mechanisms can be used. However, to date only ADBMSs that support primitive events have been used [e.g., 6, 7, 17], and thus control with complex constraints as described above is not possible within the ADBMS. For instance, the SPADE [1] environment is implemented on top of the ADBMS NAOS [7] and still uses external to the ADBMS process interpreters for process enactment. Adele/Tempo [3] is based on a DBMS providing an extended ER-Model. Interpreted temporal event-condition action rules are attached to software objects to define development policies and express integrity constraints. The supported event types are database operations and the conditions (defined as part of the events) are formulas over the past and present state of the system or database.

The work presented in [8] is similar to our approach in that it uses ECA-rules to control and organize long-lasting workflows. However, in the broker/services model introduced here, additional abstractions are introduced which —as we feel— serve the purpose of designing CPEs better than "pure" ADBMSs. Particularly, the broker/services model supports agent- or service-oriented views, which are not apparent if CPE-design and imlementation actually means programming an active database system.

Condition-action rules have also been used in PCDEs, e.g., in ALMA [18] or Marvel [2]. These approaches, however, are potentially less efficient (since events are not supported), and complex constraints on processes can be formulated, checked, and enforced in a less elegant way than is possible with a system supporting complex constraints attached directly to agents.

The integration of existing and possibly heterogeneous component systems is also a goal of the REACH project [4]. In contrast to our intended application domain, REACH focuses on real-time applications (where deadlines are much harder and more critical than in our types of processes). We consider the work done in REACH as complementary to ours since REACH so far has mainly considered the transaction management aspect (which is still open here).

7 Conclusion

We have described the broker model which we use for the realization of CPEs, namely control, communication, and coordination of CPE-components. In comparison to current approaches using process engines, the broker-based approach is more flexible and allows a more natural view of CPEs, since the relevant structures and behavior can be specified local to brokers. Thus, the contribution of this work is twofold:

- by using brokers, tasks related to control, communication, and coordination can be distributed among the brokers, and
- brokers can be easily implemented using an ADBMS such as SAMOS.

The broker model as presented here is currently under implementation on top of SAMOS. Two aspects of CPEs not investigated here, are subject to future work:

- a complete *programming environment* for customizing CPEs, and
- *autonomy of component systems* and *transaction management (TM)*.

First, we have described the use of brokers for the customization of CPEs. Clearly, a more abstract and declarative model (e.g., a graphical design tool) would be helpful. Most likely, we will not develop yet another language, but evaluate existing ones for our purposes. Functionalities such as planning, measurement, and process evolution shall be covered by such a programming environment as well. Additionally, this environment shall support process state representation and visualization.

Second, since we use brokers as wrappers for external components, interoperability and autonomy have to be addressed in the context of a suitable wrapper definition. In combination with TM, however, they pose a much harder problem. With respect to TM, we want to achieve the following:

- processes should be definable as long-lived transactions (e.g., comparable to DOM transactions [5]),
- TM on the level of CPEs should be able to integrate the local TM mechanisms of the component systems, wherever present.

TM in interoperable systems is still an open problem. We plan to investigate whether it can beneficially be implemented local to brokers (in case the wrapped system does not provide full-fledged TM) using our construction approach in terms of strategies and techniques [15], and the transformational approach for transaction structures [14]. We will also investigate whether the concept of strategy can be extended so that it can guide CPE-implementors during the wrapping and integration process in these cases where component systems already have a local transaction manager.

8   Acknowledgments

We gratefully acknowledge the comments and ideas contributed by Klaus Dittrich. We thank Stefan Scherrer for illuminating explanations of the health insurance business.

We also thank the Swiss Federal Office for Education and Science for funding our part in the ACTNET HCM-network (BBW Nr. 93.0313). The work of M. Kradolfer is funded by the Swiss National Fund in the context of the TRAMs project (Nr. 21-40440.94).

9   References

1. S. Bandinelli, L Fuggetta, C. Ghezzi, L. Lavazza: SPADE: An Environment for Software Process Analysis, Design and Enactment. In [9].
2. N.S. Barghouti: Supporting Cooperation in the MARVEL Process-Centered SDE. *ACM Software Engineering Notes,* 17:5, December 1992.
3. N. Belkhatir, W.L. Melo: Evolving Software Processes by Tailoring the Behavior of Software Objects. *Proc. IEEE Intl. Conf. on Software Maintenance,* Victoria, September 1994.
4. H. Branding, A. Buchmann, T. Kudrass, J. Zimmermann: ' Rules in an Open System: The REACH Rule System. In [20].
5. A. Buchmann, M.T. Oezsu, M. Hornick, D. Georgakopoulos, F.A. Manola: A Transaction Model For Active Distributed Object Systems. In A.K. Elmagarmid (ed): *Database Transaction Models For Advanced Applications.* Morgan Kaufmann Publishers, 1992.

6. C. Bussler, S. Jablonski: Implementing Agent Coordination for Workflow Management Systems Using Active Database Systems. *Proc. 4th Intl. RIDE: ADS Wokshop*, Houston, Texas, February 1994.

7. C. Collet, T. Coupaye, T. Svensen: NAOS: Efficient and Modular Reactive Capabilities in an Object-Oriented Database System. *Proc. 20th Intl. VLDB Conf.*, Santiago, Chile, September 1994.

8. U. Dayal, M. Hsu, R. Ladin: Organizing Long-Running Activities with Triggers and Transactions. Proc. ACM-SIGMOD Intl. Conf. on Management of Data, Atlantic City, May 1990.

9. A. Finkelstein, J. Kramer, B. Nuseibeh (eds): *Software Process Modeling and Technology*. Research Studies Press Limited, 1994.

10. S. Gatziu, A. Geppert, K.R. Dittrich: Integrating Active Concepts into an Object-Oriented Database System. *Proc. 3rd Intl. DBPL Workshop*, Nafplion, Greece, August 1991.

11. S. Gatziu, K.R. Dittrich: Events in an Active Object-Oriented Database System. In [20].

12. M.R. Genesereth, S.P. Ketchpel: Software Agents. *Communications of the ACM*, 37:7, July 1994.

13. D. Georgakopoulos, M. Hornick, A. Sheth: An Overview of Workflow Management: From Process Modeling to Workflow Automation Infrastructure. *Distributed and Parallel Databases*, 3:2, April 1995.

14. A. Geppert, K.R. Dittrich: Rule-Based Implementation of Transaction Model Specifications. In [20].

15. A. Geppert, K.R. Dittrich: Strategies and Techniques: Reusable Artifacts for the Construction of Database Management Systems. *Proc. 7th Intl. Conf. on Advanced Information Systems Engineering*, Jyväskylä, Finland, June 1995.

16. A. Geppert, S. Gatziu, K.R. Dittrich: Architecture and Implementation of an Active Object-Oriented Database Management System: the Layered Approach. TR, Computer Science Dept., University of Zurich, 1995.

17. H. Jasper: Active Databases for Active Repositories. *Proc. 10th Intl. Conf. on Data Engineering*, Houston, Texas, February 1994.

18. A. van Lamswerde: Active Software Objects in a Knowledge-Based Lifecycle Support Environment. In D. Mandrioli, B. Meyer (eds): *Advances in Object-Oriented Software Engineering*. Prentice Hall, 1992.

19. F. Leymann, W. Altenhuber: Managing Business Processes as an Information Resource. *IBM Systems Journal*, 33:2, 1994.

20. W. Paton, H.W. Williams (eds): *Rules in Database Systems*. Workshops in Computing, Springer-Verlag, 1994.

21. M. Rusinkiewicz, A. Sheth: Specification and Execution of Transactional Workflows. W. Kim (ed): *Modern Database Systems*. Addison Wesley, 1995.

22. D. Tombros, A. Geppert, K.R. Dittrich: SEAMAN: Implementing Process-Centered Software Development Environments on Top of an Active Database Management System. TR, Computer Science Dept., University of Zurich, 1995.

23. *Glossary. A Workflow Management Coalition Specification.* The Workflow Management Coalition, Bruxelles, Belgium, November 1994.

Active Databases and Agent Systems
— A Comparison

James Bailey[1] Michael Georgeff[2] David B. Kemp[1] David Kinny[2]
Kotagiri Ramamohanarao[1]

[1] Department of Computer Science
University of Melbourne
Parkville 3052, Australia
{jbailey,kemp,rao}@cs.mu.oz.au

[2] Australian Artificial Intelligence Institute
171 Latrobe Street
Melbourne 3000, Australia
{dnk,georgeff}@aaii.oz.au

Abstract. This paper examines Active Databases and Agent Systems, comparing their purpose, structure, functionality, and implementation. Our presentation is aimed primarily at an audience familiar with active database technology. We show that they draw upon very similar paradigms in their quest to supply reactivity. This presents opportunities for migration of techniques and formalisms between the two fields.

1 Introduction

In recent times, two technologies have become prominent in the database and artificial intelligence research communities. An Active Database (ADB) is a system which supplements traditional database functionality by reacting automatically to state changes, both internal and external, without user intervention. An Agent System (AS) is a software system which utilizes agents that possess certain mental attitudes which allow them to emulate "intelligent" behaviour.

Although these technologies have been developed in different fields of computer science and are designed with different applications in mind, the methods they employ to achieve their ends have much in common. It is the fact that they address the problem of generating reactive systems which draws these two seemingly disparate models together. Indeed, it is our contention that researchers in both of these areas would benefit from exposure to ideas from the other one, particularly as research in the respective communities has tended to focus on different problems.

Agent systems are usually employed in applications where complex, purpose-directed behaviour is needed in a changing environment. There are many different areas that require these abilities; air traffic control, control and monitoring of industrial processes, network management and management of business processes including workflow and automated trading, to name a few. Applications of active databases are also diverse. They can range from simple database alerters to systems that perform complex database changes.

Interestingly, initial applications of ADBs have been relatively unambitious and have concentrated on issues such as extending the handling of integrity constraints [8] and providing view maintenance [9, 21]; areas also of importance to passive databases. This reflects the inherent difficulty of reasoning about systems that react in a complicated way and perform a series of complex tasks, which is also the reason for the limited functionality of current commercial systems. Once some of these tractability problems have been overcome, however, the likelihood of advanced applications of ADBs being successfully implemented should increase. The incorporation of AI techniques may become feasible, which will result in ADB researchers confronting some of the issues that AS researchers presently face.

In this paper we identify some of the key similarities and differences between ADBs and ASs. We focus mainly upon issues in ASs of interest to the ADB community, presenting in some detail one of the more mature AS paradigms. This is not to suggest that ASs are homogeneous — there is much diversity amongst them. In fact, with the recent application by commercial vendors of the term "agent" or "software agent" to simple software offerings of limited functionality, the term is in danger of becoming just another marketing buzzword.

We commence by describing the key features of the selected agent architecture. Next, we contrast this with typical ADB architectures and identify areas of commonality. Here our emphasis is on a few key comparisons rather than an exhaustive list of similarities and differences. Familiarity with ADBs is assumed[3]. We present examples to illustrate both the expressiveness of the languages typically provided and the classes of problems where a particular language may be more suitable. After making comparisons in several other areas, we look at research trends in each field and propose topics for future research.

2 Agent System Architectures

The term *agent* has been used in AI to label a multitude of systems, ranging from simple reactive systems devoid of explicit symbolic representations [30, 1, 15, 27] through to complex heterogeneous multi-agent systems with individual and shared representations [22, 11, 14]. The term has recently achieved the status of "flavour of the month", with many commercial software developers offering or promising "software agents" that will act intelligently and autonomously to perform useful tasks. Unfortunately, as with many previous developments in AI, there is a danger that a technology that is still far from mature will be oversold, leading to a negative reaction from the marketplace.

Despite this terminological confusion, there has been considerable progress made in research in AI into the design of agents, by which we mean reactive, knowledge-based systems that are embedded in some dynamic, partially unpredictable environment. The essential requirement for such agents is that they should be able to take actions to achieve certain goals, while responding in a timely and considered manner to changes in the environment. This requires amongst other things, an ability to determine appropriate actions in a context-sensitive manner and to deal with failure and uncertainty.

---

[3] Detailed descriptions of ADBs may be found elsewhere [13, 3].

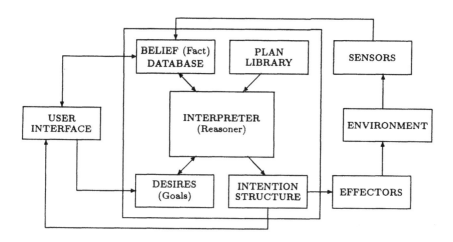

Fig. 1. BDI Agent Architecture

The goals of the agent, intrinsic or supplied by a user, may also change over time. Thus an agent must also be able to reason about which goals to pursue, how best to achieve them given the limited resources it has available, and what to do in the case of goal conflict.

In this paper we will focus on a particular approach to software agency that has achieved considerable maturity, the *Belief/Desire/Intention* (**BDI**) architecture [17, 16, 12, 28, 7, 32, 26, 29]. This architecture has its origins in the study of *mental attitudes*; namely, Beliefs, Desires and Intentions that represent, respectively, the agent's information, motivational, and deliberative state. These mental attitudes directly determine the system's behaviour and are critical for achieving adequate performance when deliberation is subject to resource bounds [6, 24].

2.1 BDI Agent Architecture

Figure 1 shows the essential structure of a typical BDI agent[4]. It consists of a *database* containing current *beliefs* or facts about the world; a set of current *desires* (or *goals*) to be realized; a set of *plans* describing how certain sequences of actions and tests may be performed to achieve given goals or to react to particular situations; and an *intention structure* containing those plans that have been chosen for [eventual] execution. An *interpreter* manipulates these components, selecting appropriate plans based on the system's beliefs and goals, placing those selected on the intention structure, and executing them.

The system interacts with its world through its database, which acquires new beliefs in response to changes in the world detected by its sensors, and through the actions that it performs via its effectors as it executes its intentions. A user of the system may directly query and update the agent's belief database.

The interpreter runs the entire system. From a conceptual standpoint, it operates in a relatively simple way. At any particular time, certain goals are established and certain events occur that alter the beliefs held in the system database.

---

[4] The architecture described is based upon PRS [18].

These changes in the system's goals and beliefs invoke (trigger) various plans. One or more of these applicable plans will then be chosen and placed on the intention structure. Finally, the interpreter selects an executable intention from the intention structure and executes *one step* of that intention. This will result in either the performance of an action, the establishment of a new subgoal, or the conclusion of some new belief. At this point the interpreter cycle begins again: the newly established goals and beliefs trigger new plans, one or more of these are selected and placed on the intention structure, and again an intention is selected from that structure and partially executed.

Beliefs An agent's belief database contains its current knowledge about the state of the world and also, possibly, some aspects of its own internal state. Typically, this will include facts about static properties of the application domain. Other beliefs are acquired by the agent itself as it executes its plans. These will typically be current observations about the world or conclusions derived by the system from these observations, and these may change over time. In a multiagent system, an agent may also need to maintain various beliefs about other agents, including beliefs about *their* mental states.

The knowledge contained in the database is often represented as ground instances in first order predicate calculus. Beliefs about internal system states are called *metalevel beliefs*. These typically describe the beliefs, goals, and intentions of the system, as well as other important control information.

Goals Goals are expressed as conditions over some interval of time (i.e., over some sequence of world states) and are described by applying various temporal operators to state descriptions. This allows the representation of a wide variety of goals, including goals to achieve, test, maintain and wait for given conditions.

A given action (or sequence of actions) is said to *succeed* in achieving a given goal if its execution results in a behavior that satisfies the goal description. Goals of achievement may succeed, vacuously, if the agent already believes that the specified state holds.

Goal descriptions are not restricted to specifying desired behaviors of the external environment but can also characterize the internal behavior of the system. Such descriptions are called metalevel goal specifications.

Plans An agent's plans are the elements of its knowledge base that describe how the agent should react when certain facts are added to its belief database, or when it newly acquires certain goals. These new facts may have arisen due to events in the external world being directly *perceived*, or by the fact being *inferred* by the agent itself; that is, by the execution of some intention. New goals, similarly, may arise as top-level (intrinsic) goals, supplied to the agent by a user of the system (or, perhaps, by another agent), or as subgoals of an existing intention.

Each plan consists of an *invocation condition*, which specifies upon which events the plan should be triggered, a *context condition*, which specifies under what situations the plan applies, and a *body*, which describes the steps of the procedure. Together, the invocation condition, context condition, and body of a plan express a declarative fact about the results and utility of performing certain sequences of actions under certain conditions.

The invocation condition is an event expression that describes what must occur for the plan to be considered for execution. Usually, this will be the acquisition of some new goal (in which case the plan is invoked in a goal-directed fashion) or some change in system beliefs (resulting in data-directed or reactive invocation).

The context condition is a state expression that describes the belief state that must hold for the plan to be executed. Often, this expression will contain free variables (which also occur in the body) that will be bound by its evaluation, thus what is intended is a particular *instance* of the plan[5].

The body of a plan is represented as a graph with one distinguished start node and possibly multiple end nodes. The arcs in the graph are labeled with the actions to be performed or subgoals to be achieved in carrying out the plan. Successful execution of a plan consists of performing or achieving each of the actions or subgoals labeling a path from the start node to an end node. This formalism allows richer control constructs (including conditional selection, iteration, and recursion) than most other plan representations.

The set of plans in a typical agent consists not only of procedural knowledge about a specific domain, but also includes *metalevel* plans — that is, knowledge about the manipulation of the beliefs, desires, and intentions of the agent itself. Metalevel plans allow the agent designer to override the default behaviour of the agent's interpreter. For example, typical metalevel plans encode various methods for choosing among multiple applicable plans, modifying and manipulating intentions, and computing the amount of reasoning that can be undertaken, given the real-time constraints of the problem domain.

Plans may also have another condition associated with them called a *maintenance condition*. Like the context condition, it must be satisfied for the plan to be invoked, but it must then remain true throughout the execution of the intention. If at any time it becomes false then the intention is terminated. Maintenance conditions provide a mechanism for preventing interference between parallel intentions, as well as guarding against change in the world that renders a particular plan no longer appropriate under certain circumstances.

The Intention Structure The intention structure contains all those tasks, called *intentions*, that the system has chosen for execution, either immediately or at some later time. A single intention consists of a top-level plan instance together with all the (sub-)plans that are being used in attempting to perform that plan. It is directly analogous to a *process* in a conventional programming system.

At any given moment, the intention structure may contain a number of such intentions, some of which may be suspended or deferred, some of which may be waiting for certain conditions to hold prior to activation, and some of which may be metalevel intentions for deciding among various alternative courses of action.

The set of intentions comprising the intention structure form a partial ordering with possibly multiple least elements (called the *roots* of the structure). An intention earlier in the ordering must be either realized or dropped (and thus disappear from the intention structure) before intentions appearing later in the

---

[5] When the context condition can be satisfied in more than one way, the interpreter must choose which instance of the plan to intend.

ordering can be executed. This precedence relationship between intentions enables the system to establish priorities and other relationships between intentions.

The intention structure captures, conceptually, the decisions an agent has made about the means to achieve its goals. Because an intention is a process, sometimes long-lived, the agent is, in a real sense, *committed* to achieve these goals in that manner. When actions fail, or the world changes in unexpected ways, the agent may need to *reconsider* these commitments. The right balance between commitment and reconsideration is an important agent design issue which depends sensitively on the properties of the world in which the agent exists [24].

3 Comparison of Architectural Features

The database component in an ADB is analogous to the belief database in an AS. The contents of the database represent the facts of the world that the system is modelling — these correspond to the agent's beliefs. Changes are made to the database by transactions to reflect the changing state of the world.

ADBs permit the enforcement of consistency on parts of the database by integrity constraints and/or triggers. ASs typically offer only limited forms of integrity constraint, but maintenance conditions may be used to terminate intentions if consistency assumptions are violated, and fact-invoked plans may be employed to maintain and recover consistency.

In an ADB, users can typically ask arbitrary queries about the contents of the database and the DBMS acts as a broker that delivers this information. The belief database in an AS can be viewed as having two "users" - the agent itself and the outside world (which may include humans and other agents).

The attainment of goals in an ADB can be achieved by rules and update procedures. In an AS, plans are the means used to achieve goals. Compared to the action languages used in ADBs, AS plan languages typically provide more powerful operators and a rich set of constructs for combining actions and subgoals.

Events in both systems are similar, with their semantics varying between implementations. Typically the events in an ADB are restricted to database operations, but this need not be the case. Some ADBs provide a rich language for combining events, but ASs tend to restrict themselves to atomic event occurrences. They do, however, possess the ability to generate a variety of metalevel events in the course of plan execution. These may be useful for allowing plans to reason about one another, an activity which is not natural for an ADB to mimic.

The occurrence of events in an ADB causes the activation of triggers which in turn evaluate conditions and possibly execute actions. Events in an AS cause the invocation of plans which are executed after placement on the intention structure.

ADBs are designed with multiple user access in mind. Users specify their needs by means of transactions and submit them to the database for execution. Conceptually, these transactions represent the top-level goals given to the database, and the statements contained within a transaction give rise to various subgoals. Transactions may cause alteration of database facts, output to the world, and change in the rule structure. They will typically compete for resources and, if the database is dedicated to a particular application, may have a fixed structure. The intrinsic goals in an AS will commonly be defined by the designer at the

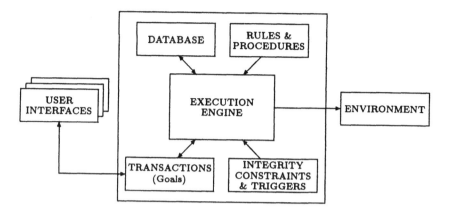

Fig. 2. Active Database Architecture

agent's conception, but may also be established at runtime by the execution of the agent's plans, a user, or other agents.

In an ADB, ACID properties [19] are an inherent part of the behaviour of transactions, whereas in an AS this functionality has to be explicitly considered in the design of plans. Multiple updates (or other actions) may be performed as a single, atomic step, but more complex sequences must employ explicit semaphores or priority-based methods to guarantee exclusion.

Atomicity is harder to achieve, however, since no notion equivalent to transaction roll-back (due to violation of integrity constraints) exists in ASs. This is because the actions performed will typically affect the external environment, and to undo these would require an ability to "roll back the real world". Concurrency is not usually a problem because agents do not share their belief database with other agents. Where agents need to update each other's beliefs (or goals), it can be accomplished by message passing. When multiple goals need to be performed concurrently, it is the responsibility of the agent designer herself to structure their execution so that data consistency is maintained.

Execution strategies are similar in both systems, being controlled by a high-level manager/interpreter. In an ADB this runs submitted transactions by drawing upon information in the database, rule and trigger repositories (see Figure 3). In an AS plans are invoked not only by goals but also by database changes and other events, resulting in a mixed top-down/bottom-up strategy.

Differences in execution strategy also exist with respect to how multiple simultaneous events and multiple triggered rules/plans are handled. For example, in an ADB, one typically wants to execute all rules that are triggered by a particular event, whereas in an AS one typically wants to invoke only one plan in order to achieve a goal — only if that plan fails will a different one be adopted.

The plans executed by an agent may be long running processes and possibly never terminate. ADB (trans)actions, conversely, are typically simple operations whose lifespan is limited. ASs have a notion of success/failure associated with actions, plans, and goals. This is typically not supported in active databases, and limits the extent to which they can interact with the outside world, where it may be necessary to make several repeated attempts to achieve a desired outcome [20].

	Active Database	Agent System	
	Events	Events	
	Event Predicate	Invocation Condition	
Rules	Condition	Context Condition	Plans
	Action	Plan Body	
	User Transactions	Intrinsic Goals	
	Database Facts	Beliefs	
	Update Procedures	Goal-invoked plans	
	Integrity Constraints and Triggers	Event- or Fact-invoked plans	

Table 1. Similar Concepts in Active Databases and Agent Systems

4 Example: MicroBlue versus BigSoft

Consider a system that tracks the stock market and is capable of sending buy and sell orders to a stock broker. Here we compare how this system might be implemented in an ADB and in an AS. The interface to the broker consists of two types of messages that can be sent to the broker and one type of message that can be received from the broker. The system can send a *trade* message (**trade**(*buyOrSell, name, amount*)) to request that the broker buy or sell a number of shares in a company. For example, **trade(sell, 'Blue', 40000)** is a request to sell 40,000 shares in the company called 'Blue'.

If the broker is unable to carry out an order — because, for example, no one is buying a stock that is offered for sale — then the broker sends an *orderFailed* message (**orderFailed**(*name*)) to the system. For example, **orderFailed('Blue')** would be received if the broker could not sell the 40,000 shares that she was requested to sell (we are assuming that we do not request the broker to both buy and sell the same shares at the same time).

The system can also send a *terminate* message (**terminate**(*name*)) to request that the broker stop trying to buy or sell particular shares. For example, **terminate('Blue')** is a request to stop buying or selling 'Blue' shares.

To give examples of how to implement this system using an ADB or an AS, we should carefully describe the syntax and semantics of the example languages that we use. Instead, we will employ here simple, intuitive languages whose semantics should be reasonably obvious from the examples. We will give here only a brief description of these languages; a full description can be found elsewhere [4].

We use the following syntax for specifying a trigger:

on *event* [**if** *condition*] **then** *action*

As well as simple insert, delete and update events on relations, we allow received messages to cause events, and events to be combined into compound events. Compound conditions may be created using **and**, **or** and **not**. Actions may be database operations (e.g. insert, delete, update), sending external messages, user defined *signalled events*, and sequences of actions (separated by **andthen**).

4.1 Buying Blue Shares

Suppose we wish the system to buy 40,000 MicroBlue ('Blue') shares if the 'Blue' share price goes from less than or equal to the BigSoft ('Soft') share price to greater than this price and stays that way for at least 5 hours.

An Active Database Solution To solve this in an ADB, we can define two events $e1$ and $e2$ which are signalled by triggers when the 'Blue' share price has gone from not greater than to greater than (respectively, greater than to not greater than) the 'Soft' share price. Here are triggers that could be used:

on update price('Blue', B) if price('Soft', S) and $B_{old} \leq S$ and $B_{new} > S$ then signal(e1)

on update price('Soft', S) if price('Blue', B) and $B \leq S_{old}$ and $B > S_{new}$ then signal(e1)

on update price('Blue', B) if price('Soft', S) and $B_{old} > S$ and $B_{new} \leq S$ then signal(e2)

on update price('Soft', S) if price('Blue', B) and $B > S_{old}$ and $B \leq S_{new}$ then signal(e2)

on not e2 in [e1, e1 + 5hours] then send trade(buy, 'Blue', 40000)

Suppose the broker cannot carry out the instruction to buy 40,000 shares, perhaps because there are none for sale. This can be handled by a rule that is triggered on an *orderFailed* event. For example, we could test to see if the price of 'Blue' shares is still greater than 'Soft' shares and stays that way for another five hours as follows:

on orderFailed('Blue') if price('Blue', B) and price('Soft', S) and $B > S$ then signal(e1)

An Agent System Solution For simplicity, we will use here a notation for plans that is as similar as possible to that used for the triggers and rules above, introducing the **while** keyword for maintenance conditions. The event predicate **addbel** is true when a tuple is added to a relation. The event predicate **modbel** is true when the value of a tuple in a relation changes. Its parameters are the previous and current values of the tuple. A suitable set of plans would be:

on modbel(price('Blue', B_{old}), price('Blue', B)) if price('Soft', S) and $B_{old} \leq S$ and $B > S$
 while price('Blue', B_{new}) and price('Soft', S_{new}) and $B_{new} > S_{new}$
 then waitfor elapsed(5hours) andthen send trade(buy, 'Blue', 40000)

on modbel(price('Soft', S_{old}), price('Soft', S)) if price('Blue', B) and $B \leq S_{old}$ and $B > S$
 while price('Blue', B_{new}) and price('Soft', S_{new}) and $B_{new} > S_{new}$
 then waitfor elapsed(5hours) andthen send trade(buy, 'Blue', 40000)

on addbel orderFailed('Blue')
 while price('Blue', B_{new}) and price('Soft', S_{new}) and $B_{new} > S_{new}$
 then waitfor elapsed(5hours) andthen send trade(buy, 'Blue', 40000)

4.2 Trade Wars

Suppose 'Blue' has two ways to deal with 'Soft' undercutting the price of 'Blue' widgets; either buy a controlling share of 'Soft', or lower the price of its widgets. Either of these ways may be suitable in the circumstances. In an AS, one could specify that both plans are triggered by the event of 'Soft' undercutting the price of 'Blue' widgets, and write a metalevel plan to actually choose between the two. The default interpreter behaviour is to try the first plan and, only if it fails — for example 'Blue' does not control 'Soft' after 2 days — to try the second plan.

An Active Database Solution Support for metalevel programming is not often provided in ADBs. Hence, if it is required that the first method be tried before the second one, then that decision must be encoded in the triggers themselves:

on update widgetPrice('Soft', S)
 if widgetPrice('Blue', B) and $S_{old} > B$ and $S_{new} < B$
 then signal(underCut)

on underCut
 if ownsPercent('Soft', X) and $X \leq 50$ and issuedShares('Soft', Y) and
 $Z = Y \times (51-X) \div 100$ then send trade(buy, 'Soft', Z)

on underCut before update ownsPercent('Soft', X)
 if $X > 50$ then send terminate('Soft') andthen signal(controlsSoft)

on not controlsSoft in [underCut, underCut + 2days]
 if widgetPrice('Soft', S) and $B = 0.9 \times S$
 then send terminate('Soft') andthen update widgetPrice('Blue', B)

By extending this example, we can highlight another feature of AS plan languages that can make them more convenient than the action languages typical of ADB systems. Observe that 'Blue' can gain control of 'Soft' by either buying 'Soft' shares or by buying a controlling fraction of companies that own shares in 'Soft'. 'Blue' may even have to sell other shares to finance this takeover. Computing what shares 'Blue' should sell and buy to gain control of 'Soft' could actually turn out to be quite a lengthy computation. Indeed, the price of 'Soft' widgets may rise above those of 'Blue' widgets before the system has actually worked out what shares to buy! In this case, the system should stop the computation.

Once again, this could be quite difficult to implement in a natural way in an ADB. One would need to make sure that the computation of what shares to buy was not implemented as one atomic operation, but instead as a series of operations with an explicit check on widget prices in between each operation. We will not even attempt to give an ADB solution to this extended problem.

An Agent System Solution We specify a maintenance condition to ensure that the plan is terminated if 'Soft' stops undercutting the 'Blue' widget price. The lengthy computation appears as a subgoal **computeOrder** which returns a list of buy/sell orders as output. Note that the body of this plan contains a conditional action with the structure **when** *condition* **do** *action* **else** *action*.

on modbel(widgetPrice('Soft', S_{old}), widgetPrice('Soft', S))
 if widgetPrice('Blue', B) and $B \leq S_{old}$ and $B > S$ and
 ownsPercent('Soft', X) and $X \leq 50$ and issuedShares('Soft', Y)
 while widgetPrice('Blue', B_{new}) and widgetPrice('Soft', S_{new}) and $B_{new} > S_{new}$
 then achieve computeOrder(X, Y, List) andthen send trade(List) andthen
 waitfor ((ownsPercent('Soft', U) and $U > 50$) or elapsed(2days)) andthen
 send terminate(List) andthen
 when test (ownsPercent('Soft', V) and $V > 50$)
 do signal(controlsSoft)
 else test widgetPrice('Soft', W) andthen update widgetPrice('Blue', $W \times 0.9$)

4.3 Atomicity and Concurrency

The absence from ASs of certain features usually found in ADBs can make them less convenient for some applications. Suppose that our stock-broker sends us messages whenever share transactions are completed. This will require a trigger to ensure that the database keeps derived relations, such as share ownership percentage, appropriately updated:

on brokerMessage(Name, Qty)
  if ownsPercent(Name, OldPC) and issuedShares(Name, Total) and
    $NewPC = ((OldPC \times Total \div 100) + Qty) \div 100$
  then update ownsPercent(Name, NewPC)

The look-up of the old value of the percentage of shares owned, the computation of the new percentage, and the update to the new value need to be done in one atomic operation to ensure that multiple updates to the same value do not result in any updates being lost.

In an ADB, the underlying transaction support would ensure that multiple updates to the same value happen sequentially, while updates to different values can happen concurrently. Currently, most ASs would offer no support for this, requiring that it be handled explicitly by the update plans.

5 Further Issues

Responsiveness Agent systems are typically designed to support time critical applications such as manufacturing/process control and air traffic control. In these systems it is necessary to impose constraints on the time taken to select and execute plans, and to guarantee that events are noticed sufficiently promptly [23]. One may need to choose a plan based on the criterion of how long it will take to execute as well as the quality of the result it produces — a sub-optimal solution within the available time is better than an optimal solution delivered too late to be useful. Furthermore, once a plan has been chosen, it may have to be abandoned due to a change in the agent's beliefs.

For example, in an air traffic control application, a particular agent's task may be to find an optimized schedule for plane landings. If more planes enter the monitored airspace, or weather conditions change, then a current intention to produce a schedule may need to be abandoned or restarted to accommodate this change in beliefs. The absence of facilities for controlling responsiveness means that these kind of dynamically changing scenarios cannot be easily supported by an ADB.

Success and Failure ASs allow one to evaluate the success/failure of actions, but it is not as easy to find out the status of an ADB action after execution. The interpreter in an AS behaves in a way that takes into account the possibility of such failures; alternative paths within a plan will be tried if actions or subgoals fail, and alternative plans will be tried on plan failure. These characteristics are essential for robust embedded applications. While such behaviour can be implemented within an ADB, it is not directly supported by the execution engine.

Persistence of Intentions Another salient feature of ASs is the long running (possibly perpetual) nature of intentions. An ADB can achieve similar behaviour through the use of an embedded application — one which interacts with the database system at regular intervals and issues the appropriate (trans)actions depending on the feedback it receives. This approach, however, can lead to inefficiencies and is less desirable from a software engineering point of view.

Another approach might be to use an active database with deductive capabilities (and hence the possibility of persistence through infinite recursion) to provide similar functionality. A different solution would be to have a complex event algebra which permitted expressions that referred to past events stored by a history mechanism.

Rollback and Recovery For performance reasons, the belief database of a BDI agent is often implemented in main memory, and only intermittently checkpointed to backing store, if at all. Usually there is no support for examining the update history. ADBs, by contrast, tend to regard the backing store as primary, and expend considerable effort to guarantee its integrity, to support rollback of transactions, and recovery to previous database states. The development of "industrial strength" applications will require the integration of such techniques into the next generation of ASs.

Metalevel Constructs Metalevel constructs are not usually provided by ADBs, whereas they are a valuable feature of ASs. Suppose an event occurs in an ADB that triggers two rules whose simultaneous execution would interfere. For example, the following rules will clearly interfere if executed simultaneously:

on update price('Blue', B)
  if price('Soft', S) and $B_{old} \geq S$ and $B_{new} < S$ then send trade(sell, 'Blue', 10000)

on update price('Blue', B)
  if price('Moon', M) and $B_{old} \leq M$ and $B_{new} > M$ then send trade(buy, 'Blue', 10000)

One approach to avoiding this problem is to hard-code logic into the rule manager, which may have a policy of always selecting the highest priority rule (e.g. by a textual ordering). Another method is to encode the necessary checking into the rules themselves so that they are mutually exclusive.

A more elegant way of handling the problem is to allow the system designer to resolve the conflict by defining a metalevel rule to make the selection. Whenever both rules are activated simultaneously, an event is generated that triggers another (higher priority) rule whose execution determines which rule is to be executed. This is the approach adopted in ASs. It is attractive because it allows localization of the rule selection strategy; one only has to alter the metalevel plan as opposed to changing the original rules or recompiling the rule manager.

ASs may also generate metalevel events to allow selection between different instances of the same plan, between different execution paths within a plan, to determine the order in which simultaneous events are processed, and to control the order of execution of concurrent intentions.

6 Research Issues and Future Directions

An obstacle to the success of both technologies is the lack of coherent system and rule/plan design methodologies. For example, in an ADB it is unclear how much functionality should be performed by the ECA triggers and how much by external applications. An inappropriate choice may incur performance penalties. Likewise, in ASs one may write complex standalone plans or else construct simple plans with a sophisticated metalevel reasoner to control them. Another issue is determining what agents are needed to solve a particular problem — this is similar to schema design in an ADB. One possibility is the adaptation of object-oriented design methodologies [31, 5] to the design of ASs; this is currently an active research area [25].

A question related to rule design is the possibility of reasoning about rule sets and testing them for certain properties. Active database research has examined properties such as confluence and termination [2], albeit in a restricted way. For agent systems these properties may be less relevant, since intentions can be persistent and hence non-terminating, but there is still much to be gained from such efforts. Another, more general approach is to look at the externally observable behaviour of the system as a whole. Does the addition of extra rules destroy the correctness of existing rule sets, or perhaps degrade system performance unacceptably? Tractable theories that address these issues will be necessary if we are to construct robust, maintainable, large-scale systems.

Another issue is the integration of the two paradigms (see [10] for an example of using both technologies co-operatively). For example, one could incorporate transactions into an AS to provide recovery and robustness. Alternatively, one could incorporate long lived processes and their associated maintenance conditions into an ADB. The purpose of these modifications is not to replace one technology with the other, but to enhance the functionality of the respective systems. Indeed these technologies have distinct application domains, one being data intensive and the other being process intensive.

Other interesting notions are to base an agent system upon an active database, or to include agents within an active database. These ideas raise important issues about the granularity of agents, but are likely to be impractical for serious use, however, until the state of the art in debugging techniques advances. The difficulties involved in verifying the correctness of concurrent systems are substantial and the coupling of both of these technologies would exacerbate the problem.

It is in the area of language syntax and semantics that we feel ASs and ADBs have the most to offer each other. As yet, there is no consensus as to what language features should be standard in either, thus there is plenty of scope for crossover of ideas. In particular, ASs could profitably adopt more powerful event languages and ADBs could utilize more plan-like action specifications. In the same way, optimization techniques such as incremental condition evaluation for ADBs and the various compilation-time optimizations employed in ASs could be utilized. Finally, real world ASs will need to adopt or adapt some of the history, rollback and recovery techniques employed in typical ADBs.

Despite the challenges presented, the rewards offered by (re)active and goal-directed functionality are great. We hope that as each field matures, researchers remain conscious of their essentially complementary nature.

References

1. Philip E. Agre and David Chapman. Pengi: An implementation of a theory of activity. In *Proceedings of the Sixth National Conference on Artificial Intelligence, AAAI-87*, pages 268–272, Seattle, WA, 1987.

2. A. Aiken, J. Widom, and J. M. Hellerstein. Behavior of database production rules: Termination, confluence and observable determinism. In *Proceedings of the ACM SIGMOD International Conference on Management of Data*, 1992.

3. J. A. Bailey and K. Ramamohanarao. Issues in active databases. In *Proceedings of the Sixth Australasian Database Conference*, pages 27–35, Glenelg, South Australia, 1995.

4. James A. Bailey, Michael Georgeff, David B. Kemp, David Kinny, and Kotagiri Ramamohanarao. Active databases and agent systems - a comparison. Technical Report 95/10, Department of Computer Science, University of Melbourne, Parkville, 3052, 1995.

5. Grady Booch. *Object-Oriented Analysis and Design with Applications*. Benjamin/Cummings, Redwood City, CA, 2nd edition, 1994.

6. Michael E. Bratman. *Intentions, Plans, and Practical Reason*. Harvard University Press, Cambridge, MA, 1987.

7. B. Burmeister and K. Sundermeyer. Cooperative problem-solving guided by intentions and perception. In *Proceedings of the Third European Workshop on Modelling Autonomous Agents and Multi-Agent Worlds, MAAMAW '91*, Kaiserslautern, Germany, 1991.

8. S. Ceri, P. Fraternali, S. Paraboschi, and L. Tanca. Putting active databases to work. In *IEEE Data Engineering*, 1992.

9. S. Ceri and J. Widom. Deriving incremental production rules for deductive data. *Information Systems*, 19(6), 1994.

10. S. Chakravarthy, K. Karlapalem, S. B. Navathe, and A. Tanaka. Database supported cooperative problem solving. Technical Report UF-CIS-TR-92-046, University of Florida, Gainesville, Florida, 1992.

11. Paul R. Cohen, Michael L. Greenberg, David M. Hart, and Adele E. Howe. Real-time problem solving in the phoenix environment. In *Proceedings of the Workshop on Real-Time Artificial Intelligence Problems at IJCAI-89*, 1989.

12. Paul R. Cohen and Hector J. Levesque. Intention is choice with commitment. *Artificial Intelligence*, 42(3):213–261, 1990.

13. U. Dayal, E. Hanson, and J. Widom. Active database systems. In *Modern Database Systems: The Object Model, Interoperabilty and Beyond*. Addison Wesley, Reading Massachusetts, 1994.

14. Keith Decker and Victor Lesser. Analyzing the need for meta-level communication. In *Proceedings of the Twelfth International Workshop on Distributed Artificial Intelligence, DAI '93*, Hidden Valley, Pennsylvania, 1993.

15. R. J. Firby. *Adaptive Execution in Complex Dynamic Worlds*. PhD thesis, Department of Computer Science, Yale University, New Haven, Connecticut, 1989.

16. R. James Firby. An investigation into reactive planning in complex domains. In *Proceedings of the Sixth National Conference on Artificial Intelligence, AAAI-87*, pages 202–206, Seattle, WA, 1987.

17. Michael P. Georgeff and Amy L. Lansky. Procedural knowledge. In *Proceedings of the IEEE Special Issue on Knowledge Representation*, volume 74, pages 1383–1398, 1986.

18. M.P. Georgeff and F.F. Ingrand. Real-time reasoning: The monitoring and control of spacecraft systems. In *Proceedings of the Sixth IEEE Conference on Artificial Intelligence Applications*, Santa Barbara, California, 1990.

19. T. Haerder and A. Reuter. Principles of transaction-oriented database recovery. *Transaction on Database Systems*, 1983.

20. E. Hanson et al. Flexible and recoverable interaction between applications and active databases. Technical Report UF-CIS-TR-94-033, University of Florida, Gainesville, Florida, 1994.

21. J. V. Harrison and S. W. Dietrich. Incremental view maintenance. In *Proceedings of the Fifth Australasian Database Conference*, Christchurch, New Zealand, 1994.

22. F. Hayes-Roth, B., R. Washington, R. Hewett, M. Hewett, and A. Seiver. Intelligent monitoring and control. In *Proceedings of the Eleventh International Joint Conference on Artificial Intelligence, IJCAI-89*, pages 243–249, Detroit, MI, 1989.

23. Felix Ingrand and Michael P. Georgeff. Managing deliberation and reasoning in real-time AI systems. Technical Report 10, Australian Artificial Intelligence Institute, Melbourne, Australia, 1990.

24. David Kinny and Michael Georgeff. Commitment and effectiveness of situated agents. In *Proceedings of the Twelfth International Joint Conference on Artificial Intelligence, IJCAI-91*, pages 82–88, Sydney, 1991.

25. David Kinny and Michael Georgeff. A design methodology for Agent-Oriented systems. Technical Report 53, Australian Artificial Intelligence Institute, Melbourne, Australia, 1995.

26. David Kinny, Magnus Ljungberg, Anand Rao, Elizabeth Sonenberg, Gil Tidhar, and Eric Werner. Planned team activity. In *Proceedings of the Fourth European Workshop on Modelling Autonomous Agents in a Multi-Agent World, MAAMAW '92*, page 20, Viterbo, Italy, 1992. Also appears as Australian Artificial Intelligence Institute Technical Note 31, Melbourne, Australia, 1992.

27. Nils J. Nilsson. Towards agent programs with circuit semantics. Technical Report STAN-CS-92-1412, Stanford University, Stanford, CA, 1992.

28. Anand S. Rao and Michael P. Georgeff. Modeling rational agents within a BDI-architecture. In *Proceedings of the Second International Conference on Principles of Knowledge Representation and Reasoning, KR '91*, pages 473–484, Cambridge, MA, 1991.

29. Anand S. Rao and Michael P. Georgeff. An Abstract Architecture for Rational Agents. In *Proceedings of the Third International Conference on Principles of Knowledge Representation and Reasoning, KR '92*, pages 439–449, Boston, MA, 1992.

30. S. J. Rosenschein and L. P. Kaelbling. The synthesis of digital machines with provable epistemic properties. In J. Y. Halpern, editor, *Proceedings of the First Conference on Theoretical Aspects of Reasoning about Knowledge*, San Mateo, CA, 1986. Morgan Kaufmann Publishers.

31. James Rumbaugh, Michael Blaha, William Premerlani, Frederick Eddy, and William Lorensen. *Object-Oriented Modeling and Design*. Prentice Hall, Englewood Cliifs, NJ, 1991.

32. Yoav Shoham. Agent0: A simple agent language and its interpreter. In *Proceedings of the Ninth National Conference on Artificial Intelligence, AAAI-91*, pages 704–709, San Jose, CA, 1991.

Recovering Active Databases

Olaf Zukunft

Universität Oldenburg, Fachbereich Informatik
Postfach 2503, D-26111 Oldenburg
zukunft@informatik.uni-oldenburg.de

Abstract. Active database systems integrate an event–based rule system into the DBMS. The rules are used to react on occurring events with the execution of transactions. In this paper, we examine which conclusions must be drawn for the active part of the DBMS if we take into account that a DBMS might fail and needs to be recovered. We propose techniques for handling different kinds of failures. These techniques result in a modified and coupling mode specific algorithm for the detection of complex events based on a log of atomic events. Finally, we use the AIDE–environment as an example to show which components of an active DBMS must be modified in order to make it recoverable.

1 Introduction

Conventional database systems are passive in the sense that they only change their state or respond to users if they receive an external stimulus. An active database system extents this behaviour by additionally incorporating an event–oriented ECA rule system. Applying these ECA–rules means to wait for the occurrence of the appropriate event, then evaluating the condition and if this evaluation yields true, executing the action. Different types of events are generated through database operations, time signalisations and user–defined events. The condition usually consists of a predicate on the database state. In the action part of the rule, all active database systems allow to use the data manipulation language. Most active database systems additionally allow to use constructs yielding a computational complete action specification language. An example of a rule which orders items if a stock quantity falls below a limit is:

```
RULE one
ON Update(Stock_Table)
IF (Stock_Table.quantity_of_hold <= 10) AND
   (NOT Stock_Table.already_ordered)
DO Order_Items(100-Stock_Table.quantity_of_hold);
   Stock_Table.already_ordered := TRUE;
COUPLING MODE Cond=Immediate, Action=Detached causally dependent
END RULE
```

Since the incorporation of the rule system is intended to add functionality to the DBMS, the traditional features of database systems should be preserved.

As one consequence of this, the system should extend the semantics of transaction processing to rule processing. In this paper, we concentrate on the recovery aspect of transaction processing. This is an important aspect, because without being recoverable, an active database system does not meet the criteria for being a database system and without offering a recoverable ECA–part, an active database system reduces itself to a passive database with a rule language. Consequently, an active DBMS has to offer recoverability for both data and activity processing. This requires to answer the following questions:

- Which aspects of recovery are not handled by today's active DBMS?
- How is recovery in active DBMS related to the specific rule–structure?
- To which extend can classical recovery techniques such as logging be used for recovery of active DBMS?
- What are the consequences of integrating external and time events into an active DBMS?

To answer these questions, the rest of this paper is organised as follows: First, the related work already done in this area is described. In section 3, we briefly describe the model we base our discussion on. Then, possible consequences of failures in an active DBMS are examined in section 4. Thereafter, a technique to recover active DBMS from failures is proposed in sections 5. The integration of a recovery component into the AIDE–workbench, a system for building active information systems, is described in section 6. Finally, section 7 gives our conclusions and some directions for further research.

2 Related Work

Papers published about transaction processing in active database systems are mostly focusing on coupling modes between rules and rule triggering transactions, i.e. the relationship between rule execution and rule triggering transactions regarding the dimensions synchronicity, abort- and commit–dependency, serialisability and object visibility (see [3], [8]). Only some papers deal with the question of recovery in active database systems. In [14] recovery is mentioned with regard to the coupling mode "detached causally dependent". There, the abort of a rule execution must be forward recovered by the system because there is no user-awareness of these transactions and hence no user responsible for restarting them. The necessity to restart them is inherent in the specification of some coupling modes and semantically useful for application areas nowadays called "workflow management". A possible reaction to the abort of a triggered transaction proposed for the nested transaction model used in HiPAC is the abort of the triggering transaction. They further discuss image–logging techniques for recovery of database actions in rule executions.

Another possible strategy for the handling of rule failures is introduced in [7]. There, the triggering transaction is not aborted but reset to that point of execution where the rule triggering event was generated. The authors argue that events signalled by transactions triggering rules in the coupling mode "causally dependent" must be recorded and recovered after a system failure. Thus, committing a transaction requires that both the database updates and the event signalisations are made persistent. The authors further distinguish between recoverable and non–recoverable events, where only database events are guaranteed to be recoverable. Beeri and Milo propose in [1] to specify the reaction on a rule execution failure orthogonal to transaction nesting. They offer four variants to handle failures of the triggered transaction, which are to ignore them, to abort the triggering transaction, to retry the triggered transaction or to start an alternative transaction. The necessity to distinguish between event compositions including effects of aborted transactions and those which don't is first mentioned in [10].

Some other comments are given in [3], where problems caused by in the incorporation of time–related events are described and the semantics of rules triggered by absolute time events is discussed. Since the REACH–system described there focuses on open systems, it also needs to handle events and operations which are non–recoverable because their consequences on the outside world can not be undone. To cope with these situations, an additional coupling mode "detached causally dependent *sequential*" is introduced, where the rule execution is performed only if the rule triggering transaction(s) has committed.

The only work explicitly dedicated to recovery aspects in active database systems known to the author is [13]. There, the issues arising from the coupling of client applications to an active database server are described and an approach based on recoverable queues is proposed. To reduce the overhead of event logging, clients can decide to bypass the recovery mechanism and use direct communication with the server.

3 Preliminaries

In order to be able to describe recovery issues in active database systems, we need an understanding of possible failures, of the transaction model offered by the DBMS and a notion of activities in the active DBMS. We give a short overview of the models used in this paper in the following.

3.1 Failure Model

In this paper, we follow the failure model proposed in [12]. The reasons causing transactions to be aborted are divided into three different categories:

Transaction–failures Transactions may fail individually for example because of incorrect input data, an explicit abort–command issued by the programmer/user or because the system needs to resolve a deadlock. To perform transaction recovery, the system can rely on all information gathered before because no information will be lost. For active DBMS, this means that no event signalisations will be missed by the event detection component.

System–failures Transactions may fail collectively after a system crash due to power–failures, processor–failures etc. In this situation, the contents of volatile memory is lost. Furthermore, events signalled by the time–subsystem or external systems during system–downtime will be lost. To perform system–recovery, the DBMS can rely on information available on persistent storage.

Media–failures Transactions may fail collectively after a system crash due to media failures. In this case, both the information on volatile storage and on persistent storage is lost. Since there are no issues specific to active database systems in media recovery, this kind of failure will not be discussed in the sequel. A survey of useful techniques for handling these situations is given in [11].

Finally, most active database systems integrate external events. Therefore, active DBMS are defined to be open systems in the sense that they have to react to or can call operations of other systems which do not operate under the control of the DBMS. These systems may fail independently.

3.2 Transaction Model

To talk about recovery, we need to define a transaction model on which we base our discussion. Since it is beyond the scope of this paper to define yet another transaction model for active databases, we use the transaction model proposed for HiPAC [14], i.e. a nested transaction model with command execution at all levels of the hierarchy and inter–transaction relationships such as causal dependencies. In this model, rule transactions are executed either as subtransactions of the rule triggering transaction or as separate transactions. Generally, recovery is used in a sense covering both the traditional undoing of operations by reestablishing the previous state through undo–operations and the logical undo through a compensating action. This extension towards an open nested transaction model is caused by the failure and the activity model, which explicitly include real–actions that can not be physically recovered.

3.3 Activity Model

The model used in the following to describe activities is based on the classical ECA model of HiPAC with extensions proposed for SNOOP in [6] and for ADL in [2]. We use the intuitive ECA–rule model from the introduction with some atomic events and a small set of operators to compose complex events from existing ones. A condition which may be associated with an event will be evaluated if an occurrence of that event is detected. If the evaluation of the condition yields true, the action is executed. For both condition evaluation and action execution we allow to specify transaction characteristics through coupling modes. It is our intention not to rely on features specific to a particular language, although it will be interesting to use some sophisticated features not available in every activity description language.

4   Recovering Active Databases

In this section, we discuss how we can react appropriately to the failures mentioned above. First, it is examined which problems related to recovery of active DBMS are already solved through a transaction oriented processing of rules. Then, open problems related to the signalling of events for both atomic and complex events are discussed.

4.1   Coupling-Modes and Recovery

Table 1. Coupling modes as proposed for REACH (HiPAC–superset)

Coupling mode	Reaction to abort of triggering Tx	Reaction to abort of triggered Tx	Example of application area
Immediate	Rule abort	Nothing or abort parent	Primary Integrity Constraints
Deferred	Rule abort	Nothing or abort parent	Secondary Integrity Constraints
Detached	Nothing	Nothing	Auditing
Causally dependent parallel	Rule abort	Redo triggered	Business Rules
Causally dependent sequential	Impossible	Redo triggered	Execution of non–compensatable actions
Causally dependent exclusive	Required	Redo triggered	Contingency Rules

The processing of rules in active database systems is usually subject to control through the transaction processing component of the DBMS. Coupling modes were introduced to offer the user rules with the necessary semantics w.r.t. transactional characteristics for different application areas. They specify values for the following dimensions of a rule:

1. Object visibility (upward– and downward–inheritance of locks between rule triggering and rule executing transactions),
2. Abort–dependencies,
3. Commit–dependencies (e.g. for ordering of causally dependent rules),
4. Synchronicity,
5. and a rule execution timepoint.

Coupling modes such as immediate, deferred, detached or causally dependent parallel assign values to these attributes for a specific application class. Table 1 shows the recovery aspects of the coupling modes proposed for the REACH system. Through coupling modes, we can guarantee that a rule executing transaction formed of either a condition evaluation or an action execution is aborted if the event raising transaction(s) aborts. Therefore, coupling modes already handle one recovery requirement in active databases, namely the causality property guaranteeing that a transaction abort results in an abort of all invalid rule executions. Through establishing such an abort dependency, coupling modes support a notion of "unsignalling an event" in current active database systems. On the other hand, the consequences of aborting a transaction which consumed an event caused by an aborted transaction is completely shifted into the transaction manager. Unfortunately, this is not sufficient. What coupling modes do generally not handle are the consequences of transaction aborts on the event composition process, see section 4.3. Here, some rule executions might become possible because of a transaction abort. To recognise these additional event composition possibilities, a modified event recognition algorithm as the one proposed in section 5.2 is required.

4.2 Recovering Atomic Events

In this subsection, we discuss recovery along the different sources for atomic events, i.e. database events, time events and external events.

Handling of Database Events. Database events are a unique kind of events w.r.t. recovery because they are only signalled when the DBMS is up and because they are completely under the control of the DBMS. This qualifies them as a good candidate for being a recoverable kind of events in an active DBMS. On the other hand, database events are generated as consequences of transactions and must hence loose their causality after a transaction abort. For rules specified with an abort–dependency, this results in an abort requirement of the rule executing transaction. As we will see in section 4.3, this requires not only to inform the transaction manager of a transaction abort, but also the event detector.

Currently, there are two kinds of facilities in active DBMS which can help in the recovery process: The first one is the regular database log which already records database updates in order to allow a recovery of the passive database. The second facility is a transaction manager aware of coupling modes, which as described in section 4.1 handles some consequences of transaction aborts on rules. Nevertheless, not all problems related to recovery of events originating in the database can be solved through these two facilities because the database log does not capture any information about queries on the database. Furthermore, database events usually carry additional parameters related to the database state and regaining that information after a crash is prohibitive expensive if we rely only on the traditional database log. Consequently, we can not use the regular database log alone to retrieve all necessary information about database events. Instead, if the recovery process requires access to database events, another facility like the event log proposed in Sect. 5.1 has to be used.

Handling of Time Events. In this subsection, the question why time events are different is answered. Time events have been introduced into active DBMS because we want to react to events modelling the semantics of an external defined environment time. This environment time has some unique features not found in any other component signalling events:

1. Time is completely predictable, i.e. no surprise will happen.
2. Time as a physical dimension is not dependent on any human controllable system.
3. Time events are used to represent the human–defined time, which is predictable, but not strongly monotonical (daylight–saving).

The time events registered in an active DBMS differ from the characterisation given above. There, a time event is signalled at a certain distance (chronon) from the last one. After a system failure, there will be a different chronon because then the time registered by the active DBMS has gaps.

The different kinds of failures introduced above result in the following situations for time events: In the case of a transaction failure, no time events will be lost. In the case of a system failure, there will be lost time events, i.e. some time events usually signalled by the time component will not be received by the atomic event detector. This case is recoverable, because through the general predictability of time any lost time event can be recovered *at a later time* given the last time event before system failure and the first event after system recovery[1]. With this knowledge, we may trigger each time event based rule which would have been triggered if the system did not have a system fault. Nevertheless, this approach generates a problem: Time events are the only events with this predictable behaviour and may be used in rule definitions with an implicit assumption that the rest of the system is working as defined.

As a consequence, we propose to offer the user two different commands to specify rules reacting on time events: A first one supports the traditional semantics, i.e. signalling a time event only if the system is up at the specified time. In a second variant, time events are always signalled either at the specified time or if the system is down then at the earliest time after a system restart. Ideally, the order of these time events would be preserved even during bulk–signalling at restart. The first version translates into an exact time w.r.t. the chronon (with equality as the matching operator) while the second means "at the exact or the first detected later time" w.r.t. the chronon and the system down–time (with $\geq$ as a once–only matching operator).

Time events which are relative to some other event, like an event specification "DB_INSERT + 15 min"[2] can be handled in a similar fashion. Relative time events can only be processed at all if they are transformable into an absolute time event before that point of time is reached. Subtractions are allowed in relative time events only if the reference event is or can be transformed

---

[1] We do not consider incorrect time event signalisations, because they can be avoided through appropriate hardware solutions.

[2] We call the database insert event the reference event.

into an absolute time event. Additions to relative time events are possible to any observable event. They can be transformed into an absolute time event (`Timestamp(event_source) + time_difference`). For recovery purposes, subtractions have to be divided into two subcases:

1. The subtracted time event is signalled, but the following reference event is lost. Since the reference event is an absolute time event, no problems arise.
2. The subtracted time event is not signalled. This case can be handled analogous to absolute time events, i.e. two options should be provided. This case is independent of the signalisation of the reference event.

For relative time events using additions, the following cases are distinguished:

1. The reference event is signalled, but the system is down at the relative time event. This case can be handled like an absolute time event.
2. The reference event is not signalled, it is a time event and the system is down when the relative event has to be signalled. This case can also be handled like an absolute time event, since both events are predictable.
3. The reference event is not signalled, it is not a time event and the system is down when the relative event has to be signalled. Since a non time event is generally not predictable, this event will not be signalizable in the general case.
4. The reference event is not signalled, it is a time event and the system is up when the relative event has to be signalled. This case is reducible to the signalisation of an absolute time event and should therefore capture the same semantics.
5. The reference event is not signalled, it is not a time event and the system is up when the relative event has to be signalled. The considerations for this case are equal to those for number 3.

Finally, some languages like SAMOS [9] offer constructs to define events which are signalled if a complex event occurs between an interval of either two definite events or within a certain period. These can be transformed into either absolute or relative time events and hence handled in a similar way.

Handling of External Events. There exist established mechanisms to handle transaction failures for rules reacting on external events. They are necessary because a transaction abort may have consequences for the action execution of causally dependent rules. These rules may execute actions in an external system which is not recoverable, either because it is executing real–world actions and hence not recoverable at all or because the external system doesn't show a transactional behaviour. Existing solutions to this problem as proposed in [3] do either request the external system to offer compensating actions or execute the action only *after* the rule triggering event set is committed, i.e. they use a decoupled sequential coupling mode.

After a system crash, events signalled by an external component may be lost. To cope with this situation, we may either use a "don't care" strategy or provide some additional mediator which might for example offer an acknowledgement protocol. Without such a facility, no guarantee can be given that any signalled event will ever be received. If an acknowledgement protocol is used, we have to take care that the same event will not be processed twice. To avoid this, either an idempotent atomic event detection algorithm has to be used or the event signalling mechanism has to offer an "exactly once" semantics.

If the external system and the active DBMS are physically distributed, then the communication between the active DBMS and the external system may fail. The handling of these failures is beyond the scope of this paper and will not be discussed in the sequel.

4.3   Recovering Complex Events

The detection of complex events has received a lot of attention in the active DB community, see for example [6] and [9]. Nevertheless, we are not aware of any papers discussing recovery issues in the proposed algorithms. To illustrate the necessity to explicitly consider transaction aborts in the complex event detection process, the following rule is used:

```
RULE two
ON   SEQUENCE (E1,E2)
IF   TRUE
DO   action1
COUPLING MODE Cond=Immediate, Action=Detached causally dependent
END RULE
```

This rule executes the transaction action1 in the causally dependent coupling mode if two events of type E1 and E2 are signalled successively. We assume that every event instance can participate only once in the event combination process for every rule and that the first matching instances of each atomic event should be combined. Now lets consider a signalisation order of events of type E1 and E2 from three different transactions as shown in table 2. In the example, three events occur: An instance of E1 at timepoint 1 and two instances of E2 at timepoints 2 and 3 respectively. These three events are signalled by the three different transactions Tx1, Tx2 and Tx3. If the rule defined for the complex event would use the detached coupling mode, then the combination of the events at the timepoints 1 and 2 would be correct even if one of the transactions aborts. On the other hand, if the coupling mode specifies an abort–dependency between rule execution and rule triggering transaction like the causally dependent parallel does, then this combination is invalid.

Coupling modes handle only one half of this situation. By defining the action as causally dependent, the transaction manager will abort the execution of the transaction. What won't be done is the combination of the event signalisations $(E1_1, E2_3)$ into a rule triggering complex event. This combination is possible only after the event signalled at timepoint 3 would have been ignored by the classical event detection algorithms. Therefore, the signalisation of the abort

Table 2. Events combined by a FIFO–strategy for the event SEQ(E1,E2)

Time	Tx1	Tx2	Tx3	Complex event detection	
				Causally dependent	Detached
1	E1			Started by consuming $E1_1$	Started by consuming $E1_1$
2		E2		$(E1_1, E2_2)$ completed	$(E1_1, E2_2)$ completed
3			E2	$E2_3$ ignored (useless)	$E2_3$ ignored (useless)
4		abort		$(E1_1, E2_2)$ loses causality	$(E1_1, E2_2)$ still correct
5			commit	$E2_3$ is now a confirmed event	
6	commit			$(E1_1, E2_3)$ *would* be causally correct	$(E1_1, E2_3)$ is still wrong

event must also be considered by the complex event detection algorithm for every rule defined in a coupling mode with an abort–dependency. Furthermore, the complex event detector must have access to events which have not been combined at their signalisation time but are usable for combinations later. Section 5.2 describes an offline–algorithm which can be used to solve this problem on the basis of an event log.

5   Techniques for Recovery

In order to be able to recover a database from failures, redundant information must be collected and made available after a restart. Active database systems introduce two new DBMS–components which need to be considered for recovery: An event detection and processing module and a rule execution module. The rule execution module has to provide reliable execution for the action part of rules. This is achieved through an extended transaction manager, where the actions of the rules are subject to the regular recovery mechanism for transactions and are additionally interconnected with rule–triggering transactions as specified through their coupling mode. Furthermore, a recoverable event detection and processing component is needed in order to provide full database functionality. Here, we have to make sure that every applicable rule is in fact triggered, even if a failure has arisen. As the discussion in subsection 4.3 has shown, this requires a mechanism capable of storing events after their signalisation time and a modified complex event detector. Therefore, a recoverable active DBMS needs to incorporate not only an extended transaction manager, but also two other additional software components: A log–facility for events which may be used to retrieve information about occurred events after a failure and a complex event detector capable of recovering. In the following, we concentrate on the two latter components. Information about extended transaction managers in active database systems can for example be found in [3, 4, 5].

5.1 A Log for Events

A log is a database system component which stores redundant information for system internal purposes. It is used during a restart after some failure occurred. Traditionally, log–information is stored in a main memory log–buffer which is dumped to disk either periodically or at commit–time. The disk–based log is used to recover from system failures when the contents of the main memory is lost. The same principles can be applied to a log of events. Additionally, various design decision have to be made for an event log. Events can for example be written to the log before an event–raising action is performed. Then, all events are fully recoverable but efficiency is low. To the other extreme, one can decide not to log events at all. This results in high efficiency but the situations and the extend to which recovery is possible is low (not null, since information from the regular database log and the inherent semantics of time events is available). Various compromises w.r.t. event logging are possible along the following dimensions:

1. Event type: We may record events caused by operations reading the database, writing it or both and may also log time events and external events.
2. Disk–write time: We may write occurring events to the log immediately after they were signalled or defer this until some other condition is fulfilled (e.g. until commit–time, until buffer–overflow, at a periodical point of time or at explicit user request (checkpoints)).
3. Exclusivity: We may use a log for events only or integrate it with the regular database log.
4. Extend: The information stored in the log may be of large or small scope (e.g. event type specific parameters may be logged, event type independent parameters like timestamp and transaction ID may be recorded).

To organise a log, one value for each of the above dimensions needs to be combined. The possible combinations of values are not completely independent, but some are connected with each other and are related to other system components like the complex event detector and the implemented recovery strategy. The event type can be restricted to events caused by read–operations on the database if we organise the regular database log in a way that all information necessary for recovery of database events can be restored from it. Using an immediate disk–write for all events is prohibitive inefficient if the same strategy is not used for the regular database log. A better option is to defer the disk–write of events until one of the conditions mentioned above is fulfilled. Since log entries should capture all the information about the system history, we either have to keep database log entries describing the database state at each event or we have to replace relative database references in event parameters. In the worst case, this could lead to the necessity to duplicate the whole database in the event log.

To avoid overhead during regular processing, a group commit strategy is used where events are grouped by transactions and event compositions.

5.2 A Supplement for Event Detection Algorithms

The event log can be the basis for a recoverable event detector. As was shown in subsection 4.3, the complex event detection algorithm needs to be modified in order to cope with recovery issues. This modification has to take into account which dependencies exist between the rule triggering and the rule executing transactions. A commit–dependency between a rule triggering and a rule executing transaction results in a forward–recovery requirement of the rule executing transaction[3]. An abort–dependency between these two as for example included in the causally dependent coupling mode leads to additional event combination strategies for complex events. Hence, the event detection algorithm must be coupling mode specific. In the following, we assume that the reader has a general knowledge of event detection techniques as described for example in [9]. The techniques described there have to be modified for transaction failures by incorporating the following algorithm:

```
IF event_consumed_from_transaction (Tx_Id) AND
   transaction_aborted (Tx_Id) AND
   rule_is_abort_dependent_on(Tx_Id)
THEN
   WHILE NOT (event_log_end_reached OR rule_composition_finished)
   DO
      reset_event_detector (MIN(Timestamp(consumed_event(Tx_Id)));
      restart_event_combination_ignoring_events_from(Tx_Id);
      IF new_matching_event_found_in_log
      THEN
         IF this_already_used_by_same_ruletype
         THEN
            IF other_using_rule_instance_combined_earlier
            THEN
               skip_this_event
            ELSE
               combine_this_event;
               reset_other_using_rule_which_combined_later(
                  Timestamp(this_event))
            ENDIF
         ELSE
            combine_this_event
         ENDIF
      ENDIF
   ENDWHILE
ENDIF
```

---

[3] Because of space limitations, the consequences of these will be ignored.

This algorithm works as follows: If a rule triggering transaction is aborted, we have to abort the triggered transaction. Furthermore, we also have to reset the event detection to that point of time where the first "aborted" event was consumed. From that point of time, we have to scan the log for matching events signalled by other transactions which were ignored before. If such an atomic event is found, we may combine it if it was not combined for the same purpose by an earlier execution of the same rule. If it was combined only later, that rule has to be aborted and we may consume the event for the recovered rule. These actions have to be performed until either the rule composition process is completed or the log has been completely scanned. Note that this algorithm does not cause cascading aborts of transactions triggered by independent rules. Note further that the timestamps of the occurred events and not the order in which the events are received by the event detection process forms the basis for the composition. This algorithmic structure needs to be incorporated into complex event detection algorithms for those rules triggered in a coupling mode including an abort–dependency between rule–triggering and rule–executing transactions.

6 Integration of a Recovery Component into AIDE

6.1 The AIDE–Environment

Since 1991, AIDE (Active Information System Development Environment) is being developed at the University of Oldenburg. It consists of a toolbox supporting all phases of the construction process of an active information system. This toolbox is structured using a three–layer architecture. The basis of the system is a bidirectional interface–layer allowing the integration of any foreign system into the active information system. Here, we use the AADT–concept of active abstract datatypes ([2]), which encapsulate the event types signalled by a system and the operations offered by it. Currently, we have integrated a relational database system and a graphical user interface toolkit. The middle layer of AIDE offers the developer a language to define the structure and behaviour of the active information system using the rule language ADL. The top layer of AIDE consists of graphical languages like browsers, debuggers and modelling tools which are provided to ease the handling of the system. Currently, the AIDE–toolbox is used to develop an active information system supporting workflow management for a software engineering environment ([15]).

6.2 A Recovery Component for AIDE

Making AIDE capable of recovering requires the following changes to be made:

- A logging module has to be introduced between the AADT–layer and the complex event detector. This logging component also records the execution of actions triggered by the rules.
- The used complex event detection algorithm has to be modified in order to support the technique for recoverable event detection described above.

- The repository needs to be extended for storing occurrences of events. This event log must be designed carefully because it could easily become a bottleneck of the active component.
- The only language–level change required was to support two different semantics for time events. We call the first one "exactly" meaning that the rule should react only if the system is up at signalisation time while the second one as the default means the earliest time after the event was detected and can syntactically be referred to as "earliest". This language–level change triggered some changes in the compiler and the time event module.

As an interesting side–effect of the event log, we are considering to offer a query facility for this log. This could significantly ease the handling of the active component because we might be able to reduce the complexity of the event algebra and use instead more powerful conditions ranging over the event log. The question whether this a realistic approach will need to be further examined. This is also valid for the integration of external systems which offer an X/Open compliant transaction behaviour (resource managers). Unfortunately, all X/Open compliant systems currently known to the author are database management systems, so that the scope of such an interface seems to be limited.

7   Conclusion and Future Work

In this paper, we have shown which problems arise when extending the notion of recovery onto the active part of a DBMS and how they can be solved. We realised that complex event detection algorithms which are capable of handling transaction aborts must be coupling mode specific. Previously proposed event detection algorithms are not able to recover correctly from transaction failures and must therefore be modified. For coupling modes with an abort dependency between the rule triggering transactions and the rule executing transaction an algorithm has been proposed. This algorithm modifies the event composition for transaction–oriented database systems based on an event log.

The future concerns of our work will focus on benchmarking the extended AIDE–system to see how much a recovery component for lightweight entities like events influences the overall performance. If the associated overhead shows to be prohibitive expensive, we intend to distinguish between recoverable and non–recoverable rules, where only the former are subject to logging and cause overhead. Furthermore, we want to implement the algorithm for complex event detection in a transaction–oriented system using the rule language itself. In this approach, only a very basic event detection technique will be hardwired into the system while any sophisticated technique is coded using ECA–rules. This is possible because aborts are regular events signalled by the DBMS and processable through rules. We expect a high degree of flexibility from this approach supporting further experiments with event detection. Finally, we want to examine whether the proposed recovery techniques can be used as a basis for the integration of mobile computers into active database systems.

Acknowledgement

I would like to thank the anonymous referees for several useful suggestions.

References

1. C. Beeri and T. Milo. A model for active object oriented database. In *Proc. Intl. Conf. on Very Large Data Bases*, pages 337–349, Barcelona, Spain, 1991.
2. H. Behrends. *Beschreibung ereignisgesteuerter Aktivitäten in datenbankgestützten Informationssystemen.* PhD thesis, Universität Oldenburg, To appear, 1995.
3. H. Branding, A. Buchmann, T. Kudrass, and J. Zimmermann. Rules in an open system: The REACH rule system. In *First Intl. Workshop on Rules in Database Systems*, Edinburgh, 1993.
4. A. Buchmann, M. T. Özsu, M. Hornick, D. Georgakopoulos, and F. A. Manola. A transaction model for active distributed object systems. In A. K. Elmagarmid, editor, *Database Transaction Models for Advanced Applications*, chapter 5. Morgan Kaufmann, San Mateo, CA, 1992.
5. A. Buchmann, J. Zimmermann, J. A. Blakeley, and D. L. Wells. Building an integrated active OODBMS: Requirements, architecture, and design decisions. In *Proc. 11th Intl. Conf. on Data Engineering (ICDE 95)*, Taipei, Taiwan, 1995.
6. S. Chakravarthy, V. Krishnaprasad, E. Anwar, and S.-K. Kim. Composite events for active databases: Semantics, contexts and detection. In *Proc. 20th Intl. Conf. on Very Large Data Bases (VLDB 94)*, Santiago, Chile, 1994.
7. U. Dayal, M. Hsu, and R. Ladin. A transactional model for long–running activities. In *Proc. Intl. Conf. on Very Large Data Bases*, pages 113–122, Barcelona, Spain, 1991.
8. U. Dayal et al. The HiPAC project: Combining active databases and timing constraints. *SIGMOD Record*, 17:51–70, 1988.
9. S. Gatziu and K. R. Dittrich. Detecting composite events in active database systems using petri nets. In *Proc. 4. Intl. Workshop on Research Issues in Data Engineering*, pages 2–9, Houston, USA, 1994.
10. N. H. Gehani, H. V. Jagadish, and O. Shmueli. Event specification in an active object–oriented database. In *Proc. Intl. Conf. on Management of Data (SIGMOD)*, pages 81–90, San Diego, California, 1992.
11. J. Gray and A. Reuter. *Transaction Processing: Concepts and Techniques.* Morgan Kaufmann, San Mateo, California, 1993.
12. T. Haerder and A. Reuter. Principles of transaction–oriented database recovery. *Computing Surveys*, 15:287–317, 1983.
13. E. N. Hanson, I.-C. Chen, R. Dastur, K. Engel, C. Xu, and V. Ramaswamy. Flexible and recoverable interaction between applications and active databases. Technical Report CIS–TR–94–033, University of Florida, 1994.
14. M. Hsu, R. Ladin, and D. McCarthy. An execution model for active data base management systems. In *3rd Intl. Conf. on Data and Knowledge Bases 1988*, pages 171–179, Jerusalem, Israel, 1988.
15. H. Jasper. Active databases for active repositories. In *Proc. 10. Intl. Conference on Data Engineering*, pages 375–384, Houston, USA, 1994.

Author Index

Lecture Notes in Computer Science

For information about Vols. 1–912

please contact your bookseller or Springer-Verlag